The Frontier Humorists

The
Frontier Humorists

Critical Views

EDITED BY

M. Thomas Inge

ARCHON BOOKS

1975

Library of Congress Cataloging in Publication Data

Inge, M. Thomas.
    The frontier humorists.

    Bibliography: p.
    Includes index.
    1. American wit and humor—Southern States—History
and criticism.   I. Title.
PS430.I5   817'.1'09   75-12698
ISBN 0-208-01509-4

© 1975 by M. Thomas Inge
First published 1975 as an Archon Book,
an imprint of The Shoe String Press, Inc.,
Hamden, Connecticut 06514

Printed in the United States of America

Dedicated

to

JOHN Q. ANDERSON

1916-1975

One of the best friends
American humor and folklore
ever had.

Contents

Preface

In the past four decades, literary historians and critics have paid an increasing amount of attention to the writings of the frontier humorists— or humorists of the Old Southwest, as they are sometimes known— because of the early seeds of realism in their work, because of their influence on later American writers like Mark Twain and Faulkner, and because of the intrinsic value of their stories on their own in style, language, and technique. While George W. Harris, Augustus B. Longstreet, Johnson J. Hooper, and William T. Thompson have received the largest share of attention, a good many of the minor writers have been evaluated and rescued from obscurity, and the entire school has received provocative assessments not always in agreement.

Most of the scholarship and criticism is found scattered through several books and lesser known scholarly journals, many of them inaccessible. The purpose of this anthology is to bring together for the first time in one volume a selection of some of the valuable and provocative historical and critical essays which have appeared on these writers who have greatly enriched America's indigenous literature.

M. Thomas Inge

Introduction

M. Thomas Inge

The group of writers who have come to be called the humorists of the old Southwest[1] were not a part of any conscious, concerted movement in American literature. But the general conditions surrounding and stimulating their development did produce a body of writing about which several generalizations may be drawn, and their achievement individually and collectively has been of definite influence on subsequent American humor and fiction.

At least three conditions were necessary to the emergence of Southwestern humor: the birth of a popular national self-consciousness, the emergence of the frontier as a social entity in the nation's mind and imagination, and the development and increasing cultural significance of the American newspaper.[2] The election of Andrew Jackson to the presidency in 1829 was but the political expression of the development of an intense interest on the part of Americans in things peculiarly American. It was a period of awakening, a "renaissance" it has been called, and on the literary front Emerson issued his clarion call for an original, national literature, no longer imitative of European models, in his address "The American Scholar," which Oliver Wendell Holmes called "our intellectual Declaration of Independence."

It was the presence of the frontier that enabled the Americans to turn their eyes from Europe and see something uniquely their own. As the frontier advanced westward, as civilization came face to face with wilderness and savagery, the influence of Europe waned, and the American character took on new and independent outlines. Frederick Jackson Turner wrote in 1893 that "The frontier is the line of most rapid and

This introduction contains material first published in *Louisiana Studies: An Interdisciplinary Journal of the South*. Copyright 1968 by the Louisiana Studies Institute and reprinted by permission of the publisher.

effective Americanization," and although his sweeping generalization—
that "to the frontier the American intellect owes its striking characteristic"—has been critically challenged, certainly much of what he says
does seem to account to a large degree for the specific nature of Southwestern humor. "The humor, bravery, and rude strength, as well as the
vices of the frontier in its worst aspect," which Turner said "have left
traces on American character, language, and literature," all have a
prominent place in these humorous writings.[3]

As frontier settlements expanded into thriving communities, an essential commodity was the local newspaper. Any community, large or
small, "that boasted a job-print-shop and a young lawyer or printer with
an itch to be an editor, supported a local news-sheet featuring humorous
sketches."[4] Frontier newspapers in 1810 comprised less than a tenth of
the total published in America, but by 1840 represented more than a
quarter of the total. It was in these journals that humorous writers first
found an audience for their productions.[5]

Given the presence of the newspapers, where humorous material was
always in demand, a certain folk custom was crucial to the actual creation
of this literature. This was the favorite frontier pastime of telling stories.
Wherever the frontiersman found himself, resting by the campfire,
traveling by boat on the river, loafing around the stove at the local tavern
or grocery, or relaxing at home before the fireside, he whiled the hours
away pleasantly engaged in vigorous "yarnspinning." As Walter Blair
has noted, "Definitely, much of this literature had its origin in the greatest
American folk art—the art of oral story-telling."[6] The conventions of
oral repetition—digressions, surprise endings, dialogue, and leisurely
pace—also became characteristic of the printed yarns of the old Southwest.

When Augustus Baldwin Longstreet recalled some of the stories he had
heard and sights he had seen as a young lawyer traveling the frontier
legal circuits, and decided to write them down for publication in a
Georgia newspaper, the humor of the old Southwest was born. His
collection of these sketches into book form in 1835 as *Georgia Scenes*
constituted "the frontier's first permanent work."[7] Longstreet's achievement lay in the fact that he had the "wit to realize that something old in
talking might look new in writing."[8]

Following a similar pattern, with publication first in periodicals and
then between hard covers, close on the heels of Longstreet came the other
classics of old Southwestern humor: *Major Jones's Courtship* (1843) by
William T. Thompson, *Some Adventures of Captain Simon Suggs* (1845)

2

by Johnson Jones Hooper, *Theatrical Apprenticeship* (1845) by Sol Smith, *The Mysteries of the Backwoods* (1846) by Thomas Bangs Thorpe, *The Drama in Pokerville* (1847) by Joseph M. Field, *Streaks of Squatter Life* (1847) by John S. Robb, *Odd Leaves From the Life of a Louisiana "Swamp Doctor"* (1850) by Madison Tensas (pseudonym of Dr. Henry Clay Lewis), *Flush Times of Alabama and Mississippi* (1853) by Joseph G. Baldwin, and *Sut Lovingood's Yarns* (1867) by George Washington Harris.

To this list should also be added two important contemporary anthologies of this humor, *The Big Bear of Arkansas* (1845) and *A Quarter Race in Kentucky* (1846), both edited by William T. Porter, the man who more than any other was responsible for encouraging this vein of writing by giving it a national circulation through his weekly journal the New York *Spirit of the Times* (1831-1861). Originally designated a "Chronicle of the Turf, Agriculture, Field Sports, Literature and the Stage," Porter's journal began to encourage its readers (a large segment of whom resided in the Southwestern states) to submit correspondence for publication. He especially solicited letters concerning sporting events in their respective areas. Soon his readers began to record the oral tales they heard, as had Longstreet, and thus unwittingly Porter became a principal instigator of the developing school of frontier humor. Except for Longstreet and Baldwin,[9] all of the above-mentioned writers published either their first efforts or their most noteworthy stories in the pages of Porter's *Spirit of the Times*. And either by the prestige of appearing there or through Porter's personal intervention and support, many of these writers were brought to the attention of northern publishing houses who issued full collections of their works.[10]

In a day when writing was not a means by which one could earn a living, none of the humorists were professional authors. Their sketches were the products of amateur effort and leisure hours, and the entire group offers a representative cross-section of nearly all possible nineteenth-century professions and vocations: Longstreet began as a lawyer and editor, and eventually became a college president; Thompson was a soldier and a journalist; Henry Clay Lewis practiced medicine; Hooper was a lawyer and editor before becoming secretary of the Provisional Congress of the Southern States; Sol Smith and Joseph M. Field both were journalists, actors and actor-managers; Thorpe was an artist, soldier and editor; John S. Robb was a printer and editor; Baldwin was a lawyer and when he moved to California became an associate judge of the Supreme Court there; G. W. Harris followed during his lifetime a multiplicity of vocations ranging from steamboat captain and farmer to railroad conductor and postmaster.[11]

Such diversity in background and heterogeneity of interests prevent much generalizing about these men further than saying that they all recognized the humorous and laughable side of life. The dangers of generalization are evident in the "biographical archetype" one critic has constructed for this literary group:

> The ideal Southwestern humorist was a professional man—a lawyer or newspaperman, usually, although sometimes a doctor or an actor. He was actively interested in politics, either as a party propagandist or as a candidate for office. He was well educated, relatively speaking, and well traveled, although he knew America better than Europe. He had a sense of humor, naturally enough, and in a surprising number of cases a notoriously bad temper. Wherever he had been born, and a few were of Northern origin, the ideal humorist was a Southern patriot—and this was important. Above all, he was a conservative, identified either with the aristocratic faction in state politics, or with the banker-oriented Whig party in national politics, or with both.[12]

George Washington Harris, among others, offers a case in point. Harris was not in the usual sense of the word a "professional man," which indicates a liberal, scientific, or artistic educational background (as in law, medicine, or theology). He was poorly educated, having attended school only a short while, and was not well traveled, having spent all his life, except for a few brief excursions, in Knoxville and Nashville, Tennessee. We don't know very much about his temper, though most found him a likable person, and a Southern patriot he was indeed—but he was a firm and faithful Democrat all his life and a great admirer of Andrew Jackson. Thus in only a couple of places does this archetypical portrait touch Harris and his career.[13]

Generalizations about the nature of the humorous material itself are equally risky. As Bernard DeVoto warned, "Frontier life across a nation and during three generations was extraordinarily complex. The humor of frontiersmen grew out of that life at every level, so that an attempt to find unity in it would be folly."[14] But DeVoto did offer a fairly safe and comprehensive definition of the frontier humorous story: "It is a narrative of a length dictated by the necessities of newspaper publication, usually based on the life immediately at hand, and working through the realistic portrayal of character toward the desired end, laughter."[15]

4

The leading characters are usually the lower-class white settlers—crackers, hillbillies, backwoodsmen, yeoman farmers, and "poor whites," although no single stereotyped figure, like that of the Yankee (which eventually reached a definite visual form in the modern portrait of Uncle Sam) or the mythological "gamecock" of the wilderness (dressed in the hunter's deerskin shirt and coonskin cap), emerged from the tales. The range of subject matter is as wide as the social life of the times. Franklin J. Meine suggested ten groupings: sketches of local customs (shooting matches, gander pullings, horse races, quiltings, frolics); courtships and weddings; law circuits and political life; hunting stories (the "Big Bears," coon hunts); oddities in character; travel (steamboat life, the new railroads, the rustic in the big city); frontier medical stories; gambling; varieties of religious experience (circuit riding preachers, Negro camp-meetings, revivalist meetings); and fights.[16]

Perhaps the best adjective which has been suggested to convey the quality of this humor is "masculine." Adapting the literature to the tenor of their life, "comic sin," trickery, and knavery are recurring themes, and "a willing suspension of morality" is frequently necessary for a full appreciation of the unbridled humor. As several critics note, "It is small wonder that the humor of the Old Southwest did not appeal to the parents of the Puritan damsels who had to read surreptitiously the popular sentimental novels still frowned upon as unwholesome fare."[17] Cruelty (especially towards the Negro or foreigner, as in some of Harris's stories or the adventures of Lewis's Swamp Doctor), and scatology find a place in this literature, and in some of the yarns of Sut Lovingood, there is a streak of ribaldry of a frankness and outspokenness unmatched in the nineteenth century (except perhaps for Twain's *1601*). Longstreet's gory description of a fight in which the combatants are irreparably maimed, Simon Suggs' pretended conversion at a camp meeting where a sensual brother works among the young women hugging and exhorting, "Keep the thing warm . . . come to the Lord, honey!", and the death of an old woman who gets in the way of a scared horse sent through the midst of a quilting party by the practical joker Sut Lovingood—these are typical events.

But deserving of equal stress is the "vitality, the sturdy strength and individualism, and above all, the high spirits and love of fun in these pioneer tales. Life on the frontier must have been good to produce so much solid enjoyment; perhaps no other early settlements in the world's history have been enlivened by such hilarity."[18]

Walter Blair was the first to describe the most common narrative method employed in the Old Southwest: first the circumstances of the telling of the tale are described with an eye towards realistic detail, then a description of the tale teller follows, at which point this narrator takes over and tells the story in his own language, at the conclusion of which the original scene of the tale telling is often briefly revisited. This "box-like structure" was comically effective because of three incongruities it underlined:

(1) Incongruity between the grammatical, highly rhetorical language of the framework on the one hand, and, on the other, the ungrammatical racy dialect of the narrator.

(2) Incongruity between the situation at the time the yarn was told and the situation described in the yarn itself. . . .

(3) Incongruity between realism—discoverable in the framework wherein the scene and narrator are realistically portrayed, and fantasy, which enters into the enclosed narrative because the narrator selects details and uses figures of speech, epithets, and verbs which give grotesque coloring.[19]

Blair also discerned on the part of the sophisticated writer in the outer framework a sense of detachment and superiority to the lower class people he has set about describing. This idea has led Kenneth S. Lynn to develop the concept of a "Self-controlled Gentleman" in the Southwestern humor, and the "frame" structure thus provided the humorists, he says, "a convenient way of keeping their first-person narrators outside and above the comic action, thereby drawing a *cordon sanitaire*, so to speak, between the morally irreproachable Gentleman and the tainted life he described."[20] Certainly such an attitude is discernible in such writers as Longstreet and Baldwin, but once again this broad generalization fails to take into account, for example, Hooper's ironical use of a fictional laudatory biographer as narrator in *Some Adventures of Captain Simon Suggs* in the creation of a "burlesque campaign biography,"[21] or the stories of Harris in which the gentlemanly George of the outer framework at no time expresses disgust or condescension towards his friend Sut Lovingood ("Take keer ove that little cackus ove yourn," says Sut to George in a moment of revealing affection, "I love you by jings"). The ultimate generalization to which Lynn is led is equally debatable: "To convert the entire community to the temperate values of Whiggery was the ultimate purpose of Southwestern humor. . . ."[22]

The most obvious importance of the humor of the Old Southwest to subsequent American literature is the fact that in this writing is to be found some of the earliest examples of what came to be called "realism," as commentator after commentator has observed.[23] "No aspect of the life in the simpler America is missing from this literature," Bernard DeVoto noted.[24] The father of the school, Longstreet, wrote that through *Georgia Scenes*, "we may be seen and heard by our posterity two hundred years hence just as we were." His aim, he said, "was to supply a chasm in history which has already been overlooked—the manner, customs, amusements, wit, dialect as they appear in all grades of society to an eye witness of them."[25] Others expressed a similar intention to report and preserve the peculiarities of the local scene, although one suspects that frequently enough this was not so much a guiding motivation in the beginning as a later rationalization with an eye cocked towards northern and eastern sales of their books. These pioneer realists are not to be confused, however, as they occasionally have been, with the local-color writers of a generation later who consciously attempted to preserve the regional eccentricities passing away with the defeated ante-bellum Southern society. Both groups achieved an accurate use of dialect and a more realistic portrayal of character, but independently and for different reasons.

As Willard Thorp suggests, perhaps the realistic aspects in Southwestern humor have been over-stressed.[26] Most of the humorists were not writing for a literary public, and knew little about contemporary literary fashions. Certainly the most important motivation for many was the simple desire to amuse. William T. Thompson has his Major Jones note that his book "was writ with no higher aim than to amuse the idle hours of my friends, and if it fails to do that, it's a spilt job."[27] And Harris has Sut Lovingood state in the preface to his book:

> Ef eny poor misfortinit devil hu's heart is onder a mill-stone, hu's raggid children am hungry, an' no bread in the dresser, hu is down in the mud, an' the lucky ones a-trippin him every time he struggils to his all fours . . . —ef sich a one kin fine a laugh, jis' one—atwixt these yere kivers—then, I'll thank God that I *hes* made a book, an' feel that I hev got my pay in full.[28]

In the course of provoking laughter, an impressive gallery of individual, memorable characters emerged from the pens of these humorists: Longstreet's Ransy Sniffle, who anticipated "in the satiric brilliance of his name, in the comic ugliness of his appearance, and in the utter malevolence of his soul—Faulkner's Flem Snopes";[29] Hooper's Simon Suggs, the most notable contribution of America to the literature of roguery; and Harris's Sut Lovingood, who stands beside Shakespeare's Falstaff and Chaucer's Wife of Bath in his spiritual freedom, his canny ability to see beneath appearances to the heart of reality about himself and the world, and his unabashed reveling in things sensual. This is to name only a few.

In its own time, the humor of the Old Southwest made its influence felt in Europe. Thackeray expressed admiration for Hooper's *Some Adventures of Captain Simon Suggs* and Baldwin's *Flush Times*, Dickens adapted John Basil Lamar's "The Blacksmith of the Mountain Pass" (the work of one of the minor humorists) for his story of "Colonel Quagg's Conversion," and Thomas Hardy based chapter xxiii of *The Trumpet Major* on "The Militia Company Drill," a sketch that appeared in *Georgia Scenes* but actually was composed by Oliver Hillhouse Prince, although Hardy got it indirectly through another source.[30] During the late 1840's, the growing interest of British readers in these sketches of American frontier and backwoods life is reflected in the frequent reprinting of pieces in the London *Bentley's Miscellany* drawn from William T. Porter's *The Big Bear of Arkansas* (1845) and Henry Clay Lewis's *Odd Leaves from the Life of a Louisiana "Swamp Doctor"* (1850).[31]

Of special significance to American literature, however, is the fact that in the early writings of Mark Twain, Southwestern humor reached its climax and provided him with basic themes and techniques that he would masterfully use in his own works with a skill and brilliance undreamed of by the frontier humorist. Following the lead of Jennette Tandy, who wrote in 1925 that "Mark Twain's indebtedness to Southwestern humor has never been fully acknowledged," the critical material exploring and substantiating this debt has grown to voluminous proportions.[32]

Once Twain enlarged upon the usefulness of the standard elements of Southwestern humor, their influence did not cease. The next American writer after Twain to use the material and techniques of frontier humor successfully was William Faulkner. How much Faulkner assimilated from growing up in the same environment that earlier nurtured the Southwestern humorists, and to what extent he actually read and imitated the humorous writings, is a moot question, but he did cite Sut Lovingood as one of his favorite fictional characters.[33] Thomas Wolfe frequently worked in the vein of the Southwestern humorists, and obviously Erskine Caldwell's "poor white" degenerates owe much to the tradition.[34] In discussing this subject, Willard Thorp has commented, "Until Carson

McCullers confesses that she has been an assiduous reader of Henry Junius Nott's *Odds and Ends from the Knapsack of Thomas Singularity, Journeyman Printer* or Johnson Jones Hooper's *Adventures of Simon Suggs*, or Flannery O'Connor admits that she treasures copies of *Odd Leaves from the Life of a Louisiana Swamp Doctor* and George Washington Harris' *Sut Lovingood Yarns* it may be impossible to document the flow of the one tradition into the other."[35]

And a strong strain of influence continues to be evident in modern fiction. The collection of stories, *Southern Fried* (1962), and two novels, *Moonshine Light, Moonshine Bright* (1967) and *Ruby Red* (1971), by South Carolina humorist William Price Fox in style and subject matter clearly suggests a knowledge of the earlier humor, as do the picaresque novels *The Ballad of the Flim-Flam Man* (1965) and *The Flim-Flam Man and the Apprentice Grifter* (1972) by Guy Owen of North Carolina, and the best-selling novelette *True Grit* (1968) by Arkansas Journalist Charles Portis. The recent short stories of Tennessean Robert Drake, collected in *Amazing Grace* (1965), *The Single Heart* (1971), and *The Burning Bush* (1974), also demonstrate that sharp and accurate ear for Southern phraseology and patterns of speech which the humorists captured so well in their sketches and tales. The influence thus persists and shows few signs of waning—a rich, strong vein of uniquely American materials continually mined by our nation's best regional writers.

NOTES

1. The title seems first to have been used by Walter Blair in *Native American Humor* (New York, 1937). Before Blair the writings were generally called frontier humor. The designated general area includes Tennessee, Georgia, Alabama, Louisiana, Mississippi, Arkansas, and Missouri, the states close to the lower Mississippi or Gulf of Mexico.

2. Will D. Howe, "Early Humorists," in *The Cambridge History of American Literature*, vol. II (New York, 1917), p. 150.

3. Frederick Jackson Turner, *The Frontier in American History* (New York, 1921), pp. 3-4, 33, 37.

4. Franklin J. Meine, ed., *Tall Tales of the Southwest* (New York, 1930), p. xxvii.

5. It is an interesting fact that most American humorists from Benjamin Franklin on have been at one time or another newspapermen. This has remained the case even in the present century. Among the sixteen modern American humorists discussed in Norris W. Yates' *The American Humorist, Conscience of the Twentieth Century* (Ames, Iowa, 1964), all were connected sometime during their careers with American newspapers and periodicals. The relationship between the American newspaper and literary humor is a subject little explored but worthy of scrutiny.

6. Walter Blair, *Native American Humor* (San Francisco, 1960), p. 70.

7. Bernard DeVoto, *Mark Twain's America* (New York, 1932), p. 96.

8. Arthur Palmer Hudson, ed., *Humor of the Old Deep South* (New York, 1936), pp. 16-17.

9. Although Walter Blair, p. 85, notes that Porter testified that Baldwin was a contributor to the *Spirit of the Times*, none of his pieces have been identified.

10. The importance of Porter to the humor of the Old Southwest has been examined in detail by Norris W. Yates in *William T. Porter and the Spirit of the Times* (Baton Rouge, 1957).

11. These details are based mainly upon the list of humorists and their vocations compiled by Walter Blair, pp. 63-64, with some additional facts gathered elsewhere.

12. Kenneth S. Lynn, *Mark Twain and Southwestern Humor* (Boston, 1959), p. 52.

13. It should be noted that when Lynn treats Harris, he recognizes these facts about him. His outline does indeed apply to several of the other humorists, but it may be misleading to present such a generalized portrait which fails obviously to cover the entire school of writers.

14. DeVoto, p. 241.

15. *Ibid.*, p. 243.

16. Meine, p. xxvi.

17. Richmond Croom Beatty, Floyd C. Watkins, and Thomas Daniel Young, eds., *The Literature of the South* (Chicago, 1952), pp. 112-113.

18. Walter Blair, Theodore Hornberger, and Randall Stewart, *American Literature, A Brief History* (Chicago, 1964), p. 161.

19. Blair, *Native American Humor*, pp. 91-92.

20. Lynn, p. 64.

21. See Robert Hopkins, "Simon Suggs: A Burlesque Campaign Biography," *American Quarterly*, 15 (Fall, 1963), 459-463. This idea was earlier suggested by Howard Winston Smith in "Johnson Jones Hooper: A Critical Study" (unpublished M.A. thesis, Vanderbilt University, 1962), p. 47.

22. Lynn, p. 65. Lynn is, of course, stressing the political to an extreme and to the detriment of an objective appraisal of the total achievement of Southwestern humor.

23. Meine, p. xxix; Blair, pp. 64-69; Robert E. Spiller, *et al.*, eds. *Literary History of the United States* (New York, 1963), pp. 609, 739; Edd Winfield Parks, "The Intent of the Ante-Bellum Southern Humorists," *Mississippi Quarterly*, 13 (Fall, 1960), pp. 163-168.

24. DeVoto, p. 98.

25. Cited in Parks, pp. 164-165.

26. Willard Thorp, "Suggs and Sut in Modern Dress: The Latest Chapter in Southern Humor," *Mississippi Quarterly*, 13 (Fall, 1960), 173.

27. Cited in Parks, p. 166.

28. George W. Harris, *Sut Lovingood's Yarns*, ed. M. Thomas Inge (New Haven, 1966), p. 26.

29. Lynn, p. 70.

30. Jennette Tandy, *Crackerbox Philosophers in American Humor and Satire* (New York, 1925), p. 95; Jay B. Hubbell, *The South in American Literature* (Durham, 1954), p. 669.

31. Milton Rickels, "The Humorists of the Old Southwest in the London *Bentley's Miscellany*," *American Literature*, 27 (1956), 557-60.

32. Tandy, p. 94; Meine, pp. xv, xxix-xxxii; DeVoto, chapters IV and X; Blair, pp. 153-162; Lynn, *passim*; Pascal Covici, Jr., *Mark Twain's Humor* (Dallas, 1962), pp. 3-36, and *passim*; Henry Nash Smith, *Mark Twain, the Development of a Writer* (Cambridge, 1962), pp. 1-21 and *passim*. These are only the more significant studies.

33. For a full discussion of this subject and a list of relevant bibliographical material, see M. Thomas Inge, "William Faulkner and George Washington Harris: In the Tradition of Southwestern Humor," *Tennessee Studies in Literature*, 7 (1962), 47-59.

34. Beatty *et al.*, pp. 624, 111.

35. Thorp, p. 170. See also Randall Stewart, "Tidewater and Frontier," *Georgia Review*, 13 (Fall, 1959), 296-307. The actual debts of modern writers to the earlier humor must be determined with some caution. For example, when the present writer asked Miss Eudora Welty, who was attending a literary symposium at Vanderbilt University on April 25, 1963, if she had read any of the humorists of the Old Southwest, she replied very apologetically that she hadn't but she must get around to it since "everybody lately is talking about them so much."

I. General Overviews

Tall Tales of the Southwest

Franklin J. Meine

Before Mark Twain and Artemus Ward it is popularly supposed that there was little or no American humor. The facts are otherwise for Mark Twain's early writings marked the climax of a rich development, rather than the beginning of one. Twain, born in 1835 of Southern parents on the Southwestern frontier, emerged out of a period (1830-60) when the humorous story and the tall tale were characteristic literary productions; and as will be seen from the last story in this collection, Mark at seventeen, setting type in the newspaper print-shop at Hannibal, was a part of that humor and contributed to it. We have lost sight of the life and literature of that earlier era because the Civil War so sharply broke off the past. At the outbreak of the war, Mark had pretty well arrived at maturity—he was twenty-six—and rooted deep in that earlier life carried over a great deal of the old Southern tradition. Instead of opening up a new vein of American humor with his first famous story, *Jim Smiley and His Jumping Frog,* in the New York *Saturday Press* (1865), he simply revived a kind of story-telling that had its home and earlier vogue in the genial South before the War. This is not a book about Mark Twain, but it is important to note that Twain was himself saturated with this frontier humor and so offers an approach to the group of Southern humorists who immediately preceded him.

Scattered through the South and Southwest during the forties and fifties there sprang up a picturesque local-color group of humorists who flourished in bar-rooms, on law circuits, on steamboats and in the wide open spaces. They were not professional humorists, but debonair settlers engaged in various tasks: lawyers, newspaper editors, country gentlemen of family and fortune, doctors, army officers, travellers, actors—

who wrote for amusement rather than for gain. "This little sketch," one of them typically prefaces, "was rit with no higher aim than to amuse the idle hours of my friends and if it fails to do that, it's a spilt job." These young men, most of whom were seeking fortune or adventure on the newly-opened, turbulent Southern and Southwestern frontier, were quick to seize upon the comic aspects of the rough life about them, and graphically sketched the humorous and colorful local happenings, the oddities in rustic or pioneer character, and the tall tales that were going the rounds of the locality. These spontaneous, hilarious pencillings, from an academic point of view, may indeed be considered nothing more than rather charcoal sketches. Yet in their way they are masterpieces: realistic, racy, written in a vein of rollicking humor, and thoroughly characteristic in tone, color, and action of that forgotten era. The age, one of the most vivid of American experiences, has no other authentic record in our literature. Nothing is more essentially American than the frontier; and these sketches, humble enough in intent, were the earliest literary realization of the frontier, and, remain its most revealing expression.

II

This early humor of the South had no counterpart in the humor of any other section of the United States. It was distinctly and peculiarly Southern; and it was provincial, wholly local. Even within the South various localities had their own peculiarities of humor which set them off. Georgia wit and humor, like Georgia watermelons, thought Joel Chandler Harris, were *prima facie* Georgian,—they were unique and there was none to compare with them. "The sun, the soil, the air, and even the spring water, seem to have something to do with it."[1]

"In the Southern states," Colonel Henry Watterson observed, "the humor turns upon character and incident. We body forth a personage out of the odds and ends of comic thought and memory, the heel-taps of current observance; we clothe this image appropriately, and then put it through a series of amusing adventures. Thus it is that our humor is anecdotal, producing such figures as Ned Brace, the practical Georgia joker; Major Joseph Jones, Esq., of Pineville, Georgia, famous lover and traveller; Captain Simon Suggs, of the 'Tallapoosy Vollantares'; Ovid Bolus, Esq., of the flush times in Alabama and Mississippi; Sut Lovingood, 'ornary' hell-raising mountaineer of the Great Smokies; and the Rev. Hezekiah Bradley, who discoursed on the 'Harp of a Thousand Strings.'

"They flourished years ago, in the good old time of muster days and quarter racing, before the camp-meeting and the barbecue had lost their power and their charm; when men led homely lives, doing their love-making and their law-making as they did their fighting and plowing, in a straight furrow; when there was no national debt multiplying the dangers and magnifying the expenses of distillation in the hills and hollows, and pouring in upon the log-rolling, the quilting, the corn-shucking, and the fish-fry an inquisitorial crew of tax-gatherers and 'snoopers' to spoil the sport and dull the edge of patriotic husbandry."[2]

III

The corner-stone of this early humorous literature was *Georgia Scenes*, 1835, by *A Native Georgian*. The pseudonym was that of Augustus Baldwin Longstreet,[3] a prominent young lawyer and newspaper editor then residing in Augusta. The collected *Scenes* comprised eighteen humorous sketches, describing "scenes, characters and incidents" of life in Georgia during the "first half century of the Republic," that had appeared previously from 1832 to 1835, over the pseudonyms *Hall* and *Baldwin* in Longstreet's local newspaper, *The States Rights Sentinel*, and other local Georgia papers. It is of bibliographical interest to note that the book was first published by Longstreet and printed at the *S. R. Sentinel Office*, Augusta, 1835.

The *Scenes* were hearty humorous sketches, by a clever story teller, of rough backwoods Georgia life and manners. Longstreet did not gloss over the crudities of frontier life, nor did he burlesque them, but with gentlemanly humor vividly described the comic, coarser aspects of the life he knew so well. The *Scenes* were consciously realistic: they showed red-necked Georgia crackers in eye-gouging, nose-biting fights, in coarse horse-trade wranglers, and in capers which even invaded funeral processions. So realistic were they in fact, that Longstreet, an ambitious young politician, published them anonymously, fearing their effects, and later when he became an elderly and godly college president, vowed that he had never written them.

In book form the *Scenes* became so popular that Harper and Brothers, New York, took over its publication and in 1840 issued a "Second Edition," with illustrations, which soon sold 8000 copies. North and

South, *Georgia Scenes* was acclaimed widely and with warm enthusiasm. Yale conferred an honorary LL.D. upon its distinguished alumnus. In the South even Poe who admittedly was "not of the merry mood" confessed that, "Seldom—perhaps never in our lives—have we laughed so immoderately over any book as over the one now before us."[4] But Poe did more than merely laugh: he appreciated Longstreet's keen insight into real, contemporary Southern life. The melancholy Poe chuckled and wrote, "The author, whoever he is, is a clever fellow, imbued with a spirit of the truest humor, and endowed moreover with an exquisitely discriminating and penetrative understanding of character in general, and of Southern character in particular. And we do not mean to speak of *human* character exclusively. To be sure, our Georgian is *au fait* here too—he is learned in all things appertaining to the biped without feathers. In regard especially to that class of Southwestern mammalia who come under the generic appellation 'Savagerous wild cats,' he is a very Theophrastus in *duo decimo*. But he is not the less at home in other matters. Of geese and ganders he is the La Bruyère, and of good-for-nothing-horses, the Rochefoucault."[5]

With *Georgia Scenes* Longstreet established a pattern that had a profound influence on all subsequent humorous writers of the South. In some instances the tradition was handed down through actual personal contact; it is interesting to note, for example, that it was Longstreet's associate in editing the Augusta *Sentinel* in the early thirties, William T. Thompson, who later secured the services of Joel Chandler Harris for the Savannah *News* in 1871. Longstreet showed the way and aroused a lively interest in the comico-ludicrous aspects of Southern and Southwestern frontier life that was enthusiastically caught up and developed, each in his peculiar way, by Thompson, Thorpe, Hooper, Baldwin, Harris and many others.

But the importance of *Georgia Scenes* was not merely sectional: it was national. In the hands of these writers the humor of the American frontier, the humor we regard as so typically American, developed rapidly and plentifully. In the local newspapers of that period there appeared literally thousands of humorous frontier stories and sketches that went the rounds of the American press. By 1860 this frontier type of American humor—so important to the understanding of John Phoenix, Artemus Ward, and Mark Twain—had been well established.

Longstreet's co-editor on the *Sentinel*, William T. Thompson, soon after (1842-43), as editor of the *Southern Miscellany*, printed a series of letters purporting to come from one Major Joseph Jones, Esq., of

Pineville, Georgia, relating in a naïve, jovial fashion the Major's court-ship of a neighbor girl, Mary Stallins. These letters were issued in book form in 1844 under the title *Major Jones' Courtship* and became ex-ceedingly popular, reaching an eighth edition in 1847.

In contrast with the *Georgia Scenes* which dealt with a wide range of subjects, *Major Jones' Courtship* is a connected series of episodes woven about the courtship theme, but revealing nevertheless contem-porary Southern plantation life, particularly that of the middle-class Georgia planters typified by Major Jones. Unlike the *Scenes*, the *Court-ship* contains nothing coarse or "brutal"; Major Jones is a simple, un-sophisticated, good-humored Georgia youth who babbles about his love for Mary, and their amusing amatory adventures.

"But Major Jones is a Georgian. He is well to do, and knows a thing or two, albeit his education in 'grammar' and 'retorick' has been ne-glected, his character, like his diction, is homespun. He is a thorough rustic, and belongs to a class which is still (1882) very large in the interior of the South."[6] In characters, quaint dialogue, and easy-going humor, the story is distinctively Southern and genuinely Georgian.

The popularity of *Major Jones' Courtship* induced the author to extend the Major's adventures in a series of travel letters (1847), describ-ing scenes, incidents and adventures in a tour from Georgia to Canada, and also induced him to gather into book form a miscellaneous lot of earlier humorous stories and sketches that he had written and printed before the Major Jones stories came out, dealing with the "nether" side of Southern life, the Georgia "Cracker." This latter collection, *Major Jones' Chronicles of Pineville*, embracing sketches of Georgia scenes, incidents, and characters was published in 1845.

The preface to this book reveals exactly the point of view of this whole group of early Southern humorists:

> Encouraged by the favour with which a recent humble attempt to depict some of the peculiar features of the Georgia backwoodsman has been received by the public, some of my friends have persuaded me to publish a few other stories illustrative of similar character, which they knew I had written. Influenced by these persuasions, I determined to brush up my old manuscripts, produce something new of the same sort, and thus endeavor to present to the public a few more interesting specimens of the genus "Cracker."
>
> I wish it to be understood that I use this term with all due respect. It belongs to a class of good people with whom it has been my des-

tiny to become intimately associated, and I know there is much to admire and respect in their characters. The lineaments of these characters are strongly marked, and they sit so fair, that he who takes rough sketches, as I sometimes do, can readly "take their picters"; but as a class they are brave, generous, honest, and industrious, and withal, possessed of a sturdy patriotism. The vagabond and the dissolute among them are exceptions to the rule, and in a few generations more, education will have made the mass a great people. When such education will have done all it is destined to effect for the American backwoodsman, it may, and will increase the sum of his happiness and usefulness in the scale of being, but it will at the same time, by polishing away those peculiarities which now mark his manners and language, reduce him to the common level of commonplace people, and make him a less curious "specimen" for the study of the naturalist. As he now is, however, I have endeavoured, in a small way, to catch his "manners living as they rise," and if I have been so fortunate as to succeed, the effort will amuse him, when he meets with it, if it should interest no one else.

I claim no higher character for my stories—some of which appeared in a literary periodical of limited circulation—than that of mere sketches, designed to amuse those who have a taste for such things, with some slight traits of peculiar character; and it may be to afford the student of human nature a glance at characters not often found in books, or anywhere else, indeed, except in just such places as "*Pineville*," Georgia.

Georgia Scenes and *Major Jones* pictured the quiet rural life of the old South, with its established and stable social order. In the *Flush Times of Alabama and Mississippi* (1853), and the *Adventures of Simon Suggs* (1845), the scene changes to the fast-shifting, turbulent Southwestern frontier. Here from 1835 to 1855 a new country was being opened up; and emigrants came streaming in from all quarters of the Union, drawn to the new frontier by exciting accounts of the fertility of its virgin lands and rumors of profitable enterprise and adventure. It was an antetype California gold rush in all except the gold.

The *Flush Times*, a collection of frontier character sketches and anecdotes, was designed "to illustrate the periods, the characters, and the phases of society" of that movement. Their author, Joseph G. Baldwin, himself an actor in the humorous and exciting life he so artistically described, was a young lawyer who had emigrated from the Old Dominion in 1836, to settle in North Alabama. His going there was, he said, " 'Urged by hunger and the request of friends.' The gentle momentum of a female slipper, too, it might as well be confessed, added its moral suasion to the more pressing urgencies of breakfast, dinner and supper. To the South West he started because magnificent accounts came from that sunny land of most cheering and exhilarating prospects of fussing, quarrelling, murdering, violation of contracts, swindling, and the whole catalogue of *crimen falsi*—in fine, of a flush tide of litigation in all of its departments, civil and criminal.[7]

"The condition of society may be imagined:—vulgarity—ignorance—fussy and arrogant pretension—unmitigated rowdyism—bullying insolence, if they did not rule the hour *seemed* to wield unchecked dominion. . . . The groceries—*vulgice*—doggeries (where beverages abounded), were in full blast in those days, no village having less than a half dozen all busy all the time: gaming and horse-racing were polite and well patronized amusements. I knew a Judge to adjourn two courts (or court twice) to attend a horse-race, at which he officiated judicially and ministerially, and with more appropriateness than in the judicial chair. Occasionally the scene was diversified by a murder or two which though perpetrated from behind a corner, or behind the back of the deceased, whenever the accused chose to stand his trial, was always found to have been committed in self-defence, securing the homicide of an honorable acquittal *at the hands of his peers*. . . . Profligacy . . . held riotous carnival. Larceny grew not only respectable, but genteel, and ruffled it in all the pomp of purple and fine linen. Swindling was raised to the dignity of the fine arts."[8]

In this setting also was written the *Adventure of Simon Suggs*, 1845,[9] by Johnson J. Hooper, who was, like Longstreet, a prominent young lawyer and newspaper editor, of Alabama. In Simon Suggs, Hooper achieved a powerful character study, bringing to a focus in one character those virulent forces of frontier life. Suggs is a sharp, shrewd swashbuckler, whose whole philosophy "lies snugly in his favorite aphorism—'it is good to be shifty in a new cuntry'—which means that it is right and proper that one should live as merrily and as comfortably as possible at the expense of others; and of the practicability of this in particular instances, the Captain's whole life has been a long series of the most convincing illustrations."[10]

The character of Simon Suggs and his significance for Southern humor have been keenly appreciated by Colonel Watterson. "In Simon Suggs," said he, "we have the Vulgarian of the South 'done' to use his

own elegant phraseology, 'to a cracklin.' . . . No one who is at all familiar with the provincial life of the South can fail to recognize the 'points'
of this sharp and vulgar, sunny and venal swashbuckler. As serio-comic
as Sellers, as grotesque as Shingle, he possesses an originality all his
own, and never for a moment rises above or falls below it. He is a gambler by nature, by habit, by preference, by occupation. Without a virtue
in the world, except his good-humor and his self-possession, there is
something in his vices, his indolence, his swagger, his rogueries, which,
in spite of the worthlessness of the man and the dishonesty of his prac-
tices, detains and amuses us. He is a representative character . . . true
to nature . . . graphic . . . picturesque."[11]

Strikingly different from any of the foregoing books were the *Sut
Lovingood Yarns*,[12] 1867, by George W. Harris, of Knoxville, East
Tennessee. Although the *Yarns* did not appear in book form until after
the Civil War, Harris was immediately contemporary with this whole
group of early Southern humorists—Longstreet, Thompson, Hooper,
Baldwin,—his first humorous sketch having appeared in the New York
Spirit of the Times in 1845.[13] Harris lived practically all his life in the
"Nobs" of "Old Knox," and loved the free, rough life of the Great Smoky
Mountains and the French Broad and Tennessee Rivers. He was a
versatile genius: silversmith, expert worker in all metals, journalist,
inventor, hunter, humorist; and in his youth, like Mark Twain, worked
on a river steamboat. Harris was a captain; Clemens, a few years later,
a pilot.

Sut Lovingood is a unique and original character in American humor.
He is a rough, lanky, uncouth mountaineer of the Great Smokies, whose
sole ambition in life is to raise "perticler" hell. As he says of himself:
"Every critter what hes ever seed me, ef he has sence enuff to hide from
a cummin kalamity, ur run from a muskit, jis' knows five great facks
in my case es well es they knows the road to their moufs. *Fustly*, that
I haint got nara a soul, nuffin but a whisky proof gizzard, sorter like the
wus half ove a ole par ove saddil bags, *Seconly*, that I'se too durn'd a
fool to cum even onder millertary lor. *Thudly*, that I hes the longes' par
ove laigs ever hung to eny cackus, 'sceptin' only ove a grandaddy spider,
an' kin beat *him* a usen ove em jis' es bad es a skeer'd dog kin beat a
crippled mud turkil. *Foufly*, that I kin chamber more cork-screw kill-
devil whisky, an' stay on aind, than enything 'sceptin' only a broad bottum'd
chun. *Fivety*, an' las'ly, kin git intu more durn'd misfortnit skeery scrapes,
than enybody, an' then run outen them faster, by golly, nor enybody."[14]
Sut relished the prospect of driving a mad bull into a wedding party, or
poking out a hornets' nest into a negro camp-meeting, or stuffing a bag

22

of lizards up the "passun's britches-laig when he were a-ravin' ontu his tip-toes, an a-poundin' the pulpit wif his fis'." Such were Sut's pranks, with his constant companion, his whisky flask, slung at his side.

Sut's humor is always robust and hearty; sometimes rough, possibly coarse, yet he is vastly funny; and the *Yarns* are full of comic situation, plot and phrase. Sut reveals the author's spirit in his keen delight for Hallowe'en *fun*,—there is no ulterior motive (except occasionally Sut's desire to "get even"), no rascality, no gambling, no sharping as in *Simon Suggs* or the *Flush Times*. Sut is simply the genuine naïve roughneck mountaineer riotously bent on raising hell.

Harris makes no pretense of literary style. He tells his story in his own way directly and swiftly. Although writers of his time generally tacked morals to most of their stories, Harris was satisfied to tell a story which tickled men's funny-bones and consigned morals to "suckit" riders. The *Yarns* are fresh, racy and packed with action. Harris rises above the level of merely objective description of humorous characters or incidents, and concocts with "owdacious" flights of fancy all sorts of grotesque schemes to display Sut's peculiar talents. For vivid imagination, comic plot, Rabelaisian touch, and sheer *fun*, the *Sut Lovingood Yarns* surpass anything else in American humor.

In addition to these single works there were three notably good collections of tall tales; two edited by Wm. T. Porter, editor of the New York *Spirit of the Times*, *The Big Bear of Arkansas*, 1845, and *The Quarter Race in Kentucky*, 1846; and a third edited by T. A. Burke, a Georgia journalist and humorous writer, *Polly Peablossom's Wedding*, (c. 1851). Each collection contained from twenty to thirty stories or sketches, by approximately as many writers, that had achieved popularity in going the rounds of the press for the previous five or ten years. These tall tales touched every phase from the mildly humorous to the utterly ludicrous in Southern and Southwestern frontier life. Of all these stories the most notable perhaps was T. B. Thorpe's *Big Bear of Arkansas* (1841),[15] which was characteristically Western and vastly amusing. It was a match for Münchhausen.

"Stranger," said the man of Arkansaw, "it took five niggers and myself to put that carcase (of the big *bar*) on a mule's back. . . . 'Twould astonish you to know how big he was: I made a bed-spread of his skin, and the way it used to cover my mattress, and leave several feet on each side to tuck up, would have delighted you. It was in fact a creation bar, and if it had lived in Samson's time, and had met him, in a fair fight, it would have licked him in the twinkling of a dice box."

The "Big Bar" was typical of the whoppers that were told when hunters and frontiersmen gathered in bar-rooms and sat around camp fires. When it was published, many similar yarns followed it into print. It is interesting to note the similarity of these tall tales of the early frontier to the yarns still popular in such regions as the Colorado mining towns, the mountains of Kentucky, and the North woods.[16]

IV

The subjects of these tales and humorous sketches are fairly typical of the whole Southern and Southwestern group of picturesque local-color humorists who flourished in the thirties, forties and fifties. They touched on the most entertaining subjects imaginable, the social life of their times; and yet these faithful and delightful pictures of those times have been elegantly ignored by most of our writers on American history. They are a treasury, inexhaustible and untouched, of information about the life of the frontier; and yet even social history has ignored them. The indifference of historians is matched by that of students of American literature, who have been, for the most part, either ignorant of this field or superior to it.

The range of subjects is indicated by the following rough groupings,—

1. *Sketches of local customs*
   Shooting matches, gander pullings, horse races, militia drills, quiltings, frolics
2. *Courtships and weddings*
3. *Law circuits and political life*
   The bench and bar, legislatures in the frontier states, stump speeches and buncombe political electioneering, the circuit courts, with all their "attractions of criminal trials, poker-playing lawyers, political caucuses and possible monkey-shows"
4. *Hunting stories*
   The "Big Bears," the bee hunters, turkey running, coon hunts, ferocious "painters" (panthers)
5. *Oddities in Character*
6. *Travel*
   Steamboat life on the Ohio and Mississippi, the new railroads, the rustic in the big city
7. *Frontier medical stories*
   Visits in the wilderness, cupping, pulling teeth, surgery with Bowie knives

8. *Gambling*
9. *Varieties of religious experience*
   Circuit riding preachers, negro camp-meetings, Millerites, Mormons, revivalist meetings, burlesque sermons
10. *Fights*

V

These stories and sketches appeared originally in newspapers and popular periodicals. American humor has always been a spontaneous part of everyday American life; and so the newspaper, chronicler of daily doings and local life, has offered a quick and easy vehicle for all manner of humorous anecdotes, stories and tall tales. The American newspaper as we know it today—the "penny press"—began gathering momentum shortly after 1830; and during the period 1830-60, especially in the South and Southwest, its growth was notably rapid. Stories of steamboat life on the Ohio and Mississippi, and tall tales of the frontier naturally and quickly found their way to the flourishing river-town dailies of New Orleans, Cincinnati, Louisville and St. Louis. Many a smaller community that boasted a job-print-shop and a young lawyer or printer with an itch to be an editor, supported a local news-sheet featuring humorous sketches. Humorous material was always in demand; and so the growth of the newspaper encouraged the local humorist. Not infrequently the humorist in turn scored a national reputation for his paper. The *Georgia Scenes,* it will be remembered, were contributed by Longstreet to his own and other local Georgia papers. So too, Hooper's *Simon Suggs* and Thompson's *Major Jones* first appeared locally—to mention only a few. Once in print these tales and sketches went the rounds of the American press, and frequently were later gathered into book form.

The most popular humorous journal of this period was the New York *Spirit of the Times,* founded and edited by William T. Porter, 1831-56. As its subtitle indicated, it was a weekly *Chronicle of the Turf, Agriculture, Field Sports, Literature and the Stage.* Started originally as a sporting journal, it had become by 1845 the outstanding humorous weekly as well, and had a national circulation.

"The novel design and scope of the *Spirit of the Times* soon fixed attention," wrote its editor, Wm. T. Porter, in 1845,[17] "and ere long it became the nucleus of a new order of literary talent. In addition to correspondents who described with equal felicity and power the stirring incidents of the chase and turf, it enlisted another and still more numerous class, who furnished most valuable and interesting reminiscences of the pioneers of the far West—sketches of thrilling scenes and adventures in that then comparatively un-known region, and the peculiar and sometimes fearful character-istics of the 'squatters' and early settlers. Many of these descriptions were wrought up in a masterly style; and in the course of a few years a generous feeling of emulation sprang up in the South and South-west, prompted by the same impulses, until at length the corre-spondents of the *Spirit of the Times* comprised a large majority of those who have subsequently distinguished themselves in this novel and original walk of literature."

After Porter's death, George Wilkes, associate editor of *Porter's Spirit of the Times*,[18] furnished the following interpretative sketch[19] of Porter and the *Spirit of the Times*: "William Porter," he said, "moved among the Livingstons, Hamptons, Stevenses, Stocktons, Joneses, Wad-dells, Longs, etc., making all happy by his cheerful spirit, and distributing favor by his presence, rather than receiving patronage. The merit of his paper, and the high character of these voluntary associations, not only drew around him the most distinguished writers and correspond-ents of the time, both at home and from foreign lands, but brought out a new class of writers, and created a style which may be denominated an American literature—not the august, stale, didactic, pompous, bloodless method of the magazine pages of that day; but a fresh, crisp, vigorous, elastic, graphic literature, full of force, readiness, actuality and point, which has walked up to the telegraph, and hardly been invigorated or improved by even the terse and emphatic lightning. This literature was not stewed in the closet, or fretted out at some pale, pensioned laborer's desk, but sparkled from the cheerful leisure of the easy scholar—poured in from the emulous officer in the barracks, or at sea—emanated spon-taneously from the jocund poet—and flowed from every mead, or lake, or mountain—in the land where the rifle or the rod was known."

The purely humorous story, as distinguished from the mildly humor-ous sporting sketch, and the tall tale from the frontier were entirely congenial to the sporting interests of the *Spirit*; and its columns were crowded full of fresh, original and facetious articles from the raciest pens of the country. Its contributors were drawn from all walks of life, lawyers, explorers, doctors, journalists, river boatmen, officers of frontier

Army posts, editors, and even members of Congress. In February 1851 Porter boasted eighteen correspondents in both houses of Congress. Porter with his genial disposition and love of laughter gathered about him, both as contributors and as personal friends, some of the liveliest wags of that day,—men like T. B. Thorpe, Johnson J. Hooper, Wm. T. Thompson, Sol Smith, C. F. M. Noland, J. M. Field, George W. Harris, and literally hundreds of other humorous writers throughout Alabama, Mississippi, Louisiana, Arkansas, and Texas. In addition to original stories the *Spirit* reprinted the best yarns from such papers as the New Orleans *Picayune*, the St. Louis *Reveille*, the Montgomery *Mail*, the Cincinnati *News*, the Louisville *Courier*,—to mention only a very few of the "snappiest" newspapers that were inexhaustible sources of humorous stories and American oddities. The number of stories in this collection that appeared originally or as reprints in the *Spirit*, as noted in the footnotes, will serve to show how William T. Porter through the medium of the *Spirit of the Times* fostered and encouraged what has appropriately been called the Big Bear school of American humor.[20]

VI

These early frontier humorists have a two-fold importance for American literature: they were our first realists and they have exerted a far-reaching influence on later American humorists, notably Mark Twain.

Beginning with Longstreet this whole group of Southern and Southwestern humorists were realists. In the preface to his *Georgia Scenes* Longstreet wrote, "They [the sketches] consist of nothing more than fanciful combinations of real incidents and characters; and throwing into those scenes, which would be otherwise dull and insipid, some personal incident or adventure of my own, real or imaginary, as it would best suit my purpose; usually real, but happening at different times and under different circumstances from those in which they are here represented."[21]

Georgia Scenes, aside from being the first Southern humorous masterpiece, was the first realistic interpretation of Southern character and manners, and it was recognized as a far more truthful and satisfactory picture than the old romantic treatments that preceded it. "The romancers of the Old South wrote extravagantly of the cavaliers, the chivalry, the noble lords and beautiful ladies of the past, but the humorists described lovingly the Jack-legged lawyer, the gambling, lying

45075

renegade, the simple but shrewd backwoodsman and the unadorned, bashful country lass of the present. The humorists were the realists, and with all their exaggeration, probably drew a truer picture of life than the romanticists."[22]

In the wake of Longstreet followed Thompson, Hooper, Harris, Thorpe, Sol Smith, and many other local-color humorists who like Longstreet wrote in a boldly realistic vein. Their humor, spontaneously bubbling forth from everyday life, dealt with *real* incidents and *real* characters. With the gigantic exaggeration of the tall tale, the use of dialect and grotesque dialogue, leisurely digressions, and surprising twists, these frontier humorists developed the characteristic "tricks" of American humor; and it was this typical humor of the wide open spaces that prepared the way for the "Wild Humorist of the Pacific Slope."

It was this humor—the humor of the South and Southwest—to which Mark Twain was born.[23] From his boyhood he heard it from the mouths of rivermen and wherever the villagers talked together in the leisurely waterside town of Hannibal. Through the printing shop where he was apprenticed and the office of his brother's newspaper passed the flood of "exchanges" from all over the county. Editors and devils laughed over the productions of "J. Cypress Jr.," "Sugartail," or "Major Jones" and then reprinted them, mostly without credit. A good story might ripple from New Orleans to New York and back again in twenty or thirty reprintings. This popularity was significant to a young printer who would some day experiment with literature at the other end of the case. Nor was he ever out of touch with it, for in St. Louis, Philadelphia, New York, Cincinnati and Keokuk, where he practised his trade, the same papers published the same sort of literature and were accorded the same popularity. Later, on the steamboats, the papers were available and, by now, the more ambitious of their productions were bound up in paperbacks and sold to the travellers whose literary taste invariably offended British tourists.

It was a humor instinct with the life of the frontier, wild and robust and male. Most of all, it gave to young Sam Clemens the interesting example of material immediately at hand translated into literature or, perhaps, into writing on the threshold of literature. The life here pictured had been his, the characters were men and women whose counterparts he saw every day. These people, then, could be written about! When young Sam Clemens took to writing, he had to look for a model no farther than the nearest newspapers and for material no farther than the boiler deck. Mr. Meine's excavation of the earliest sketch known to have been Mark Twain's, therefore, inevitably fits into the *genre*. Mark Twain was utilizing the material at hand in the way that had been shown him.

Consider the austere ideal of justice upheld by Captain Summons of the steamboat *Dr. Franklin*, in the sketch called "Breaking a Bank." Always solicitous of the comfort and enjoyment of his passengers, he is "determined that they shall amuse themselves as they d—n please." He scrupulously assists at the Sabbath services of clergymen travelling on his boat, and just as wholeheartedly puts himself at the disposal of those who care to dance or "pass the time in playing poker." Dancers, players, or parsons, they have the captain's good will and shall drink with him. "All sorts of passengers are accommodated on the *Dr. Franklin*—the rights of none are suffered to be infringed." A group of revivalists board the boat and proceed to hold services day and night, gravely protected by Captain Summons from disturbance by unbelievers. Meanwhile, to the shocked displeasure of the godly, other passengers are engaged in gambling. The circuit riders wait on the Captain and request him to put a stop to this immorality . . . Clearly, we are dealing with a Mark Twain conception. The situation is his, and Captain Summons may well be a foretaste of Captain Ned Blakely or even of Captain Stormfield. The conviction is reinforced by Captain Summons' reply to the clergymen:

"Gentlemen, amuse yourselves as you like; preach and pray to your hearts' content—none shall interfere with your pious purposes; some like that sort of thing, *I* have no objection to it. These men prefer to amuse themselves with cards; let them—they pay their passage as well as you, *gentlemen*, and have as much right to *their amusements* as you have to *yours*, and they shall not be disturbed. Preach, play cards, dance cotillions—do what you like, *I* am agreeable; only understand that all games, preaching among the rest, must cease at ten o'clock."

The voice is unquestionably the drawl of Mark Twain, the disarming humor that masked the most penetrating knowledge of "the damned human race" yet revealed in American literature? So it would seem. And yet "Breaking a Bank" is only a typical item in this widely diffused, sub-literary humor of the frontier. It is by Sol Smith, the actor-manager, and was published in 1846 in *The Quarter Race in Kentucky*, edited by Wm. T. Porter.

If Mark's earliest recovered sketch belongs to this literature, his far Western period displays a flood of it. "The Massacre at Dutch Nick's" and "The Petrified Man" are typical "tall tales" and might have appeared in *The Spirit of the Times* as fittingly as in the Virginia City *Enterprise*. He had found other mediums of humor when he reached San Francisco, but he filled columns of the *Californian* with similar tales, some of his own invention, others long weathered in newsprint or in pilot houses. In Jim Gillis' cabin on Jackass Hill he either did or did not meet the history of the jumping frog. But at least he later remembered that he did, and whether in his pocket or someone else's, the frog had made the journey from the Mississippi bottoms to Caleveras County. With its publication, the "tall tale" reached a kind of climax, having climbed from anecdotal folk humor to universality. But Mark Twain was not done with it. The device served him handsomely in *Innocents Abroad*. By *Roughing It* he had moulded it into a sort of narrative interlude, such as the story of the cat who ate coconut, the genuine Mexican plug, and that other cat at Jackass Hill who was named Tom Quartz. Through all his books thereafter he makes use of the framework, constantly refining it and constantly enriching it with the flashes of human insight that gave his characters body and breath. As late as *Joan of Arc*, the Paladin is richly embroidering his inventions in a manner that comes straight from the foibles of river folk glimpsed from the door of a pilot-house and straight from the pages of forgotten newspapers over which men had laughed along the river within the hearing of Sam Clemens, printer's devil . . . It was not only the mechanism of humor that these vanished writers gave him. So far as literary parentage is not a fiction, so far as there is any truth in notions of literary influence, these humble humorists made a realist of Mark Twain.

NOTES

1. Harris, J. C. *Stories of Georgia*, p. 240.
2. Watterson, Henry. *Oddities in Southern Life and Character*, preface, p. vii.
3. For a complete discussion of Longstreet and the *Georgia Scenes* see his biography, *Augustus Baldwin Longstreet*, by J. D. Wade, 1927.
4. Poe reviewed *Georgia Scenes* in the *Southern Literary Messenger*, March 1836.
5. Poe, *Southern Literary Messenger*, March 1836.
6. Watterson, *Oddities*, p. 134.
7. Baldwin, *Flush Times*, p. 47. For further amusing recital of this frontier life see the sketch in this collection, "How the Times Served the Virginians."
8. *Ibid.* p. 85, p. 89.
9. Carey and Hart, Philadelphia. A small portion of *Simon Suggs* and one or two of the other sketches in the volume had already appeared in Hooper's paper, *The East Alabamian*, Lafayette, Chambers County; and in the New York *Spirit of the Times*. A second volume of humorous sketches by Hooper, *A Ride with Old Kit Kuncker*, was published by Slade in Tuscaloosa, 1849. This collection is more generally known by the title of the Philadelphia reprint, *Widow Rugby's Husband*, A. Hart, 1851.
10. Hooper, *Simon Suggs,* p. 12.
11. Watterson, *Oddities*, pages 39, 134, adapted.
12. Dick and Fitzgerald, New York, copyright 1867. Dick and Fitzgerald was a cheap publishing house, specializing in "Books for the People," and like the Petersons of Philadelphia usually did not date their title-pages. I have never seen a copy of *Sut* with dated title-page. I suspect an earlier edition perhaps in Cincinnati in pamphlet form. At the time of his death, 1869, Harris had ready for the printer a second collection of *Sut* stories but these seem to have disappeared.
13. *The Knob Dance.* See p. 55. The first Sut Lovingood yarn, *Sut Lovingood's Daddy Acting Horse*, appeared originally in the *Spirit*, 1854.
14. Harris, *Sut Lovingood Yarns*, p. 172.
15. *The Big Bear of Arkansas* first appeared in the New York *Spirit of the Times*, 1841 March 27. It was later reprinted in the collection of that title edited by Wm. T. Porter (1845), and also included in Thorpe's own volume of collected sketches, *The Hive of the Bee-Hunter* (1854).
16. Witness the *Tall Tales of the Kentucky Mountains* by Percy Mackaye, the *Paul Bunyan* yarns; and note also the stories about Mike Fink, the last of the Ohio River keel-boatmen which, although earlier, are of much the same nature.
17. Porter, *Big Bear of Arkansas*, Preface.
18. In 1856 Wm. T. Porter left the editorship of the old *Spirit* to start his own journal, *Porter's Spirit of the Times*.
19. From a memorial article on Porter by Wilkes in *Porter's Spirit*, 1858 July 24.
20. DeVoto, Bernard, *Saturday Review*, 1929 June 1.
21. Longstreet, *Georgia Scenes*, Preface. The italics are Longstreet's.
22. King. J. L., *Dr. George William Bagby*, 127, p. 62.
23. Summarized from *Mark Twain: A Preface*, by Bernard DeVoto.

Southern Humor

John Donald Wade

Long ago, at the sanguine age when one hopes at length to know every-thing, I had it as my business once to write something about a man who was notable as a humorist. My first obligation seemed to me to find out what humor, after all, was—what its sources were, what its charms. Or, more simply, to find out what makes a thing funny, and why, indeed, we are pleased to have funny things brought to our attention, whether rele-vantly or not.

I read much, then, on that score, and the result was like most results, not satisfying; I was left for all my effort not much the wiser. Incongruity, contrast, from what I could make out, seemed to be the bed-rock found uniformly by all pundits seeking humor's origin. What bed-rock was found by those seeking its fascination, remains to me to this day unknown, as it apparently did to my masters, in spite of their profound method of saying so. What I had been able to reckon for myself, I found after irk-some suspense to be what other people also had reckoned. What I had not been able to reckon—why humor is delightful—I found after irksome suspense was a question that other people also had found always beyond them.

Naturally, one hazards guesses, and the guesses about the fascination of humor group themselves for the most part either about the conscien-tious motive of correction or the quite unconscientious one of escape. To jeer at a person or a state of affairs leads the jeerer, with more or less earnest inimicalness on his part, into satire or irony. But some of us fell short, somehow, of acquiring our just endowment of inimicalness, and we have come to cherish the idea that a mordant earnestness on our part about other people's activities is an impulse to be eschewed. People of

From *Culture in the South*, edited by W. T. Couch. Chapel Hill: University of North Carolina Press, 1934. Reprinted by permission of the publisher.

this stripe laugh, certainly; they cannot go about sighing always. They regard the story's butt not with detestation, but with affection, and they do not cherish hope of remodeling anybody or anything very speedily—not even themselves.

These by all rules are life's ineffectuals; but their justification in humanity is that without them humanity would take on an aspect too horrible to contemplate, too indubitably governed by dullness or malice for anybody to wish its continuance. And if facts are regarded and not rules, it is these people who bring about for us, all the betterments we ever get.

As for *Southern*, that qualifies Humor in my title, I have put some thought on that for a long time. I learned the word early, and as a child in a Georgia village-school yearned at times to emulate some of my less restrained peers and punch out with a pencil-point the eyes of the northern generals pictured in my text-books. Restrained, I comforted myself by inscribing encomiumistic phrases under the pictures of southern generals. Later I learned better than to wish to occupy myself so barbarously. But I knew by then, and I know still, how to look at a book and without reading it to be aware, somehow, of every word on the pages that remotely looks like *southern*. I conceived it as my duty, once, over many years, to inspect that word every time it occurred on a page and to ascertain the veracity or falsehood of the sentence containing it. Sometimes the sentence said merely that on the southern slope of these mountains the climate is mild—and that was indeed disappointing. But I was powerfully affected if it declared the southern temperament sluggish, or, on the other hand, if it declared it generous.

I rehearse this autobiography in my anxiety to show that the word southern has long had its importance in my consciousness. Has it a meaning, really, other than the geographic one? It has been fashionable to think so for many years, and if the legend which in the beginning ascribed it meaning was at first legend merely, it is not likely by now legend merely, any more. A dog badly named, or well named, for that matter, will justify what is said of him, and a people will doubtless do as much. So in my mind there is a body of notions that hold their hands up and answer present when one says southern; yet to define those notions (since in definition one must be definite) is more than I can do in this essay, or more than anybody could do, I judge, except by implications and overtones and suggestions that nobody in this swift-moving time would trouble to follow, or, indeed, would trouble in the first place to set down.

And now, writing this article, I review in my mind not merely what has been the course of southern humor historically. I wonder what it is, in essence, and whether it is in fact different from any other humor in anything except in its setting and in the types of people it concerns itself with.

The historical phase of my activity need not cost me great effort. The extent of the contribution southern writers have made to the merriment of this nation and of other nations is a matter chiefly of research, and research students here and yonder have unearthed much information about it—with a solemnity that one must pronounce marvelous.

But the essence of southern humor, and the possibility of distinguishing it from other humor (except, as I have said, by perfectly objective tests) —that, truly, is a horse of a different color.

As the earliest of southern humorists, consider William Byrd, that good Briton. Young, he was a debonair blade of a fellow, as familiar in London as in Virginia; old, when sickness had him, and the inevitable knowledge that he would not come to as much as he had hoped to, he was very tragical. He noted the antics of his contemporaries and wrote about them, not as himself an antic-doer, but as one superior, remote. On one side is his sophistication and his fastidiousness; on the other, their ignorance and blundering. That contrast was accidental; it was not a device of his to make the situation more amusing. His characters seemed to him ludicrous enough, himself not ludicrous at all.

Everything of his that has been published waited, in manuscript form till Byrd was a hundred years dead. That late, his writings were no longer capable of proving a literary influence; times had changed so greatly, toward libertarianism in politics, toward finical delicacy in social intercourse, that his writings lay neglected for almost a further hundred years. So much for what he wrote. What he said, in its influence upon people who knew him personally, was almost surely more influential—and that disparity between what was written and what said is interesting not of itself only, but as an early instance in southern life of a disparity that marks all life, everywhere, but particularly, I think, marks life in the South.

After Byrd, there are few echoes of southern laughter for a long time. Laughter there was, doubtless, and gayety enough, but the soberness of Revolutionary times together with the eighteenth-century ideal of decorum, and the widespread influence of evangelicalism, kept most of this gayety vocal, forbade it the dignity of being written. When Revolutionary earnestness had burnt itself out in a scene of incandescent triumph, when the old aim of decorum had slumped before the new democracy, when evangelicalism, in its ardor to save everybody, had lowered its bars to admit everybody, then there was a new day. The old heaven and the old earth of Byrd or of Franklin or of Timothy Dwight had passed away, except, perhaps, in the heart of Washington Irving. And Irving, the stranded soul, put out soon for Europe and ever afterward in general stayed there.

The new country was above all else hopeful. Democracy in politics and arminianism in religion and free land in economics gave it hardihood to set beneath all of its amusement at the grotesque, the assumption that most grotesqueness would soon end. And the same assumption humanized all the jokes because they had in them always the implication that the superiority of the joker was largely accidental, largely a matter of his having shared more fully than his humorous puppets in wholesome opportunities that would soon be open to everyone. The old story tellers are at constant pains to make this clear. I record all this now, they keep saying, because it is so ludicrous, and because soon the very clowns I write about will be behaving as punctiliously as anybody—their children turning out to be—who knows?—perhaps president. From a time as early as 1825 onward till 1900 this song was never silent in American life; and it is not silent yet—though it is audible, now that the twentieth century is a third gone, principally in the success magazines and in the sophisticated weeklies published in New York.

The Revolution was well over. Old colonials and fresh immigrants were pushing westward. And then cotton as a great commercial possibility came to tempt them all southward. Georgia for a moment became the West, and it was soon, thanks to cotton, a West that was relatively rich, relatively well ordered—though retaining the violent contrasts in cultural groups (southerner, Yankee, immigrant, Negro) that make for humorous situations. Funny, all of this, people kept saying; record it now, set it down now; it is so transient (else it would be sad); it will be gone soon; it is, indeed, already gone.

So they set it down—Longstreet with his horse swappings and his eye-gougings, Thompson with his tobacco-spitters, R. M. Johnston, and Sidney Lanier and Bill Arp Smith and Joel Chandler Harris—all in Georgia. Hooper and Baldwin wrote of Alabama, Crockett and G. W. Harris of Tennessee, Prentice of Kentucky, Thorpe and Opie Reed and Mark Twain of the South bordering the Mississippi. Even Virginia—that urbane place—offered its quota of natural men to be pictured by the romanticized and romanticizing Dr. Bagby. Even South Carolina—that sedate place—offered its quota to be pictured by the robustious Simms and the much less robustious (oh, much!) Mrs. Gilman.

And except for Mark Twain, who had the advantage of having been born later as well as innately superior to the rest of them, they all said

35

very much the same thing. Their literary form: mostly Addison-like essays or fanciful letters, with an increasing deviation from Addison as it became the practice to introduce more and more dialect, more and more bad spelling. Their subject: unsophisticated country-folk (mostly white at first but at last mostly Negro) in contact with a world unfamiliarly urban. Their attitude: enjoy with me, reader, you who are cultivated, as I am, the foibles of these men and women, all of whom, as you and I both know, have hearts of gold beneath their superficial crudities.

Over and over this went on, and people everywhere found it delectable. America had at last come free of Europe's shadow; and this humor was really the humor of the nation at large at the time when the frontier was the nation's dominant interest. So far was it from sectional merely that its reception was equally clamorous in Philadelphia and in Peoria and in Vicksburg; and the fact is that of the eight southern humorists discussed in *The South in the Building of the Nation* (the eight, I mean, who died before 1900) four were bred and born in the North and one was educated there. The victories this humor won were identical in all sections; the re-buffs it met, ineffectual rebuffs such as the disgust felt for it by females and refined gentlemen, were also identical. It went marching on, and if it had more proponents North than it did South after 1860; so much the more demonstrably was it in the current, in the torrent, indeed, of national development.

For it is worth noting that the Civil War and early post-Civil War pro-ponents of the old humor persisted not in the new America that had taken form along the north Atlantic coast nor freely in the new America that had been driven to take form along the south Atlantic coast. It persisted in the western north, and as soon as the western north lost its distinctive-ness the old humor languished there also.

Now certainly as early as the 1830's forces were at work which render the South unable and unwilling to float its raft on the broad stream of national development. In the light of that time the democractic theories of 1800, and the arminianism so dear then, seemed less and less tenable. Negroes, it seemed, so far as this world went, at least, were outside that picture; and as the poor whites hardened in their resentment against their betters, becoming less amenable, they also were excluded. The southern oligarchy tended to become logically both aristocratic and Calvinistic. That is what it became *logically*. What it became actually is a different story.

There was a condition to be reckoned with that inevitably rides down, at last, most schedules of what one ought to believe in deference to one's own purely selfish interests. This consideration was that in the South, because it was a sparsely settled, farming region, people in the various classes, white and black, knew one another personally, intimately. Most often, as a result—one can risk saying so—they had a sort of affection for one another; but even if they had instead a sort of hatred, no one sinned so pointedly as to mistake people for mechanisms.

In the great North, the case went by contraries. There democracy and free-will had all the official endorsement they could ever need, but the unofficial, dominating conviction of individuals endorsed far different doctrines. As industrialism proceeded men became specialists, and as population grew denser it became necessary for every man to rule out from his consciousness the ups and downs of most of the people he had contact with. It became necessary, in short, for people to act as if they believed other people made out of metal rather than of flesh and blood.

What prophet could have foreseen this—fuddled as prophets must always be by the stir about them? South, all roads led *from* America, it was said; North, all roads turned back on themselves toward the ideals of the 1776 Declaration, or toward some vague place that was perhaps Heaven, and that was in any case very nice indeed. But as plain as those roads were, the travelers on them arrived, at last curiously—one group in Paterson, New Jersey, let us say; the other, in Macon, Georgia—cities both of which Jefferson might have understood, but only one of which he might possibly have commended.

In the South, the forces likely to break up the old humor were largely theoretical, and any of them that were more than theoretical were broken in upon by the personal intimacies that characterize a rural civilization. Further, any hard and fast program of social stratification that might have dehumanized and standardized society there, crumbled before the spectacle of reconstruction, with its pulling down of what had been high and its exaltation of what had been low. When Marie Antoinette (for all her saying "let them eat cake, then") is forced at last to beg crusts from her jailer, the situation is so poignantly tragic that the mind cannot last it out; it must save itself by laughter. So one's very poverty in the South in the 1870's—and in more years than those—was often the theme of one's best stories, the nucleus of ten thousand situations calculated to stir merriment.

Reconstruction, then, with its harsh anarchy, made humor mandatory. Desolate and lacking cheer, one was the more bound to simulate it—to shun madness, for simple sanity's sake, *bound*. Reconstruction with its anarchy broadened, also, the *field* of humor. Cousin Lucius, in his patched breeches, rehearsing Horace; Cousin Mintora, in homespun, fanning herself with jeweled ivory—both were figures one could not be wholly solemn about. And the laughter one accorded them, with themselves leading in it, was not far different from the laughter accorded the rough-and-ready catch-as-catch-can citizenry of Longstreet's *Georgia Scenes*. Black Sambo and his lady, the poor white and his, the colonel and his—each with his valid claim upon absurdity. And, to make the gamut complete—put in mind of doing so, perhaps, by the Negro's personification of animals and his humanization of deity—one recognizes as valid (out of neighborliness if nothing else) the claims, out absurdity-way, of beasts on the one hand, of divinity on the other. Uncle Remus' Brer Rabbit and Mr. Roark Bradford's God join hands indiscriminately with mankind, and the trio will likely as not, if a fiddle twangs, do some trick steps worth a body's trying to catch on to.

Even fine abstractions, programs for salvation, sacrosanct now in so many places, are not likely to meet in the South with much decorousness of reception. There, there is remembrance still of a fine program that came to nothing, for all that General Lee could do to make it prevalent —it was absurd, perhaps, ever to hope it would prevail—not soon will another program obtain one's whole endorsement. A lofty pronouncement, as a pronouncement, is a marvelous thing meriting one's admiration. As something more than a pronouncement, as a signal for action, it evokes less iron resolution than it does skeptical, half-sorrowful, amusement. Life is volatile—the grave running into the comic, the comic into the grave, each perhaps dependent upon the other for its being. This ponderous listing of grievances, this meticulous study of how to rectify them, this deep drumming to organization and to action—if necessary, to violent action. Are lister, studyer, drummer really quite solemn—more actually solemn than Cousin Lucius with his Horace, than Jesus in Reverend Sambo's praying? (Come, Lenin, and say so if you will—take care when you do lest your beard bob.) *And, besides Mr. Lenin, I know Cousin Joe —as well as one man can know another,—made his money curiously too, I heard said. But Lord, more than likely he hardly knew what he was up to. And he's mighty kind to all his folks, sir, and I expect that's being kind to half the county—helped me out, personally, more than once. You talk fine, sir, to a fellow down and out like me, but you can see, I judge, how Cousin Joe being in the family, and all, I'd naturally rather look to him for help than to a man outside the family—especially, if you'll excuse me for saying so, to a foreigner.*

Through the last of the eighteen hundreds much of the recorded humor of America ran in the old channels set before the Civil War. In the South, one could observe Bill Arp and Joel Harris, both of them in many ways reminiscent of old Longstreet—could observe in the West a parallel reminiscence in Mark Twain, as long as Mark Twain stayed in the West, and as long incidentally, as there was a West, any longer, in the historic sense to stay in Mark Twain.

A glib man gifted in grimacing and mimicry, touched with sentimentality, did not need capital to insure profits in the South till a time that only yesterday, it seems, became the past. For long years, there, people relished incalculably the yarns of semi-professional funny-men, some of whom, when they were not delivering their hilarious "lectures" (admittance, say, 25 cents), filled in their time acceptably as ministers of this or that evangelical denomination.

They were the court-jesters of a homogeneous culture and they are extinct now not because the culture they represented has crumbled utterly, but because it has grown self-conscious and ashamed, wistful to be cosmopolitan. En route, as it were, to extinction, they lived for years in the smoking compartments of railway trains and gabbed there interminably, to their own joy and with cost to nobody. Cosmopolitanism, with its creed of efficiency and its experience of human depravity, warned all travelers at length with printed bulletins to beware of all other travelers and Prohibition left those who were warned ready to heed the warning and often half ready to justify them.

But even in 1932, in the effectible privacy and brevity of a newspaper perusal, one can catch (and many are intent to catch) the echoes of that old buffoonery in the comic-strip depiction of one Hambones, true son of frontier America. Except for Hambones, then, and such-like, the old humor is gone—that is, in its professional aspect. In its non-professional aspect it has waned little to this day.

For consider, now, such a group of people as comes together at countless places in the South to celebrate Christmas by heavy eating. There is grandfather first. The mossy marble has these many years been all anybody has seen of grandmother,—but not all that anybody has heard of her. That lady's sayings, her eccentricities (always whispered about), her preferences in dress and food and flowers, are well understood by her descendants regardless of whether or not they ever had the happiness of seeing her. And there is grandfather's friend, invited in for dinner, a retired small-merchant he; grandfather, a retired farmer. Between the two, so far as one can discern, there is one point of congeniality: they are both upwards of eighty. How they enjoy each other!

Besides these two are mother and father (he, a lawyer) and uncles and aunts, wed and unwed, farmers, doctors, merchants, a mail-carrier, a teacher, a knitter of knit bed-spreads. And there are countless cousins, male and female, conventional for the most part, some unconventional —but none so unconventional as not to know better than to offend this agglomeration of good nature. One cousin conducts a gallery of modern art in Chicago; one, Sorbonne trained, teaches French at Vassar. One, absent, is represented by a note from him saying how sorry he is; he for his part is in Russia, finding out for some great foundation or other about the doings of the Soviets.

Here are all these people, gorged at last, and called upon by six or eight stray diners, as diverse as they, from another family. These people are constrained to talk about something, for along with the fundamental prohibitions (don't walk pigeon-toed, don't pick your teeth, child, in public) they were all given a fundamental admonition—keep, oh, whatever you do keep the occasion *moving*. Moving, my dear, lest we think perchance of how weakness comes at last, and pain, to all of us; lest we think too wrackingly of those whom weakness and pain already shove with brutal deliberation to their end, moving, lest a recognition of our own inadequacy—as persons, as a people—sere us here into sighers only.

Would it do, here, for Cousin Julius to talk of Proust's analyses, for Cousin Mary to tell of Epstein, for Uncle Tom to make Bergson clear, for someone else to echo Swift's mordancy, Wilde's glitter? I ask this question unabashedly as rhetorical. It would never, never do.

This is the challenge—tell a story now, you, that mail-carrying Uncle Jack and Proust-teaching Cousin Julius will both think so pointed, that knit-bed-spread-knitter Aunt Susan can endure without fainting, that Rabelaisian Uncle Rob can endure without nodding. Scour your memory, sir; let's hear from you; it is your time now, everybody else has said something—what were you born for, anyway? Slash in where you can, echoing that word of Aunt Susie's, giving it an emphasis that she did not mean to give it, making her disclose more than she meant to, covering her with confusion, while the table roars.

"How was it, Dick, that your mother used the field glasses at the beach. . . . Yes, we have most of us heard but Julius hasn't and besides we want to hear it again." "Now father," protests Dick's mother, Emma, "now, *father*!" And Dick tells it again, and they all shout again.

"Now that," says John, "reminds me of what old Mr. Pixley said" . . . "And Lord, Lord," says grandfather, "when have I thought of old Mr. Pixley? Why John, that man died before ever your mother and father got married." "None the less," says John, "I shall tell you about old Mr. Pixley. . . ." "Wait," says Henry. "Have you all heard about Res biting Tom Johnson's leg?" (There, naturally, everybody knows both characters. Res is short for Resaca de la Palma, a dog-name in the household since the Mexican War; Tom Johnson is an esteemed but emaciated neighbor.)

"Actually bite him?" asks Howard.

"No, just snapped at him."

"I'm glad of that," says Walter, "but what odd taste of Res in the first place!"

"But," George exclaims, "*wasn't* Res an unpractical idealist trying to locate it!"

"Now, boys," says Aunt Mattie, "I have the real truth of it. When Res's tooth struck Tom's breeches, it naturally slid off. . . ."

"How was it, Carrie," asks father, "that old black Bella set you straight about the Family when you first married into it and came here from Boston?"

"What was it, Red, the Yankee said when you bumped into him after coming back from your schooling in England? *I'm sorry*, you said—what was it he replied?"

"Uncle John," says Red, "the Yankee said 'What fer.'"

"What was it, Andrew, that little rapscallion said when he encountered for the first time—and too late at that—quinine with his natural milk?" "Uncle John," says Andrew, "it was like this. The child's name was Micajah, and when he became aware of the quinine he made a wry face and said this: 'Pappy,' says he, 'give me a chaw er baccer, Mammy's been a-eatin' bitter weed.'"

And so it goes, the old Abductor, the old destroyers, torturers, weakeners, frightened for a moment to other spheres.

Now all of the people at this Christmas dinner know one another, and the fact that they know, already, most of the stories they hear told does not make those stories blunt for them. Somehow the story itself is not primarily the thing one laughs at. If that were true a story read or told by a radio-entertainer or by a boresome man with a good memory would be as amusing as one heard acceptably. The important part of a story is the effect it has on the teller, and one must naturally know the teller well to perceive what that effect is. That is why a funny thing captured so that it can be drawn forth and exhibited at will by one man as by another, loses often, all its force.

That is why uninitiated northern persons often find themselves impatient at the zest with which southern persons—as sophisticated as themselves, apparently, listen to one Negro story after another, through an entire evening. They do not recognize how largely the point of such stories depends upon outside considerations. When they are aware of those considerations, when they know intimately the garrulous raconteur and his mannerisms, their impatience yields readily. For the initiated understand well enough that the teller, in the telling, is himself the main point of his story. They know that the southerner is in many ways bilingual, bi-mental, bi (if I may say so) attituded, he speaks his own language and the dialect, his own thoughts and the Negro's thoughts; he has a sentiment for the Negro that the northerner cannot diagnose except as detestation and at the same time a sentiment for him that the northerner cannot diagnose except as affection. It is the interplay of all these traits that makes the yarn worth listening to.

The humor of the Negro, too (I mean as displayed by Negroes), is dependent upon a sympathetic comprehension. The point is always in what the teller is really, contrasted with what he tells, and contrasted with his relation to the white man whom he placates and with a complete understanding by each of the other, often hoodwinks.

All of this, I think, suggests with some adequacy the present-day, generally unrecorded type of humor current in the South. The South at large represents in its basic economy the persistence of a tradition long superseded elsewhere, and its humor does too. That economy, obsolete in dominant America, stimulated a social tradition that is as yet obsolescent only, and that is indeed not clearly doomed to extinction, ever. It is a tradition which insists that human beings must quite inescapably remain humorous if they are to remain human, and one may well believe that it will reassert itself.

Even New York, for example, as late as the nineteen-hundreds, found itself as greatly amused by tar-heel O. Henry as pioneer Georgia in its time was amused by Longstreet. And most of O. Henry's merits arise from restatements of the old fundamental theme of American humor, which is in 1932 perhaps less fashionable than it has ever been. I think that it will be fashionable again after a while and that O. Henry would be fashionable again also if it were not for the tawdry newfangledness which he proudly affected and which his contemporaries vulgarly admired.

Newfangledness makes slow headway in the South, and humor there is still at base rural, and all the clanging urbanism of Atlanta or of Birmingham has not been able to make most southerners feel quite at home in the brothel of modish slang—with how great a loss to them let him who will figure. For Atlanta and Birmingham are close, still, to the fields and woods surrounding them, and the bright young people of those cities, let them strive ever so faithfully, are rarely able to pronounce "Sez you," for instance, with a conviction deep enough to keep it from proving nauseous. Most of them luckily have a better wit about them than to try. In the main, when they undertake to be mirthful, they behave themselves as much as they can like Andrew mimicking his young Micajah, or like Dick teasing his mother Emma.

But a discernible amount of southern humor such as Mr. Cohen's Slappey saga, has sprung from sections (more social than geographic in boundary) that are in thoroughgoing fashion both urban and industrialized. This, it turns out, has been most frequently indistinguishable from the humor current in, say, Akron, Ohio,—a humor sprigs of which have been brought South and set in soil as much like that of Akron as its admirers could possibly search out.

On occasion another type has sprung up, indigenous, I think though sophisticated beyond a doubt, and by many tests urban. Miss Ellen Glasgow, for instance, is almost wholly dependent in her subject matter upon the sources of humor which I have suggested as being somewhat definitely southern; and it is obvious that all of the assumptions behind her hard, bright wit are authentically local. Cabell and Frances Newman and even Mencken must be reckoned with as belonging to the South. Consider those names, and pair them, not with the names Richmond, Atlanta, Baltimore, but with Detroit, Cleveland, Omaha. The pairing most manifestly will not stand. For these people too are country people, who do not manage to be at home in whirring cities. Cabell's interests are in districts that are surely not crowded; Frances Newman's were in a social plane dominated still by the ideas of Miss Winnie Davis. Mencken's interests are keener in his yokel, apparently, than in most other things—and particularly in that brand of yokel (found seldom in greater verdancy than in the South) whose folly evinces itself most notably in religion. What is more, Mencken attacks his victim with a stampeding directness which David Crockett, could he have heard it, would have mightily exulted in, which is as distant from the knowing, metropolitan Walter Winchell as if New York and Baltimore were seven universes apart. And it must not be forgotten that Cabell and Mencken, at some inconvenience to themselves, doubtless, continue living where they do, and that Frances Newman, a little while before her death, came very definitely to the notion that her place was South or nowhere.

It is properly terrifying to observe that as time runs, the number of things a man may be merry over is gradually diminished. "The year is dying," the poet said—and, philosophically—"let it die." So I say here—this number is diminishing—let it diminish. But the year passes, the number falls, with results that no degree of willingness on our part to have them change, can keep from being in part bad. We can not laugh ever again with a free heart at physical deformity or at madness as people—and very good people, too—did everywhere until very recently. Those sources of laughter are not sources of laughter any longer—they are gone from that list and will not be put back there, and I should be as unwilling as anybody else to see them put back. None the less, we laugh less. Ignorance may go off next; next, the "pain" (so hypersensitive we become) Dick caused his mother about the field glasses.

We progress toward a Heaven, it appears, of unrelieved earnestness and propriety. But there are happily many people who would be unhappy at this prospect, and they are probably the same people who would be most upset at the prospect of their having the opportunity again to exhibit kindness. Doubly hard, then, is their lot, for they are, unless all signs fail, sentimentalists—and the sentimentalist, like the humorist without a mission, is an ineffectual, and his only shadow of justification in life is that without him life would be so very little preferable to death that few would prize it.

For such reactionary persons, I think the South a good place. Many contrasts are deeply rooted here, and they promise to stay rooted. Not soon will the industrialized piedmont regions *completely* overlord the lowlands, nor the forces of modern education (which may conceivably be bad education) overwhelm *completely* in the mind of either barber or bishop the notion that white people and Negroes are somehow not identical.

More progressive sections than ours may actually reach, *via* standardization, before the world ends, that Heaven of deadly uniformity which I am apprehensive of. But I am sure that such a Heaven must be very disagreeable, and that no one of cultivated sensibilities would desire it were it not for the gullibility, latent in the best of us, which teaches men to desire anything which calls itself by an agreeable name.

Many of us would find on attaining such a Heaven that the mere name was insufficient. We should want still a tightening of the heart, at times, with pity, or with indignation, a loosening down of the whole structure of our being, at times, with gigantic mirth.

Humor of the Old Southwest

Walter Blair

Contemporaneous with the humor of life Down East, the robust humor of the Old Southwest revealed the comedy of background, custom, and character in Tennessee, Georgia, Alabama, Louisiana, Mississippi, Arkansas, and Missouri. In these states, ways of living differed greatly among the inhabitants not only because many peoples mingled but also because various stages of civilization naturally were juxtaposed in stretches between settled sections and frontiers. Here, therefore, flourished striking contrasts which furnished excellent stuff for humor. Using these materials, a boisterous band of humorists produced a body of amusing narrative unsurpassed by any group in American literature.

A few biographical facts about some of the members of this group will suggest some interesting generalizations. Typical and important were:

Augustus Baldwin Longstreet (1790-1870), author of *Georgia Scenes*, published in newspapers (1832-1835) and in book form (1835)—lawyer, legislator, judge, and editor.[1]

Madison Tensas, M.D. (pseudonym—real name unknown), who summarized part of his life thus: "I was scarcely sixteen, yet I was a student of medicine, and had been, almost a printer, a cotton-picker, a ploughboy, gin-driver, gentleman of leisure, cabin-boy, cook, scullion, and runaway. . . ." The sentence is from his *Odd Leaves of a Louisiana "Swamp Doctor"* (1843).

Johnson J. Hooper (1815-1863) of Alabama, author of *Adventures of Simon Suggs*, published in part in newspapers and periodicals before it appeared in book form (1845)—lawyer, political office holder, and editor of various newspapers.[2]

Sol Smith (1801-1869) who, according to a friend, was successful as "editor, actor-manager, preacher and lawyer." His books were *Theatrical Apprenticeship* (1845) and *Theatrical Journey Work* (1854).

Thomas Bangs Thorpe (1815-1878), whose work was collected from periodicals to take book form in *The Mysteries of the Backwoods* (1846) and *The Hive of the Bee Hunter* (1854)—painter, soldier, newspaper editor.

William T. Thompson (1812-1882) of Georgia whose *Major Jones's Courtship* (1843), *Chronicles of Pineville* (1845) and *Major Jones's Sketches of Travel* (1847) were collections of newspaper stories—soldier, printer, law student, and journalist.

Joseph M. Field (1810-1856), St. Louis actor, actor-manager, and journalist, whose newspaper and periodical sketches made up *The Drama in Pokerville* (1847).

John S. Robb, also of St. Louis, journeyman printer and, later, editor, whose newspaper and periodical sketches went into *Streaks of Squatter Life* (1847).[3]

Joseph G. Baldwin (1815-1864), who wrote of his experiences as a young frontier lawyer in *Flush Times of Alabama and Mississippi*.[4]

George W. Harris (1814-1869) of Tennessee, jeweler's apprentice, river boat captain, silversmith, political writer, postmaster, hunter, inventor, and a frequent contributor to periodicals of humorous writings, some of which appeared in *Sut Lovingood* (1867).[5]

Even such brief notes as these show what a remarkable species these men were. Before they became authors, most of them had knocked around from place to place, from job to job, seeing much of the teeming life of the sections they portrayed. They were not scholars who emerged from libraries, blinking as they carried manuscripts into the light of day.[6] They were lawyers who wrote their stories between swings around the circuit, journalists who scratched out their yarns on desks around which eddied the life of a newspaper office, soldiers and doctors who jotted down their tales during lulls in strenuous activity.

Their literary training, as one would expect, was varied; and one soon discovers that they patterned their work upon the writings of various schools. And the characters whom they pictured were of many kinds: though they knew the ring-tailed roarer of the sort repeated frequently during the century, these men, steeped in the life of their sections, preferred as a rule to limn more individualized characters. Nevertheless, one will discover several qualities common to the writings of all of them.

For one thing, writing with an eye cocked towards the East, where sooner or later their books were published, and to which they wanted to "interpret" their section, they were all, consciously or unconsciously, local colorists, eager to impart the flavor of their particular locality. There was no gradual development of this desire, as there was in the East. From the beginning, their humor, as Mr. Meine, who knows it better than any modern scholar, has pointed out, "was provincial, wholly local"[7] —localized in space and time. Tied up with this aim was a desire to write truthfully, authentically.

The title page of the first and most influential book of Southwestern humor emphasized the fact that it contained "*Georgia* Scenes, Characters, Incidents, &c. *in the First Half Century of the Republic*," emphasized the fact, too, that these scenes were authentic, since they were "By a *Native* Georgian."[8] In his preface, the author, A. B. Longstreet, indicated that he was eager to present to his countrymen a vivid account of an interesting phase of history: in his book, he spoke of "Georgia language" and "Georgia humor."[9] As he talked about the book, the author stressed his desire to write authentically about a particular place at a particular time:

> The design of the "Georgia Scenes" has been wholly misapprehended by the public. It has been invariably received as a mere collection of fancy sketches, with no higher object than . . . entertainment . . . whereas the aim of the author was to supply a chasm in history which has always been overlooked—the manners, customs, amusements, wit, dialect, as they appear in all grades of society to an ear and eye witness to them. But who ever tells us the comments of the wits and the ways of the common walks of life, in their own dialect, upon the victors and the vanquished in the public games? Could we hear them, we would find a rich fund of amusement in their remarks upon the dresses of their characters, the horses, their mode of driving, and their blunders; upon the pugilistic combatants, their appearance, their muscle, their remarks, and gruntings and groanings . . . ; their own private games, quarrels, and fights, and the manner in which they were conducted . . . I have chosen the first fifty years of our republic . . . To be sure . . . I have not confined myself to strictly veracious historic detail; but there is scarcely one word from the beginning to the end of the book which is not strictly *Georgian* . . . "The Gander Pulling" actually occurred at the very place where I locate it. The names of the persons who

figure in it are such as were well known in Richmond County at that time, and the language which I put in the mouths of my actors was just as was common at such exhibitions. . . . Again, take "The Wax Works." The exhibition actually came off in Waynesboro, Burke County, Ga. Every character introduced actually existed . . . performing precisely the part ascribed to him . . . "The Fight" . . . is a description of a combat which was not uncommon in almost every county in Georgia, at almost every one of which there was a Ransy Sniffle, a little more ludicrous in form and figure, and made rather more conspicuous in this fight than the real Ransys were. In person, however, he answered very well to many of the poorer class whom all Georgians have seen in the sterile pine woods of that State. These may serve as examples of how far the sketches were actually true and how far fanciful.[10]

The preface similarly asserted that the sketches "consist of nothing more than fanciful *combinations* of *real* incidents and characters; and throwing into those scenes . . . some personal incident or adventure of my own, real or imaginary, as it would best suit my purpose; usually *real* but happening at different times and under different circumstances from those in which they are here represented."[11] "I have not always," he continued, "taken this liberty. Some of the scenes are as literal as the frailties of memory would allow them to be." Longstreet asserted to his friends that he hoped that through his writings "we may be seen and heard by our posterity two hundred years hence just as we are."[12]

William Tappan Thompson, a disciple of Longstreet,[13] shared his attitude toward writing and attempted similarly to display the Georgia Crackers as "a genus of bipedulus animals *sui generis* . . ."[14] His first book, *Major Jones's Courtship* (1844) was an attempt, he said in his preface, "to depict some of the peculiar features of the Georgia backwoodsman." His second book, *Major Jones's Chronicles of Pineville* (1845) contained, the Preface asserted, "other stories illustrative of similar character . . . [designed] to present a few more interesting specimens of the genus Cracker." The Cracker, he continues, has "strongly marked" lineaments, easy for even a beginner to catch. The author has tried "to catch his 'manners living as they rise' . . . to afford the student of human nature a glance at characters not often found in books, or anywhere else, indeed, except in just such places as '*Pineville*,' Georgia."

Though Longstreet and Thompson indicated more clearly than others their literary theories, obviously humorists who followed them had in mind the same localized and realistic portrayal. Wrote T. B. Thorpe of a book whose very title indicated concern with locality: "An effort has been made, in the course of these sketches, to give those personally acquainted with the scenery of the Southwest, some idea of the country, of its surface, and vegetation."[15] The purpose of Baldwin's *Flush Times in Alabama and Mississippi* was largely "to illustrate the periods, the characters, and the phases of society, some notion of which is attempted to be given in this volume."[16] John S. Robb stresses the value of the originality of the Western life he portrays to the humorist:

> The west abounds with incident and humor. . . . It would indeed seem that the nearer sundown, the more original the character and odd the expression, as if the sun, with his departing beams, had shed a new feature upon the back-woods inhabitants. This oddity and originality has often attracted my attention and contributed to my amusement. . . .[17]

The preface to the most famous collection of humorous tales from the Southwest stressed the fact that the book "furnished most valuable and interesting reminiscences of the pioneers of the far West—sketches of thrilling scenes and adventures in that then comparatively unknown region, and the extraordinary characters occasionally met with—their strange language and habitudes . . ." and the subtitle of the book called attention to the fact that the sketches were "illustrative of Characters and Incidents in the Southwest."[18] The very titles of the stories had local flavoring—"Jones' Fight, a Story of Kentucky by an Alabamian," "That Big Dog Fight at Myers's, a Story of Mississippi by a Mississippian," and so on. And the popularity of this volume led to the compilation of a similar volume "Illustrative of Scenes, Characters, and Incidents, throughout 'the Universal Yankee Nation.' "[19] Henry Watterson, learned in the lore of the South and its humor, speaks of the "local tone" of these writings, pointing out that scenes portrayed by Thompson "might possibly be laid in Tennessee or Alabama, but not in Virginia or Mississippi" and that "Sut Lovingood belongs to a class which is but little known in the South. The gulf between him and Simon Suggs," he continues, "is impassable. He is no relation to Major Jones, or even to Ransy Sniffle [portrayed by Longstreet]."[20]

These local colorists, in their attempt to satsify what a discerning editor called "the eager curiosity to know more of the distinguishing traits of character of the denizens of . . . the West and Southwest,"[21] typically amassed many details concerning the life about them. As Bernard De Voto points out, as a part of his excellent study of their writings,

> No aspect of the life in the simpler America is missing from this literature. The indigo tub and the bearskin rug are here, as well as the frontier gentry's efforts to speak French. In the solitude of the upper rivers, trappers practice their ferocity . . . in the solitude of hither-Illinois, Ole Bull meditates on his art. Jackson, Van Buren, Harrison, Benton, Taylor, Tyler, Douglas, and such worthies entertain the electorate; so do such humbler worthies as Big Bear of Arkansas, Kit Kuncker, Dick McCoy, Billy Warrick, and Cousin Sally Dilliard. The panorama of religion passes: camp meetings, christenings, Millerism, Mormonism, spiritualism. So does the comedy of the land—claim jumpers, false locators, Regulators, auctions, surveyors, roof-raisings, husking bees—and of the law courts, the bench and bar, sheriffs, muster days, legislatures, election campaigns. The folk boil over in Texas and the literature swarms with dragoons and infantry, recruits, West Pointers, and Rangers. Itinerants pass by, those strange travellers from abroad, peddlers, actors, singers, mesmerists, prophets, temperance agitators, physicians, census takers, circus clowns, bear leaders, accordionists. The folk labor at their vocations in the fields and the woods, the doggeries, the still-houses, the swamps, the bayous; at the spinning wheel, the loom, the churn. They frolic always, and if Betsy Smith, the fair offender, isn't married to John Bunce, why, jedge, "we oughter been, long ago." . . . Cataloguing is futile. Here is the complete life of the frontier.[22]

Alike in making their writings local, authentic, and detailed, these humorists were also alike in imparting to their stories a zest, a gusto, a sheer exuberance. In part, of course, the materials handled by them made for racy narration: one could not write of the staccato gambolings of frontiersmen in a tranquil style. A writer in a periodical of 1851, though he caricatured the liveliness of the frontier, caught something of its galloping tempo when he said:

> "Out West" is certainly a great country . . . there is one little town in "them diggins" which . . . is "all sorts of a stirring place." In one day, they recently had two street fights, hung a man, rode three

men out of town on a rail, got up a quarter race, a turkey shooting, a gander pulling, a match dog fight, had preaching by a circus rider, who afterwards ran a footrace for apple jack all round, and, as if this was not enough, the judge of the court, after losing his year's salary at single-handed poker, and licking a person who said he didn't understand the game, went out and helped to lynch his grandfather for hog stealing.[23]

This sprightly passage manages to indicate why a picture of folk "out West" never could be as idyllic as a picture of the folk in "Down East" Downingville or Jalaam.

But more important as a cause for gusto perhaps was the manner of the origination of much of this humor. Definitely, much of this literature had its origin in the greatest American folk art—the art of oral story-telling. The fact is worthy of attention because the oral tale had an important influence upon the matter of most Western tales and upon the manner of them.

An Englishman in 1889 perceived more clearly than many Americans the importance of oral story-telling. "All over the land [in America]," said Andrew Lang, "men are eternally 'swopping stories' at bars, and in the long endless journeys by railway and steamer. How little, comparatively, the English 'swop stories'! . . . The stories thus collected in America are the subsoil of American literary humour, a rich soil in which the plant . . . grows with vigour and puts forth fruit and flowers."[24]

The art of oral narrative noted by the British critic, not unknown in New England, where it influenced the almanacs of Robert B. Thomas[25] and some of the periodical literature,[26] and not foreign to other sections of the United States or even to Canada,[27] flourished particularly in the West and the Southwest. Evidence of this fact is missing from many travel books, presumably because many of the genteel folk who visited America did not consort with the tellers of tales; but visitors who kept their ears open and many an American left records of the widespread art. As Lang suggests, the telling of yarns was particularly well adapted to travelers by stagecoach or boat. James Hall and his party, floating down the Ohio on a flatboat in the twenties, were delighted, he records, by a visit from a weatherbeaten old keelboatman called "Pappy," whose "affected gravity, drawling accent, and kind, benevolent manner . . . marked him as . . . a humorist." Pappy entertained the travelers by telling "merry and marvelous tales."[28] James P. Beckwourth, drifting down the Missouri, about 1824, with a group of soldiers, "had a jovial time of it, telling stories, cracking jokes, and frequently making free with Uncle Sam's 'O be joyful' . . . The soldiers listened with astonishment to the wild adventures of the mountaineers, and would, in turn, engage our attention with recitals of their own experience."[29] A British captain on an Ohio river steamboat in the thirties heard, so he said, fine stories of "high life in Kentucky" and an oral account of a yarn Longstreet had told in *Georgia Scenes*.[30] Tall tales, exuberant combinations of fact with outrageous fiction which came to be thought of as typical of much oral narrative in the West, whiled away the time of a group with which J. S. Buckingham rode in a stagecoach between Wheeling and Zanesville in the forties. His companions, he said, exercised their wit "in the exaggerated strain so characteristic of Western manners":

> The unhealthy condition of some of the Western rivers, the Illinois in particular, was the subject of their discourse; when one asserted, that he had known a man to be so dreadfully affected with the ague, from sleeping in the fall on its banks, that he shook . . . all the teeth out of his head. This was matched by another, who said there was a man from his State, who had gone to Illinois to settle, and the ague seized him so terribly hard, that he shook off all his clothes . . . and could not keep a garment whole, for it unravelled the very web, thread by thread, till it was all destroyed! The climax was capped, however, by the declaration of a third, that a friend of his who had settled on the banks of the Illinois, and built a most comfortable dwelling . . . was seized with an ague, which grew worse and worse, until its fits . . . at length shook the whole house about his ears, and buried him in its ruins! Such is the kind of wit in which the Western people especially delight, and which the Southern and Western newspapers feed and encourage, by racking their invention for the supply of new extravaganzas.[31]

But travelers by boat and stagecoach were not the only tellers of tales. William Tappan Thompson, down in Florida to campaign against the Seminoles in 1836, assembled around the campfire with other soldiers after tattoo, to listen to comic yarns.[32] George Wilkins Kendall, a contributor to Southwestern humorous literature, told of tales related by campfires on an expedition to Santa Fé—"long yarns about border forays, buffalo hunts, and brushes with Indians on the prairies" in the course of one of which an old-timer innocently asserted that, on one occasion, he saw "between two and three million" buffaloes. In Texas,

Kendall heard widely told tall tales about a mythical White Steed of the Prairies.[33] This was in 1841. Four years later, when Hall visited Texas, stories about the same handsome steed were still going the rounds.[34] In country stores in Illinois,[35] in the gunsmith's shop or Larkin Snow's mill in Fisher's River in North Carolina,[36] in a log hotel in Kansas territory,[37] by a bear hunters' campfire in Tennessee,[38] the story-teller told his yarns.

History has fortunately informed most of us of at least one great story-teller of the frontier, Abraham Lincoln. The coonskin tales which he collected came to him everywhere he went, it seems, until he left Springfield—at Anderson Creek ferry, in the log store at New Salem, on a raft drifting down the great river, and in taverns at night when he foregathered with other lawyers in swings around the circuit. The lawyers, in particular, cherished good stories in which the vernacular figured prominently. Wrote Philip Paxton, in 1853:

> The origin and perpetuity of many of our queer and out-of-the-way phrases, may be traced to the semi-annual meetings of the gentlemen of the bar at the courts of our Southern and Western States.
>
> These gentlemen, living as they do in the thinly inhabited portion of our land, and among a class of persons generally very far their inferiors in point of education, rarely enjoying anything that may deserve the name of intellectual society, are apt to seek for amusement in listening to the droll stories and odd things always to be heard at the country store or bar-room. Every new expression and queer tale is treasured up, and new ones manufactured against the happy time when they shall meet their *brothers-in-law* at the approaching term of the district court.
>
> If ever pure fun, broad humor, and "Laughter holding both his sides," reign supreme, it is during the evening of these sessions. Each one empties and distributes his well filled budget of wit and oddities, receiving ample payment in like coin, which he pouches, to again disseminate at his earliest opportunity.[39]

Of the ten Southwestern humorists listed above, four—Longstreet, Hooper, Smith, and Baldwin—were all, at one time or another, lawyers. Longstreet was one of a jolly group of tellers of tales on the circuit which included Oliver H. Prince, author of the laughable "Militia Drill"; A. S. Clayton, believed by some to have had a hand in Davy Crockett's racy writings;[40] the humorous Judge Dooley, and others. Many years later, a contemporary wistfully recalled hilarious evenings in an old tavern where "assembled at night the rollicking boys of the Georgia bar . . . Humor and wit, in anecdotage and repartee, beguiled the hours."[41] Presumably other lawyer-humorists, like Longstreet, heard scores of yarns at night-time gatherings of the bench and bar. Certainly Ovid Bolus and Cave Burton, described by Baldwin, were typical tellers of tales. Certainly Johnson H. Hooper averred that he secured at least one of his stories, "Shifting the Responsibility," while "attending court in the adjoining county of Randolph" from "a friend who is fond of jokes of all sorts, and who relates them almost as humorously as 'His Honour . . .' "[42] and at least four of his yarns bear the earmarks of circuit origin.[43]

But neither Hooper nor the others of the period needed to go to gatherings of lawyers to hear amusing tales. On a hunting trip, Hooper listened to a series of anecdotes told by the guide, and when they stopped overnight, their host entertained them with a tall tale. A visit with old Kit Kuncker yielded another yarn.[44] Joseph M. Field testified that one of his tales—his best, in fact—was a patchwork of oral narratives about a frontier hero which he had heard in barrooms or by firesides in five cities over a period of fifteen years.[45] T. B. Thorpe's description of a tale-telling session aboard a Mississippi steamboat is vivid enough to convince one that he was no stranger to the art of the oral story-teller. It seems reasonably probable that all the humorists of the old Southwest could, if they chose, learn something about narrative materials and method from oral story-tellers.

What they learned about materials to some extent limited and to some extent enlarged the subject matter with which the humorists dealt. Since fireside story-telling in the Southwest, as elsewhere, was largely a rugged masculine pastime, no subtle psychological depictions were likely to develop as a result of its influence. Certain important elements of life were likely to be neglected: there was no equivalent here for Mrs. Partington or Widow Bedott. Longstreet and Thompson were the only two outstanding humorists who concerned themselves much with the tenderer domestic scenes. And despite Longstreet's exceptional desire to portray "all grades of society,"[46] he and others who were concerned with subject matter like that of the oral tale were more concerned with the lower social groups than the higher ones. Masculine pastimes, such as hunting, fishing, gambling, drinking, and fighting, and the trades of the doctor, the editor, the lawyer, the politician, the actor, the boatman, and the soldier received attention to the neglect of some other phases of life. Too, a large amount of the humor, as C. Alphonso Smith suggests,[47] derived from physical discomfort, which often, apparently, was more hilariously amusing than it is today.

But despite these limitations suggested by oral art, the vistas of adventure and character opened by tale-spinners were wide enough to give the Southwestern literature richness. As Mr. De Voto's catalogue indicates, interesting materials were not lacking. The hairbreadth adventures, the feverish competition of sports and commercial enterprise, the heterogeneous mingling of characters in the new country gave the humor, as George E. Woodberry noted, a picturesque quality: "It was as if all the world had gone on a picaresque journey by general consent in various quarters, and at the chance roundup for nightly rest and refreshment fell to telling what, and especially whom, they had met with."[48] Tales which told what happened in the bustling section, sometimes factually, sometimes in a hilariously exaggerated fashion, and character sketches of the highly varied figures who lived in the settled districts or on the frontier or who moved restlessly from place to place had plenty of variety.

It is more difficult to generalize about the effect of the oral tale upon the manner of these humorists. The chief general effect has been indicated— a zestful exuberance entered into the narratives. Stories he heard told in the Western country, John Neal noted, had "a decided character"— "*live* stories I should call them," he said. They were "brimful of energy and vivacity . . ."[49] But some of the humorists, naturally, were more affected by the oral art than others.

It was to be expected that Longstreet, the first of the group, despite his appreciation of "the comments of the wits . . . in their own dialect, upon the victors and the vanquished in the public games," would be influenced particularly by the methods of earlier narrators. Quite correctly, his latest biographer points out that Addisonian echoes were quite frequent in *Georgia Scenes*.[50] In the *Spectator* tradition, though rather more heavily, he moralizes about the vices he portrays. Fighting, baby talk, drunkenness, modern dancing, duelling, horse racing, and the undomestic wife are reprimanded severely.[51] Several of his sketches later appeared in a book labeled, not inappropriately, *Stories With a Moral*. Humor, he asserted, should improve the reader by correcting his errors or leading him to reflect upon them; he saw ridicule as a weapon against vice.[52] More important than this attitude was the essay-like quality of much of the material. "The Dance," "The Song," "The Charming Creature as a Wife," "The Mother and Her Child," and "The Ball" are Americanized *Spectator* papers. In the last of these, such characters as

Misses Mushy, Feedle and Deedle and Messrs. Boozle and Noozle play parts in a fable which proves the folly of duelling.

The style often echoes eighteenth-century writings. "Some passages," Poe remarked, "in a certain species of sly humor, wherein intense observation of character is disguised by simplicity of relation, put us forcibly in mind of the Spectator."[53] In at least half of the volume, the language has the cadences, the rhetorical quality, at best the elegance, of the older essays. The character, "designated," Longstreet says ponderously, "by the appellation of Ned Brace," is introduced in lines reminiscent of the older style:

> This man seemed to live only to amuse himself with his fellow-beings, and he possessed the rare faculty of deriving some gratification of his favorite propensity from almost every person whom he met, no matter what his temperament, standing, or disposition. Of course he had opportunities enough of exercising his uncommon gift, and he rarely suffered an opportunity to pass unimproved. The beau in the presence of his mistress, the fop, the pedant, the purse-proud, the over-fastidious and sensitive, were Ned's favorite game. These never passed him uninjured, and against such he directed his severest shafts. With these he commonly amused himself, by exciting in them every variety of emotion, under circumstances peculiarly ridiculous.

And so on. Ned Brace, thus characterized, is a contemporary of Pindar Cockloft, an Addisonian humorist, a link between the humor of the eighteenth and the nineteenth centuries[54]—and the manner is unmistakably reminiscent. Thompson, reviewing the book, noted, "As to the *style*, except where the author quotes the language of his characters, it is *throughout* remarkably pure, flowing and beautiful";[55] and he cited several passages of a similar sort. Longstreet's liking, doubtless, was for the essay.

To modern taste, these passages are the least admirable in the book; and one regrets their frequency—not because they are bad but because Longstreet's predecessors did such things better. We are much more amused by the talk of the characters, especially when, as is often the case, it is valuable in humorous characterization. The adolescent bellicosity of the hero of "Georgia Theatrics," Hiram Baugh's elaborate alibi for his poor shot and Billy Curlew's acute and sly humor in "The Shooting-Match" (though the latter is sometimes too derivative from commonplace oral

tale formulae); the learned talk of yerbs and curses by the old women in
"A Sage Conversation"; the boastful bargaining of the Yellow Blossom
from Jasper in "The Horse-Swap"—perfect for portraiture—are in Longstreet's best vein. So, too, are his vivid descriptions of some of the characters—Ransy Sniffle, for example, and the animals in his tales. "Of
geese and ganders," Poe observed, "he is the La Bruyère, and of good-
for-nothing horses, the Rochefoucault."[56] And at its best, with the sometimes lengthy rhetorical introduction out of the way, Longstreet's narration moves along swiftly, in the manner of a well-told anecdote which
leads up to an explosive conclusion.

Of course, various fictional creations of the time made use of some of
these same devices, and Longstreet was not unacquainted with the
literature of his day. As Poe pointed out, one scene in Longstreet's book
is quite reminiscent of a scene by Miss Edgeworth.[57] But Longstreet had
learned the art of the oral tale. An "inimitable story-teller," a contemporary recalled, at circuit tale-swapping sessions he was "usually the
center of a listening, laughing, admiring crowd. His tone, gesture, and
play of feature gave his narratives a peculiar zest and charm."[58] Stories
incorporated in *Georgia Scenes* he told with "indescribably amusing
mimicry."[59] And since mimicry of speech (particularly for purposes of
characterization), humorous depictions of men and beasts, and the
development of a story with a point are important in the art of oral story-
telling, it seems fairly reasonable to suggest that what was best in *Georgia
Scenes* was at least in part derived from the method of the oral tale.

Even more than Longstreet, Baldwin, in his writing, is influenced by the
older essay style; four-fifths of his book takes that form. In *The Flush
Times in Alabama and Mississippi*, the lawless life of the new country, the
strange ways of its inhabitants, are presented in a generalized style.
Primarily an essayist, outside of reports of court room speeches, Baldwin
makes little use of direct discourse. At times, this is a handicap, as when,
in an essay about a liar, the author lyricizes about the liar's artistry
amusingly but fails to do the thing most needful—give us a specimen, in
the man's own words, of the lie told "from the delight of invention and
the charm of fictitious narrative."[60] Or consider another sketch entirely
concerned with a story-teller, "Cave Burton, Esq., of Kentucky." In a
generalized passage, Baldwin dilates upon the way Cave tells yarns. But
when the time comes for Cave to tell one of his interminable narratives,
Baldwin says, "We can only give it *our* way, and only such parts as we
can remember, leaving out most of the episodes, the casual explanations
and the slang; which is almost the play of Hamlet with the Prince of

Denmark omitted."[61] Of course it is. And too often, Baldwin, omitting specific detail of this sort, falls short of heights he might have achieved.

This, of course, does not entirely condemn him, since he has other abilities. Despite the fact that he writes in a style at times too leisurely, too polished, for an account of the brisk frontier and its rough inhabitants, he is a diverting essayist. Observant, he laughingly perceives the comic topsy-turvy quality of law in a relatively lawless country. He enjoys himself hugely as he writes the record of the strange assortment of men, ranging from rascals to statesmen, who inhabit Alabama and Mississippi. There are at least touches of admirable characterization. And he accomplishes his purpose as he himself announces it: he does record—as a highly readable contemporary historian—the chief aspects of those two states during the flush times.[62]

The oral anecdote affects his writings but little. Some of the details of Ovid Bolus's yarns, though they are presented in indirect discourse, have the flavor of frontier oral humor. And some of the practical jokes Baldwin tells about have plots of the sort which pleased fireside audiences—tales of how a young lawyer was befooled by an old lawyer, how a horse thief persuaded a drunken sheriff to allow him to escape, how a lover of oysters was kept talking until his friends in an adjacent room had eaten three barrels of the bivalves, how a slick lawyer outwitted a tricky publisher. And now and then, a paragraph in the midst of a lengthy exposition takes the form of a pointed anecdote: there are three such in "Ovid Bolus, Esq."

To some extent, then, oral literature molded the work of Longstreet and Baldwin. Other humorists of the period and of the section, however, were influenced in a much more tangible fashion either by the fireside yarn or by writings which had been flavored and fashioned by it. Even while Longstreet's sketches were appearing in newspapers, writings very directly affected by oral humor were beginning to find their way into print— stories in varied publications about comic legendary heroes of the frontier, and stories about Southwestern happenings by yarn spinners who simply put campfire talk in ink for newspapers or for the periodical which was the most important influence of the day in American humor.

"The narratives of the frontier circle, as they draw around their evening fire," said Flint, "often turn upon the exploits of the old race of men, the heroes of the past days, who wore hunting shirts, and settled the country."[63] Of such men,[64] predecessors of Paul Bunyan,[65] anecdotes translated from fireside talk into printed form began to appear in newspapers in the late twenties. Davy Crockett (1786-1836), for example, shrewd politician, great hunter, fighter, drinker, and tall talker, had been the source of many tales, some printed, some orally circulated, after 1828, when he entered Congress. An idea of the way oral tales clustered about him is given by an English captain who, traveling through Kentucky, heard many a story of the comically godlike hero of the canebrakes:

> Every thing here [he said] is Davy Crockett. He was a member of Congress. His voice was so loud it could not be described—it was obliged to be drawn as a picture. He took hailstones for "Life Pills" when he was unwell—he picked his teeth with a pitchfork . . . fanned himself with a hurricane. . . . He had a farm, which was so rocky, that, when they planted the corn, they were obliged to shoot the grains into the crevices with muskets. . . . He could . . . drink the Mississippi dry—shoot six cord of bear in one day. . . .[66]

Passages like this, wherein the humor of Western "tall talk," of exaggeration, reached fantastic heights, appeared in a long series of popular "Crockett" almanacs (1835-1856) which were widely circulated.[67] And tales closer to fact, told by Crockett himself or by others who assumed the role of Crockett, printed in a series of books,[68] had a wide sale.[69] These books, at their best, told in the toothsome vernacular of the people and the happenings of the frontier: in the second volume of the series, a Western critic pointed out in 1834, "the events are such . . . as we have seen acted over and over, and heard repeatedly recited by the firesides of our hardy backwoodsmen."[70]

Into the magazines, newspapers, and books, too, beginning in 1828 and on down to the end of the century, came transcriptions of oral tales about Mike Fink (1770?-1823?), whose picturesque and picaresque career carried him from Pittsburgh, where he was born, along with the shifting frontier until he died violently in Missouri. Mike, the king of the keelboatmen on the Mississippi and Ohio, talked tall, fought mightily, shot with uncanny skill, and manifested great affection for women, whisky, and adventure in a series of at least thirty yarns, republished widely, many of which pretty clearly derived from oral narratives.[71] The first two lengthy accounts of his career, published in Cincinnati in 1828 and 1829, were admittedly based on tales told respectively by a steamboat pilot and a fur-trader;[72] one anecdote hinted at but not recounted in the second of these bobbed up, with full details, in an almanac published in 1839 in Nashville,[73] and another which had merely been sketched was told, with many added details, in a St. Louis newspaper in 1847.[74] And the story of Mike's death escaped becoming fixed in print so well that when eleven versions of it at length appeared, they differed concerning where he died, why he died, and who killed him.[75]

Newspapers all over the country published humorous tales about Crockett, Fink, or others celebrated in oral lore during the thirties and forties, the New Orleans *Picayune* and *Delta* and the St. Louis *Reveille* being particularly productive in the Southwest. These were important in the development of oral humor in print. But more important than any other publication was a weekly paper appearing in New York—*The Spirit of the Times* (1831-1861), edited by William T. Porter (1809-1858).

This unique periodical, a "Chronicle of the Turf, Agriculture, Field Sports, Literature and the Stage," as its subtitle proclaimed, had a racy masculine flavor. One who sought out its editor, if he had poor luck at the editorial office, did well to move a few doors away to Frank Monte-verde's saloon, the unofficial editorial sanctum. In the cosy anteroom, there would be clustered around the tall figure of Porter a crowd of jockeys, trainers, doctors, race-track patrons, hunters in fustian jackets and corduroy pantaloons, artists,[76] authors,[77] dandies, actors—all "discussing the merits of the drama, the turf, and the chase, interrupted only by the monotonous clang of domino pieces."[78] These men were a sampling of the magazine's varied readers and its contributors. Scattered over the face of the earth "from Hudson's Bay to the Caribbean Sea, from the shores of the Atlantic to the Pacific,"[79] subscribers included men of many backgrounds and many occupations—soldiers and sailors at every American post,[80] farmers, planters, lawyers, doctors, newspaper editors, and so forth. Reasonably common interests, apparently, were an affection for sports of all kinds—horse-races, cock-fights, hunting, and fishing, an enthusiasm about fine dogs, fine horses, and fine cattle, and a love for good comic stories.

From some of these readers came the "original contributions" to the *Spirit*, small in number during the early years of the publication, but increasing until, in 1846, Porter proudly announced: "Last week's 'Spirit of the Times' contained nearly Seven Pages of Original Matter, from the pens of no less than *thirty-three correspondents!*"[81] These came from every section of the country, but particularly from the old Southwest. And they came from men of many sorts—army officers,[82] "country gentlemen, planters, lawyers, &c. 'who live at home at ease,' " denizens of the frontier with "exteriors 'like the rugged Russian bear' . . . gifted with . . . good sense and knowledge of the world . . . fond of whiskey

. . . characterized by . . . their fondness for story-telling." Their stories, which "refer," said Porter, "to characters and scenes of recent date—to men who have not only succeeded 'Mike Fink, the Last of the Boatmen,' but 'Col. Nimrod Wildfire,' and originals of his stamp,"[83] had the qualities of Southwestern humor which have been suggested: they were local, authentic, detailed, zestful;[84] they were distinctly masculine, and they dealt largely with the lower classes.[85]

Perhaps because, as a recent commentator suggested, "they had the wit to realize that something old in talking might look new in writing,"[86] or perhaps—as seems more probable—because they saw in the oral tale the only artistic form dealing to their satisfaction with the problems they had to solve, the contributors to the *Spirit* more clearly than any other group embodied in their writings the matter and the manner of the oral story. Now and then a subscriber would write gleefully about hearing a story from the lips of a contributor, sadly pointing out that the written version was inferior to the oral version.[87] Tales which showed changes characteristically associated with oral transmission appeared frequently. In 1841, a yarn which had appeared in a New England almanac at the beginning of the century was sent in, not from New England, but from Buffalo, where the correspondent's grandfather had told it, changed in many details.[88] A little later, a man in East Baton Rouge, trying to top the yarn of the Buffalo narrator, sent in his yarn about a similar incident, including details which had been in the New England version but not in the Buffalo version, and adding new details.[89] Thus the magazine became a medium for the swapping of tall tales—and this sort of thing happened frequently. Furthermore, time after time, an author would indicate where he had listened to the story he told—on a steamboat on the Mississippi[90] or on the Ohio River,[91] on a boat on the Chattahoochee in Florida, in an old log cabin in Louisiana wherein a party of hunters had taken shelter for the night, by a Missouri hunter's campfire,[92] or by the fireside after a coon hunt in Texas.[93]

How large the circulation of Porter's periodical was during its best days in the middle forties it is impossible to say, but it was probably more than forty thousand, a huge subscription list for that time.[94] Not only did its stories reach many subscribers directly; in addition, they were widely reprinted: the Rutland (Vermont) *Herald* estimated that "the original communications of the 'Spirit' furnish matter for half the papers in the Union,"[95] and the Boston *Times* asserted that Porter, as editor of his periodical, had "done more to develop and foster the humorous genius of his countrymen than any man alive."[96]

That the oral humor of the Crockett tales, the Fink tales, the *Spirit of the Times*, and kindred publications affected the writings of many Southwestern humorists seems reasonably sure. Of the ten listed above, at least three—T. B. Thorpe, Joseph M. Field, and John S. Robb—told tales about Mike Fink, tales which were evidently based upon oral lore.[97] And all of the ten except Longstreet wrote material which appeared in Porter's magazine.[98] Evidence of the influence of the oral tale upon the writings of these men is plentiful.

Consider Hooper's book, *Widow Rugby's Husband*,[99] for example. Almost every tale in it might well be preceded by the quotation which prefaces "The Res Gestae of a Poor Joke" (pp. 142-145)—"We tell the tale as 'twas told to us." A series of little yarns told by a guide are reported in "Dick McCoy's Sketches of His Neighbors" (pp. 35-40); "A Night at the Ugly Man's" (pp. 41-51) is a tall tale told by a host, full, as Mr. De Voto has pointed out, of oral lore, some of it particularly linked with Crockett;[100] four stories are pretty clearly derived from yarn-spinning sessions on the law circuit;[101] "A Ride with Old Kit Kuncker" (pp. 86-96) is a reported oral yarn; "The Evasive Soap Man" (pp. 109-111) is made up chiefly of the spiel of a peddler, and "Captain McSpadden" (pp. 112-120) is a tall tale recounted by an Irishman. Less specifically acknowledged sources in oral tales are discoverable in three of the other sketches in the volume.

It is at least possible, furthermore, that without the example of the Crockett tales, the Fink stories, and the yarns in the *Spirit*, Hooper never would have written his masterpiece, *Adventures of Simon Suggs* (1845). This is a notable American contribution to the literature of roguery as defined by Frank W. Chandler.[102] Hooper's book is an admirable account of a crafty rascal, Simon Suggs, who gorgeously lived up to his motto, "It is good to be shifty in a new country," by cheating or hoodwinking as many of his Alabama neighbors as possible. A series of chapters are given unity because they all reveal hawk-nosed, watery-eyed Simon Suggs brilliantly duping people. They are given variety because the backgrounds and the characters change as the hero—"as clear cut a figure as is to be found in the whole field of American humor"[103]— moves around the frontier, cheating his father at cards, collecting money on false pretenses from an over-anxious claim-filer, passing himself off as a rich uncle in Augusta, cozening the godly folk at a camp meeting by simulating repentance. They are humorous because they ludicrously display a series of comic upsets of poetic justice shrewdly arranged by a downright rascal who, in Hooper's words, "lives as merrily and comfortably as possible at the expense of others" by taking advantage of the frailties of human nature.

Three forces, conceivably, may be back of this book: the influence of European picaresque fiction, the influence of life on the frontier, and the influence, direct or indirect, of oral literature. How much Hooper knew of the literature of Europe which detailed the adventures of rogues it is impossible to say, and it is likewise impossible to presume that, even if he knew this literature, he would have been any quicker to imitate it than most of his countrymen were.[104] But it is possible to perceive that with nothing except a knowledge of life on the frontier and acquaintance with Southwestern humor, Hooper could have learned how to draw Simon Suggs.

For in the United States the frontier was to a large degree responsible for such a character as Hooper's shifty hero. As Miss Hazard has suggested, "To find the American picaro we must follow the American pioneer; the frontier is the natural habitat of the adventurer. The qualities fostered by the frontier were the qualities indispensable to the picaro: nomadism, insensibility to danger, shrewdness, nonchalance, gaiety."[105] As Watterson said of Suggs, "His adventures as a patriot and a gambler, a moralizer and cheat, could not have progressed in New England, and would have come to a premature end anywhere on the continent of Europe."[106] And in the oral literature of the frontier—literature which idolized Mike Fink for swigging a gallon of whisky without showing effects, for flaunting justice at the St. Louis court house, for stealing from his employer, for maltreating his spouse, and for cheating a gullible farmer, restraints which limited the stuff of other American fiction had disappeared.[107] Professor Boynton discerningly calls attention to the change:

> In all the accounts of the real figures of the frontier in South and Southwest the point is in one respect utterly different from that of the older North and East. The conscious literature was consciously edifying; it was not only polite but also moral. The Saxon insistence on ethical motivation was seldom relaxed at any section of the Atlantic seaboard. But the unconscious, or unliterary, literature of the backwoodsman, plainsman, riverman, was frankly unethical, amoral. The prevailing practice is summed up in Simon Suggs's favorite saw, "It is good to be shifty in a new country" . . . Crockett boasted of his shiftiness as proudly as of his shooting prowess. Ovid Bolus is presented . . . with great gusto . . . as a natural liar. . . . If it

is pertinent to refer to these tales as savoring of folk literature, it is pertinent to suggest that guile prevails in all of it, and that Reynard the Fox and Brer Rabbit move on the same plane as Simon Suggs. On the open, fluid frontier the ethics implicit in these stories is the ethics of success. . . .[108]

The most notable precedent for Hooper's volume is the literature, oral and printed, about Fink and—to some extent—Crockett. Their tales, too, are told in loosely linked yarns, since oral narrative fosters episodes and anecdotes rather than thoroughly integrated plots. Their histories reveal wandering heroes who, like Suggs, despise book larnin', who know that mother wit is the best asset of a man in a new territory, and who consistently display their common sense in their dealings with others. And the book about Simon, like the first book about Crockett, is a campaign biography.

Thompson's Major Jones letters are, of course, in the literary tradition of the Downing letters, and their greatest merit, it may be, is that they approach, in their limning of Pineville, the Down East Yankee's depiction of community and domestic existence: graphically they portray the interior life of Georgia.[109] As Watterson says, they "possess a value as contemporaneous pictures beyond and above their humor, abundant as that is."[110] The major is a believable figure, and those who appear in his tales are likewise convincing. In addition, Thompson is a capable storyteller.[111] His capability as a teller of tales, and a dialect more flavorsome than that even of the admirable Major, however, are better displayed in the yarns which were brought together in book form in 1872,[112] although some of them were written in the fifties[113]—such tales as "A Coon Hunt in a Fency Country" and "Beginning to Practice."

These are "mock oral tales," that is, reproductions in print of yarns told in the vernacular by a narrator of the sort who might delight a fireside audience. The influence of the unwritten form of the *raconteur* here is indeed a strong one. Whereas the loose commentary of the letter or the highly mannered style of most short stories of the time encouraged diffuseness, this form encouraged, among other things, directness. Oral tales, as Neal pointed out, were likely to be told "with a straightforwardness and simplicity . . . irresistibly impressive."[114] An oral story-teller could not hold his audience if he employed the leisurely and heavily rhetorical manner of even some of the best nineteenth-century narratives. Vivid phrases, drawn from the racy vernacular, here were likely to replace rambling descriptions; a striking figure of speech or a single well-chosen verb quickly recorded an action,[115] and the narrative moved along. Thumbnail sketches of characters and the use of much direct quotation which caught peculiarities of speech were bound up with the art.[116]

Some of these qualities are displayed in "A Coon Hunt in a Fency Country." The setting is meager; the characters are introduced simply as "the two greatest old coveys in our settlement for coon-huntin"; and after their fondness for liquor is revealed, the story moves forward rapidly, consistently holding interest. Vivid phrases catch the action: "After takin a good startin horn, they went out on their hunt, with their lightwood torch a blazin, and the dogs a barkin and yellin like they was crazy." They paused now and then to drink one another's health "until they begun to feel first-rate"; and a little later "they begun to be considerable tired and limber in their jints." Then Tom, "kerslash! . . . went into the water up to his neck. Bill heard the splash, and he clung to the fence with both hands like he thought it was slewin round to throw him off." Nothing could seem more artless and at the same time be more vivid, lively, direct, or more in keeping, than such phrases as these. The tale ends, as an anecdote should, with a point. In this and similar tales, palpably derived from the art of the fireside yarns, perfectly fulfilling their purpose, Thompson was at his best.

Whether or not this story appeared in the *Spirit*, it was typical of many yarns which did appear there. Typically, the stories in Porter's publication told of amusing characters who had their comic experiences while traveling, while attending to some sort of business in town, while enjoying a boisterous frolic or—most frequently—while on a hunt. But incidentally, to demonstrate the sophistication, the culture, of the author, and, even more important, to go one step farther in catching the pleasant quality of a fireside yarn, many of the correspondents of the periodical put their mock oral tales into an evocative framework. The circumstances of the telling of the tale were set forth, often with appreciative detail. Perhaps the yarn was told after an exciting hunt and a big meal, with all the company comfortable around the fire. A typical passage would describe the situation:

> Our saddles furnished a glorious pillow, and our buffalo skins a glorious bed . . . You may talk about your soirées, and your déjeuners, and all that sort of . . . social refinement, but let me tell you . . . for true-hearted benevolence, for that freedom of expression that conveys and leaves no sting, for an unreserved intercourse . . . commend me to a hunting-party in a half-faced camp.[117]

Then the teller of the tale would be described. In the story just quoted, he was a broad-shouldered, gigantic bear-hunter named Tom Wade. Then, in the words of the narrator thus introduced, the tale itself—a reported oral yarn—would be presented. The story-teller would begin slowly, philosophizing, perhaps, as if he had no intention of telling a tale, but incidentally introducing his characters and meandering up to the beginning of the events he described. With the introduction out of the way, the story itself moved rapidly through its big scene or scenes to its conclusion. At the end, the fireside scene of the opening paragraphs might again receive attention.

This box-like structure, a common enough device in fiction, was probably the best humorous narrative method employed in the Southwest. It was not new: one might allege that it derived from Chaucer, Boccaccio, or the *Arabian Nights*. One might even point to more recent antecedents, Scott's "Wandering Willie's Tale" in *Red Gauntlet* (1824), Downing's passage about his grandfather (1833), or Haliburton's enclosed Sam Slick monologues.[118] But it seems reasonable to guess that its best qualities in Southwestern humor simply derived from oral story-telling. However it came into being, it proved to be one of the best devices for telling a humorous story of the sort then and later prevalent.

Most important, it was admirable because it effectively characterized the story-teller, through direct description, through indirect description (i.e., the depiction of the effect he had upon his listeners), and through a long and highly characteristic dramatic monologue in which, revealingly, the imagination of the yarn-spinner was displayed. The vividness of the presentation of the narrator gave the narrative illusive power. It was also admirable because, as it was used, it seemed artless. The realistic setting given at the beginning, the detailed description of scene and narrator, gave an impression of naturalness just as it does when Kipling or Conrad presents a tale in such a framework. And from the standpoint of comic appeal, the method was particularly rich in its underlining of three types of incongruity:

(1) Incongruity between the grammatical, highly rhetorical language of the framework on the one hand and, on the other, the ungrammatical racy dialect of the narrator.

(2) Incongruity between the situation at the time the yarn was told and the situation described in the yarn itself. Far less amusing than the contrast provided by the first type of incongruity, this contrast was never-theless important for comedy, since it helped to remove the happenings

described by the tale-teller from the realm of harassing reality, to render them less disturbing, more amusing. Recounted in the atmosphere of the quiet, peaceful fireside, even the most harrowing episodes of a frontier tale might become comic.

(3) Incongruity between realism—discoverable in the framework wherein the scene and the narrator are realistically portrayed, and fantasy, which enters into the enclosed narrative because the narrator selects details and uses figures of speech, epithets, and verbs which give grotesque coloring.

Such was the artistry particularly developed by the *Spirit of the Times*—an artistry discoverable in tales by Madison Tensas, Johnson J. Hooper, Sol Smith, T. B. Thorpe, John S. Robb, George W. Harris, and dozens of others. Such was the art which at its best is revealed in a story thus introduced by William T. Porter: "Our readers must on no account fail to read an article . . . under the head of the 'Big Bear of Arkansas' . . . the best sketch of backwoods life, that we have seen in a long while."[119]

This tale, the masterpiece of T. B. Thorpe, begins with a vivid description of the heterogeneous crowd on a Mississippi steamboat, men of many sections and of many levels of society, crowded together in the cabin of the "Invincible." They were startled by the voice of the yarn-spinner booming from the social hall, uttering fragments of his boast. Then—

. . . the "Big Bar" walked into the cabin, took a chair, put his feet on the stove, and looking back over his shoulder, passed the general and familiar salute of "Strangers, how are you?" . . . in a moment every face was wreathed in a smile. There was something about the intruder that won the heart on sight. He appeared to be a man enjoying perfect health and contentment: his eyes were as sparkling as diamonds and good-natured to simplicity. Then his perfect confidence in himself was irresistibly droll.

The Big Bear started to talk, meanderingly at first, long enough for one to become acquainted with him. Then he launched, naturally, into a fantastic tall tale—the tale of how he battled to conquer a huge bear—a creation bear, and how, after epic struggles, the bear died. "'Twould astonish you," said the yarn-spinner, "to know how big he was: I made a *bed-spread of his skin*, and the way it used to cover my bar mattress, and leave several feet on each side to tuck up, would have delighted you." The yarn ended, and in the cabin there was deep silence, as Thorpe cogitated about the story. The yarn-spinner broke the silence by jumping up and suggesting a nightcap. Thus the simple story ends.

But during the course of its telling, Thorpe takes advantage of its possibilities for incongruity. In the framework, there are pedestrian sentences such as: "Starting from New Orleans in one of these boats, you will find yourself associated with men from every state in the Union, and from every portion of the globe; and a man of observation need not lack for amusement or instruction in such a crowd, if he will take the trouble to read the book of character so favourably opened before him."[120] With such ponderous phraseology still ringing in one's ears, one appreciates the refreshing contrast furnished by the illiterate narrator's "Strangers, the dog knows a bar's way as well as a horse-jockey knows a woman's: he always barks at the right time, bites at the exact place, and whips without getting a scratch." Similar incongruity is furnished by the juxtaposition of the interruptions by the Hoosier, the timid little man, and the Englishman, with the Big Bear's remarks before and after them. And the framework not only throws into relief the comic qualities of the Westerner's talk but also makes the scene vivid, reveals the quaint personality of the yarn-spinner, and moves the possibly distressing details of the contest with the bear out of the realm of harassing realism into the realm of comedy.

The comedy, furthermore, is developed fully because, side by side with the realistic depiction of a commonplace scene—a steamboat cabin jammed with a jostling crowd, there is told a tale colored by details which belong not in realism but in fantasy. Here the world of fact is a revealing background for a wildly imagined world—a world in which potato hills grow so large that they are mistaken for Indian mounds, in which a bear becomes so hot that steam spurts out of a bullet hole in his body, in which a bear walks over a fence, "looming up like a black mist, he seems so large." This fantastic world is one of mythical splendors and poetic mysteries:

> . . . he walked straight towards me. I raised myself, took deliberate aim, and fired. Instantly the varmint wheeled, gave a yell, and walked *through the fence* like a falling tree would through a cobweb. I started after . . . I heard the old varmint groaning in a thicket near by, like a thousand sinners, and by the time I reached him he was a corpse. Stranger, it took five niggers and myself to put that carcase on a mule's back, and old long-ears waddled under his load, as if he was foundered in every leg of his body, and with a common whopper

of a bar, he would have trotted off, and enjoyed himself . . . It was in fact a creation bar, and if he had lived in Samson's time, and had met him, in a fair fight, it would have licked him in the twinkling of a dice-box. But strangers, I never liked the way I hunted, *and missed him*. There is something curious about it, I could never understand, —and I never was satisfied at his giving in so easy at last. Perhaps, he had heard of my preparations to hunt him the next day, so he jist come in, like Captain Scott's coon,[121] to save his wind to grunt with in dying; but that ain't likely. My private opinion is, that that bar was an *unhuntable bar, and died when his time come*.

Rich in detail, in contrast, in fancy, Thorpe's sketch is a delightfully humorous achievement. And it reveals a splendidly realized character— a character who is memorable because the reader learns not only how he looked, how he talked, how others reacted to him, but also how his mind worked, and, more important, how his imagination worked. The framework and the reported narrative combine to make possible this splendid achievement.[122]

Such is the artistry of Thorpe at its best. Unfortunately the tale is not typical of him. More often, he wrote passably good but essentially dull essays about various aspects of the frontier—about bee-hunters or buffalo hunts or the like. Only in "The Disgraced Scalp-lock," "A Piano in Arkansaw," "Bob Herring, the Arkansas Bear Hunter," and perhaps in other stories discoverable solely in old newspapers and periodicals, does Thorpe forsake his heavily literary style and employ the more direct artistic methods of oral narrative. And in no other tale known to be by him, does he approach the level of his masterpiece.

Other contributors to the *Spirit* used the highly effective framework technique more frequently.[123] It is quite tellingly employed by many anonymous contributors as well as by John S. Robb, for example, in "The Standing Candidate" and Madison Tensas in "A Tight Race Considerin'."

But the author who most consistently uses the framework narrative method to portray his chief character is George W. Harris. His book, *Sut Lovingood* (1867), the product of a man who himself was as adept at oral story-telling[124]—a book which is typical of Southwestern humor because it is full of local color, exuberant, masculine, "the nearest thing to the undiluted oral humor of the Middle West that has found its way into print,"[125] has never had the widespread appreciation it deserves,

partly, perhaps, because its artistry has never been sufficiently appreciated, partly because its faults have been overemphasized by oversquea-
mish critics.[126] Nevertheless, this volume which, in a sense, may be
thought of as a picaresque novel in the form of anecdotes within a framework, represents a highly artistic use of the formula employed by Thorpe
in his masterpiece.

Harris's tales have all the qualities made possible by this technique. So
artless do they seem that even such a discerning critic as Watterson takes
for granted that any reader will observe that in Sut's yarns there is "little
attempt at technical literary finish, either in description or proportion . . . ; the author is seemingly satisfied to aim merely at his point,
and, this reached, to be satisfied to leave it work out its own moral and
effect."[127] Yet a careful study will reveal that there is sufficient artistry
splendidly to reveal Sut's character and to underline various incongruities. In the framework, Sut is revealed by direct description—a
"queer looking, long legged, short bodied, small headed, white haired,
hog eyed" youth, who comes into view at the beginning or the conclusion of various sketches—reining up his bow-necked sorrel in front of
Pat Nash's grocery or Capehart's Doggery to tell a yarn to a crowd of
loafing mountaineers, weaving along the street after a big drunk or a big
fight, or stretching his skinny body at full length by a cool spring at noon.
Indirectly, too, by showing the reactions of those who listen to Sut's tales,
Harris reveals his hero's character. A rat-faced youth who is conquered by
Sut's badinage (p. 21),[128] "George" (Harris), who claims that a part of a
tale is not true (p. 120), or who tolerantly encourages Sut's yarns, even
when he is awakened to hear them (p. 122), the book agent who is insulted
and frightened by Sut's onslaught (p. 244), others affected in various ways
by Sut's talk, help us to understand the manner of person he is.

Sut's character is also revealed, moreover, by the tales he tells about
himself, tales which display "his keen delight for Hallowe'en *fun*—there
is no ulterior motive (except occasionally Sut's desire to 'get even'), no
rascality, no gambling, no sharping as in *Simon Suggs*. . . . Sut is
simply the genuine naïve roughneck mountaineer riotously bent on raising hell."[129] They indicate his chief passions—telling stories, eating good
food, drinking "corkscrew kill-devil whisky," hugging pretty girls, and
"breeding scares among darned fools" by playing pranks. Just as revealing
are his dislikes: Yankee peddlers, Yankee lawyers, Yankee scissor-
grinders—any kind of Yankees, sheriffs, most preachers, learned men
who use big words or flowery language, tavern keepers who serve bad

food, and reformers. His idea of what is funny shows us what kind of person he is: a comic situation, according to this son of the soil, is usually one in which a character of the sort he hates, or preferably a large number of characters, get into highly uncomfortable circumstances.[130] Comic to him, too, are the procreative and bodily functions, the animal qualities in humans and the human qualities in animals.

The language he employs in his monologues helps reveal his character —a language polished little by book larnin', Rabelaisian, close to the soil, but withal poetic in an almost Elizabethan fashion.[131] The very figures of speech he employs have more than comedy to recommend them. They are conceits, comic because they are startlingly appropriate and inappropriate at the same time, devices for characterization because they arise with poetic directness from the life Sut knows. Consider these passages, redolent of Sut's knowledge of nature and of liquor groceries:

> Bake dwelt long on the *crop* of dimes to be *gathered from that field*; [saying] that he'd make *more than there were spots on forty fawns in July*, not to speak of the *big gobs* of reputation he'd bear away, *shining* all over his clothes, *like lightning bugs on a dog fennil top*. (p. 62)

> . . . her skin was as *white as the inside of a frogstool*, and her *cheeks and lips as rosy as a perch's gills in dogwood blossom time*—and such a smile! why, when it struck you fair and square it felt just *like a big horn of unrectified old Monangahaley, after you'd been sober for a month, attending a ten horse prayer meeting twice a day, and most of the nights.* (p. 76)

> Wirt had changed his *grocery range*, and the spirits at the new *log-lick* had more *scrimmage seed* and *raise-devil* into it than the old *boiled drink* he was used to, and three horns *hoisted his tail*, and *set his bristles about as stiff* as eight of the other *doggery juice* would. So when court sat at nine, Wirt was about as far ahead as *cleaving*, or *half past that*. The *hollering stage of the disease* now struck him, and he roared one good *ear-quivering roar* . . . (p. 249)

> [Of a man howling in fear and pain:] The noise he made sounded *like a two-horse mowing-machine, driven by chain-lightning, cutting through a dry cane brake on a big bet.* (pp. 268-269)

Recited in Sut's drawl, with far more touches of dialect than are here revealed, in fact, in "the wildest of East Tennessee jargon,"[132] these passages and others in Sut's stories contrast amusingly with the rhetorical framework language. Harris seemed to realize the possibilities of ludicrous antitheses in language, for he liked to put Sut's talk alongside of flowery passages[133] or of learned language in which big words predominated.[134] Humorous, too, is the contrast between the circumstances under which Sut tells his tale and the harrowing scenes he describes. Incidentally, most of the happenings about which Sut tells never could be amusing unless they were removed by several steps from reality.

But the great incongruity in the tales, only partly exploited by Harris, is that between the realistically depicted world of the framework and the fantastically comic world created by Sut in the highly colored, highly imaginative enclosed narrative. His is a world in which the religious life of the Smoky Mountains is grotesquely warped until all its comedy is emphasized, a cosmos wherein the squalor in which the Lovingoods live—squalor without alleviation, without shame—somehow becomes very jolly. It is a world in which the crowds at a camp meeting, a frolic, or a quarter race[135] are revealed in postures and garbs as amusing as those of the earthy and lively figures that throng a canvas by Peter Breughel. Startlingly, it is a world in which scent, sound, form, color, and motion are not only vividly lifelike but also hilariously comic. Here is a mare in that strange country, whose rider has just shouted "Get up!":

> Well she did "get up," right then and there, and staid up long enough to light twenty feet further away, in a broad trembling squat, her tail hid between her thighs, and her ears dancing past each other, like scissors cutting. The jolt of the lighting set the clock [which her rider was carrying and which prodded her unmercifully] to striking. Bang-zee-bang-zee-whang-zee. She listened powerful attentive to the three first licks, and they seemed to go through her as quicksilver would through a sifter. She waited for no more, but just gave her whole soul to the one job of running from under that infernal Yankee, and his hive of bumble bees, rattle snakes, and other awful hurting things, as she took it to be. (p. 40)

Here is a bull on a rampage in the public market:

> . . . just a-tearing, a thirteen hundred pound black and white bull, with his tail as straight up in the air as a telegraph pole, and a chest-

nut fence rail tied across his horns with hickory withes. He was a-toting his head low, and every lick he made . . . he'd blow whoff, outen his snout . . . He'd say whoff! and a hundred and sixty pound nigger would fly up in the air like unto a grasshopper, and come back spread like a frog . . . Whoff! again, and a boy would turn ten somersaults towards the river. Whoff! and an Amherst woman lit a-straddle of an old fat fellow's neck, with a jolt that jumped his tobacco out of his mouth and scrunched *him*, while she went on down hill on all fours in a fox trot . . . A little bald-headed man, dressed in gold specks and a gold-headed walking stick, was a-passing . . . he looked like he was a-ciphering out a sum . . . in his head . . . Whoff! and the specks lit on the roof of the market house, and the stick, gold end first, sat in a milk can sixty feet off. As to bald head himself, I lost sight of him, while the specks were in the air; he just disappeared from mortal vision somehow, sort of like the breath from a looking-glass. (pp. 126-127)

In such passages as these, in passages which use conceits even more grotesque than those quoted above,[136] in passages of imaginative exaggeration,[137] of strangely linked entities,[138] the world of Sut's stories, tremendously different from the world where Sut's whisky flask flashes in the sun, takes its queer shape to delight the reader. And from the passages about Sut, and from his imaginative tales, emerges a character, coarser and earthier, perhaps, than any other in our literature during the nineteenth century, but at the same time, understandably true to life, an ingratiating mischief-maker, America's Till Eulenspiegel,[139] in his own right a poet and a great creator of comedy.

In *Sut Lovingood*, the antebellum humor of the South reaches its highest level of achievement before Mark Twain. The author of this book, like his contemporaries, was a man of the world who became an author almost by accident. Like them, he wrote tales full of authentic local color, zestful yarns which blossomed from the rich subsoil of oral humor. Encouraged by the *Spirit of the Times* and other publications, he learned to employ the best method for telling a story developed by members of a highly artistic group, making the most of the framework technique for setting forth a mock oral tale, making the most, too, of the mock oral tale itself, with its colloquial richness, its disarming directness, its vivid comic detail. If his writings were better than the rest, they were better because he had more sense of incongruities, more exuberance, more imagination, and because he had greater genius than his contemporaries for transferring the unique artistry of the oral narrative to the printed page.

NOTES

1. See John Donald Wade, *Augustus Baldwin Longstreet* (New York, 1924).

2. See Marion Kelley, *The Life and Writings of Johnson Jones Hooper* (Unpublished Master's Dissertation, Alabama Polytechnic Institute, 1934).

3. For data concerning Thompson, Thorpe, Field, and Robb, as well as others of the group, see Franklin J. Meine's admirable *Tall Tales of the Southwest* (New York, 1930). For treatments of Robb, Smith, and Field, see Carl Brooks Spotts, "The Development of Fiction on the Missouri Frontier," *Missouri Historical Review*, XXIX, 100-108, 186-194 (1935).

4. See George F. Mellen, "Joseph Glover Baldwin," *Library of Southern Literature* (New Orleans, n.d.), I, 175-181.

5. A monograph on Harris is being prepared by Mr. Meine. Unless Harris's writings were collected many years after they were written, it is highly probable that the date 1867 indicates a reprint rather than a first edition. He contributed to *The Spirit of the Times* as early as 1845, and at least three of the Sut Lovingood yarns were written in the fifties.

6. For additional comment on this point, see W. P. Trent, "Retrospect of American Humor," *Century*, LXIII, 50-52 (November, 1901).

7. *Op. cit.*, p. xvi.

8. Printed in Augusta in 1835, in New York in 1840 and thereafter.

9. 1840 edition, pp. 72, 200.

10. Quoted in Bishop O. P. Fitzgerald, *Judge Longstreet. A Life Sketch* (Nashville, 1891), pp. 164-166. The italics are Longstreet's.

11. The italics are Longstreet's.

12. Review by William T. Thompson, *Southern Literary Messenger*, VI, 573 (July, 1840). See also the review in *The New-Yorker*, IX, 157 (May 23, 1840). At one point in his book (p. 47), Longstreet voiced regret that fidelity to history forced him to record profanity.

13. Associated with Longstreet as a newspaper editor, he admired his predecessor heartily, and was flattered when a book of his was attributed to the author of *Georgia Scenes*—Wade, *op. cit.*, pp. 165-166.

14. The phrase is used by "Uncle Solon" in "Sketches of Piney Woods Character," *Spirit of the Times*, XXI, 79 (April, 1851). The writer links Longstreet's and Thompson's books as accurate portrayals of Georgians.

15. *The Mysteries of the Backwoods; or Sketches of the Southwest including*

Characters, Scenery and Rural Sports (Philadelphia, 1846), p. 8. "Mysteries" here apparently refers to occupations. Reviewers mentioned the historical value of Thorpe's writings frequently.

16. Published in New York, 1853, p. v.

17. *Streaks of Squatter Life and Far Western Scenes. A Series of Humorous Sketches Descriptive of Incident and Character in the Wild West* (Philadelphia, 1846), p. viii. He mentions Thorpe, Hooper, Field, and Sol Smith as predecessors.

18. *The Big Bear of Arkansas* . . . (New York, 1843).

19. *A Quarter Race in Kentucky* . . . (New York, 1846).

20. *Oddities in Southern Life and Character* (Boston, 1882), pp. viii, 134, 415.

21. Preface to *The Big Bear of Arkansas*, p. xi.

22. *Mark Twain's America* (Boston, 1932), p. 98. *Georgia Scenes*, most influential of the humorous books of the section, typically dealt with country and ballroom dancing, horse swapping, racing, fox-hunting, the militia drill, the shooting-match, the fight, the gander-pull, the debating society meeting, and the gossipy matrons of Georgia.

23. *Spirit of the Times*, XXI, 205 (June 28, 1851). Compare Baldwin's note on conditions in *Flush Times of Alabama and Mississippi* (New York, 1853), pp. 84-85: "The pursuits of industry neglected, riot and debauchery filled up the vacant hours. . . . Even the little boys caught the taint of the general infection of morals; and I knew one of them . . . to give a man ten dollars to hold him up to bet at the table of a faro-bank. . . . The groceries—*vulgice*—doggeries, were in full blast in those days, no village having less than a half-dozen all busy all the time: gaming and horse-racing were polite and well patronized amusements. I knew of a Judge to adjourn two courts (or court twice) to attend a horse-race, at which he officiated judicially and ministerially, and with more appropriateness than in the judicial chair. Occasionally the scene was diversified by a murder or two . . ."

24. "Western Drolls" in *Lost Leaders* (London, 1889), pp. 186-187. See also De Voto, *op. cit.*, pp. 92-94.

25. Neighbor Freeport in the sketch reproduced hereafter (pp. 199-200) was famed as a story-teller. The tall tales from the almanac, reproduced pp. 199, 201-202 are probably recorded oral tales.

26. See, for example, "Big Connecticut Pumpkins," *Spirit of the Times*, XXI, 350 (September 13, 1851).

27. Haliburton was the only notable humorist to win fame as a portrayer of a famous Yankee comic figure who drew much upon oral story-telling. See V. L. O. Chittick, *Thomas Chandler Haliburton*, pp. 182-183. In *The Attaché*, II, 18, Sam Slick tells of collecting material in fireside conversations.

28. *Letters from the West* (London, 1828), pp. 181-182.

29. T. D. Bonner, *The Life of James P. Beckwourth*, ed. Bernard De Voto (New York, 1930), p. 55.

30. *Echoes from the Backwoods* (London, 1849), pp. 28-30. The Longstreet story was "Georgia Theatrics," but the author did not indicate any acquaintance with the written version.

31. J. S. Buckingham, *The Eastern and Western States of America* (London, [n.d.]), pp. 271-273.

32. *John's Alive* (Philadelphia, 1883), p. 176.

33. *Narrative of the Texan Santa Fé Expedition*, ed. Milo M. Quaife (Chicago, 1929), pp. 87, 91-93, 108-110. The book was first published in 1844.

34. *The Wilderness and Warpath* (New York, 1846), pp. 160-170.

35. Charles B. Johnson, *Illinois in the Fifties* (Champaign, 1918), pp. 58-61.

36. [H. E. Taliaferro], *Fisher's River (North Carolina) Scenes and Characters* (New York, 1859), pp. 51, 58. Uncle Davy, the gunsmith, "had a great fund of long-winded stories and incidents, mostly manufactured by himself—some few he had 'hearn'—and would bore you or edify you, as it might turn out, from sun to sun, interspersing them with a dull, gutteral, lazy laugh. He became quite a proverb in the line of big story-telling. True, he had many obstinate competitors, but he distanced them all . . . Uncle Davy's mind was trained in a sort of horsemill track, and would pass from one story to another with great naturalness and ease."

37. G. Douglas Brewerton, *The War in Kansas* (New York, 1855), p. 240.

38. Joseph S. Williams, *Old Times in West Tennessee* (Memphis, 1873), p. 115.

39. *A Stray Yankee in Texas* (New York, 1853), pp. 113-114. For an excellent characterization of circuit story-telling in Georgia, see R. M. Johnston, "Middle Georgia in Rural Life," *Century*, XLIII, 739-740 (March, 1892).

40. John D. Wade, "Authorship of Davy Crockett's Autobiography," *Georgia Historical Quarterly*, VI, 265-268 (September, 1922). See also Constance Rourke, "Davy Crockett: Forgotten Facts and Legends," *Southwest Review*, XIX, 149-161 (January, 1934).

41. W. H. Sparks, *The Memories of Fifty Years*. Third edition. (Philadelphia and Macon, 1872), p. 483. See also Edward Mapes. *Lucius Q. C. Lamar*, p. 39, quoted by Tandy, *op. cit.*, p. 75.

42. Printed in *Polly Peablossom's Wedding*, ed. T. A. Burke, and recently reprinted in *Tall Tales of the Southwest*, pp. 299-301.

43. "The Bailiff that 'Stuck to His Oath,' " "Jim Bell's Revenge," "Mrs. Johnson's Post Office Case," and "The Fair Offender," in *The Widow Rugby's Husband* (Philadelphia, 1851), pp. 64-86.

44. These will be cited later, p. 86.

45. "Mike Fink, the Last of the Boatmen," St. Louis *Reveille,* June 14 and June 21, 1847.

46. Fitzgerald, *op. cit.*, p. 164. Lonstreet did treat the upper classes more than most of his contemporaries.

47. "Johnson Jones Hooper," *Library of Southern Literature* (New Orleans, 1909), VI, 2490.

48. *America in Literature* (New York, 1903), p. 159.

49. "Story-Telling," *New York Mirror*, XVI, 321 (April 6, 1839). "Of all the stories I meet with," testified Neal, "none are so delightful to me as those I *over-hear* on board a steamboat or a stage-coach." He cited several thus overheard.

50. Wade, *Augustus Baldwin Longstreet*, pp. 157-160.

51. Percy H. Boynton, *Literature and American Life* (Boston, 1936), pp. 437-438.

52. *Master William Mitten* (Macon, 1864), p. 185.

53. *Southern Literary Messenger*, II, 289 (March, 1836).

54. The ability of a cultured, well-balanced gentleman to perceive eccentri-

city, carefully cultivated by many of the humorists of the South, was important particularly in the earlier humorous writings.

55. *Southern Literary Messenger*, VI, 572 (July, 1840).

56. *Southern Literary Messenger*, II, 287 (March, 1836).

57. *Southern Literary Messenger*, II, 289. "The Turn Out" reminded him of Miss Edgeworth's "Barring Out."

58. R. H. Rivers, quoted by Fitzgerald, *op. cit.*, pp. 169-170.

59. John B. Gordon, *Reminiscences of the Civil War* (New York, 1905), p. 93.

60. "Ovid Bolus, Esq.," *The Flush Times in Alabama and Mississippi* (New York, 1853), pp. 1-19.

61. *The Flush Times in Alabama and Mississippi*, p. 162.

62. Miss Tandy, *op. cit.*, p. 83, concludes her illuminating criticism of Baldwin with an excellent summary: "Baldwin is the amateur story teller, the professional lawyer and historian. His talent and wit are carelessly displayed. Nevertheless his pictures of the era of inflation are faithful and valuable."

63. *Recollections of the Last Ten Years* (Boston, 1836), p. 161.

64. Captain Sam Brady, Pennsylvania Regulator; the Wetzel family, Indian exterminators in West Virginia; Kit Carson of Texas, mountain man; Jim Bridger of Utah, trapper and guide; Wild Bill Hickok of the cattle frontier were examples.

65. Paul Bunyan, giant lumberman about whom some of the finest tall tales of all were told, is not represented in this volume simply because none of the yarns about him were printed until this present century. The best collection is Esther Shephard, *Paul Bunyan* (Seattle, 1924).

66. R. G. A. Levinge, *Echoes from the Backwoods; or, Scenes in Transatlantic Life* (London, 1849), II, 12. This is only a portion of Levinge's report. He quotes two stanzas of a ballad in which Crockett's boast is set forth in rhyme.

67. A fine bibliography of these is available in Constance Rourke, *Davy Crockett* (New York, 1934), pp. 251-258. The same volume (pp. 259-270) contains the best study of the tangled problem of the authorship of the *Sketches and Eccentricities* and the books attributed to Crockett which are listed in the next footnote.

68. *Sketches and Eccentricities of Col. David Crockett* (New York, 1833), published in Cincinnati the same year as *The Life and Adventures of Colonel David Crockett of West Tennessee*, followed by *A Narrative of the Life of David Crockett, of the State of Tennessee* . . . (Philadelphia, 1834); *An Account of Col. Crockett's Tour to the North and Down East* . . . (Philadelphia, 1835); and *Col. Crockett's Exploits and Adventures in Texas* (Philadelphia, 1836). The best parts of the last three of these are available in *The Autobiography of David Crockett*, ed. Hamlin Garland (New York, 1923).

69. The first went through at least twelve editions in the thirties, and the others were probably even more popular.

70. *Western Monthly Magazine*, II, 278 (May, 1834). The reviewer, it is interesting to note, scouted the idea that Crockett was a humorist. "But the colonel," he said, "is 'barking up the wrong tree,' when he sets up for a man of humor. Whatever he may be in conversation . . . it is not that quality which will give him fame as a writer. The dullest parts of his book are those intended to produce a laugh . . ."

71. See Walter Blair and Franklin J. Meine, *Mike Fink, King of Mississippi*

Keelboatmen (New York, 1933), pp. 273-277, for a list of the stories. In print, many of the tales were definitely given the form of oral yarns.

72. "The Last of the Boatmen," *Western Souvenir* (Cincinnati, 1828), and "Mike Fink, the Last of the Boatmen," *Western Monthly Review*, July, 1829, pp. 15-19.

73. *Crockett Almanac for 1840* (Nashville, 1839) reveals how Mike shot at a target held by his wife. The earlier narrator felt "compelled to omit the anecdote altogether."

74. "Trimming a Darky's Heel," St. Louis *Reveille*, January 25, 1847.

75. See Blair and Meine, *op. cit.*, pp. 176-239, for an examination of the various versions of the story of his death.

76. Such as Henry Inman, Robert Clark, Charles Elliot.

77. Fitz-Greene Halleck, William Gaylord Clark, and any contributors to the *Spirit* who happened to be in New York, such as T. B. Thorpe, Albert Pike, G. W. Kendall.

78. Francis Brinley, *Life of William T. Porter* (New York, 1860), pp. 86-100, gives a lengthy account of the *Spirit* crowd at Monteverde's.

79. Brinley, *op. cit.*, pp. 78-79. This is to be taken literally.

80. In the issue of the *Spirit* for February 22, 1851 (XXI, 1), Porter said: "We are not aware of a single Military or Naval station of the United States, in any clime, where the 'Spirit of the Times' is not to be found."

81. *Spirit of the Times*, XVI, 277 (August 15, 1846).

82. In the issue of the *Spirit* for August 22, 1846 (XVI, 303), Porter stated with pride that fourteen correspondents had received army promotions "since the glorious achievements on the Rio Grande."

83. *The Big Bear of Arkansas*, pp. xii, ix.

84. Porter often commented on the way these stories "illustrated," as he said in the preface to *A Quarter Race in Kentucky*, "character and incident in the south and south-west." In the *Turf Register* for April, 1841, Porter asserted that American sporting literature was better than that of England, because there was an exhaustless fund of adventure. To this, to "incidents of travel over prairies and mountains hitherto unknown by the white man, the singular variety of manners in the different States, springing from differences of origin, in climate and product, peculiarities unhackneyed by a thousand tourists, to this is attributed the greater freshness and raciness of American sketches."

85. The quotation on the title page of *The Big Bear* collection, aptly selected by Porter, was Dogberry's "This is your charge; you shall comprehend all vagrom men."

86. Arthur Palmer Hudson, "Introduction" to *Humor of the Old Deep South* (New York, 1936), pp. 16-17.

87. See "Familiar Epistle from Mississippi," *Spirit of the Times*, XV, 63 (April 5, 1845): "Mr. P[orter]—Sam has been here for a few days past setting up with 'Jim and Bill,' and when he was fairly through last night we made him *tell* the story about 'That Big Dog Fight at Ned Myers's,' and then after two or three whiskey punches he was prevailed upon . . . to give the *true* account of the 'Tooth Pulling' as related by 'Uncle Johnny.' It is unfortunate for you that Sam lives such a long way off—he *tells* a story much better than he writes it—he gives the *action*, the pantomimic part of a good anecdote inimitably; without being a buffoon he is certainly one of the most delightful *raconteurs* in the state." Both

of the stories mentioned were by P. B. January, "a country gentleman of Mississippi" and a highly admirable story-teller, according to the testimony of Porter. Both, too, were reprinted in *The Big Bear* collection. See also the reference to Harris as a story-teller, p. 96.

88. The almanac story is reprinted in this book, p. 199 [refers to original book from which this excerpt is taken]. The Buffalo version appears in the *Spirit of the Times*, XI, 205 (July, 1841).

89. *Ibid.*, XI, 288 (August 21, 1841).

90. "Driving a Parson Ashore"—reprinted from the *Spirit*—in *Stray Subjects* (Philadelphia, 1848), p. 110.

91. *Spirit of the Times*, XVI, 374 (October 3, 1846).

92. *Ibid.*, XXI, 55 (March 22, 1851); 194 (June 14, 1851).

93. *Ibid.*, XVI, 331 (September 5, 1846); XXI, 19 (March 1, 1851).

94. Definite statistics are not available. However, in 1856, well past the peak of the magazine's popularity, when Porter allowed his name to be associated with another periodical, *Porter's Spirit of the Times*, by the time the new publication reached its eighth number, it was "backed by a circulation of 40,000 copies." —Brinley, *op. cit.*, p. 266.

95. Quoted in the *Spirit of the Times*, XVI, 618 (February 20. 1847).

96. *Ibid.*, XI, 540 (January 2, 1840).

97. T. B. Thorpe, "The Disgraced Scalp-lock," *Spirit of the Times*, July 16, 1842, reprinted frequently; J. M. Field, "The Death of Mike Fink," St. Louis *Reveille*, October 21, 1844, and "Mike Fink, the Last of the Boatmen," *Reveille*, June 14, 21, 1847; John S. Robb, "Trimming a Darky's Heel," *Reveille*, January 25, 1847. Field's stories are based in part upon oral narratives of Charles Keemle, a former trapper, in part, says Field, upon many tales heard in many places. Robb's story is a version of a story merely hinted at as early as 1823.

98. None of the stories written by Baldwin have been identified, although Porter testifies that he was a contributor. It would be interesting to discover how much Baldwin modified his style when he wrote for the racy pages of the *Spirit*.

99. First published as *A Ride with Old Kit Kuncker* (Tuscaloosa, 1849), but generally known by the title given above, published in Philadelphia in 1851, since no copy of the first edition has been discovered.

100. De Voto, *op. cit.*, pp. 93-94. Crockett makes much of his ugliness, alleging that he can bring a coon from a tree by grinning at it. Hooper's hero is so ugly that flies avoid lighting on his face even when he is a baby, so ugly that his wife has to practice before she can manage to kiss him, so ugly that a whole crowd of men who have been told to give their knives to any man uglier than they are shower knives upon him.

101. "The Bailiff that 'Stuck to His Oath' " (pp. 64-70), "Jim Bell's Revenge" (pp. 71-79), "Mrs. Johnson's Post Office Case" (pp. 80-82), and "A Fair Offender" (pp. 83-86).

102. *The Literature of Roguery* (Boston, 1907), I, 2-6.

103. C. Alphonso Smith, "Johnson Jones Hooper," *Library of Southern Literature* (New Orleans, 1909), VI, 2491.

104. Teague, in *Modern Chivalry*, is hardly worthy of the tradition. Birdofredum Sawin came later. The best American predecessor of Simon is discoverable in Henry Junius Nott's *Novelettes of a Traveller* (1834) wherein the South

Carolina author displayed the farcical adventures of Thomas Singularity. Singularity, as Professor Wauchope pointed out, is "a sharper 'deadbeat' and unscrupulous rascal—a lineal descendant of the earlier picaresque romances."—*The Writers of South Carolina* (Columbia, S.C., 1910), p. 59. But Nott's book is pretty generalized, pretty pallid, and rather dull.

105. Lucy L. Hazard, "The American Picaresque," *The Trans-Mississippi West* (Boulder, 1930), p. 198.

106. "The South in Light and Shade," in *The Compromises of Life* (New York, 1903), p. 78. Simon receives high praise from Watterson: "He is to the humor of the South what Sam Weller is to the humor of England, and Sancho Panza is to the humor of Spain . . . he stands out of the canvas whereon an obscure local Rubens has depicted him as lifelike and vivid as Gil Blas of Santillane."

107. Blair and Meine, *op. cit.*, p. x.

108. *Op. cit.*, pp. 614-615.

109. De Voto, *op. cit.*, p. 257.

110. *The Compromises of Life*, p. 72. For additional comment on Thompson, see Watterson's *Oddities of Southern Life and Character*, pp. 134-135, wherein the provincial qualities of the fiction are stressed.

111. Robert Cecil Beale, *The Development of the Short Story in the South* (Charlottesville, 1911), p. 38.

112. *Major Jones's Courtship* . . . [and] *Thirteen Humorous Sketches* (New York, 1872).

113. "A Coon Hunt in a Fency Country" appeared in the collection, *Polly Peablossom's Wedding* (1851), and "The Hoosier and the Salt Pile," ascribed to another author in Burton's *Cyclopedia of Wit and Humor* (New York, 1858).

114. *New York Mirror*, XVI, 321 (April 6, 1839).

115. Note the opening paragraph of "The Hoosier and the Salt Pile," reproduced hereafter, wherein travel by rail "whar people are whirled along 'slam bang to eternal smash,' like they wer so many bales and boxes" is compared with travel by stagecoach, which allows one to enjoy "the rattle of the wheels over the stones . . . the lunging and pitching into the ruts and gullies, the slow pull up the steep hills."

116. In "The Hoosier and the Salt Pile," the second paragraph quickly and vividly pictures seven characters, including "a dandy gambler, with a big diamond breast-pin and more gold chains hangin round him than would hang him; and old hardshell preacher . . . with the biggest mouth and the ugliest teeth I ever seed," and "a cross old maid, as ugly as a tar-bucket." The conversation in later paragraphs is highly characteristic of the various characters.

117. "Tom Wade and the Grizzly Bear," by Phil, *Spirit of the Times*, XXI, 194 (June 14, 1851). For other tales which are told in this fashion in the *Spirit*, see those cited in footnotes 90-91 above, and several in each of the collections edited by Porter and Haliburton.

118. The framework form was adopted by Haliburton, probably, so that the sketches might be written from the viewpoint of a Canadian, although Sam was always quoted at length. Like the writer of the Southwest, Haliburton too was no doubt eager to display cultural superiority.

119. *Spirit of the Times*, XI, 37 (March 27, 1841). The story was first printed in this issue.

120. Compare the opening sentences of "The Hoosier and the Salt Pile," by Thompson, rather clearly influenced by Thorpe's famous sketch.

121. The reference is to Captain Martin Scott who, legend had it, made a coon give up by looking at him, so certain was his aim. The legend also was attached to Boone and Crockett, though it is impossible to know who was the original hero.

122. Some of these comments parallel—except for emphasis and terminology —Mr. De Voto's comments on Jim Baker's blue-jay story—*op. cit.*, p. 251. Mr. De Voto's suggestive criticism is the only one I have seen dealing with the value of the framework technique for humorous narrative.

123. In Porter's collections of favorite stories, *The Big Bear of Arkansas* and *Quarter Race in Kentucky*, there are twenty-one framework narratives and thirty-two which do not use the framework. Of the latter, seven are letters or mock oral tales in the vernacular.

124. See Charlie's letter from "Out West," in which he tells how Harris came charging down the street to tell a "cock and bull story" about a steamboat explosion. "The story is very good," he concludes, "particularly when you hear it told by S—1 [Harris's pen name] . . ."—*Spirit of the Times*, XVIII, 73 (April 8, 1848).

125. Napier Wilt, *Some American Humorists* (New York, 1929), p. 130.

126. The book has three faults: (1) Sut employs a dialect which some readers think too hard to translate. (2) Sometimes the details about the plights of the victims or details incidental to the tales are coarse, in bad taste, and unfunny. (3) The repetition in his tales of the motif of physical discomfort is so frequent that it becomes monotonous. None of these faults, in my opinion, should damn the book. Sut's dialect is mastered after a little effort. Harris suggested that those who were troubled by the second fault would be those who had a wholesome fear of the devil, and ought to, and those who hadn't a great deal of faith that their reputation would stand much of a strain; and "fur a gineral skeer—speshully for the wimen," quoted the words, "Evil to him that evil thinks." The point is well taken: the stories are no coarser than highly admired stories by some of the greatest writers. And the richness of the detail may well atone for the monotonous resemblances between situations.

127. *Oddities of Southern Life and Character*, p. 415.

128. Page references here and hereafter are to the 1867 edition. In some excerpts given later on, the dialect will be simplified for purposes of illustrating points.

129. Meine, *op. cit.*, p. xxiv.

130. A host of wasps or bees which interfere with the business or social activities of various people, a wild bull on a rampage, lizards surreptitiously introduced into the pantaloons of a preacher, who thereupon disrupts a camp meeting—these and similar agencies are likely to be the inciting forces in Sut's little comedies.

131. In Sut's speech better than elsewhere, one may see what George H. McKnight meant when, in Chapter X of *Modern English in the Making* (New York, 1928), he spoke of Shakespeare's language being enriched by common speech. "The effect produced," he said, "is like that of the renewed metaphors to be heard in modern times in the speech of the frontier, where, free from the blighting influence of learning, forms of language are created afresh."

132. Watterson, *The Compromises of Life*, p. 66.

133. *Sut Lovingood*, pp. xiii, xiv, 114-115, 244.

134. *Ibid.*, pp. 19, 21, 29, 48-49, 65, 75, 87, 159, 210, 231, 232, 243-244, 264, 276. An example is this passage on p. 232:

"'. . . an' that very nite he tuck Mary, fur better, fur wus, tu hev an' to hole to him, his heirs, an'—'

'Allow me to interrupt you,' said our guest; 'you do not quote the marriage ceremony correctly.'

'Yu go to *hell*, mistofer; yu bothers me.'

This outrageous rebuff took the stranger all aback, and he sat down.

'Whar wer I? Oh yes, he married Mary tight an' fas', an' next day he were abil to be about . . .'".

135. Harris's masterpiece; among all the stories I have seen, a number of which have not appeared in book form, is "Bill Ainsworth's Quarter Race," in the Knoxville *Press and Messenger*, June 4, 1868.

136. For example, this description of a clever man (p. 38): "Why he'd have held his own in a pond full of eels, and have swallowed the last darned one of them, and then set the pond to turning a shoe-peg mill."

137. Sut's maw, for example, when frightened, "out-run her shadow thirty yards in coming half a mile," (p. 68), and of a man's big nose, Sut remarked that "the skin off of it would have covered a saddle, and was just the right color for the job, and the holes looked like the bow-ports of a gun boat"—and several lines of exaggeration of a similar sort follow.

138. The incongruous catalogue delights Sut. One example: a horse, running inefficiently, suggests this: "The gait . . . was an assortment made up of dromedary gallop, snake sliding, side winding, and old Virginia jig, touched off with a sprinkle of quadrille . . ." (p. 291).

139. Eulenspiegel, too, liked to get people tangled up in conflicts, enjoyed particularly disrupting churchly gatherings by discomforting priests, and played tricks which were gross, coarse, and sometimes brutal. Sut's story, "Well! Dad's Dead!"—in the Knoxville *Press and Messenger*, November 19, 1868, has the theme but none of the details of the anecdote about Eulenspiegel's burial: "He was strange in his life, he wants to be so after his death"; like several of Sut's yarns, it poetically combines the macabre and the grotesque. Enid Welsford, in *The Fool—His Social and Literary History* (London, 1935), p. 47, summarizes Eulenspiegel's career in words which might apply equally well to Sut's career: he "indulges in an occasional wit-combat, but his main purpose is 'to live joyously for nothing,' he makes mischief for the fun of the thing, and slips away before he can be made to suffer the consequences. This is something elvish about him . . ." Nevertheless, it is very improbable that Harris ever heard of Sut's medieval predecessor.

II. Authors and Works

Augustus Baldwin Longstreet
William Tappan Thompson
George Washington Harris
Joseph Glover Baldwin
Harden E. Taliaferro

Georgia Scenes

Edgar Allan Poe

*Georgia Scenes, Characters, Incidents, &-c. in the First
Half Century of the Republic. By a Native Georgian. Augusta, Georgia.*

This book has reached us anonymously—not to say anomalously—yet it
is most heartily welcome. The author, whoever he is, is a clever fellow,
imbued with a spirit of the truest humor, and endowed, moreover, with
an exquisitely discriminative and penetrating understanding of *character*
in general, and of Southern character in particular. And we do not mean
to speak of *human* character exclusively. To be sure, our Georgian is *au
fait* here too—he is learned in all things appertaining to the biped without
feathers. In regard, especially, to that class of southwestern mammalia
who come under the generic appellation of "savagerous wild cats," he is
a very Theophrastus in duodecimo. But he is not the less at home in other
matters. Of geese and ganders he is the La Bruyere, and of good-for-
nothing horses the Rochefoucault.

Seriously—if this book were printed in England it would make the
fortune of its author. We positively mean what we say—and are quite
sure of being sustained in our opinion by all proper judges who may be
so fortunate as to obtain a copy of the *"Georgia Scenes,"* and who will
be at the trouble of sifting their peculiar merits from amid the *gaucheries*
of a Southern publication. Seldom—perhaps never in our lives—have
we laughed as immoderately over any book as over the one now before
us. If these *scenes* have produced such effects upon *our* cachinnatory
nerves—upon *us* who are not "of the merry mood," and, moreover, have
not been unused to the perusal of somewhat similar things—we are at
no loss to imagine what a hubbub they would occasion in the uninitiated
regions of Cockaigne. And what would Christopher North say to them?—

From *Southern Literary Messenger*, 2 (March 1836), 287-292.

ah, what would Christopher North say? that is the question. Certainly not a word. But we can fancy the pursing up of his lips, and the long, loud, and jovial resonation of his wicked, and uproarious ha! ha's!

From the Preface to the Sketches before us we learn that although they are, generally, nothing more than fanciful combinations of real incidents and characters, still, in some instances, the narratives are literally true. We are told also that the publication of these pieces was commenced, rather more than a year ago, in one of the Gazettes of the States, and that they were favorably received. "For the last six months," says the author, "I have been importuned by persons from all quarters of the State to give them to the public in the present form." This speaks well for the Georgian taste. But that the publication will *succeed*, in the bookselling sense of the word, is problematical. Thanks to the long indulged literary supineness of the South, her presses are not as apt in putting forth a *saleable* book as her sons are in concocting a wise one.

From a desire of concealing the author's name, two different signatures, Baldwin and Hall, were used in the original *Sketches*, and, to save trouble, are preserved in the present volume. With the exception, however, of one scene, "The Company Drill," all the book is the production of the same pen. The first article in the list is "Georgia Theatrics." Our friend *Hall*, in this piece, represents himself as ascending, about eleven o'clock in the forenoon of a June day, "a long and gentle slope in what was called the Dark Corner of Lincoln County, Georgia." Suddenly his ears are assailed by loud, profane, and boisterous voices, proceeding, apparently, from a large company of ragamuffins, concealed in a thick covert of undergrowth about a hundred yards from the road.

"You kin, kin you?

"Yes I kin, and am able to do it! Boo-oo-oo-oo! Oh wake snakes and walk your chalks! Brimstone and fire! Dont hold me Nick Stoval! The fight's made up, and lets go at it—my soul if I dont jump down his throat, and gallop every chitterling out of him before you can say 'quit!'

"Now Nick, don't hold him! Jist let the wild cat come, and I'll tame him. Ned'll see me a fair fight—won't you Ned?

"Oh yes; I'll see you a fair fight, my old shoes if I dont.

"That's sufficient, as Tom Haynes said when he saw the Elephant. Now let him come!" &c. &c. &c.

And now the sounds assume all the discordant intonations inseparable from a Georgia "rough and tumble" fight. Our traveller listens in dismay to the indications of a quick, violent, and deadly struggle. With the intention of acting as pacificator, he dismounts in haste, and hurries to the scene of action. Presently, through a gap in the thicket, he obtains a glimpse of one, at least, of the combatants. This one appears to have his antagonist beneath him on the ground, and to be dealing on the prostrate wretch the most unmerciful blows. Having overcome about half the space which separated him from the combatants, our friend Hall is horror-stricken at seeing "the uppermost make a heavy plunge with both his thumbs, and hearing, at the same instant, a cry in the accent of keenest torture, 'Enough! My eye's out!' "

Rushing to the rescue of the multilated wretch the traveller is surprised at finding that all the accomplices in the hellish deed have fled at his approach—at least so he supposes, for none of them are to be seen.

"At this moment," says the narrator, "the victor saw me for the first time. He looked excessively embarrassed, and was moving off, when I called to him in a tone emboldened by the sacredness of my office, and the iniquity of his crime, 'come back, you brute! and assist me in relieving your fellow mortal, whom you have ruined forever!' My rudeness subdued his embarrasment in an instant; and with a taunting curl of the nose, he replied; you needn't kick before you're spurred. There 'ant nobody there, nor ha'nt been nother. I was jist seein how I could 'a' *fout*! So saying, he bounded to his plow, which stood in the corner of the fence about fifty yards beyond the battle ground."

All that had been seen or heard was nothing more nor less than a Lincoln rehearsal; in which all the parts of all the characters, of a Georgian Court-House fight had been sustained by the youth of the plough *solus*. The whole anecdote is told with a raciness and vigor which would do honor to the pages of Blackwood.

The second Article is "The Dance, a Personal Adventure of the Author" in which the oddities of a backwood reel are depicted with inimitable force, fidelity and picturesque effect. "The Horse Swap" is a vivid narration of an encounter between the wits of two Georgian horse-jockies. This is most excellent in every respect—but especially so in its delineations of Southern bravado, and the keen sense of the ludicrous evinced in the portraiture of the steeds. We think the following free and easy sketch of the *hoss* superior, in joint humor and verisimilitude, to anything of the kind we have ever seen.

"During this harangue, little Bullet looked as if he understood it all, believed it, and was ready at any moment to verify it. He was a horse of goodly countenance, rather expressive of vigilance than fire; though an unnatural appearance of fierceness was thrown into it, by the loss of his ears, which had been cropped pretty close to his head. Nature had done but little for Bullet's head and neck, but he managed in a great measure to hide their defects by bowing perpetually. He had obviously suffered severely for corn; but if his ribs and hip bones had not disclosed the fact he never would have done it; for he was in all respects as cheerful and happy as if he commanded all the corn cribs and fodder stacks in Georgia. His height was about twelve hands; but as his shape partook somewhat of that of the giraffe his haunches stood much lower. They were short, straight, peaked, and concave. Bullet's tail, however, made amends for all his defects. All that the artist could do to beautify it had been done; and all that horse could do to compliment the artist, Bullet did. His tail was nicked in superior style, and exhibited the line of beauty in so many directions, that it could not fail to hit the most fastidious taste in some of them. From the root it dropped into a graceful festoon; then rose in a handsome curve; then resumed its first direction; and then mounted suddenly upwards like a cypress knee to a perpendicular of about two and a half inches. The whole had a careless and bewitching inclination to the right. Bullet obviously knew where his beauty lay, and took all occasions to display it to the best advantage. If a stick cracked, or if any one moved suddenly about him or coughed, or hawked, or spoke a little louder than common, up went Bullet's tail like lightning; and if the *going up* did not please, the *coming down* must of necessity, for it was as different from the other movement as was its direction. The first was a bold and rapid flight upwards usually to an angle of forty five degrees. In this position he kept his interesting appendage until he satisfied himself that nothing in particular was to be done; when he commenced dropping it by half inches, in second beats—then in triple time—then faster and shorter, and faster and shorter still, until it finally died away imperceptibly into its natural position. If I might compare sights to sounds, I should say its *settling* was more like the note of a locust than any thing else in nature."

"The Character of a Native Georgian" is amusing, but not so good as the scenes which precede and succeed it. Moreover the character described (a practical humorist) is neither very original, nor appertaining exclusively to Georgia.

"The Fight" although involving some horrible and disgusting details of southern barbarity is a sketch unsurpassed in dramatic vigor, and in the vivid truth to nature of one or two of the personages introduced. *Uncle Tommy Loggins*, in particular, an oracle in "rough and tumbles," and Ransy Sniffle, a misshapen urchin "who in his earlier days had fed copiously upon red clay and blackberries," and all the pleasures of whose life concentre in a love of fisticuffs—are both forcible, accurate and original generic delineations of real existences to be found sparsely in Georgia, Mississippi and Louisiana, and very plentifully in our more remote settlements and territories. This article would positively make the fortune of any British periodical.

"The Song" is a burlesque somewhat overdone, but upon the whole a good caricature of Italian bravura singing. The following account of Miss Aurelia Emma Theodosia Augusta Crump's execution on the piano is inimitable.

"Miss Crump was educated at Philadelphia; she had been taught to sing by Madam Piggisqueaki, who was a pupil of Ma'm'sell Crokifroggietta, who had sung with Madam Catalani; and she had taken lessons on the piano, from Signor Buzziuzzi, who had played with Paganini.

"She seated herself at the piano, rocked to the right, then to the the left—leaned forward, then backward, and began. She placed her right hand about midway the keys, and her left about two octaves below it. She now put off the right in a brisk canter up the treble notes, and the left after it. The left then led the way back, and the right pursued it in like manner. The right turned, and repeated its first movement; but the left outrun it this time, hopt over it, and flung it entirely off the track. It came in again, however, behind the left on its return, and passed it in the same style. They now became highly incensed at each other, and met furiously on the middle ground. Here a most awful conflict ensued, for about the space of ten seconds, when the right whipped off, all of a sudden, as I thought, fairly vanquished. But I was in the error, against which Jack Randolph cautions us—'It had only fallen back to a strong position.' It mounted upon two black keys, and commenced the note of a rattle-snake. This had a wonderful effect upon the left, and placed the doctrine of snake charming beyond dispute. The left rushed furiously towards it repeatedly, but seemed invariably panic struck, when it came within six keys of it, and as invariably retired with a tremendous roaring down the bass keys. It continued its assaults, sometimes by the way of the naturals, sometimes by the way of the sharps, and sometimes by a zigzag, through both; but all its attempts to dislodge the right from its strong hold proving ineffectual, it came close up to its adversary and expired."

The *"Turn Out"* is excellent—a second edition of Miss Edgeworth's "Barring Out," and full of fine touches of the truest humor. The scene is laid in Georgia, and in the good old days of *fescues, abbiselfas,* and *anpersants*—terms in very common use, but whose derivation we have always been at a loss to understand. Our author thus learnedly explains the riddle.

"The *fescue* was a sharpened wire, or other instrument, used by the preceptor, to point out the letters to the children. *Abbiselfa* is a contraction of the words 'a, by itself, a.' It was unusual, when either of the vowels constituted a syllable of a word, to pronounce it, and denote its independent character, by the words just mentioned, thus: 'a by itself *a,* c-o-r-n, *acorn'*—e by itself *e,* v-i-l vil, evil. The character which stands for the word *'and'* (&) was probably pronounced with the same accompaniment, but in terms borrowed from the Latin language, thus: '& *per se* (by itself) &.' Hence anpersant."

This whole story forms an admirable picture of schoolboy democracy in the woods. The *master* refuses his pupils an Easter holiday; and upon repairing, at the usual hour of the fatal day, to his school house, "a long pen about twenty feet square," finds every avenue to his ingress fortified and barricadoed. He advances, and is assailed by a whole wilderness of sticks from the cracks. Growing desperate, he seizes a fence rail, and finally succeeds in effecting an entrance by demolishing the door. He is soundly flogged however for his pains, and the triumphant urchins suffer him to escape with his life, solely upon condition of their being allowed to do what they please as long as they shall think proper.

"The Charming Creature as a Wife," is a very striking narrative of the evils attendant upon an ill-arranged marriage—but as it has nothing about it peculiarly Georgian, we pass over without further comment.

"*The Gander Pulling*" is a gem worthy, in every respect, of the writer of "The Fight," and "The Horse Swap." What a "*Gander Pulling*" is, however, may probably not be known by a great majority of our readers. We will therefore tell them. It is a piece of unprincipled barbarity not unfrequently practised in the South and West. A circular horse path is formed of about forty or fifty yards in diameter. Over this path, and between two posts about ten feet apart, is extended a rope which, swinging loosely, vibrates in an arc of five or six feet. From the middle of this rope, lying directly over the middle of the path, a gander, whose neck and head are well greased, is suspended by the feet. The distance of the fowl from the ground is generally about ten feet—and its neck is consequently just within reach of a man on horseback. Matters being thus arranged, and the mob of vagabonds assembled, who are desirous of entering the chivalrous list of the "Gander Pulling," a hat is handed round, into which a quarter or half dollar, as the case may be, is thrown by each competitor. The money thus collected is the prize of the victor in the game—and the game is thus conducted. The ragamuffins mounted on horseback, gallop round the circle in Indian file. At a word of command, given by the proprietor of the gander, the pulling, properly so called, commences. Each villain as he passes under the rope, makes a grab at the throat of the devoted bird—the end and object of the tourney being to pull off its head. This of course is an end not easily accomplished. The fowl is obstinately bent upon retaining his caput if possible—in which determination he finds a powerful adjunct in the grease. The rope, moreover, by the efforts of the human devils, is kept in a troublesome and tantalizing state of vibration, while two assistants of the proprietor, one at each pole, are provided with a tough cowhide, for the purpose of preventing any horse from making too long a sojourn beneath the gander. Many hours, therefore, not unfrequently elapse before the contest is decided.

"*The Ball*"—a Georgia ball—is done to the life. Some passages, in a certain species of sly humor, wherein intense observation of character is disguised by simplicity of relation, put us forcibly in mind of the Spectator. For example.

"When De Bathle and I reached the ball room, a large number of gentlemen had already assembled. They all seemed cheerful and happy. Some walked in couples up and down the ball room, and talked with great volubility; but none of them understood a word that himself or his companion said.

"Ah, sir, how do you know that?

"Because the speakers showed plainly by their looks and actions, that their thoughts were running upon their own personal appearance, and upon the figure they would cut before the ladies, when they should arrive; and not upon the subject of the discourse. And furthermore, their conversation was like that of one talking in his sleep—without order, sense, or connexion. The hearer always made the speaker repeat in sentences and half sentences; often interrupting him with 'what?' before he had proceeded three words in a remark; and then laughed affectedly, as though he saw in the senseless unfinished sentence, a most excellent joke. Then would come his reply, which could not be forced into connexion with a word that he had heard; and in the course of which he was treated with precisely the civility which he had received. And yet they kept up the conversation with lively interest as long as I listened to them."

"*The Mother and Her Child*," we have seen before—but read it a second time with zest. It is a laughable burlesque of the baby 'gibberish' so frequently made use of by mothers in speaking to their children. This sketch evinces, like all the rest of the Georgia scenes—a fine dramatic talent.

"*The Debating Society*," is the best thing in the book—and indeed one among the best things of the kind we have ever read. It has all the force and freedom of some similar articles in the Diary of a Physician—without the evident straining for effect which so disfigures that otherwise admirable series. We will need no apology for copying *The Debating Society* entire.

****

"*The Militia Company Drill*," is not by the author of the other pieces but has a strong family resemblance, and is very well executed. Among the innumerable descriptions of Militia musters which are so rife in the land, we have met with nothing at all equal to this in the matter of broad farce.

"*The Turf*," is also capital, and bears with it a kind of dray and sarcastic morality which will recommend it to many readers.

"*An Interesting Interview*," is another specimen of exquisite dramatic talent. It consists of nothing more than a fac-simile of the speech, actions, and *thoughts* of two drunken old men—but its air of truth is perfectly inimitable.

"*The Fox-Hunt*," "*The Wax Works*," and "*A Sage Conversation*," are all good—but neither as good as many other articles in the book.

"*The Shooting Match*," which concludes the volume, may rank with the best of the Tales which precede it. As a portraiture of the manners of our South-Western peasantry, in especial, it is perhaps better than any.

Altogether this very humorous, and very clever book forms an aera in our reading. It has reached us per mail, and without a cover. We will have it bound forthwith, and give it a niche in our library as a sure omen of better days for the literature of the South.

Augustus Baldwin Longstreet

A Southern Cultural Type

John Donald Wade

A certain lady long ago wrote a cook-book that attained wide popularity throughout the South. Canny person that she was, this author was rich in her suggestions of alternatives. "Use," she would say, "the juice of three lemons—or, if lemons are not at hand, vinegar may be substituted."

It is a puzzle to find out how often a good Georgian in mixing the patrio-historic dressing for his life is bound to resort to second choices. What magnificent rich cherry is there which he can impress for garnishment, what quite inimitable sprig of parsley, what watercress? We have Alexander Stephens to show, and we have Lanier. The disposition is strong to acclaim others; if one garnishment is not at hand, why, then—

Then Longstreet. He was of us, for us, with us. To name the impulses that bore him on, and to trace his stout, at last unavailing resistance to those impulses imply the blocking out of a sketch that one would swear inconsequential did not the hasty lines of it inevitably keep falling into shapes that are tragic and even noble. Tragic, chiefly because he was brave; noble, chiefly because he was true. Bravery he manifested in common with the pioneer nation to which he belonged; truth he manifested most strikingly apart from it.

The dominion of candor is apparently not yet established anywhere in this world. In the United States, and particularly in the South, its claims upon human allegiance seem rather less strong than they do elsewhere. It is safe to say that our condition did not occultly rise up out of hell to stifle us; it developed from many great and slight causes. Some of these

From *Southern Pioneers in Social Interpretation*, edited by Howard W. Odum (Chapel Hill: University of North Carolina Press, 1925), pp. 117-140. Reprinted by permission of the publisher.

94

are cosmic in import and need not be discussed; but it is as well in passing to single out at least one of them, perhaps the chief, namely, the wicked and deceitful heart of man. That, we can hardly at this time, very comfortably put from us.

There are some other considerations, however, which can be pretty definitely isolated and examined. One of them is the Puritan's refusal to attach importance to any craving that has its origin in the senses. Another is the pioneer's refusal to admit the existence of anything which might discourage immigration. Still another, more evident in the post-bellum South than elsewhere, is the instinctive refusal of any man to throw a burden of unfavorable opinions upon a fellow creature already struggling for life.

What, in principle, would have been the judgment of, say, Cotton Mather, upon the importance of substituting vinegar for lemon juice? He would probably have thought the whole matter too trivial for his attention, but if compelled to say just why it was too trivial, he would have reasoned this way: it is all an affair of sensuous enjoyment, and concern about it would only take up time that ought to be spent pondering eternal mysteries. Now most pioneer Americans were largely brought up on Mather's own catechism. They feared God quite as much as he did.

And they loved man and what man makes somewhat more than he did. These American forests were lonesome and dangerous; and there was much sentiment in early times (as there is in Miami and Los Angeles in these times) toward going any length to further pleasant report of the new lands, in districts naturally looked upon as reservoirs of population and wealth.

Governor John Winthrop in his history of New England gives the edifying story of some caitiffs who in 1642 abandoned Massachusetts and returned to England. On their voyage they spoke reproachfully of the people and the country they had left. Straightway storms broke upon them. "Then they humbled themselves before the Lord, and acknowledged God's hand to be justly out against them. Only one of them had not joined the rest, but spake well of the people and of the country; upon this, it pleased the Lord to spare their lives. Yet the Lord followed them on shore. One had a daughter that presently ran mad. Another, a schoolmaster, had no sooner hired an house, and gotten in some scholars, but the plague set in and took away two of his children."

Bad "religion," then, to indulge oneself in changes that would gratify only temporal demands; bad "patriotism" to admit publicly that all is not precisely as it should be. In both of these matters Longstreet was fortunate. In "religion," he was skeptical, and in "patriotism," too devoted to believe that his country needed prescriptive adulation. He was inherently frank, and he was endowed with the perspective that came of a long residence away from home. He was also fortunate in that his principal activities began just at the moment when Georgia at large was most buoyantly self-confident—long enough after the state had obviously got under way for a prosperous voyage, long enough before the seas had been made choppy by the unwearied suspirations of the abolitionists.

As a boy about Augusta, Longstreet was aggressive in everything except intellectual attainment, but when he was about seventeen years old he came under the influence of a young fellow named George McDuffie, a sort of intellectual prodigy who was so amiable that Longstreet decided to be as nearly like him as possible. That decision necessitated a brand of education different from any he had yet known.

It was generally conceded that the Reverend Doctor Moses Waddel, who was then conducting a back-woods school some miles above Augusta, could give out learning according to unique and effective methods. With contagious enthusiasm he aimed to apply reason starkly, to life as well as to education, but he did not stint the perverse humor of his mind which was always showing him how absurdly, on occasion, his program might work out.

Longstreet became a student at this school; and he was influenced there, profoundly, by Waddel himself, and by the numerous promising young men with whom he formed friendships. But most of all, he was influenced by John C. Calhoun, Doctor Waddel's brother-in-law, then just back from his educational ventures in New England. He, too, seemed to Longstreet the very pink of amiability, worthier of imitation, perhaps, than McDuffie.

Calhoun had been a student at Yale, and later, in Litchfield, Connecticut, at a law school which was then the best of its kind in this country. Longstreet followed him. After about two years at each place he returned to Georgia, and when he was twenty-five years old entered upon the practice of law. This was in 1815.

Two years more, and Longstreet removed from Augusta to Greensboro, a village about seventy-five miles away toward the now rapidly retreating frontier. His parents had followed this movement from New Jersey to Georgia and it was natural that he, in turn, should follow it also; but it is likely that the definite cause of his going to Greensboro was his marriage to a young woman of that place.

Frances Eliza Parke was eighteen years old, an heiress in her own right;

and one of the items of her wealth was about thirty slaves. Longstreet's marriage with her did two things for him. It enmeshed him in the blissful coils of a domesticity that at last wrested—or allured as to brighter worlds—his naturally free-thinking religious impulses into the most conforming orthodoxy. It also involved him straightway, rich man now that he was, in the almost equally blissful coils of an economic order which, everywhere more and more assailed from without, was beginning to demand of its votaries a compliance more and more absolute.

Before he was led away from himself into the castle of respectable formalism, then still in the building, he struggled so manfully that one finds it hard ever to leave off loving him. And indeed throughout his life, as a sort of royal prisoner, he was always, from time to time, uttering whoops of derisive laughter or mirthful sympathy that must have seemed very unmannerly to his house-mates.

Fannie Parke's father and mother found themselves captivated by their new son-in-law. And everybody else was captivated. The young man was extremely well informed, and his manners were ingratiating. He was garrulous and given to much joking, distinctive, but not too conspicuously an original to be respectable. He believed that the American Revolution was the crowning event of all history, and he felt himself, in his simple capacity of American citizen, "standing above the rest of the world on a lofty peak of moral elevation." Such sentiments were popular.

Now it is obviously not a stimulant to effort to consider oneself thus far superior to one's fellows, but Longstreet was above everything companionable—not only, in actuality, with his neighbors, but, in fancy, with any living creature his imagination might confront him with. It seems sure that he indulged himself in his vision of superiority more fully when he was mounted on some rostrum for campaign purposes, than he did while he was whittling out picture frames, or grafting his apple trees, or pottering away with his silk worms, or conducting his little loan business.

Lofty patriotic sentiment, it is true, he probably reserved most generally for lofty rostrums, but patriotic utterances, nevertheless, played their sure part in sending him to the state legislature in 1821, and in procuring for him a year later a position as Judge of the Superior Court. In 1824, he became a candidate for election to the national congress, and every chance seemed moving as he would have it.

Then, in the midst of his campaign, he suffered the death of his little son, Alfred. He withdrew from the race and entered upon a religious inquiry, which resulted most satisfactorily. He had been a skeptic; within a fortnight, he says, all his doubts vanished. Within three years he became a member of the Methodist Church; within ten years more, a minister.

But Longstreet found trouble in being anything unreservedly. The Methodists of his time were cold to sensuous appeal, deaf to many claims to virtue advanced by people whose religious dogma (it was reported) did not coincide with the dogma which (it was reported) was the lodestar of Methodism. The new convert had heard much argument about it up to his thirty-eighth year, before he capitualted, and he was not so easily to give over the rigidness of his convictions. There were some points he preferred about the Methodists, and some others about the Baptists. He said so. As for the conventional animosity he ought to feel for the Baptist denomination, he simply could not rise to it—he had wandered too long in darkness ever quite to get the knack of things. For the life of him he could never understand why if a Catholic prayed a good prayer it was improper for him to chime in with Amen—he went that far.

As for asceticism, he wondered how a thing so rarely practiced could be so generally preached. "I cannot," he says, "think that the interest of religion is served by cutting off any one innocent enjoyment." Dangerous talk that, from a temperance agitator, particularly from one who would not himself become a "teetotaler."

Longstreet lived in Greensboro ten years before again taking up his residence in Augusta. Those ten years, and what he learned in them, their friendliness and informality of intercourse, their slapdash versatility of attainment, their disposition to revere standard virtues—and neglect other virtues—these forever thereafter created the Judge's unique spiritual stock-in-trade. They are attributes that do not lose their freshness if they are properly cured; and frankness is among the best of all salts.

To many people it is not a tasteful salt; but a mature man who has truth clamoring in his heart cannot hold his counsel always out of regard for popular sensibilities.

During the early 1830's, Longstreet set forth, in a series of half-actual half-fictitious newspaper sketches, his observations on the social development of Georgia. They are kindly and humorous, but they do not gloss over any defects, nor do they weaken their indictment with any confession of burlesque—on the contrary, the author states explicitly that they are not burlesque. No one could tell how they would be received. They were printed anonymously, but the secret of their authorship soon transpired, and Longstreet was generously praised everywhere. He had kept off the subjects that important people are traceably connected with, and everyone was able to think that the sketches had reference to his neighbors rather than to himself. They were excessively popular throughout the United

States up to the period of the Civil War; and to the present, under their collective title, *Georgia Scenes*, they retain significance as one of the earliest examples of American realism.

People are willing enough to accept social comment made under a veil of humor, but the more direct type of criticism that finds itself nagging the world toward exertion is less welcome. When Longstreet began nagging, his contemporaries soon found instinctively what to do with him; they put him at the head of a boys' school where nagging is held salutary, and where it cannot be resented. Their liberality in tolerating him even in that fastness was remarkable. It was due somewhat, of course, to the fact that he had become a preacher—and preachers are supposed to quarrel—but it was due more largely to the fact that the evils he named were then too patently in way of remedying themselves to need either denial or justification. A little earlier, or a little later, this could not have been the case.

But Longstreet was not so easily shut up. He had some very definite suggestions as yet to make about politics.

Nationally, he thought Georgia should adopt Nullification. His advice was disregarded, and he divulged his opinion that a good many states would probably surprise some people before long by withdrawing from the then existing Union and associating themselves with a Union formed about Texas as a nucleus. They would, in short, go west.

Locally, politics did not suit him much better. The idealism he once observed, or thought he observed, was somewhat absent. He was in position to see the corrupt courses of government and he thought it incumbent on him to speak his knowledge. The way to be elected to office in Georgia, he says, is to "treat liberally, ape dignity here, crack obscene jokes there, sing vulgar songs in one place, talk gravely in another." And the legislature, filled with mountebanks and demagogues, "has enacted measures which for extravagance and folly have no parallel in the codes of enlightened nations." For Longstreet's part, he was independent. He held it the "bounden duty of a candidate openly to avow his sentiments, particularly those which are averse to the prevailing opinion of those to whom he offers himself." It is hardly necessary to set down the result of his various candidacies.

Logic left him only one retort: the people were not fit to govern themselves, anyhow. Whither, then, might they look for guidance? Hardly to any crown-heads; hardly to Judge Longstreet; perhaps, then, to God.

When Longstreet was a little boy in Augusta his father took him to a show at which, it developed, one of the actors was so presumptuous as to make Mr. Longstreet, Sr., the subject of a facetious ballad. The gentleman withdrew from the theater in great heat; the fresh air outside was more to his liking. The son never forgot the magnificent method of rebuke.

The political theater of Georgia in the late 1830's was ribald, and the man who as a little boy had once seen his father withdraw so effectively, now began picturing himself as outside this house altogether, bathed in the fresh air of moral and mystical speculation. "Human laws and governments," he wrote, "have ever failed and ever must fail of their ends. The Christian religion would supersede them all."

In accord, then, with youthful memories, as well as with pioneer instinct, whenever one place grew insupportable, Longstreet moved on to another. He became a minister of the Methodist Church in 1838. Entering a new realm, he carried over with him no contrivances to mollify the buffetings he might encounter. A plague fell upon the city of Augusta, but he remained there, faithful to the nicest whispers of his conscience, exposing himself to the disease unguardedly whenever he could make himself useful.

A year later, at nearly fifty, he accepted the presidency of Emory College, a Methodist institution only a few months in operation. Here, as his wont had been, the Judge was frank and adventurous, and by consequence, at times quarrelsome. But youth is very tolerant of frankness and venturesomeness—more tolerant than age, with its accumulation of secret misdeeds and its stiff joints, can well afford to be—and it was accordingly in his contact with youngsters that Longstreet did the best work of his life. If a policy of his, helpful in that it restrained his students, at times restrained him also in its operation, he stood to his position and bore his punishment. This engaging procedure, so rarely observed among mature persons, seemed to the bizarre judgment of youth, not folly, but very worshipful honesty. And he had a way of thought comprehensible to people who have yet before them some fifty or sixty years in which to accomplish things. "Merit, like water," he told his students, "will find its level, though it may have to wind through many a loaming vale, and leap many a rugged precipice before it does so."

The President further won the regard of his students by his attitude toward the important matter of enjoying oneself. Hard to please as he was, he seldom talked of what is forbidden—those things he made clear by example, his way of living. As for precept—through that, one heard chiefly of bright virtues to which any true man might lift up his heart passionately.

With what eager pride his following of boys must have gabbled over the long debate, between their idol and another minister, with reference to the iniquity of employing instrumental music in divine services. Longstreet thought music would really help, and he said so, earnestly, vigorously, but with unvarying dignity. His opponent was so violent, so ranting, that only a very spiritless young fellow could have witnessed the fray without having his sympathies stirred in behalf of a fighter who was too brave to adopt the barbarous tactics of his adversary.

But not students only admired Longstreet's course at the General Conference of the Methodist Church held in 1844. Even the numerous good Southerners who had always thought him dangerous were bound after that event to consider him a benefactor. Amid the rasp and bickering of that obscene week, Longstreet stood cool and helpful and conciliatory. But patience has its limits. At last, he decided, with his bloc, that the free air of the slave-owning South was more to his liking than any air contaminated with Northern breathings could be, ever. And from the theater of that Conference he withdrew in great heat.

So was the Methodist church—representing the phase of American life which is spiritual—divided, its parts alienated (certainly for as long as eighty years) over an issue which later (for only four years) entered wedge-fashion into the phase of American life which is political. But this rather indecent contrast would not have been embarrassing to Longstreet. In effect, the Northern delegates at that Conference had sung mocking ballads about causes that were sacred to him—primarily about the conscientiousness of Bishop Andrew, his neighbor and dear friend, and for his part, he was through with those delegates quite permanently. He became one of the most violent of all separatists; he doubted whether there was a good Methodist in the entire North.

In 1848 the President of Emory College in Georgia became for a few months the President of Centenary College in Louisiana. And then for several years he was President of the University of Mississippi. On any map those places are both west of Georgia, and that alone gave them some fascination in Longstreet's mind. Before entering the ministry he had long been haunted with an idea that if he could only move west he could speedily get rich. And on Longstreet's map, at least, the business of being head of a state school lay somewhat west of the business of being head of a church school. Who was he, by a wilful fixity, to be hindering, perhaps thwarting, the Course of Empire? And beside, there was the consideration of a wider field of usefulness—of course, there was that.

In Mississippi, it was held that to manifest an interest in politics is incompatible with the ideally cloistered life of a scholar. To get Longstreet into a cloister, however, was more than all the trustees and all their horses could accomplish. He saw the Know Nothing Party becoming powerful, and he believed it a great menace. It seemed to him cowardly and false, utterly divorced from any good. Trustees might tug till they grew tired. He would denounce cowardice and falsehood so long as he had breath, God helping him. If they tugged to the extent of annoying him, he threatened to resign, and they desisted. He had saved the school from ruin and made it powerful, and it was good tactics to retain him. Once, however, they went too far, and the old man in exasperation executed his threat, withdrawing shortly afterwards to a nearby farm on which he hoped to end his days, peacefully.

In little over a year he was in South Carolina, President of the State College at Columbia. Know Nothings had ceased from troubling him, but his unwearied spirit had found rest altogether intolerable. He was only sixty-eight, and Yankee abolitionists were menacing the peace of this continent. Their policy seemed to him cowardly and false, utterly divorced from any good. He would denounce cowardice and falsehood so long as—and so forth. Trustees we have with us always. There was one at hand to remonstrate—it happened a personal friend of old standing. Letters were exchanged. The one from the President stated that the writer loved his correspondent dearly, and was always interested to learn the opinions of a friend; the suggestions of a trustee, however, regarding a matter of non-official conduct—were these not a little intrusive? But more people, doubtless, than one lone trustee considered the old man outside his bounds.

There were troubles also within the college. The discipline of the institution had so declined that it could be restored only by very drastic measures. On that score, too, there was complaint. It was whispered that the president was not vitally interested in his classes. Damocles remembered his magic formula, and busied himself whetting a resignation, but before he could hoist it, new circumstances turned dissent into a din of acclamation.

He had had such luck before this. The acclaim this time had its genesis in London. Longstreet was there in 1860 as the representative of the United States at a gathering of scientists—it was a politician, one should state, who appointed him, not by any means the Lord God, not even Agassiz. When the scientists were assembled, a negro was introduced to them, and they were indiscreet enough to cheer. Longstreet simply would not abide it; in the grandest possible manner he stalked out of that convention. Cautious and sensible trustees thenceforth might reason as they would, but their reasoning had best be done inside their own heads, and

102

kept there. President Longstreet was canonized; he was a grand old man, and Yankees and upstart niggers were equally despicable, and there was little chance of holding off a war anyway.

Little chance? Little wish to hold it off.

Then it comes, explosive, crashing, insatiate. The world tumbles in before it, and old Longstreet, set off frantically, goes hurtling round, catching vainly at all manner of things which suddenly turn as unstable as himself. Hold it off? He would give his life to hold it off. Who dreamed the disagreement would come to this? Who dreamed it? For the South to be fighting the North, that truly was an occurrence greatly to be deprecated, but for young John Heyward to be going out to let some wretches shoot the life out of him, for young George Rhett to be going —(how that boy will keep reminding one, somehow, of little Alfred Longstreet, dead now these forty years!)—did one dream these boys would be so foolish? South and North, all right; but John Heyward and George Rhett—No! No! No! We know what the hysteria came to. John Heyward knew, also, before the year was out; and George Rhett, likewise. And others knew.

Once Longstreet recognized the war was inevitable, he furthered his section's cause in every way at his command. His nephew, James Longstreet, and his son-in-law, L. Q. C. Lamar, were figures of great prominence in the struggle, and he himself was throughout the long four years associated with the most important functionaries conceivable. He ranged over the country from South Carolina to Mississippi, and in spirit he ranged the whole earth and all past time seeking everywhere some sure swift strategem whereby he could foil the wicked power of the oppressor. His activity was unbounded. Letters to Lamar, letters to nephew James, manifestoes to the Southern Armies, went from him constantly. He was busy, too, with the social obligations which naturally devolve upon a distinguished man who unremittingly chooses distinguished people for his hosts. And he was busy preaching to the soldiers, busy mistrusting President Davis, busy wishing General Lee would use his spade less and his gun more, busy teaching arithmetic to little white and negro children, busy praying God, fervently, fervently, not to hear the prayers ascending to Him daily in behalf of Grant.

Then Appomattox. His dear South lay quite broken. It was as if at the end of some dark foreboding he had come upon the mangled body of a sweet child, a delicate girl, whom he had loved with utmost tenderness. Life was so flat to him. Every syllable of reprimand that he had ever spoken to her rose to his mind to sear it. O God, if you will spare her, spare her, never, never while I live will I say aught to her except in way of praise!

And every neighbor of his, every friend, was bowed in equal grief. Never, never against the names of people who had suffered so unjustly could he again let his swift mind enregister one fault. He could only love them, and, on Sundays, preach to them of bright Heaven and its joys of reunited love, sing to them, upon occasion, in the course of his sermons, hymns whose rolling cadences seemed at times to bear them all up well-nigh against the gleaming ramparts of Paradise.

But at last that stricken child regains her strength, and certain people, remembering her past hoydenish enterprises, think it well to shake a finger, and say that recklessness and folly may always expect an over-throw. But to Longstreet and his kind, the barest hint of blame is heinous sacrilege. At all costs, that kind of talk must be silenced forthwith, con-clusively. That, then, was a thing to live for. And so the old weary pro-cesses, re-exhilarated by the wine of a new aim, begin afresh.

Books to read, vindications to establish, invectives to hurl, Bible manu-scripts to translate, grandchildren to teach the art of flute-playing, land records to make unmistakable, God, always, to be prayed to. How the days go!

One morning a friend saw him grafting appletwigs. "Judge," he inquired, "do you ever expect to eat any apples off that twig?" "No," the old man answered, "but someone else will."

Soon now, he knew well, he would be moving on. What of it? Across the world he had left his trail of apple trees—in Augusta, in Greensboro, around Emory College, in Louisiana, in Mississippi. Always he had planted in full knowledge that he might reap no benefit—so shifting a world it is—but he had never therefore planted the less faithfully. . . . It is a trait to be very glad over.

* * *

In the summer of 1870, the old transient cleared out, definitely, his face beaming as with a vision, his lips—obeying the dictate of a still resilient mind—calling aloud, "Look! Look!" What fine new country a little west, there, did those eyes behold?

"The Big Bear of Arkansas"

T. B. Thorpe and His Masterpiece

Walter Blair

Fred Shaw, late Professor of English in the University of Miami, in mid-summer 1954 got word that he was to show William Faulkner around Miami during a stopover between planes. Shaw and a graduate student met America's greatest living novelist and at once escorted him to the nearest air-conditioned bar. The student mentioned that he was writing a dissertation about a relationship not yet much explored—between Faulkner and antebellum Southwestern humor. Faulkner spoke of his great admiration for that humor and in particular

> paid a fine compliment to Thomas Bangs Thorpe's "The Big Bear of Arkansas." The student said he thought he could detect similarities between that story and Faulkner's "The Bear." Faulkner looked surprised. Then: "That's a fine story. A writer is afraid of a story like that. He's afraid he'll try to rewrite it. A writer has to learn when to run from a story."[1]

Faulkner's reaction to talk about resemblances was a typical writer's response, and no doubt he was unconscious of any. Just the same, there are enough likenesses between his greatest short story and Thorpe's to provide impressive catalogues.

Important as an influence, "The Big Bear" also merits praise as a classic. On its first appearance, William T. Porter, knowledgeable editor of the

This is a revised version of "The Technique of The Big Bear of Arkansas," *Southwest Review*, 28 (1943), 426-435, original portions of which are reprinted here with permission of the Southern Methodist University Press. The essay will appear in a forthcoming history of American humor by Walter Blair and Hamlin Hill, tentatively entitled *To Get to the Other Side* and to be published by Oxford University Press.

leading outlets for such a story, warned readers "on no account" to miss "the best sketch of backwoods life, that we have seen in a long while." Porter printed the story in both *The Spirit of the Times* and a second periodical he edited, and a few years later featured it in a collection of his favorites—*The Big Bear of Arkansas and Other Sketches*. Meanwhile, the piece had been reprinted in sporting magazines and newspapers throughout the United States and Europe. And thereafter, down to the present, it would be published and hailed as a masterpiece again and again.

The subtitle of Porter's anthology, itself a landmark in the history of American humor, suggested the nature of an important appeal of Thorpe's story and others like it: "Illustrative of Characters and Incidents in the South and the Southwest." Porter's introduction praised "a new order of literary talent" for blazing "novel and original" trails by writing "in a masterly style . . . valuable and interesting reminiscences of the pioneers." The new breed of authors, Porter said, were men "who live at home at ease" in the midst of the life which they portray. Porter borrowed his epigraph from Dogberry: "This is your charge; you shall comprehend all vagrom men." Like the vagrom men about whom they wrote authentically, Porter said, his writers had "exteriors 'like the rugged Russian bear,' " were "gifted with . . . good sense and knowledge of the world," "fond of whiskey" and loved telling stories.

To the rough exterior, the description fit Thorpe: "a poor little fellow with an awful face," a friend called him, looking "like an embodiment, in semi-human form, of a thick fog on the Mississippi, at half past three in the morning to a man who has just lost his last dollar at poker." The friend perhaps exaggerated, but even portraits—usually flattering—show that Thorpe was short and pudgy, with a big flat nose, auburn hair and a sour phiz; he resembled a pug dog with russet sideburns.

But his attractive personality helped him comprehend vagrom men, as did his knowledge of the world. The friend went on to say that Thorpe's "grave and saturnine countenance quite belies a kind and playful spirit that seems to live in light and loveliness beneath the madness and gloom of his character." And at twenty-five, when he wrote his masterpiece, Thorpe had had varied experiences. Though born a Yankee, he had lived during most of his childhood and youth in Albany and New York City. In Manhatten he studied painting under a pupil of John Wesley Jarvis, John Quidor; and starting in his teens, Thorpe exhibited—and even sold —paintings. More important for his writing, from the time he was an adolescent, he sat in on story-telling sessions of artistic Bohemians— Gilbert Stuart, Henry Inman, the ubiquitous Jarvis, and others. During more than fifty years, every now and then he praised in print this group, particularly the three men mentioned—their mimicry, their "fluency in speech, their happy manner of description and story-telling." As late as 1872 he recalled the feat of one artist: "Ingham was only remarkable for telling one story, and that one only at the regular meetings of the National Academy. And this story, for a long period of time, was absolutely told every twelve months with mathematical precision as to circumstance, manner, and words."

For a couple of years, Thorpe went to Wesleyan University in Connecticut. Then bad health, invitations by fellow students from the South who liked him, and chances for portrait commissions led him to move to Louisiana. By 1841, he had married, settled down in Feliciana Parish on the Mississippi River, and launched a career as both painter and writer.

In addition to the oral stories of Jarvis and his pals, he knew Irving's writings "by heart." (Like his teacher, Quidor, he had painted illustrations for Irving's comic narratives.) He had read sketches and books by and about Davy Crockett, sermons by critics urging his countrymen to create a national literature, and guesses that the frontier might produce The American Character. He had seen at first hand life in New Orleans, aboard river boats and on riverside farms and plantations. Thanks to the hospitality and breezy ways of his neighbors, he was hunting, getting sozzled, and swapping stories with Feliciana planters, and between jollifications, painting portraits of his friends, their wives, and their daughters. On a recent visit to New York, he had called on a couple of editors, sold one a painting, and got orders from both for magazine pieces. He had placed writings with *Knickerbocker Magazine* and *Spirit of the Times*. "The Big Bear of Arkansas" first appeared in the March 27, 1841 issue of the latter magazine.

In this piece, the high point of a long and prolific career, young Thorpe discovered new possibilities for a vernacular style, comic characterization, and imaginative invention. A look at it may suggest why, despite its brevity and its look of artlessness, it caused scholars to dub a whole group of great humorists "The Big Bear School."

II. Contrasting Narrators

Like units in Boccaccio's *Decameron* and Chaucer's *Canterbury Tales*, "The Big Bear of Arkansas" is a story enclosing a story. It has two narrators, a writer who tells about the gathering of an audience aboard a riverboat, and an oral narrator who unfolds an enclosed tale about a bear hunt.

The first sentence is: "A steamboat on the Mississippi frequently, in making her regular trips, carries between places varying from one to two thousand miles apart; and as these boats advertise to land passengers and freight at 'all intermediate landings,' the heterogeneous character of the passengers on one of these up-country boats can scarcely be imagined by one who has never seen it with his own eyes." The language—even for a day when most writings were quite formal—is stilted and unimaginative: its lightest touch is a drab quotation from an advertisement. The ponderous tone, the big words, and the sentence construction show up the first narrator as a bit stuffy. So does his next sentence, also high-falutin, its sole figure of speech (here italicized) smelling of the lamp: "Starting from New Orleans in one of these boats, you will find yourself associated with men from every state in the Union, and every portion of the globe; and a man of observation need not lack for amusement or instruction in such a crowd, if he will take the trouble to read *the great book of character so favourably opened before him.*" As he continues, this narrator proves to be the sort that marks off phrases barely edging towards slang—e.g., "latest paper" and "social hall"—in apologetic quotation marks.

Nevertheless, he soon shows he relishes the motley steamboat crowd and popular nicknames: "Here may be seen jostling together the wealthy Southern planter, the pedlar of tin-ware from New England—. . . a venerable bishop and a desperate gambler—. . . Wolverines, Suckers, Hoosiers, Buckeyes, and Corn-crackers, besides a 'plentiful sprinkling' of the half-horse and half-alligator species of men, who are peculiar to the 'old Mississippi' . . ." And when he boards the *Invincible* for a brief trip from New Orleans, he at once notices that the crowd is as miscellaneous as usual and decides that, because of special circumstances, he will not, on this trip anyhow, peruse "the great book of character" they open.

When the second narrator, Jim Doggett, arrives, the writer tells of his offstage shouts, describes and quotes him at length, remarks his pleasant effect on the crowd, and—because he will only see "so singular a personage" briefly—persuades him to tell a long story. Jim's yarnspinning skill delights him:

His manner was so singular, that half of his story consisted in his excellent way of telling it, the great peculiarity of which was the happy manner he had of emphasizing the prominent parts of his conversation. As near as I can recollect, I have italicized them, and given the story in his own words.

Once Jim gets going, the writer quotes him without interrupting. When Jim ends, he describes an interesting aftermath. Stuffy though his language makes him appear, then, this narrator, no aloof and prissy Whig gentleman, has a lively interest in his fellow passengers and an even livelier one in Jim.

Jim first lifts his voice at the bar, shouting stock frontier boasts. "Hurra for the Big Bar of Arkansaw! [I'm a] horse! [I'm a] screamer! [Alongside me] lightening is slow!" Having noisily identified himself the Big Bear strolls into the cabin, sits, hoists feet onto the stove, greets the crowd, says he feels at home, and soon charms his motley audience:

> Some of the company at this familiarity looked a little angry, and some astonished; but in a moment every face was wreathed in a smile. There was something about the intruder that won the heart on sight. He appeared to be a man enjoying perfect health and contentment: his eyes were as sparkling as diamonds, and good-natured to simplicity. Then his perfect confidence in himself was irresistably droll.

Clearly no clownish caricature, this is an interesting personality attractive to men of all "creeds and characters," of all classes and parts of the country.

So close to the stodgy utterances of the writer, Jim's quoted words, phrasings and rhythms are by contrast informal, idiosyncratic, and imaginative. His homage to his dog Bowie-knife is typical:

> . . . whew! why the fellow thinks the world is full of bar, he finds them so easy. It's lucky he don't talk as well as think; for with his natural modesty, if he should suddenly learn how much he is acknowledged to be ahead of all other dogs in the universe, he would be astonished to death in two minutes. Strangers, the dog knows a bar's way as well as a horse-jockey knows a woman's; he always barks at the right time, bites at the exact place, and whips without getting a scratch. I never could tell whether he was made expressly to hunt bar, or whether bar was made expressly for him to hunt; any way, I believe they were ordained to go together as naturally as Squire Jones says a man and woman is, when he moralizes in marrying a couple.

Jim's zest creates hyperbole and the flood of details that support wild claims. Affection helps Jim read Bowie-knife's mind and endow the beast with human virtues—intelligence and modesty.[2] One of the unhackneyed similes, the trope which cites the well-informed horse-jockey, signals his wordly wisdom. His praise of the timing of Bowie-knife's bark and bite, and his use of "whips" show his precise knowledge of a great hunting dog's tactics. His philosophical discourse about the predestination of either the hunter or the hunted is distinctive. So is a respect for what is "natural" which comes out two other times as he tells his story.[3]

In addition to being exuberant, an acute observer, and a do-it-yourself philosopher, Jim is a superb yarnspinner. He orders expository details and events in a masterful fashion and marshals hosts of particulars and witty comments on them. Although his story (in large part because of its salty style) seems artless, it steadily mounts to its climax and then ends.

III. Little, Bigger, Biggest

The introduction of the two narrators, of Jim's audience, and the detailing of Jim's initial talk with the crowd occupies more than half of Thorpe's pages before The Big Bear begins his account of his greatest hunt. These preliminaries initiate a pattern which Doggett's yarn develops and completes—essentially one of contrasts and expansion.

After saying that he feels entirely at home among the cosmopolitan steamboat crowd, Jim launches talk about a contrast that is analogous to that between his vernacular style and the formal style of the writer:

> "Perhaps," said he, "gentlemen, . . . you have been to New Orleans often; I never made *the first visit before*, and I don't intend to make another in a crow's life. I am thrown away in that ar place, and use-less. . . . Some of the gentlemen thar call me *green*—well, perhaps I am, said I, *but I arn't so at home*; and if I ain't off my trail much, the heads of them perlite chaps themselves wern't much the hardest; for according to my notion, they were the real *know-no things*, green as a pumpkin vine—couldn't, in farming, I'll bet, raise a crop of turnips; and as for shooting, they'd miss a barn if the door was swinging . . ."

Jim has had trouble talking with these dandies. If they speak of "game," they mean not "Arkansaw poker and high-low-jack" but fowl and wild animals, which Jim calls "meat." Moreover, New Orleans game is tiny stuff, "chippenbirds and shite-pokes"—"trash" that Arkansans think beneath contempt. Jim says that at home he will not shoot a bird weighing less than forty pounds.

Arkansas is "the creation state, the finishing-up country. . . . Then its airs—just breathe them, and they will make you snort like a horse." Even when Jim admits that mosquitoes there are enormous, he defends them in a way underlining the contrast between Arkansas and the rest of the world. Natives or settlers are impervious to them, and the one injury they caused was to a Yankee—"a foreigner" who "swelled up and busted, . . . su-per-ated . . . took the ager . . . and finally took a steamboat and left the country."

To end his argument, Jim lists his state's features in the order of their size: mosquitoes, and then—"her varmints are large, her trees are large, her rivers are large." Next—as if climactically—he comes to the bears. They differ not only from bears anywhere else but of any other time: "I read in history that varmints have their fat season and their lean season. That is not the case in Arkansaw, feeding as they do upon the *spontenacious* productions of the sile, they have one continued fat season the year round" and running one "sort of mixes the ile up with the meat," and if you shoot one, "steam comes out of the bullet hole ten feet in a straight line." When a "foreigner" asks, "Whereabouts are these bears so abundant?" Doggett introduces the greatest district in this marvelous Cockayne, Schlaraffenland, Lubberland, Arkansas—"Shirt-tail Bend" on the Forks of Cypress—Jim's own clearing.

Shirt-tail Bend is called "one of the prettiest places on the old Mississippi," but soon this mild claim gives way to claims that "the government ain't got another such place to dispose of" and that three months after planting beets are mistaken for cedar stumps, potato hills for Indian mounds. *Planting in Arkansaw is dangerous*," Jim warns. Dangerous for bears are Doggett, "the best bar hunter in the district"; his gun, "*a perfect epidemic among bar*; if not watched closely, it will go off as quick on a warm scent as my dog Bowie-knife will," and the aforesaid super-dog.

Soon after Jim has jocosely praised his settlement, two paragraphs in the highfalutin style of the writer return to the contrasting steamboat cabin. There skeptics briefly dispute with him, but the first narrator asks for "a description of some particular bear hunt," describes the Big Bear's singular manner, then without interrupting, lets him give his account in his own salty words.

Repeating the pattern of contrast and enlargement, Jim mentions two

ordinary hunts—ordinary, that is, for the Forks of Cypress—then promises to give "an idea of a hunt, in which the greatest bar was killed that
ever lived, *none excepted.*"

A customary hunt for Jim is "about as much the same to me as drinking." "It is told," he says, "in two sentences—a bar is started, and he is
killed." This hunt, by contrast, requires many sentences, since the varmint
was the giant beast which eluded Jim, his epidemic gun, and the incomparable Bowie-knife two or three long years.

Jim first learns about this critter by measuring the height of bite marks
made on sassafras trees—marks which, experience proves, show "the
length of the bar to an inch." These are "about eight inches above any in
the forest that I knew of. Says I, 'them marks is a hoax, or it indicates
the d-----t bar that was ever grown.' In fact, . . . I couldn't believe it
was real, and I went on. Again I saw the same marks, . . . and *I knew the
thing lived.* That conviction came home to my soul like an earthquake."

Jim tells about hunting the bear and wasting away in flesh because of
his frustration over many months before he again happens to mention
the critter's size. This time the beast is "a little larger than a horse." Still
later, when Jim gets a final shot at him, the bear "loomed up like a *black
mist*, he seemed so large." After Jim's shot, "the varmint wheeled, gave
a yell, and *walked through the fence* like a falling tree would through a
cobweb." Thus, like Cypress Forks beets and potatoes, the bear of bears
grows at an astonishing rate.

IV. Topping A Climax

Though this account has traced the bear's growth by degrees in Jim's
narrative to his greatest size, it has not noticed a second climactic development that is not made explicit until the very end.

Soon after that earthquake conviction has proved to Jim that the giant
animal lives, he has a startling thought: "Says I, 'here is something a-
purpose for me: that bar is mine, or I give up the hunting business.' " The
way everything goes wrong during the first pursuit of the bear is disquieting because it is "past my understanding." Other happenings prove
to be just as inexplicable. Jim's flesh begins to waste away "faster than
the ager." He becomes obsessed—sees the bear in everything he does.
But when at last he gets close enough to see the beast plainly, he reacts
strangely, exclaiming, "But wasn't he a beauty, though? I loved him
like a brother."

A companion's shot strikes the animal's forehead: "The bar shook his head, . . . and then walked down from that tree as gently as a lady would from a carriage. 'Twas a beautiful sight. . . ." Now Jim takes careful aim "at his side just back of his foreleg" and pulls the trigger; his gun snaps. The bear leaps into a lake, has a fight in the water with the dog, sinks, and stays submerged. Jim dives, brings up the carcass, and thinks all is over. But—

> "Stranger, may I be chawed to death by young alligators, if the thing I looked at warn't a she bar, and not the old critter after all. The way matters got mixed . . . was onaccountably curious, and thinking of it made me more than ever convinced that I was hunting the devil himself. I went home that night and took to my bed—the thing was killing me. . . . I grew as cross as a bar with two cubs and a sore tail."

Kidded by his neighbors, Jim decides "to catch that bar, go to Texas, or die," and he makes preparations for a final hunt. But the day before that hunt is planned, at a most inopportune moment the bear comes along. Jim manages to fire a shot. The beast wheels, walks away, and Jim hears him "groaning in a thicket nearby, like a thousand sinners." When Jim reaches him, he is dead.

At this point, ending his story, Jim states a deduction for which his yarning has prepared:

> ". . . strangers, I never liked the way I hunted and *missed him*. There is something curious about it, I never could understand,—and I never was satisfied at his giving in so easy at last. Perhaps, he had heard of my preparations to hunt him next day, so he just come in, like Capt. Scott's coon, to save his wind to grunt with in dying; but that ain't likely. My private opinion is, that that bar was an *unhuntable bar, and died when his time come.*"

So the biggest bear in Shirt-tail Bend, domicile of the biggest bears in Arkansas, a state which itself is greater than any other country—such a bear in the end is slain not by bullets but by the inscrutable fate which has brought him and the Big Bear of Arkansas together. And from the first sentence to this point a parade of details in the story prepare for this climax.

This climax has some relevance to remarks that Faulkner made during his talk with Professor Shaw and the student about bear stories. Shaw had suggested that the bear in bear stories was "the big test—the medieval dragon." Faulkner agreed: "Yes, the bear was a symbol; he was the wilderness. On the frontier . . . things could be pretty hard. Here was a farmer trying to beat back the woods, trying to make a crop, and not having a very easy time of it; and here was the bear. If he could kill him, he had licked the wilderness."

The comment provides a useful gloss on the work about which Faulkner was talking, his own "The Bear." But since that superb story is a serious one which uses symbols to convey its profound significations, the remarks have relevance to Thorpe's story only as much as a solemn treatise on Mississippi farming would have to Faulkner's hilarious "Spotted Horses." For however noteworthy are the realism and the characterization of "The Big Bear of Arkansas," in essence it is a comic story. Its different narrators and styles, its incongruities and expansions, its fantastic imaginings as well as its initial reception and subsequent history make this clear to all readers except a few solemn, thesis-ridden scholars.

Important aids to achieving the humorous effect are the changes in Jim's attitude and that of his listeners while he tells his tall tales, and two strategically placed anticlimaxes.

En route to the cabin, Jim pauses at the bar. Soon he is shouting a cheer for himself, boasting that he is a horse and a screamer, and alleging that compared with him lightening is slow. After he joins fellow passengers, they are at first startled or irritated. But soon "something about the intruder"—his *joie de vivre*, his *Gemütlichkeit* and his "irresistably droll" self-assurance—win every heart and cause everyone to smile. As he joyously pours out one whopper after another, the listeners' reactions show that they know very well that he is putting them on. When he talks about shooting only forty-pound turkeys, "twenty voices in the cabin at once" proclaim disbelief. When he piles on details about the fatness of one of these birds, "a cynical-looking Hoosier" asks "Where did all that happen?" and a bit later he interrupts Jim's claim that Arkansaw is without a fault by saying, "Excepting mosquitoes." Undeterred, Jim makes even more outrageous claims, whereupon a gentlemanly Englishman, "foreigner" though he is, laughs and voices disbelief, and "a 'live sucker' from Illinois . . . has the daring to say that our Arkansaw friend's stories 'smell rather tall.'"

Jim argues with this skeptic surely in a playful spirit with no hope that he will close yawning credibility gaps. And though the listeners do not interrupt Jim's yarn about his biggest hunt, as he launches it they cannot be unaware of Jim's exaggerations or unappreciative of his witty way of phrasing them.

But as the story moves along, Jim's attitude and that of his listeners change. At the start, fresh from the bar, Jim is high spirited, jocose, humorous. His eyes sparkle as he invents and exaggerates wildly improbable details. But signs that he and his listeners are amused decrease. When he finishes, both he and his audience are solemn:

> When his story was ended, our hero sat some minutes with his auditors in a grave silence; I saw there was a mystery to him connected with the bear whose death he had just related, that had evidently made a strong impression on his mind. It was also evident that there was some superstitious awe connected with the affair,—a feeling common with all "children of the wood," when they meet with any thing out of their everyday experience.

The picture is of a man who tells a beautiful lie—such a superbly imagined and performed work of art that he convinces not only his audience but also himself. Fantastic Cypress Forks, which Jim has created out of thin air (and a fact or two) becomes a reality for him. The bear, which he has imaginatively enlarged beyond all reason and even gifted with supernatural powers, has overawed Jim's auditors and—still more impressive—Jim himself. Thanks to his own soaring eloquence, paradoxically, Jim has confused the real and the imagined.

Overwhelmed though he is, Jim manages to recover before his silenced listeners: "He was the first one, however, to break the silence, and jumping up, he asked all present to 'liquor' before going to bed,—a thing which he did, with a number of companions, evidently to his heart's content."

As the style indicates, after Jim ends his story, his salty language gives way to the stuffy style of the first narrator—latinate words, apologetic quotes, long sentences. Simultaneously, Jim and his audience are plopped down again in the mundane cabin. The final sentence of "The Big Bear of Arkansas" rounds out the contrast between Jim's clearing and the world of the writer: "Long before day, I was put ashore at my place of destination, and I can only follow with the reader, in imagination, our Arkansas friend, in his adventures at the 'Forks of Cypress' on the Mississippi."

The shift in style marks an anticlimax. Another anticlimax which occurs earlier was probably even more impressive in 1841.

The period, recall, was by modern standards an incredibly prissy one when the slightest hint of blasphemy or obscenity shocked Americans beyond belief. An instance: Jim, in a passage quoted a few paragraphs back, said that his gigantic bear groaned "like a thousand sinners." Because the simile somehow sounded irreligious, the words were cut out of a number of early reprintings. Whole books have been written about taboos in force against references to sex. Following the publication of Herman Melville's *Typee*—five years after Thorpe's "Big Bear"—so many wails would be raised about its frankness that numerous passages would be excised from subsequent editions—passages which readers today often study with complete bewilderment, unable to imagine what the readers of those quaint times found suggestive in them. Even rarer than references —including vague ones—to sex were scatalogical passages. Melville, in the final chapter of *The Confidence Man* (1857) would write about what a character called "a life preserver"—described as "a brown stool with curved tin compartment underneath" which smells bad—and alert readers somehow managed to discover that the passage refers to a toilet seat. In our own dear enlightened era when folk are daily uplifted by televised Curses on Constipation and Paeans to Regularity or by bits about bodily functions in respected books, plays, and movies, we need a translation for a passage that in 1841 was unique—part of Jim's story:

". . . I went into the woods near my house, taking my gun and Bowie-knife along, *just from habit*, and there sitting down also from habit, what should I see, getting over my fence, but *the bar*! Yes, the old varmint was within a hundred yards of me, and . . . he walked . . . towards me. I raised myself, took deliberate aim, and fired. Instantly the varmint wheeled . . . I started after, but was tripped up by my inexpressibles, which either from habit, or the excitement of the moment, were about my heels. . . ."

This translates: Accompanied by his dog and carrying his gun, as usual, Jim entered the woods to take his daily crap. Squatting there, he looked up, saw the bear approaching, and fired at him. The bear turned. Jim started after him, but his pants ("inexpressibles" in 1841!) fell about his heels and tripped him. Combined with this account, shockingly frank for 1841, were phrases that are indicated above by dots: "the way he walked *over that fence*—stranger, he loomed up like a *black mist*, he seemed so large," and "he *walked through the fence* like a falling tree would through a cobweb." In other words, at the very moment when Jim's imagining carries the picture of the bear to a climax of physical grandeur, he also tells about having a bowel movement, letting his pants fall, and being tripped up by them. And the clauses following the quoted passage are those which tell about the bear's groaning and his mysterious death.

This combination of the earthy with the fantastic makes for a superb anticlimax—an incongruous coalescence that is not only typical of American humor and the tall tale but also one of their superb achievements.

Bibliographical Note

Discussions of the relationship between Thorpe's story and Faulkner's "The Bear" include Carvel Collins, "Faulkner and Certain Southern Fiction," *College English*, 16 (November 1954), 96, and Francis Lee Utley, "Pride and Humility," in *Bear, Man and God* (New York, 1971), pp. 170-171. Early discussions of "The Big Bear" which were drawn upon include Walter Blair, *Native American Humor* (New York, 1937; San Francisco, 1960), pp. 91-95, and "The Technique of 'The Big Bear of Arkansas,' " *Southwest Review*, 28 (Summer, 1943), pp. 426-435. A fine biography, supplemented with a detailed bibliography, usefully discusses the story—Milton Rickels, *Thomas Bangs Thorpe, Humorist of the Old Southwest* (Baton Rouge, 1962), pp. 49-62. Norris W. Yates, *William T. Porter and the Spirit of the Times* (Baton Rouge, 1957), subtitled "A Study of the 'Big Bear' School of Humor" and Richard Boyd Hauck's University of Illinois doctoral dissertation, "Literary Content of the New York Spirit of the Times" (1965), are good on the tall tale as a genre and on Thorpe's masterpiece. The latter discussion of the story (pp. 226-232) differs somewhat from the one offered here.

NOTES

1. Letter from Shaw to Walter Blair, September 8, 1954.
2. Compare Simon Wheeler's tribute in Mark Twain's story to Smiley's famous jumping frog: "You never see a frog so modest and straightfor'ard as he was, for all he was so gifted."
3. Jim says that he and his neighbors "were driven to hunt naturally"; he also says "I go according to natur. . . . I never find fault with her."

The Humorous Works of
George W. Harris

Donald Day

Critics have noticed that *Sut Lovingood's Yarns* (1867) by George W. Harris (1814-1869) is typical in many ways of the humor of the ante-bellum Southwest.[1] Yet Mr. Franklin J. Meine, comparing Harris's work with that of the other humorists, has stated that it is "strikingly different."[2] The purpose of this paper is to see how Harris resembles other humorists of the time and how he differs from them.[3] The study therefore may be enlightening as a detailed consideration of the claim that "in *Sut Lovingood* the ante-bellum humor of the South reaches its highest level of achievement before Mark Twain."[4]

I

Harris's life was that of a typical humorist of the section and of the period. Such a humorist was a man of varied backgrounds and experiences, having some acquaintance with books but usually more with the life that inspired the boisterous humor of the Old Southwest. Like the rest, Harris was more indebted to experience than to books for his materials.

Born in Allegheny City, Pennsylvania (now a part of Pittsburgh), on March 20, 1814, Harris was taken to Knoxville, Tennessee, when he was still a youngster.[5] Knoxville, where he lived most of his days, was to some extent shut off until the 1850's from the bustle and stir of westward expansion by the Cumberland and Smoky Ranges. Yet the confluence of the Holston and French Broad rivers into the Tennessee furnished not only a connection with the outside world but also the essential condi-

From *American Literature*, 14 (January 1943), 391-406. Reprinted by permission of Duke University Press.

tions of a "river" community. At the same time the mountains, particularly the Great Smokies, offered a magnificently contrasting way of living. Harris, therefore, had ample opportunities for "seeing humanity in all its varieties," as he states in an early sketch.[6]

Harris's schooling was meager, probably not exceeding eighteen months, but he learned to be a careful workman in metals by serving an apprenticeship in the jewelry shop of his half-brother, Samuel Bell.[7] When he came of age he worked three years as captain of a steamboat plying the Tennessee and Holston rivers;[8] farmed for an equal period in the foothills of the Smokies;[9] and then established a metal-working shop in Knoxville which he operated for seven years, making and repairing anything from the smallest screw to a steam engine.[10] During the 1850's he established and managed a glass works,[11] again captained a steamboat,[12] established a sawmill,[13] surveyed and managed the Ducktown (Hiwasse) copper mines,[14] served as postmaster at Knoxville,[15] became an important political figure in the state,[16] and in the late years of the decade turned to railroading, which held him until the outbreak of the war.[17] After the war he again took up railroading, rising to a position as superintendent of construction for the Wills Valley Railroad.[18]

This background and experience certainly qualified Harris with enough knowledge of the life of the section to follow the literary manifesto of this "boisterous band of humorists" as set forth by Augustus B. Longstreet in these words: ". . . the aim of the author was to supply . . . the manners, customs, amusements, wit, dialect, as they appear in all grades of society to an ear and eye witness to them."[19] Throughout life Harris followed the dictum laid down by Longstreet: he had the same interest in showing the life of his region. Typifying his attitude is a statement found in a sketch published in 1843: "I mounted my nag and started for the Knob, having seen some odd specimens of humanity; though such specimens are to be met with frequently in this mountain region."[20] Earlier in the sketch he describes some of the "odd specimens," together with the "manners, customs, amusements, wit, and dialect" of the region.

When Harris wrote his first full-length yarn, "The Knob Dance,"[21] he took material of the same sort from his experience, organized it, and put it into the mouth of a narrator, Dick Harlan. He also turned to his experience for vivid metaphors which he was to use so effectively in his later writings. His "A Snake-bit Irishman"[22] relates an incident which supposedly happened while he was on a hunt in the mountains of Morgan County with a party from Knoxville. The days of his youth, when he "was sent into the upper counties" of Tennessee on "a trip of business," furnished the background and setting for "A Sleep Walking Incident."[23] "There's Danger in Old Chairs"[24] records "a most amusing incident" which happened "not long since at one of the first class hotels, in a western city." Certainly by 1854, when "Sut Lovingood's Daddy 'Acting Horse' " first bodies Sut forth, Harris had encountered most of the material which went into his yarns.

II

Longstreet, in spite of his dictum, depended to a great extent on the Addison-Goldsmith-Irving tradition for his literary form. In this he was followed by other humorists of the South, particularly by Joseph G. Baldwin in *The Flush Times of Alabama and Mississippi*, and to some extent by Harris. In "How to Marry," published in the *Spirit* in 1854, Harris wrote a sketch which might have been hatched under the wing of N. P. Willis.[25]

Although he did not have much formal education Harris evidently read a considerable number of books. When farming at the age of twenty-five he possessed at least seventy-five books in addition to a Bible.[26] He was treasurer of a literary society in Knoxville whose library was said to already contain "many Standard works" and was "constantly receiving valuable acquisitions." Mrs. Raymond stated that her father was quite fond of reading and spent a great deal of time with books.

In "How to Marry" there are several allusions to the Bible; the Queen of Sheba is used for a comparison in "A Snake-bit Irishman"; Sut invokes Joseph as the "foredaddy" of the Lovingoods in "Sut Lovingood at Sicily Burns's Wedding";[27] Harris states in a note to Porter [editor of the *Spirit*] that "it is the general impression hereabouts that your 'Spirit' has played the Dickens with 'Boz.' "[28] He took the central idea in "Old Skissim's Middle Boy"[29] from *The Pickwick Papers*, as Sut admits in these words: "Charley Dickins's son, the fat boy, mout been es ni kin tu him es a secund cuzzin, ef his mam wer a pow'ful wakeful 'oman." In addition, Harris mentions Byron,[30] Burns,[31] Elizabeth Barrett,[32] and Longfellow.[33] There are also allusions to Mahomet's coffin[34] and to "Alborax."[35]

It must not be inferred, however, that Harris was vitally affected by literary influences. Probably his reference to Longfellow may be taken as a guide. Sut is singing a folk-song when George (Harris) asks him to stop the noise. Sut replies:

Well, I be durn'd! Calls superfine singin ove a hart-breakin luv song, what's purtier by a gallun an' a 'alf than that cussed fool thing *yu* wer a-readin, jis' arter supper 'bout the youf what toted a flag up a mountin by hissef ove a nite, wif 'Exelcider' writ ontu hit. . . .[36]

After more arguments Sut attempts to prove his song is a love song, then adds this illuminating criticism on Longfellow:

Now yu's a cussin at my luv song, I wants tu say a word about that 'Excelcider' youf ove your'n, what sum Longfeller writ. I say, an' I'll swar tu hit, that eny feller, I don't keer hu the devil ne is, what starts up a mountin, kiver'd wif snow an' ise, arter sundown, wif nuffin but a flag, an' no whisky, arter a purty gal hed offer'd her bussum fur a pillar, in a rume wif a big hath, kiver'd wif hot coals, an' vittils . . . am a dod durn'd, complikated, full-blooded, plum nat'ral born durn'd fool; he warn't smart enuf tu fine his mouf wifout a leadin string; he orter froze es stiff es a crow-bar, an' then been thaw'd out by the devil; dod durn him.

This passage shows Sut's and his creator's preference for the stuff of life rather than that of romance. And it is not surprising that other models of form than those supplied by Longfellow's poetic creations were followed by Harris in his humorous narratives.

Far more powerful in the development of Harris as a humorist was the influence of the oral tale. And since oral storytelling "had an important influence upon the matter of most Western tales and upon the manner of many of them,"[37] his literary kinship with the humorists of his time and his section is best suggested by this fact.

The spinning of a tale became an art, and the material for these tales was inexhaustible. Eventually, most of them found their way into newspapers, popular periodicals, and books. The most popular humorous journal of the period was William T. Porter's New York *Spirit of the Times*, and in almost every case the better humorous stories sooner or later appeared in its columns. Harris gives evidence of this when he asks in the introduction to "The Knob Dance" if "your [Porter's Mississippi friend "In the Swamp"] . . . was at 'ar-a-frolick' while in East Tennessee?" He then promptly answers his own question by saying, "I reckon not or you would have hearn of it before now in the 'Spirit of the Times.'" Thus, it was quite natural that Harris began writing humorous sketches for the *Spirit* and learned much of his technique from writers for its columns.

Harris's wide experience and interests must have constantly thrown him into contact with oral tales. His "ragged, thoughtless boyhood," untrammeled by schools, kept him among people. His earliest writings were reports of gatherings and experiences where stories were likely to have been encountered. His nostalgic remembrances of later days include "the old stone Court-house," quarter races, camp meetings, quiltings, cornshuckings, frolics—all gatherings where the telling of stories constituted one of the chief means of entertainment.

Harris loved a good story well told, and, according to the evidence, he was a good storyteller himself. When the "Patlander" in "A Snake-bit Irishman" tells long dry yarns, all having a more or less remote bearing on his own prowess, he is guilty of a definite violation of frontier etiquette and hence is suitably and properly punished.[38] A correspondent of the *Spirit* gives evidence that a "story is very good, particularly when you hear it told by S——l [Harris's pen name]."[39]

The development of Harris's technique shows definitely his dependence upon the oral tale. His earliest known humorous writings appear in the *Spirit* over the pseudonym of "Mr. Free" as "Sporting Epistles."[40] This form of writing, appearing in almost every issue of the *Spirit*, usually catalogues happenings in various sections of the country and almost invariably includes a transcribed version of an oral tale. Following this form in his writings, Harris gradually reduces the epistolary part and increases the importance of the transcribed oral tale, finally developing a framework or "box-like structure" which takes the place of the epistolary part and becomes, in general, an introduction and a conclusion. This permits him to emphasize the incongruities between the telling of the tale and the fantastic world into which the tale moves.

Other writers of pieces for the *Spirit* mastered the technique, and one at least (T. B. Thorpe in "The Big Bear of Arkansas") is as artful in creating a framework and its contrasting fantastic world. But Harris does more in his *Sut Lovingood Yarns*. An obvious advantage comes from the use of Sut as the narrator and George (Harris) as his "stooge" in a series of sketches. This eliminates the characterization of a new narrator each time and progressively rounds out both Sut and George as characters, thereby moving the reader into the world of fantasy with the maximum of belief (or perhaps suspension of disbelief).[41]

A generalized statement of technique, however, will not explain Mr. Meine's conclusion that Harris is "strikingly different." Nor will it explain this statement by F. O. Matthiessen:

He [Harris] brings us closer than any other writer to the indigenous and undiluted resources of the American language, . . . Harris possesses on the comic level something of what Melville does on the tragic, the rare kind of dramatic imagination that can get movement directly into words.[42]

The explanation of this well-deserved praise can only come from an analysis of Harris's writings which will bring to the surface characteristics that are uniquely his. For convenience the analysis will be made under the conventional headings of character, setting, action or situation, and language. Harris's satirical comments on the foibles of humanity, mixed into his stories like "two pints of bald-face in a quart flask on a hard trotting hoss," will be considered in a separate section.

III

Characters appear in Harris's yarns on two levels: first, those who are in the framework; and, secondly, those who are in the yarn told by Sut. The connection between the two groups is maintained by Sut; George (Harris) never enters the world of fantasy as a character (except in "Eavesdropping a Lodge of Free Masons").

The framework characters help Sut get the yarn under way, relieve the monotony of the monologue, underline the incongruity, and then help bring the setting back from the world of fantasy to the world of realism. George, in particular, helps make this "queer looking, long-legged, short-bodied, small-headed, white-haired, hog-eyed, funny sort of a genius," appropriate for the strange tales he is going to relate. Here is how George qualifies Sut to tell his famous shirt story:

"Why, Sut, what's wrong now? You look sick."

"Heaps wrong, durn my skin—no my haslets—ef I hain't mos' ded, an' my looks don't lie when they hints that I'se sick. I is sick—I'se skin'd."

"Who skinned you—old Bullen?"

"No, hoss, a durnder fool nor Bullen did hit; I jis skin'd myself."

"What in the name of common sense did you do it for?"

"Didn't du hit in the name ove common sense; did hit in the name, an' wif the sperit ove plum natral born durn fool."[43]

123

When the yarn is under way Sut operates in situations on three levels, each of which demands a different type of character: first, in situations dealing with his Dad's world of "fooldom" (from which Sut stems) in which Sut helps his Dad to merited punishment; secondly, situations in which Sut gets out of his "nat'ral born fool" occupation and thereby comes to grief; and, third, situations in which "Sut's nat'ral born durn'd fool" endowments are pitted against supposedly respectable and intelligent members of society who are in reality hypocrites and whose intelligence cannot save them from his devastating punishment.

"Sut Lovingood's Daddy 'Acting Horse,'" as it appeared in the *Spirit* November 4, 1854, the first of the Sut yarns, deals with Dad's world of "fooldom" and gives to Sut the following significant kinship:

> Well, thar we was—Dad an' me (counting on his fingers)—Dad, and me, and Sall, an' Jake (Fool Jake we called him fur short), an' Jonass, an' Phineass, and me, and Callime Jane, and Sharlotteean, an' Simeon Saul, an' Cashus Henry Clay, an' Noah Dan Webster, an' me, and the twin gals, an' Cathrine the Second, and Cleopatry Antony, an' Jane Lind, and Tom Bullion, an' the baby an' the prospect, an' mam herself. . . .

Obviously, this kinship, presided over by Dad, the "king fool" of them all, is tremendously important in the characterization of Sut. Significantly, Harris places this sketch first in the *Yarns* and then ends the book with another story of the same sort, "Dad's Dog School," in which Sut insists that it

> happen'd ur ruther tuck place apupus, in our famerly; hit cudn't a-been did by eny urther peopil on this yeath but us, fur hit am plum clarified dam fool, frum aind tu aind. Dad plan'd hit; an' him, an' mam, an' Sall, an' Bent, an' me—oh, yas! an' the pup.[44]

Sut describes his first effort to leave his proper sphere in "Sut's New-Fangled Shirt."[45] He errs by following the advice of Betts Carr, who is "the cussedes' oman" he ever saw "fur jaw, breedin, an' pride." She persuades Sut to put on a "pasted" shirt and in getting out of it, after he has perspired and the shirt has dried, Sut loses a goodly portion of his skin. He swears "never again," but in "Blown up with Soda"[48] George says:

> Sut's hide is healed—the wounds received in his sudden separation from his new shirt have ceased to pain, and, true to his instincts, or

124

rather "a famerly dispersion," as he calls it, he "pitches in," and gets awfully blown up by a wild mountain girl.

Obviously, the supporting characters in the first two types of yarns are those suitable for bringing about a merited punishment for Sut's Dad or for Sut. In the third type the chief character (always a hypocrite) is to be punished and is given characteristics which merit that punishment. These characters are usually introduced by Sut in thumbnail descriptions such as that in which Parson Bullen is designated a "durnd infunel, hiperkriti- kal, pot-bellied, scaley-hided, whisky-wastin, stinkin ole groun'-hog" who preaches like this:

> He tole 'em how the ole Hell-sarpints wud sarve em if they didn't re- pent; how cold they'd crawl over thar nakid bodys, an' how like ontu pitch they'd stick tu 'em es they crawled; how they'd rap thar tails roun' thar naiks chokin clost, poke thar tungs up thar noses, an' hiss intu thar years. This wer the way they wer tu sarve the men folks. Then he turned ontu the wimmen: tole 'em how they'd quile intu thar buzzims, an' how they *wud* crawl down onder thar frock-strings, no odds how tite they tied 'em, an' how sum ove the oldes' an wus ones wud crawl up thar laigs, an' travil *onder* thar garters, no odds how tight they tied 'em, an' when the two armys ove Hell-sarpints met, then. . . .[47]

Mrs. Yardley is put "ahine a par ove *shiney* specks," and Sut warns that such a woman "am dang'rus in the extreme" because she is "a great noticer ove littil things, that nobody else ever seed" such as "that yaller slut ove a hen, a-flinging straw over her shoulder" of which she promises:

> I'll disapint *her* see ef I don't; I'll put a punkin in her nes', an' a feather in her nose. . . . An' sakes alive, jis' look at that ole sow; she's a- gwine in a fas' trot, wif her empty bag a-floppin agin her sides. . . . what a long yearnis grunt she gin; hit cum from way back ove her kidneys. . . . sich kerrying on means no good.[48]

As a usual thing Sut works alone in his punitive endeavors. However, at times, he has assistants. Bake Boyd is a good helper because "thar wur durn'd little weevil in his wheat, mity small chance ove warter in his whis- ky, and not a drap ove streakid blood in his veins." But it is Wirt Staples, directly out of the rip-roaring frontier tradition, who is the best. Wirt brags:

I's jis' a mossel ove the bes' man what ever laid a shadder ontu this dirt. Hit wilts grass, my breff pizens skeeters, my yell breaks winders, an' my tromp gits yeathquakes. . . . An *I kin spit a blister ontu a washput ontil the flies blow hit*.[49]

And Wirt is just about that good. Sut says that if the state fair will begin to give prizes for men, as it does for jackasses, he will enter Wirt and win the prize every time.

In Sut's fantastic world animals assume human characteristics. Squire Haney's horse

wer ove a pius turn ove mine, ur ole Haney wudn't a keep him a day. Nobody ever see him kick, gallop, jump a fence, smell uther hosses, ur chaw a bridil. He wer never hearn squeal, belch, ur make eny onsightly soun.[50]

Ole Mill's bull, with "fat, an' stumpy, an' cross-grained Old Burns" clutching tight to his back and with his teeth clamped onto his tail, reasons like this:

Ole Mills [the bull] dident begin tu onderstan' what wer atop ove 'im; hit were sumthing sartin what hed bof claws an' teeth, an'— *painter*, flash'd ontu his mine wif all the force the bill holt ontu his tail cud give hit. Dredful, dredful, tho't! His pluck wilted, an' he jis' turn'd tail tu the battil groun, an' went aimin fur North Caliney. . . .[51]

These few examples give a hint as to the dazzling array of characters found in Harris's yarns. As has been shown, they operate in two worlds, one quiet and peaceful and the other teeming with action. Certainly, Harris faces a difficult problem in making the peaceful setting of the framework blend with one for his fantastic world so that his stories will not bog down in descriptions. He does this with such consummate artistry that his settings hardly seem to exist.

The necessary accompaniments for Sut's telling a story consist of a flask well filled with whiskey, a place to lie flat in the shade, or a log to sit on. The framework setting, then, may be "among a crowd of mountaineers" at "Pat Nash's grocery" or "beside a cool spring." Often the story is told to a group gathered around a campfire or while George is waiting for his "fool chain kerriers."

The setting for Sut's oral tale is seldom more complicated. Harris's criterion seems to have been to keep the setting down to an absolute minimum. With his uncanny facility for noting details, he could have described elaborate and minute settings, and in some of his stories (particularly "Bill Ainsworth's Quarter Race") he does so. He seems to have operated on a formula: the more fantastic the tale, the simpler the setting. For example, here is the setting for "Mrs. Yardley's Quilting":

> The morning cum, still, saft, sunshiney; cocks crowin, hens singin, birds chirpin, tuckey gobblin—jis' the day tu sun quilts, kick, kiss, squeal, an' make love.
>
> All the plow-lines, an' clothes-lines was straiched tu every post an' tree. Quilts purvailed. Durn my gizzard ef two acres roun that ar house warn't jis' one solid quilt, all a-sunnin, an' tu be seed. They dazzled the eyes, skeered the hosses, gin wimin the heart-burn, an perdominated. . . .[52]

Note how little of this passage is actual setting and how much of it performs other functions. It is particularly important to note that these quilts are to be combined later with action to create a situation around which the story is built. Sut, operating behind them as a screen, prepares for a general "momoxing" of things by fixing a horse so he can break loose, then he

> tore off a palin frum the fence, an' tuck hit in bof hans, an' arter raisin hit 'way up yander. . . . fotch hit down. . . . an' hit acksidentally happen'd tu hit Wall-eye, 'bout nine inches ahead ove the root of his tail.[53]

The resulting situation must be read about to be appreciated.

In other cases Sut uses situation merely for the humor which emerges from its incongruities. Old Burns, after an "onspeakabl bull ride," is thrown by the bull, his saddle gets caught on a limb, and Old Burns's feet, still in the stirrups, suspend him in midair so that

> he foun his sef hung up by the heels like onter a ded hog, an two bulls a fitin round im, his voice wer changed mitely, fur his guts (and he hed a few ove em) bore down towards his hed, and hit sounded like he wur down in a well, ur hed a locust in his throat. He bemoaned his condishun powful, cussed . . . an talked orfull about shot guns, clubs, grave yards, and the brimstone works onder the kere ove the devil. I tell yu hit were tremenjus, comin frum a man ove family hung

up by the heels tu a tree, whar two dredful ole bulls wer at war. Wun got a running go onter tuther an backed him again Ole Burns at the rate ove pidgin flying, an toted the ole feller way out tu wun side, es fur as the ropes let em; an tu make it wus, he'd grabbed a deth holt onto a tail, and hilt es long es he cud stan hit fur his ankils. Then he let go and swung—tick, tick, like ontu a durnd ole clock what wur behine time an tryin tu ketch up. . . .[54]

These examples indicate quite clearly that it is situation, rather than setting, which enlivens Sut's world of fantasy.

With a representative picture of character, setting, and situation, both in the framework and in Sut's world, in mind, the reader can see what an enormous responsibility and load language must carry, if these are adequately translated to the reader. In addition, his language must make up for gestures and vocal intonation with which the oral tale was enlivened.

Harris is a master of vivid metaphors. Lizzards running up Old Bullen's legs make a noise "like squirrels a-climbing a shell-bark hickory"; Sut's mam gets hostile and soaks "hickory ile intu" his back "ontil hit" greases his "shut buzzum"; and cursing runs out of an old Dutchman "in a solid sluice as thick es a hoe handil." The metaphors are reinforced by a vigorous use of verbs. When mam tangles with Mis' Simmons, they "fit, an' they fout, they scratch'd, an' they claw'd, they grab'd, and they snatch'd, they knock'd, an' they hit, they grunted, an' they groaned. . . ."

As important as the vivid metaphors is the painstaking use of detail. When Sut describes a situation, he makes the whole come to life by a few details. See how this very complex situation unfolds its tremendous activity in a few words:

A monstrous cloud ove dust, like a harykane hed cum along, hid all the hosses; an away abuv hit yu cud see hosses tails an ends ove fence rales a flyin about, an now and then a par ove brite hind shoes wud flash in the sun like two sparks, an away a head wur the baskit [in Old Burns's hand on top of a run-away·bull], circklin roun' an about at random. A heap of brayin, sum nickerin, the bellerin ove the bull, clatterin ove runnin hoofs, an a monstrous rushin soun made up the nize.[55]

Sut also uses details to bring out more subtle points. When he wants to picture his unrest in the presence of Sicily Burns he says:

My toes felt like I wer in a warm krick wif minners a-nibblin at em; a cole streak wer a racin up an' down my back like a lizzard wif a turky hen arter 'im; my hans tuck the ager, an' my hart felt hot an onsatisfied like. . . .[56]

Thus language is used by Harris to fuse the other elements into a whole and bring them to life, and is itself made exactly appropriate to the character or situation, whether it be in the framework or in Sut's world of fantasy. Harris literally seems to breathe life and gestures and intonations and experience into cold words so that they blend with character and situation—so that they become men in action. But he is not content to stop there. After his matter is deftly spun into yarn, then wound into a ball of the correct size (or as Sut says, "I ain't like ole Glabbergab; when I'se spoke off what I knows, I stops talking"), he then sews it into a more compact and durable sphere by his satires on the foibles of mankind.

IV

In his earlier writings Harris is content to amuse. The gauge for "The Knob Dance" is "fun" which is appropriate to "a regular bilt frolick in the Nobs of 'Old Knox.' " Although amusement continues to be the primary purpose in his yarns, beginning with "Sut Lovengood's Daddy 'Acting Horse,' " he adds lusty licks at the foibles of mankind. In order to do this without freighting his stories with moral preachment, he gives to Sut's reasoning processes this characteristic:

Well, I thinks peopil's brains what hev souls, am like ontu a chain made outen gristil, forkid at wun aind; wun fork goes tu the eyes, an' tuther tu the years, an' tuther aind am welded tu the marrer in the backbone, an' hit works sorter so. Thar stans a hoss. Well, the eyes ketches his shape, jis' a shape, an' gins that idear tu the fust link ove the chain. He nickers, an' the years gins that tu tother fork ove the chain, a soun, nuffin but a soun. Well, the two ruff idears start along the chain, an' every link is smarter nur the wun ahine hit, an' dergests em sorter like a paunch dus co'n, ur mash'd feed, an' by the time they gits tu the back-bone, hit am a hoss an' yu *knows* hit. Now, in my case, there's a hook in the chain, an hits mos' ove the time onhook'd, an' then my idears stop thar half made. Rite thar's whar dad failed in his 'speriments; puttin in that durn'd fool hook's what made me a natral born fool. The breed wer bad to, on dad's side; they all run tu durn'd fools an' laigs powerful strong.[57]

This is not a very abstruse explanation for a psychologist, but is a highly appropriate way to have Sut characterize himself. With this random kind of "hooking" provided for, Harris can "hook" that chain in Sut only when it makes the satire of a desired sort possible. Furthermore, it provides for a strange or unusual moral kind of "hooking." A "morril an' sensibil way" of running a quilting for Sut—one that is "good fur free drinking, good fur free eating, good fur free hugging, good fur free dancing, good fur free fiting, an' goodest uv all fur poperlating a country fas' "—differs from the ideas of "the ole mammys."

Whiskey plays an important part in Sut's world. This "barlm of life" is a sort of gateway, an approach, to the good things in life and it is itself the best thing in life: it is not to be enjoyed by those who damn other amusements. With this as a criterion for hypocrisy, the "Hardshell" in "Bart Davis's Dance" who lets his "shove-shaped onder lip" drop outward "like ontu the fallin door ove a stone coal stove" and upsets a gourd of whiskey "inside ove his teef" so that the liquid goes down his throat "like a snake travelin thru a wet sassige gut," is welcome. But when he puritanically tries to interfere with the "innercent mucement" of dancing which follows, he is appropriately punished.[58] This indicates Harris's chief hatred: hypocrites.

His satires, made effective by Sut's punishment, fall on many classes: women, circuit riders, lawyers, sheriffs, dandies, politicians, temperance workers, tavern "perpryiters," professors, pedigree hunters, and many other odious specimens of humanity. But it is at women and circuit riders —two groups which he particularly feels should not be hypocrites—that he aims his most frequent and best directed satires. A few examples of satires at these two groups will indicate his method.

Deceitful women are satirized in the person of Sicily Burns.[59] Delicacy is not the proper attribute of a woman, for as Sut snorts: "There never was a durnder humbug on earth than it is, except the delicates themselves, an' their appurtinances. Oh! its jist so."[60] But a strong-minded woman is worse. If such a woman gets after a man, Sut advises:

. . . jist you fight her like she wore whiskers or run like hell, ef you dont, ef she dont turn you inter a kidney worm'd hog what cant raise bristiles in less nor a month, you are more or less ove a man than I takes you to be. Ove all the varmints I ever seed I's feardest of them.[61]

Old Bullen is Sut's particular hate among the many circuit riders whom he meets. The chief "pint" of this worthy is "durn'd fust rate, three bladed, dubbil barril'd, warter-proof, hypockracy, an' a never tirein appertite fur bald-face." He not only drinks whiskey, which he shouldn't, but also makes and sells whiskey, of which Sut says:

> . . . he puts in tan ooze . . . an' when that aint handy, he uses the red warter outen a pon' jis' below his barn; makes a pow'ful natral color, but dont' help the taste much. Then he correcks that wif red pepper; hits an orful mixtry, that whisky ole Bullen makes. . . .[62]

Balanced against this odious group in Sut's fantastic world is a group of "right folks." For instance, Sut has a definite use for women. He thinks that "men folks wur made jist to drink, eat, and stay awake in the early part of the night," and that the women are made "tu cook the vittils, mix the liquor, and help the men tu du the staying awake." Here is his selection for a "helper":

> But then, George, gals an' ole maids haint the things tu fool time away on. Hits widders, by golly, what am the rale sensibil, steady-going, never-skeering, never-kicking, willin, sperrited, smoof pacers. . . . They hes all ben tu Jamakey an' larnt how sugar's made, an' knows how tu sweeten wif hit; an', by golly, they is always ready tu use hit. . . . Nex tu good sperrits, an' my laigs, I like a twenty-five year ole widder, wif roun ankils, an' bright eyes, honestly an' squarly lookin intu yurn, an' saying . . . I hes been thar; yu know hit ef yu hes eny sense, an' thar's no use in eny humbug, ole feller—cum ahead!
> Widders am a speshul means, George, fur ripening green men, killin off weak ones, an' making 'ternally happy the soun ones.[63]

In the final analysis, then, Harris writes humor which is "strikingly different" and which reaches "the highest level of achievement before Mark Twain" simply because he is able to take the same material and the same forms and to do more with them than the other humorists of the Old Southwest. After the war, when life which he has satirized becomes life which he hates and blasts, in one nostalgic effort he writes a sketch about the "good old days" with only the subtlest ironies replacing his usual satire. This sketch, "Bill Ainsworth's Quarter Race,"[64] gathers together the excellences of Harris, both in his selection of material and use ot technique, mellows and softens his robustness without the loss of any of his strength, and, perhaps, rests at a peak of attainment in American humor.

NOTES

1. George W. Harris, *Sut Lovingood's Yarns* (New York: Dick & Fitzgerald, 1867). Hereinafter this work will be designated as the *Yarns*. See Walter Blair, *Native American Humor (1800-1900)* (New York: American Book Company, 1937), pp. 62-101; Franklin J. Meine, *Tall Tales of the Southwest* (New York: Alfred A. Knopf, 1930), pp. xv-xxxii. The region designated as the Southwest includes Kentucky, Tennessee, Georgia, Alabama, Mississippi, Louisiana, and Arkansas.

2. Meine, *op. cit.*, p. xxiii.

3. The scope of this study does not include Harris's political satires, which have not as yet been collected in book form. It does not include *Sut Lovingood Travels with Old Abe Lincoln*, ed. Edd W. Parks (Chicago, 1937).

4. Blair, *op. cit.*, p. 101.

5. Information furnished by Mrs. Amanda Pillow Harris Raymond, daughter of George W. Harris, hereinafter designated as Mrs. Raymond.

6. New York *Spirit of the Times*, June 17, 1843. Hereinafter this publication will be designated as the *Spirit*.

7. George F. Mellen, "Samuel Bell," Knoxville *Sentinel*, Oct. 12, 1916.

8. George F. Mellen, "George W. Harris," Knoxville *Sentinel*, Feb. 13, 1909.

9. Records of Blount County, Maryville, Tenn., for the years 1839-1842.

10. Knoxville *Argus and Commercial Herald*, Feb. 1, 1843; Knoxville *Register*, June 26, 1846.

11. *Spirit*, May 26, 1849; Knoxville *Register*, Sept. 29, 1849.

12. Knoxville *American Statesman*, Feb. 10, 1854.

13. Knoxville *Standard*, Aug. 30, 1858.

14. Information furnished by Mrs. Raymond.

15. Letter from 1st Assistant Postmaster General to J. Cleveland Harris, April 19, 1928.

16. Nashville *Union and American*, March 17, 1859 ff.

17. *Ibid.*, Oct. 2, 1859. Corroborated by Mrs. Raymond.

18. Letter from Ben T. Brock to J. Cleveland Harris, dated June 15, 1928.

19. O. P. Fitzgerald, *Judge Longstreet: A Life Sketch* (Nashville: Methodist Publishing Co., 1891), p. 164. In a sketch written in 1848 Harris states that what follows "would take the pen of a Longstreet to describe" (*Spirit*, July 29, 1848). Whether he was familiar with *Georgia Scenes* during his early writing days is not known.

20. *Spirit*, April 15, 1843.

21. *Ibid.*, Aug. 2, 1845.

22. *Ibid.*, Jan. 17, 1846.

23. *Ibid.*, Sept. 12, 1846.

24. *Weekly Nashville Union*, Oct. 6, 1847.

25. There is evidence that he wrote a number of such sketches. Another sketch which is probably his appeared in the *Spirit* for October 28, 1854, under the title of "How They Do Things in Tennessee."

26. Book "Q," p. 155, Records of Blount County, Maryville, Tenn., Dec. 23, 1840, records an indenture which includes "seventy-five books and a Bible" in a list of Harris's personal property.

27. Nashville *Union and American*, April 15, 1858.

28. *Spirit*, April 15, 1843.

29. *Yarn*, p. 67.

30. *Spirit*, June 24, 1848.

31. *Ibid.*

32. Knoxville *Press and Messenger*, Sept. 29, 1869.

33. *Yarns*, p. 124.

34. Chattanooga *Daily American Union*, Nov. 27, 1867.

35. Nashville *Union and American*, Aug. 10, 1866.

36. *Yarns*, pp. 123-124.

37. Blair, *op. cit.*, pp. 70 ff.

38. *Spirit*, Jan. 17, 1846. This version of the yarn must not be confused with the one appearing later in the *Yarns*.

39. *Spirit*, Jan. 17, 1847.

40. *Spirit*, Feb. 11, 1843; April 15, 1843; June 17, 1843; and Sept. 2, 1843.

41. Of course other humorists in the region used a continuing comic character as, for example, Johnson J. Hooper's Simon Suggs. He, however, does not use the "framework" technique.

42. *American Renaissance* (New York: Oxford University Press, 1941), p. xiii.

43. *Yarns*, p. 29.

44. *Yarns*, p. 277.

45. *Ibid.*, p. 29.

46. *Ibid.*, p. 75.

47. *Ibid.*, pp. 52-53.

48. *Ibid.*, pp. 135-136.

49. *Ibid.*, p. 250.

50. *Ibid.*, p. 288.

51. *Ibid.*, p. 103.

52. *Ibid.*, pp. 139-140.

53. *Ibid.*, p. 143.

54. Nashville *Union and American*, April 22, 1858.

55. Nashville *Union and American*, April 16, 1858.

56. *Yarns*, p. 80.

57. *Ibid.*, pp. 210-211.

58. *Ibid.*, pp. 181-188.

59. *Ibid.*, pp. 75-79.

60. Chattanooga *Daily American Union*, Nov. 28, 1867.

61. Nashville *Union and American*, June 30, 1858.
62. *Yarns,* p. 86.
63. *Ibid.,* pp. 141-142.
64. Knoxville *Press and Messenger*, June 4, 1868.

Sut Lovingood

Brom Weber

Commenting on George Washington Harris in his anthology of Southwestern frontier humor, Franklin J. Meine wrote: "For vivid imagination, comic plot, Rabelaisian touch, and sheer *fun,* the *Sut Lovingood Yarns* surpass anything else in American humor." The judgment is not mere hyperbole, for the combination of virtues found in Harris's writing is genuinely unique. Nonetheless, this is the first full-length collection of his work to appear in almost a century.

The reasons for neglecting the monologues of Sut, the Southern mountain youth, might virtually be descriptions of their valuable qualities. Permeating the stories throughout is an unadulterated determination to evoke laughter and to reveal the delight of animality. This is achieved by picturing the doings of Great Smoky Mountain folk with racy details and generous sympathy, in a language more faithful to the vernacular and its poetry than most American literature written since has contained. Furthermore, Harris loved to tell a good story and did so with an extraordinary narrative zest.

The dominant literary interests of the pre-Civil War period in which Harris wrote were the New Englanders. These men looked askance at stories whose main stress was on humor, in which the common man figured as a central character, whose style was speech as he spoke it, which mercilessly ridiculed sentimentality and gentility, in which there were no taboos on the robust expression of the funny and the pleasurable. Such stories were surely the epitome of Jacksonian democracy, composed by someone flaunting his coarseness, ignoring the canons of good taste, abysmally unaware of respectable culture, and probably uneducated too. If Harris was disregarded on these counts by the guardians of the

From *Sut Lovingood* by George Washington Harris, edited by Brom Weber. New York: Grove Press, 1954. Reprinted by permission of the author.

cultural temple, it was not because they even bothered to read him. Work like his was simply outside their province, of no interest to their publishers and magazines, and undoubtedly not even submitted to them. As for the South, where Harris lived, its genius was resolutely permitted to go elsewhere or subsist in obscurity unless caught up in propagandizing for slavocracy.

Yet it was Southern politics which ultimately nurtured the ribald humor of Harris, even though political disquisition on a higher level represented the South's conception of virtuous literary art. Aloof though a gentleman might be, he still had to depend on the vote of the common man. And since party newspapers were anxious to appeal to the latter, they provided space for a literature centered on folk experience. More than expediency was involved, of course; gentlemen, despite disclaimers, usually stemmed from the lower classes and shared a mutual interest in the South's indigenous humor with them, as well as in the sport and conviviality which played a large role in it.

Until a quarter of a century ago, however, Harris remained almost completely forgotten. The post-Civil War period witnessed an intensification of the values proscribing Harris and his fellow frontier humorists in the North. When Mark Twain, the greatest of these men, finally came East, he was greeted with a disturbed queasiness which never quite vanished. In the South, meanwhile, writers and men of affairs argued over whether to accept the harsh socio-economic lessons of Northern victory or to romanticize the departed days of plantation society. While this crucial debate proceeded, some writers turned to an exploitation of the quaint and exotic local color of their region. Mary Noailles Murfree ("Charles Egbert Craddock") created fiction based on the mountain region previously treated by Harris. Generally speaking, there was nothing in Miss Murfree's polite work to prevent its publication in the genteel magazines. Except for its dialect, there was little to invite comparison with the realistic and earthy Sut Lovingood yarns. A few perceptive scholars paid some incidental attention to Harris and the frontier humorists. However, not until the publication of Meine's *Tall Tales of the Southwest* (1930), Constance Rourke's *American Humor* (1930), and Bernard DeVoto's *Mark Twain's America* (1932) were Harris and frontier humor re-incorporated into the main stream of American literature.

II

Mark Twain could not possibly have been overlooked by the Bostonians. He was the spokesman for a portion of the nation larger in size than New England, more vital in spirit. Men and women had flowed from one shore of the vast continent to the Pacific at its other shore. All that had transpired in those years of journey and settlement was blended into his writings. Much of it bore the direct stamp of Harris; Twain had reviewed *Sut Lovingood* in a San Francisco newspaper and the book's influence is traceable in his own work. Beyond that, the fantasy of Harris, his grotesque humor and satirical imagination, his sensitive reproduction of ordinary language are also characteristics of Twain. With all their similarities, however, Harris was fated to be overshadowed. Twain was prolific for a greater number of years; he went beyond the short newspaper piece of Harris into the complex form of the novel; he was a man of the world rather than a provincial like Harris; and, at the last, the equalitarian strain in Harris was enriched with humanity in Twain.

The smaller compass of Harris, however, fostered a lyric intensity which reflects itself in his prodigious outpouring of poetic similes and metaphors. Characters and situations may at times be repetitive in outline, but they are vivified and transcended by imagery which practically never repeats itself. Details flash by at breathless speed; their insight into motive, their re-creation of the sensuous texture of life plunge the reader deep into the heart of Sut's strange world. Working intensively within a limited scope, Harris veritably embraced almost every aspect of his chosen reality and, as will be discussed later, seems to have gone beyond it too. There is not elsewhere in American literature, certainly not in the Nineteenth Century and not even in Twain's masterpiece, *Huckleberry Finn,* a similar portrait of primitive, insular man in all his bestiality, glory, and humor. Nor, for that matter, has anyone equalled the concentrated richness of his style.

A writer's appropriateness for subsequent ages may be measured by the extent to which his fundamental elements have reappeared discernibly. By this test, Harris surely belongs to us. The influence of Twain is undoubtedly responsible in part. In greater part, however, those major artists who resemble Harris—Thomas Wolfe, Erskine Caldwell, and William Faulkner, Southerners all—do so because the American frontier tradition is ineradicable. The continuity may be seen at once in the basically-identical plot structure of Harris's uncollected "Well! Dad's Dead" and

Faulkner's *As I Lay Dying*. It is more subtly comprehended in Wolfe's largeness, Faulkner's violence, and Caldwell's antic peasantry, though this curt catalog by no means exhausts the similarities. To a limited extent, all three modern writers have composed humor in various forms— grotesque and ironic in Faulkner, grandiose in Wolfe, nostalgic and eccentric in Caldwell—and they have all written in the common tongue. But their humor is pallid, generally without the joyousness of Harris. Their language, which may be brilliant as in Faulkner's "Spotted Horses," is frequently marred by banal and pompous rhetoric in both Wolfe and Faulkner, has been stripped of poetry in Caldwell. There is no intention of suggesting that these men be replaced by Harris, merely a reminder that his refreshing mirth offers relief from their grimness and so merits our gaze.

III

The life of George Washington Harris was unsettled, made turbulent by political and sectional controversy terminating in civil war, punctuated by the defeat of his ideals and the inability to acquire worldly success. Nonetheless, this experience, coupled with his temperament, was to provide him with the foundation responsible for his distinctive humor.

The son of a native Virginian, he was born in Allegheny City, Pennsylvania, on March 20, 1814. About 1820, however, the family migrated to Knoxville, virtually a frontier village in Scotch-Irish East Tennessee with less than a thousand inhabitants. The frontier impinged on young Harris in the pioneers who passed through Knoxville for more distant lands. Perhaps even more important in shaping Harris was the frontier tradition embodied in a man like Davy Crockett of Tennessee, soon to become the epitome of the frontiersman in oral and written literature.

Apprenticed during his youth to metalworker and jeweler, Harris at twenty-one became the captain of one of the first steamboats plying the Tennessee River in the trade between Knoxville and the lower South. For a brief period, too, he aided the government in transporting the Cherokee Indians being removed from their lands to settlements further west. The most significant of these formative years in their effect on his writing, however, were the three or four he spent as a farmer in the foothills of the Great Smoky Mountains. There Harris's interest in "seeing humanity in all its varieties" fed itself on the language and character of the country folk whom he later sketched in his stories. The quiltings, dances, weddings, and religious meetings which made up their social life proved vastly entertaining and left a residue of situations for subsequent development. Nor, apparently, did he miss the more profound concerns which underlay their rude existence.

The personality that emerged during Harris's young manhood also contributes some illumination of his restless career and the humor he created. "A little fellow" with a "quick, nervous way," he was physically courageous and exceptionally proud, asserting his decisions without fear of authority or consequence. Balancing his aggressiveness, however, was much personal charm, as well as a proclivity for good fellowship, joking, and yarn spinning. These attributes won him friends; even those who later supported him in ventures proving unprofitable merely deplored his business ineptitude but remained constant to him.

Apparently Harris's combination of vigor and gregariousness was recognized as a valuable asset, for almost at the inception of his farming career he began his lifelong association with the rough-and-tumble politics of Tennessee. Political activity provided Harris with an initial opportunity for literary expression; it guided him in the assumption of a critical temper. The party journalism of the period barred neither invective nor caustic frankness when dealing with an opponent. In the polemical pieces which Harris began contributing to the Knoxville *Argus and Commercial World* in 1839, for example, a major theme was the hypocrisy of those men who had betrayed their party allegiance for cash or office. Perhaps because of this uncompromising tone, his political career, engrossed and devoted though he might be, did not bring him the rewards which more tactful men obtain. It could not be said that he lacked the necessary acumen: in one of his political satires during the 1850's, Harris sagaciously predicted the results of the 1856 presidential campaign and the dissolution of the Know-Nothing party. Nor, indeed, was Harris averse to the rigors of campaigning, finding enjoyment in stumping, baby-kissing, and handshaking at corn huskings and other gatherings. The only appointive office he ever held, however, was that of Postmaster in Knoxville; his stay in that post was limited to seven months.

The party with which Harris had aligned himself was the Democratic Party of Tennessean Andrew Jackson, the party which had traditionally espoused the interests of both artisans and farmers. It was a choice consistent with his own background, one which he affirmed in other ways as when joining with a group of Knoxville artisans in the 1840's to protest the competition of goods produced by prison labor. Unfortunately, East Tennessee was changing from a region of independent artisans and small farmers slowly but perceptibly. Men were arising in it who welcomed industrialism, wished to exploit the mineral resources of the area, and strove to develop large-scale trade and commerce. Furthermore, the businessman's Whig Party was dominant in East Tennessee. Harris's prosperous half-brother Samuel Bell, for example, was active in Whig politics and served as Mayor of Knoxville for two terms in the 1840's. Harris remained loyal to the Democratic Party, however, as it continued to lose power locally and nationally, writing in its official organ in 1839 and accepting election to the Democratic State Central Committee in 1856. To complicate his politics still more, Harris early advocated secessionism though East Tennessee was strongly Unionist and antislavery. In addition to Harris's love for the Southern way of life, this choice may have stemmed from the artisan's fear of free Negro competition, from party regularity or a belief in States' rights. Whatever its origins, it partially explains Sut's contemptuous references to Negroes, abolitionists, Yankee peddlers, and Abraham Lincoln. Of course, some of these butts were antipathies of the common man quite apart from secessionist sentiments, as were "foreigners" like Jews and Catholics, and exist as such even in the works of Northern humorists like "Sam Slick" and Artemus Ward.

Though Harris opposed the Whigs and supported the Jacksonian Democrats, he nevertheless tried for many years to establish himself as both businessman and manufacturer. The record is one of failure on the whole, first as an independent craftsman operating a metalworking shop, then as glass manufacturer and sawmill manager. These sorties as an entrepreneur were interspersed with periods of employment as metalworker, steamboat captain for a second time, and surveyor of copper mines. The final years of his life were spent as a railroadman in various jobs, the last one involving planning and construction of railroads being laid out in the New South after the Civil War. There is paradox in Harris's participation in the industrialization and expansion which he otherwise resisted because it threatened to eliminate the leisurely and convivial spirit of the South. There is perversity in his unwillingness to embrace a political party whose connections would have enabled him to succeed in business. Finally, there is tragic irony in this spectacle of a man who, though temperamentally unsuited and intellectually antagonistic, was pushed by the tide of his times to engage in undertakings where personal victory was unlikely. The disappointments of such a man go far toward explaining the fierce delight evinced in his limning of the gusto, the irresponsibility, and the grotesquerie of a wild creature like Sut Lovingood.

IV

During his lifetime, Harris received a recognition for his humorous and satirical writings which did much to compensate for his worldly ill-luck. Newspapers eagerly presented his stories to their readers. His pieces are to be found in important anthologies of antebellum American humor such as W. T. Porter's *A Quarter Race in Kentucky* (1846) and T. C. Haliburton's *The Americans at Home* (1854). By the latter year, in fact, Harris was one of the most valued contributors to Porter's New York *Spirit of the Times,* a weekly sporting paper famous for its publication of humor. Harris's first fictional sketch had appeared in the *Spirit* in 1845; it contained many of the racy details, lusty characters, and stylistic touches which distinguish the Sut Lovingood tales. Nine years later, in 1854, the fantastic Sut himself frolicked into being in the *Spirit*, relating the adventures of "Sut Lovingood's Daddy, Acting Horse."

The weight of Harris's imagination and thought was thereafter carried by Sut. But it was not only in the evocation of pure laughter that Sut became a willing instrument. The Democratic newspapers of the South, which published most of the Sut stories after the first one had appeared in the *Spirit*, were caught up in the increasing fury of partisan strife. The popularity of Sut induced Harris to utilize him in satirical pieces of the kind which was then common in American humor and found a country bumpkin commenting wisely and acidly on issues and personalities. Sometimes, too, the bumpkin meandered on to Washington or his state capital in order to take a personal hand in affairs and straighten out an intolerable mess.

The Lincoln trilogy in this book, which appeared in the Nashville *Union and American* of February 28, March 2, and March 5, 1861, has been selected to represent Harris as a satirist. Lincoln, the frontier humorist who as President found relaxation in the satirical pieces of Orpheus C. Kerr, Petroleum V. Nasby, and Artemus Ward, might not have enjoyed Harris's satires of him as much as a secessionist would. But he would have understood their context; as a politician Lincoln had made effective use of the homely image, mimicry, the tall story, and pitiless caricature to devastate his opponents. He would have laughed at the exaggeration of ugliness so customary in frontier humor, at the charge of excessive drinking from a toper like Sut, and at the distortion of his wise caution into stupidity. He probably would have viewed Harris's satire as rather mild when set beside the mass of sober abuse which followed upon his surreptitious entrance into Washington.

When Harris's *Sut Lovingood,* his only book, was published by a New York firm in 1867, obvious satires like the Lincoln pieces were not included. Stressing humor alone, the book was subtitled "Yarns Spun by a Nat'ral Born Durn'd Fool" and bore the following epigraph: "A little nonsense, now and then,/Is relished by the wisest men." The stories, from which those in this book were selected, amply fulfilled Harris's prefatory intention of giving the reader "such a laugh as is remembered with his careless boyhood." Two years later, while returning to Alabama from a business trip into Virginia, Harris fell ill on the train. He was at first apparently mistaken for a drunk, and ignored. At Knoxville, however, he was carried off the train and given medical treatment in the city. Shortly before he died on December 11, 1869, perhaps in truth and perhaps as a final joke, Harris whispered the word "poisoned." No post-mortem was made, and the cause of his death remains unknown.

V

An understanding of why the Sut Lovingood stories possess the character they do is facilitated by a brief glance at the frontier tradition to which Harris was subjected. The phrase "a new country" is one key to the frontier, and it occurs in Harris's writing as well as in those of other frontier humorists. It found a place in Harris because the spirit of the frontier kept washing back upon relatively-settled lands like East Tennessee and kept their frontier heritage alive. Most significantly for Harris, it returned in the form of written versions of oral anecdotes. These rough transcriptions gradually became more artful and, like his own work, took on the lineaments of a mature literature. In the *Spirit of the Times,* for example, or in the books of men like Johnson J. Hooper, Augustus B. Longstreet, and Madison Tensas, Harris read the earlier humor of the frontier and absorbed much of its technique and content.

The frontiersman had made light of the new country's hardships by enveloping his misfortunes in a mocking humor. A stubborn pride had encouraged him to glory in adversity, to perversely seize upon difficulty as the cause of heroic action, to grossly and sardonically exaggerate qualities which enabled a man to triumph over circumstances: coarseness, endurance, decision, brutality, shrewdness, trickiness, speed, strength. Weakness, sentimentality, stupidity, regret, thoughtfulness, and respectability were handicaps for survival in a new country, therefore characteristics of the ludicrously inept and worthy only of contempt and ridicule. Yet behind the bravado of the frontier lay a profound fear of the supernatural and the mysterious.

Frontier life influenced the form of its humor as well as its nature. The storyteller could be certain of his audience's attention if he concerned himself with the realities of daily life. Since delayed reactions lessened his entertainment value, he specialized in physical action rather than psychological subtleties, generally developing character by means of objective behavior and descriptive details rather than analysis. The pace of the tale was kept rapid so as to accord with the tempo of existence, though digressions might occur for purposes of emphasis and ironic effect. It was related in the common tongue, where figures of speech which compressed, heightened, and toyed with experience were frequent since life was exuberant and varied. Finally, to underscore the proximity of the homely and the heroic, the extravagant was cloaked in understatement testifying to the narrator's lack of surprise at what he assumed his audience knew was only natural and to be expected.

The events and interests of Harris's life also left their impress on the Lovingood yarns. Primarily, Harris aimed to present imaginary characters in invented situations with all the humor and genius at his command. On the other hand, Sut obviously functions as a device to carry forward a satirical discussion of political and economic affairs, as well as Harris's thoughts about such matters as religion, temperance, women, and sentimentality. These wide-ranging intentions of Harris's overlapped, inevitably so because he was unable to devote himself exclusively to either fiction or journalism. The result was a mixing of themes and emphases which at first sight appears to negate some of the humor, but actually roots it so firmly that the comic prevails at every level.

The integrated artistry of Sut can be illustrated in his scathing treatment of the circuit-riding preachers whom Sut despises with ceaseless virulence. A member of the Presbyterian church, Harris found it desirable in his satire proper to use "Methodistic" as a term of opprobrium. As it happened, the Methodists (and Baptists, too) dispatched the greatest number of circuit riders into the country and the mountains.

These men were not always distinguished for their intelligence, education, or personal behavior. Harris may thus have had sober grounds for his displeasure with them. When Sut undertakes to tangle with them, however, the sobriety of Harris is imbedded in shrewd and homely details which are appropriate for a rebellious character like Sut. The prayerful, supplicating gesture introducing Clapshaw in "Blown Up with Soda" is the man ignobly concealing his fright in a ritual motion, but the hypocrisy implicit in the act and under attack has been made laughable because of the ridiculous incongruity of Sut's condensed description.

There are indications that, consciously and unconsciously, Harris intended Sut and his world to be that fusion of the mundane and the cosmic of which an American comic mythology was constructed in the first half of the Nineteenth Century. The geography of mountains, rivers, and states is scrambled together so that Sut bestrides the Appalachians from Virginia down through North Carolina and Tennessee into Georgia, and is everywhere at once. The physical background is vague, though Sut is fully capable of precise description. Recurrent figures and relationships offer the ingredients of a social pattern to some extent, but the resultant society is depicted far too mistily and only the peregrinations and predicaments of Sut bring it into even temporary focus. Sut, like his fellows, has his skirmishes with oppressive forces such as law and religion, but is unhampered by any occupation or home which would call forth definitively-drawn relationships. The very origin of Sut is shrouded in an ambiguity going beyond the needs of simple comic effect; it is likely that Sut is indeed the offspring, not of his "king fool" father, but of the sandhill crane who pursued Mrs. Lovingood and cornered her under the bed one day.

Into that swirling mythological backdrop, with its admixture of the fantastic and the whiskey flowing through Sut's body, Harris wove the particularity of detail and largeness of substance which rescue Sut from the charge that he is merely a poor-white degenerate. With sure comic insight, Harris created a character who boasts of his scariness, his tendency to flee from the very whiff of trouble, his "natural born durned fool" spirit, his petty trickiness, and his conscienceless infliction of pain and discomfiture. Yet out of the seeming chaos and meanness of Sut's personality and actions there gradually arises a superstructure revealing that a morality and a philosophy have been in existence always; that they contain, ironically enough, numerous traditional and wholesome values.

In practically every story, except those in which he is at the receiving-end of the joke, Sut functions as a catalytic agent. The chain of events which he sets in motion is prankish and hilarious, speeded up by Sut's appearance at opportune moments as concealed devil or heavenly messenger with keen knowledge of the secret lives of his fellows. Though sketched with incisive detail, these characters are usually broad portraits of a human trait or a social institution, sometimes both. Characters standing for authority and religion, or such failings as hypocrisy and injustice, usually become Sut's victims and are meted out the retribution which he believes they deserve. In contrast to the objects of Sut's vengeance, there are also characters who embody attributes wholly admirable: Wirt Staples, for example, is the embodiment of American physical grandeur and ready to roar challenges against the law; his wife typifies the woman who is both lover and housewife, simple in bearing, fun-loving, in tune with her husband's appetites. Scattered through the work, furthermore, are observations by Sut expounding his ideas about the cannibalism of society, the fraud of sentimentality, and the like.

It should be kept in mind that the characters, though broad in import, are not always visible as such at first glance because of their individuality as people. Furthermore, the work is kept from the dry realm of allegory by the fact that the plot events are exciting, the interaction of the characters absurd and amusing, and Sut's presence a stimulus to complications. Ultimately, however, the mythic universalities such as heroism, fertility, masculinity, and femininity emerge over a bedrock of elemental human values which Sut has carved out in the course of his adventures, values such as love, joy, truth, justice, etc. These are only some of the positive concepts which Sut has admired and championed, and it is no small feat that they emerge from behind a protagonist who has ironically been deprecated by his creator. This is humor on a grand scale.

Sut Lovingood

Edmund Wilson

One of the villains of Lanier's novel *Tiger-Lilies* is a poor white from Tennessee named Gorm Smallin, who deserts from the Confederate army and becomes a Yankee agent. He has been forced into the army by the hero's father, a country gentleman named John Sterling, and when the Yankees, invading Tennessee, have been burning down houses there, he swears revenge upon Sterling for involving him in this disaster. " 'Hit's been a rich man's war,' " he says to himself, " 'an' a poor man's fight long enough. A eye fur a eye, an' a tooth fur a tooth, an' I say a house fur a house, an' a bullet fur a bullet! John Sterlin's got *my* house *burnt*, *I*'ll get *his'n* burnt. John Sterlin's made *me* resk bullets, I'll make *him* resk em! An' ef I don't may God-a-mighty forgit me forever and ever, amen!' " And he eventually burns down Sterling's mansion, which has been made by Lanier, in his fable, to stand for the old way of life in the South.

The malignant Tennessee "cracker" had already been introduced into literature by the Tennessee journalist George Washington Harris, who invented a comic character called Sut Lovingood and exploited him for fifteen years as a narrator of fantastic stories and as a mouth-piece for political satire. These sketches, of which the first appeared in 1854, were printed not only in the local press but also in a New York sporting paper. Sidney Lanier may have known Harris: he was something of a public figure in Knoxville, which is only fifteen miles from Montvale Springs, where Sidney Lanier's grandfather Sterling Lanier, whose Christian name he had used for the family name of his hero, possessed the impressive estate which is also made to figure in *Tiger-Lilies*; and he must certainly have known about the Lovingood stories. These stories were collected,

Reprinted with the permission of Farrar, Straus & Giroux, Inc. from *Patriotic Gore: Studies in the Literature of the American Civil War* by Edmund Wilson. Copyright 1962 by Edmund Wilson. First published in *New Yorker*, 31 (May 7, 1955), 150-159.

in 1867, in a volume called *Sut Lovingood: Yarns Spun by a Nat'ral Born Durn'd Fool*, which was reviewed by Mark Twain in a San Francisco paper and to which he perhaps owed something; but Harris's work, after his death in 1869, seems to have been soon forgotten, and it was only in the thirties of the present century that—in the course of the recent excavations in the field of American literature—such writers as Bernard De Voto, Constance Rourke and F. O. Matthiessen began to take an interest in Sut Lovingood.

Bernard De Voto thought that it might be a good idea to have the Lovingood stories "translated" out of the dense hillbilly dialect in which Harris had tried phonetically to write them, and this suggestion was taken up by Professor Brom Weber, who published in 1954 a selection of the Lovingood pieces slightly expurgated and transposed into a more readable language. This version was not, however, an entire success. In attempting to clean up Sut Lovingood and make him attractive to the ordinary reader—an ambition probably hopeless—Mr. Weber has produced something that is not of much value to the student of literature. He is correct in pointing out that Harris, in trying to render Sut's illiterate speech, has inconsistently mixed written misspelling, intended to look funny on the printed page—though Sut has never learned to write—with a phonetic transcription of the way he talks; but the writing does have a coarse texture as well as a rank flavor, and to turn it, as the editor has done, into something that is closer to conventional English, and to dilute it with paragraphs and strings of dots, is to deprive it of a good deal of this. By the time Mr. Weber gets done with him, Sut Lovingood hardly even sounds like a Southerner; it is fatal to the poor-white dialect to turn "naik" and "hit" into "neck" and "it." What is worst, from the scholarly point of view, is to comb out "words [that] are obsolete and others [that] are probably meaningless to all but a handful of contemporary readers." If the book was to be reprinted, the text should have been given intact, and the unfamiliar words as well as the topical allusions explained. Mr. Weber makes no effort to do this, nor—though Harris, at the time of his death, was preparing a second volume—does he add any new material except for three little lampoons on Lincoln. Sut himself is depicted on the jacket as a stalwart and bearded mountaineer, a portrayal that has nothing in common with the dreadful, half-bestial lout of the original illustrations.

One is also rather surprised at the editor's idea of deleting "three lines of an extremely offensive nature." One of the most striking things about *Sut Lovingood* is that it is all as offensive as possible. It takes a pretty strong stomach nowadays—when so much of the disgusting in our fiction is not rural but urban or suburban—to get through it in any version. I should say that, as far as my experience goes, it is by far the most repellent book of any real literary merit in American literature. This kind of crude and brutal humor was something of an American institution all through the nineteenth century. The tradition of the crippling practical joke was carried on almost to the end of the century with *Peck's Bad Boy*, and that of the nasty schoolboy by certain of the writings of Eugene Field, a professional sentimentalist, who, however, when working for the Denver *Tribune*, betrayed a compulsive fondness for puerile and disgusting jokes: cockroaches and boarding-house hash and colly-wobbles from eating green peaches. But the deadpan murders and corpses of Mark Twain's early Far Western sketches are given an impressive grimness by the imperviousness to horror their tone implies, and the nihilistic butcheries of Ambrose Bierce derive a certain tragic accent from his background of the Civil War. The boorish or macabre joke, as exploited by these Western writers, does perform a kind of purgative function in rendering simply comic stark hardships and disastrous adventures. The exploits of Sut Lovingood, however, have not even this kind of dignity. He is neither a soldier nor a pioneer enduring a cruel ordeal; he is a peasant squatting in his own filth. He is not making a jest of his trials; he is avenging his inferiority by tormenting other people. His impulse is avowedly sadistic. The keynote is struck in the following passage (I give it in the original Tennessean):

"I hates ole Onsightly Peter [so called because he was selling encyclopedias], jis' caze he didn't seem tu like tu hear me narrate las' night; that's human nater the yeath over, an' yeres more univarsal onregenerit human nater: ef ever yu dus enything tu eny body wifout cause, yu hates em allers arterwards, an' sorter wants tu hurt em agin. An' yere's anuther human nater: ef enything happens sum feller, I don't keer ef he's yure bes' frien, an' I don't keer how sorry yu is fur him, thars a streak ove satisfackshun 'bout like a sowin thread a-runnin all thru yer sorrer. Yu may be shamed ove hit, but durn me ef hit ain't thar. Hit will show like the white cottin chain in mean cassinett; brushin hit onder only hides hit. An' yere's a littil more; no odds how good yu is tu yung things, ur how kine yu is in treatin em, when yu sees a littil long laiged lamb a-shakin hits tail, an' a dancin staggerinly onder hits mam a-huntin fur the tit, ontu hits knees, yer fingers *will* itch to seize that ar tail, an' fling the littil ankshus son ove a mutton over the fence amung the blackberry briars, not tu hurt hit, but jis' tu disapint hit. Ur say, a littil calf, a-buttin fus' under the cow's fore-laigs, an' then the hine, wif the pint ove hits tung stuck out, makin suckin moshuns, not yet old enuf tu know the bag aind ove hits mam frum the hookin aind, don't yu want tu kick hit on the snout, hard enough tu send hit backwards, say fifteen foot, jis' tu show hit that buttin won't allers fetch milk? Ur a baby even rubbin hits heels apas' each uther, a-rootin an' a-snifflin arter the breas', an' the mam duin her bes' tu git hit out, over the hem ove her clothes, don't yu feel hungry tu gin hit jis' one 'cussion cap slap, rite ontu the place what sum day'll fit a saddil, ur a sowin cheer, tu show hit what's atwixt hit an' the grave; that hit stans a pow'ful chance not tu be fed every time hits hungry, ur in a hurry?"

In view of this, the comments on Sut Lovingood by our recent academic critics are among the curiosities of American scholarship. We find Mr. Franklin J. Meine, in *Tall Tales of the Southwest*, speaking of this hero's "keen delight for Hallowe'en *fun* [italics the author's]—there is no ulterior motive (except occasionally Sut's desire to 'get even'), no rascality, no gambling, no sharping. . . . Sut is simply the genuine naïve roughneck mountaineer, riotously bent on raising hell," and again, "For vivid imagination, comic plot, Rabelaisian touch and sheer *fun*, the 'Sut Lovingood Yarns' surpass anything else in American humor." "Ultimately," asserts Mr. Weber, "the mythic universalities such as heroism, fertility, masculinity, and femininity emerge over a bedrock of elemental human values which Sut has carved out in the course of his adventures, values such as love, joy, truth, justice, etc. These are only some of the positive concepts which Sut has admired and championed, and it is no small feat that they emerge from behind a protagonist who has ironically been deprecated by his creator. This is humor on a grand scale."

Now, Sut Lovingood can be called "Rabelaisian" only in the sense that he is often indecent by nineteenth-century standards and that he runs to extravagant language and monstrous distorted descriptions. Unlike Rabelais, he is always malevolent and always excessively sordid. Here is an example of his caricature at its best:

"I seed a well appearin man onst, ax one ove em [the proprietors of taverns, evidently carpetbaggers] what lived ahine a las' year's crap ove red hot brass wire whiskers run tu seed, an' shingled wif har like ontu mildew'd flax, wet wif saffron warter, an' laid smoof wif a hot flat-iron, ef he cud spar him a scrimpshun ove soap? The 'perpryiter' anser'd in soun's es sof an' sweet es a poplar dulcimore, tchuned by a good nater'd she angel in butterfly wings an' cobweb shiff, that he never wer jis' so sorry in all his born'd days tu say no, but the fac' were the soljers hed stole hit; 'a towil then,' 'the soljers hed stole hit;' 'a tumbler,' 'the soljers hed stole hit;' 'a lookin glass,' 'the soljers hed stole hit;' 'a pitcher ove warter,' 'the soljers hed stole hit;' 'then please give me a cleaner room.' Quick es light com the same dam lie, 'the soljers hed stole hit too.' They buys scalded butter, caze hit crumbles an' yu can't tote much et a load on yer knife; they keeps hit four months so yu won't want to go arter a second load. They stops up the figgers an' flowers in the woffil irons fur hit takes butter tu fill the holes in the woffils. They makes soup outen dirty towils, an' jimson burrs; coffee outen niggers' ole wool socks, roasted; tea frum dorg fennil, and toas' frum ole brogan insoles. They keeps bugs in yer bed tu make yu rise in time fur them tu get the sheet fur a tablecloth. They gins yu a inch ove candil tu go tu bed by, an' a littl nigger tu fetch back the stump tu make gravy in the mornin, fur the hunk ove bull naik yu will swaller fur brekfus, an' they puts the top sheaf ontu thar orful merlignerty when they menshuns the size ove yer bill, an' lasly, while yu're gwine thru yer close wif a sarch warrun arter fodder enuf tu pay hit, they refreshes yer memory ove other places, an' other times, by tellin yu ove the orful high price ove turkys, aigs, an' milk. When the devil takes a likin tu a feller, an' wants tu make a sure thing ove gittin him he jis' puts hit intu his hed to open a cat-fish tavern, with a gran' rat attachmint, gong 'cumpanimint, bull's neck variashun, cockroach corus an' bed-bug refrain, an' dam ef he don't git him es sure es he rattils the fust gong. An' durn thar onary souls, they looks like they expected yu tu b'leve that they am pius, decent, an' fit tu be 'sociated wif, by lookin down on yu like yu belonged tu the onregenerit, an' keepin' a cussed ole spindel-shank, rattlin crazy, peaner, wif mud daubers nestes onder the soundin board, a-bummin out 'Days ove Absins' ur 'the Devil's Dream,' bein druv thar too, by thar long-waisted, greasey har'd darter, an' listen'd to by jis' sich durn'd fools es I is."

As for the "fun" of Sut Lovingood, it is true that Harris explained his aim as merely to revive for the reader "sich a laugh as is remembered wif his keerless boyhood," and that he liked to express his nostalgia for the dances and quiltings of his youth; but even in one of Harris's pre-Lovingood sketches that deal with one of these, the fun seems mainly to consist of everybody's getting beaten to a pulp, and in the Lovingood stories themselves, the fun entirely consists of Sut's spoiling everybody else's fun. He loves to break up such affairs. One of his milder devices is setting bees and hornets on people. In this way, he ruins the wedding of a girl who has refused his advances and dismissed him with an unpleasant practical joke, and puts to rout a Negro revivalist rally—for he runs true to poor-white tradition in despising and persecuting the Negroes. He rejoices when his father, naked, is set upon by "a ball ho'nets nes' ni ontu es big es a hoss's hed" and driven to jump into the water. Sut gloats over "dad's bald hed fur all the yeath like a peeled inyin, a bobbin up an' down an' aroun, an' the ho'nets sailin roun tuckey buzzard fashun, an' every onst in a while one, an' sum times ten, wud take a dip at dad's bald hed." This leaves the old man "a pow'ful curious, vishus, skeery lookin cuss. . . . His hed am as big es a wash pot, an' he hasent the fust durned sign ove an eye—jist two black slits." Sut, who supposes himself to be his mother's only legitimate child, has nothing but contempt for his father as an even greater fool than himself, who has bequeathed to him only misery, ignorance and degradation. Most of all, however, his hatred is directed against anybody who shows any signs of gentility, idealism or education. On such people, under the influence of bad whisky, to which he refers as "kill-devil" or "bald face," he revenges himself by methods that range from humiliation to mayhem. His habit of denouncing his victims as hypocrites, adulterers or pedants is evidently what has convinced Mr. Weber that Sut Lovingood cherishes "values such as love, joy, truth, justice, etc." But he is equally vicious with anyone who happens for any other reason to irritate him. In the case of an old lady who loves to make quilts, he rides into her quilting party with a horse he has driven frantic, ripping up all the quilts and trampling the hostess to death. This is Sut's only recorded human murder, but animals he has more at his mercy, and he loves to kill dogs, cats and frogs. It is not in the least true, as another of Sut's encomiasts has said, that pain does not exist in Sut Lovingood's world. On the contrary, the sufferings of his victims are described with considerable realism, and the furtively snickering Sut enjoys every moment of them. It is good to be reminded by Mr. Meine that his hero is never shown as addicted to gambling or sharping.

Nor is it possible to imagine that Harris is aiming at Swiftian satire. It is plain that he identifies himself with Sut, and his contemporaries referred to him as Sut, just as Anatole France in his day was referred to as M. Bergeret. "Sometimes, George, I wishes," says Sut, addressing his creator, "I could read and write just a little." George Harris himself had had—apparently at intervals—but a year and a half of schooling, and it is obvious that he is able to express himself a good deal better as Sut than he can in his own character. He had been steamboat captain, farmer, metalworker, glassworker, surveyor, sawmill manager, postmaster and railroad man—none of them for very long and none with any great success. It is not known how Harris got along during the years of the Civil War.

He seems to have dragged his family from pillar to post in Tennessee, Alabama and Georgia. His wife died in 1867, leaving him with three small children. He is evidently speaking of himself, in his preface to *Sut Lovingood*, when he makes his hero explain that he will "feel he has got his pay in full" if he can rouse to a laugh "jis' one, eny poor misfortinit devil hu's heart is onder a mill-stone, hu's raggid children are hungry, an' no bread in the dresser, hu is down in the mud, an' the lucky ones a-trippin him every time he struggils tu his all fours, hu has fed the famishin an' is now hungry hisself, hu misfortins foller fas' an' foller faster, hu is so foot-sore an' weak that he wishes he wer at the ferry."

George Harris had anticipated both the protest and the plea of Helper's *The Impending Crisis*. He represented the same stratum as Helper: that of the white "non-planter" who had got himself some education. We know nothing of Harris's early life except that he had once been a jeweller's apprentice; but his origins seem to have been humble—it is not known what his father did or what became of his parents—and he shared with what were called the "poor white trash" something of their consciousness of limitation and of their bitterness against those who did not want them to escape from it.

In Unionist eastern Tennessee, George Harris never wavered from his original allegiance to the Democratic party, which in the South represented the artisans and farmers as against the industrializing Whigs. But he failed in an attempt at farming as well as at his several industrial projects—his sawmill, his glass manufactory, his metal working shop—and it is plain that a sense of frustration—"flustratin' " is one of Sut's favorite words—is at the root of the ferocious fantasies in which, in the character of Sut, he likes to indulge himself. Yet he also uses Sut as a spokesman for his own sometimes shrewd observations, and this rather throws the character out as a credible and coherent creation, since he is made to see the world from a level which in reality would be beyond him. The effect of it is more disconcerting than if Sut were simply a comic monster, for it makes one feel that Sut's monstrous doings really express, like his comments on the local life, George Harris's own mentality. It is embarrassing to find Caliban, at moments, thinking like a human being.

But the book is not without its power, the language is often imaginative, and Sut is a Southern type, the envious and mutinous underling, which it is well no doubt to have recorded, and which Harris could do better than Lanier. Mr. Weber says truly that Harris has something in common with Caldwell and Faulkner. He is thinking of the tradition of "folk humor"; but what is more fundamental is that these writers are all attempting to portray various species of the Southern poor white. Sut Lovingood is unmistakably an ancestor of Faulkner's Snopses, that frightening low-class family (some of them stuck at Sut's level, others on their way up), who, whether in success or in crime or both, are all the more difficult to deal with because they have their own kind of pride —who are prepared, as Mr. Weber points out in connection with their predecessor, to "take on the whole world." All that was lowest in the lowest of the South found expression in Harris's book, and *Sut Lovingood*, like A. B. Longstreet's *Georgia Scenes*, with its grotesqueries of ear-chewing, eye-gouging fights and yokelish hunts and balls, is needed, perhaps, to counterbalance those idyls of the old regime by Kennedy, Caruthers and Cooke and the chivalrous idealism of Sidney Lanier.

The dreamy nobility of a man like Lanier and the murderous clowning of Harris are products of the same society, and the two men have something in common. George Harris did not share Helper's politics: he was all in favor of secession. Nor was his Sut disaffected like Lanier's Gorm Smallin, who burned down his master's mansion. From the moment of Lincoln's nomination, George Harris turned Lovingood loose on the Unionists. Here is a passage from one of his libels on Lincoln—to call them satires would be to give them too much dignity—of which still another infatuated editor, Mr. Edd Winfield Parks, has said that "though good-humored, they reveal his [Harris's] feelings," and of which Mr. Weber, who includes them in his volume, has said that Lincoln "might not have enjoyed [them] as much as a secessionist would" but that "he would have laughed at the exaggeration of ugliness so customary in frontier humor." Sut Lovingood is supposed to be accompanying Lincoln on the latter's incognito journey through Baltimore on his way to the inauguration, and Lincoln is supposed to be terrified by the threats of the Maryland secessionists: "I kotch a ole bull frog once an druv a nail through his lips inter a post, tied two rocks tu his hine toes an stuck a durnin needil inter his tail tu let out the misture, and lef him there tu dry. I seed him two weeks arter wurds, and when I seed ole Abe I thot hit were an orful retribution cum ontu me; an that hit were the same frog, only strutched a little longer, an had tuck tu warin ove close tu keep me from knowin him, an ketchin him an nailin him up agin; an natural born durn'd fool es I is, I swar I seed the same watry skery look in the eyes, and the same sorter knots on the backbone. I'm feared, George, sumthin's tu cum ove my nailin up that ar frog. I swar I am ever since I seed ole Abe, same shape same color, same feel (cold as ice) an I'm d_____ ef hit ain't the same smell."

Sut's tirades after the defeat of the South are vituperative on a level that almost makes the passage above seem the work of a sensitive artist. A new rancor, a new crushing handicap have been added to his previous ones. He can only spew abuse at the Yankees. The election of Grant seems a death-blow. According to Professor Donald Day, the principal authority on Harris, one of the last of the Lovingood stories, called *Well! Dad's Dead*, which appeared in a Tennessee paper on November 19, 1868, was inspired by this event. I am not sure that I can accept Professor Day's idea that Sut Lovingood's moronic father has here come to stand for the Old South. He passes, in any case, without lament: "Nara durn'd one ove 'em [the neighbors] come a nigh the old cuss, to fool 'im into believin' that he stood a chance to live, or even that they wanted him to stay a minit longer than he were obleeged to. . . . That night [after they had buried him], when we were hunker'd round the hearth, sayin' nothin' an' waitin for the taters to roast, mam, she spoke up—'oughtent we to a scratch'd in a little dirt, say?' 'No need, mam,' sed Sall, 'hits loose yearth, an' will soon cave in enuff.' " Sut has always claimed that his father sired him as "a nat'ral born durn'd fool," and his habitual falling back on this as an excuse for both his oafish inadequacies and his sly calculated crimes strikes the only touching note in these farces.

The creator of Sut himself did not long survive Sut's father. Returning from a trip to Lynchburg, where he had gone on railroad business and to try to arrange for the publication of a second Sut Lovingood book, he became very ill on the train, and so helpless that the conductor at first thought him drunk. He was carried off at Knoxville, and died there. His manuscript disappeared. The cause of his death is not known, but it is reported that just before he died, he whispered the word "Poisoned!"

The Imagery of George Washington Harris

Milton Rickels

Few of our minor writers have shown a more unusual command of the American language than George Washington Harris, and perhaps no one has created so pessimistic an account of the American backwoods settlement. In the darkness of his vision he is comparable to Mark Twain, and in his preoccupation with physical ugliness to Jonathan Swift, although these particular qualities have passed almost unnoticed because of the indirection with which he communicates them.

Walter Blair has observed that Harris's "writings were better than the rest," but that his book, *Sut Lovingood's Yarns*, "has never had the widespread appreciation it deserves, partly, perhaps, because its artistry has never been sufficiently appreciated. . . ."[1] Of the frontier humorists in whose tradition Harris wrote—A. B. Longstreet, T. B. Thorpe, William Tappan Thompson, Johnson Jones Hooper, and others—Harris was among the least interesting in the variety of his plots, but at the same time the most intense in his vision, and the most self-conscious in his use of language: "well, when I larns tu spell an' pernounce the flavor ove a ded hoss," his story-telling protagonist, Sut, promises hopelessly, "play the shape ove a yeathen war-jug [water-jug?] ontu a fiddil, ur paint the swifness ove these yere laigs ontu a clap-board, then I'll 'scribe [describe] the nise ove that meetin."[2] Harris's imagery is the medium through which he projects, indirectly, his vision of the American backwoods—the cabins, doggeries, and clearings of Frog Mountain, Rattlesnake Spring, and Lost Creek. It is a strange, subtly perceptive, dark vision, projected through a varied, complex, and tonally consistent body of images.

It is misleading, as Henry W. Wells observes in *Poetic Imagery*, to con-

---

From *American Literature*, 31 (May 1959), 173-187. Reprinted by permission of Duke University Press.

sider symbolism a phase of rhetoric.[3] Imagery at its best is not simply a matter of literary technique; for Harris, it embodies his philosophy, his religion, his humor—in short, his knowledge of the world. Harris's work provides an unusual opportunity to observe an example of the function imagery serves in providing a counterpoint to surface meaning, because what his images communicate is not the same thing that his plots and characters communicate. The stories themselves are examples of wildly exuberant humor, full of cruel practical jokes and a childlike, or savage, delight in inflicting discomfort on one's enemies. Coarse and impish on the surface, the tales celebrate the joy of physical movement, delight in food, drink, and sexual experience, and the excitement of wild confusion. But the careful reader is early aware that the tone of the tales is not one of sheer fun, of masculine delight in slapstick.

Harris knew that he had something to say, a vision of backwoods life to present that was altogether unusual in the 1850's and 1860's, a striking obverse to the Adamic myth, as R. B. W. Lewis calls it: the idea of "the authentic American as a figure of heroic innocence and vast potentialities."[4] Since Crèvecoeur the American frontier had been accepted as the creator of the truest American. But Harris was hopeless that he could command any audience worth communicating his counter-vision to—if, indeed, he believed any such audience existed.

From the first, Harris warns his readers that his stories have a moral point of view. In his dictated Preface, Sut forecasts that his book will not "sit purfeckly quiet ontu the stumicks ove sum pussons" and those are "—them hu hes a holesum fear ove the devil. . . ." But Sut has no hope of reforming the hypocritical and the wicked: "They hes been preached to, an' prayed fur, now ni ontu two thousand years an' I won't dart weeds whar thuty-two poun shot bounces back" (p. x). Prefaces themselves, Sut argues, are to no purpose: "Smells tu me sorter like a durned humbug, the hole ove hit—a littil like cuttin ove the Ten Cummandmints intu the rine ove a warter-million; hits jist slashed open an' the inside et outen hit, the rine an' the cummandmints broke all tu pieces an' flung tu the hogs, an' never tho't ove onst—them, nur the 'tarnil fool what cut em thar" (p. ix). The purpose of the book, Harris has Sut say, is to comfort "eny poor misfortinit devil hu's heart is onder a mill-stone . . ." (p. xi) by making him laugh. But the laughter must come from the poor plots; the style, the imagery, communicates an infernal country in which no man could take joy.

I

Most apparent in Harris's images is the frequency with which he uses epithets and complexly developed metaphors and similes. The similes are often extended by elaborate addition and qualification of detail. Almost every line of the book contains some kind of imagery. The detail used in the comparisons is concrete, closely packed, and graphic.

The first effect of this frequency of imagery is speed and intensity. The reader is whirled into the illusion of sheer delight in motion and wild action. Racy colloquialism, nonce words, corruptions of names and of bookish terms, compression of detail, astonishing expansion of connotation, and controlled changes in the tensions of the action and of the language, shifting from litotes to the wildest hyperbole, give a constant illusion of speed and movement. Images are expanded by piling detail upon detail until the reader is bewildered in a complexity of emotions and ideas.

The subject matter of Harris's images shows that his concrete world of reference was limited but closely and intensely observed. The great body of metaphors and similes can be classified into a few broad categories.

The largest group, constituting well over one-third of all images employed, is made up of animal images—mammals, birds, fish, and insects. Usually these are unpleasant, whatever the animal. Harris use horses, mules, and asses most frequently: a woman may be as "ugly es a skin'd hoss" (p. 36); Sut, Harris's protagonist, has a starched shirt that stands like "a dry hoss hide" (p. 32); words may fall from one's lips "sorter like a ole heart-broken hoss slobbers" (p. 61); an attractive woman can do more devilment than "a loose stud hoss et a muster groun' " (p. 77); and a deceitful woman may look as "solemn es a jasack in a snowstorm when the fodder gin out" (p. 80).

The next largest group within the animal category consists of comparisons to bulls and cows. Sut's starched shirt sat as close to his skin "es a a poor cow dus tu her hide in March" (p. 33); a reformed creature may become as "morril es a draft-steer" (p. 104); and, of the naked Parson Bullen, "his belly wer 'bout the size an' color ove a beef paunch" (p. 57).

The third sub-group is made up of insects, usually poisonous or verminous—mosquitoes, hornets, ants, bees, locusts, lightning bugs, bed bugs, weevils, cockroaches, fleas, and others. After insects come comparisons to dogs and cats, followed and approximately equaled by those to hogs and sows. For example, the victim of one of Sut's practical jokes lies as "quiet as a sick sow in a snowstorm" (p. 44). A strong minded woman may browbeat her man until she changes him into "a kidney worm'd hog what cant raise bristles in less nor a month."[5] Many of the comparisons to domestic beasts are to skinned carcasses or bloody parts of butchered animals. Whiskey goes down a circuit rider's throat "like a snake travelin thru a wet sassidge gut" (p. 185). Another man might have a mouth "es red es a split beef" (p. 199), or a foot that "wer the biggest chuck ove meat an' knotty bones I ever seed tu have no guts intu it" (p. 37).

Miscellaneous animals make up the rest of the sample: alligators, elephants, lizards, snakes, worms, eels, rats, fish, ganders, sheep, squirrels, panthers, wolves, buzzards, ferrets, and weasels. A fish image may illustrate Harris's stranger conceits. He imagines his political enemies in hell, where the devil sorted them from the "common cusses," took "up a needil as long as a harpoon, and with a big quile of trace chain . . . threaded . . . it and strung em on the chain . . . then hung the whole bunch over the aidge of the boat into the brimstone. Jehosephat, how they sizzled, an' sloshed, an' dove, and sprinkled hot iron about wif thar tails. A string of sun pearch would have been jist no whar."[6]

At times the image refers to no specific animal but merely to general animal characteristics. A practical joker watches for opportunities "jist es clost es a ole 'oman what wer wunst onsanctified hersef, watches her darters when a suckus ur a camp meetin am in heat" (p. 61). Sut says of a Yankee whom he hates: "He wer hatched in a crack . . ." (p. 37). And Sut's starched shirt, with bits of his skin clinging to it, "looked adzactly like the skin ove sum wile beas' tore off alive . . ." (p. 35).

The total effect of Harris's animal imagery is unpleasant. It implies speed, wild action, grotesque appearance, bloody flesh, and suffering.

Next to animals, the second largest category, accounting for perhaps one-fifth of Harris's similes and metaphors, is that of machinery and implements: steam engines, locomotives (a pair of angry bulls clash "like two drunk locomotives," p. 99), threshing machines, pumps, steamboats, sawmills, grist mills, cotton gins, whiskey stills, corn shellers, welding torches, knives, axes, and the like. The pictures they create are of motion, frequently of powerful, fearsome, and mindless action.

The third most frequent group of images has to do with human actions, trades, and professions. An act may be "quick es an 'oman kin hide a strange hat" (p. 239), or one may be a "pow'ful b'lever, not a sarcumsized b'lever, but a lie b'lever" (p. 198). Or animal characteristics and human trades may be combined: Sut says he may "turn buzzard, an' eat ded hosses fur a livin" (p. 171). Of a dog fight, Sut says, "When the ballunce ove the dorgs cum up, (human like,) they all pitched into the poor helpless devil . . ." (p. 106), and of critics, "Then thar's the book-butchers, orful on killin an' cuttin up, but cud no more perjuce a book, than a bull-butcher cud perjuce a bull" (p. x). Thus Sut's characters are compared to the church-goers, circuit riders, congressmen, soldiers, rough-and-tumble fighters, drunks, auctioneers, farmers, butchers, tailors, coffin-makers, and other classes and trades of the backcountry.

The category next in size is made up of references to household goods and utensils. A fat man may be "a tub ove soap-grease" (p. 51) or pot-bellied (p. 51); women are quilts (usually old quilts) (pp. 105, 22); an unconscious man may be "es cold es krout" (p. 73); while another may have a head "es big es a wash pot" (p. 28).

Various smaller categories can be set up, including those referring to the appearance and power of whiskey, called skin-gut, fester gut, rot-gut, popskull, churn brain, limberleg, tangle-leg, tangle-foot, kill-devil, etc. (pp. 31, 85, 113, 173, 199, etc); of the imagined actions and looks of the devil and of hell; of vegetables and plants; of gunpowder, poisons, and diseases.

Many incongruous or incommensurate comparisons, common in American humor, appear in Harris's descriptions. One may be "a bigger fool nor ole Squire Mackmullen, an' he tried tu shoot hisef wif a onloaded hoe-handle" (p. 58). Retribution may be "es big es a car shed" (p. 179). A Negro camp meeting, disrupted by Sut, "looked like forty-eight cords ove black cats a-fitin . . ." (p. 167). Sheriff Doltin purses his mouth to blow out "a whistil seven foot long" (p. 240), and Sut, singing.

> Daddy kill'd the blind bull,
>   Human nater, human nater!
> Mammy fried a pan full,
>   Sop an' tater, sop an' tater, (p. 123)

claims that the song is prettier than Longfellow's "Exelcider" "by a gal-lun an' a 'alf" (p. 123).

II

Several generalizations are possible after Harris's imagery is abstracted and classified. First, it is neither attractive nor pleasant. The effect of images of flayed and butchered animals, of mindless and rapidly running machinery, and of the utensils of the backwoods kitchen is generally ugly or grotesque.

However, it is equally apparent that the effect is not merely ugly. Harris's imagery is formally varied and complex. Usually it is concrete and graphic, but at times it conveys no picture at all. It becomes cryptic and intellectual, communicates ideas and judgments. One example of such sunken imagery[7] is Sut's mother's invitation to the local deacon to leave her home: "We's got no notes tu shave, nur gals ole enuf tu convart . . ." (p. 289). Thus Harris implies that the circuit rider's interest in girls is sexual rather than spiritual. The image comprehends too much for simple visualization. It approaches abstraction. Specifically, it compares a child to a nubile adolescent, and then, shifting the object of the comparison, suggests that a minister can have no interest in children. Such sunken imagery exists for its content of ideas. Its generalization is expansive. Recurring images of circuit riders as fathering illegitimate children, seducing girls, fleeing irate husbands, and the like, communicate a graphic impression of the hill country preacher as ignorant, immoral, and as baldly hypocritical as Chaucer's Pardoner or Boccaccio's Friar Onion. Explicitly Harris does not argue this. But behind the comic fantasy of his plots plays the counterpoint of the imagery, sounding the discordant notes of the American Eden.

However, Harris's vision of evil had no complementary vision of good. Without hope he could do not more than mourn that his knowledge and his art should die, as his image of the Mosaic law hints: "a littil like cuttin ove the Ten Cummandmints intu the rine ove a war-ter-million; hits jist slashed open an' the inside et outen hit, the rine an' the cummandmints broke all tu pieces an' flung tu the hogs . . ." (p. ix).[8] Although the tables of the law are broken, Harris's image is unsentimental and hard: only fools offer laws to swinish mankind.

Next, the imagery reveals that Harris was blessed with an expansive, myth-making imagination which functioned with natural ease and telling effect in symbols and allegories. The excesses of the language, wild, vigorous, and compelling, match the vaultings of a large and strange imagination, an imagination at times irrational and compulsive but bodying forth from a microcosm of homely images a macrocosm of emotions and ideas.

III

Perhaps the consistency, the artistry, and the meanings communicated by the imagery may be illustrated further by examining in some detail those associated with Sut, with Sut's father, and with two minor female characters. The first picture of Sut is of "a queer looking, long legged, short bodied, small headed, white haired, hog eyed, funny sort of a genius, fresh from some bench-legged Jew's clothing store" (p. 19). When Sut swears, he says "durn my skin—no, my haslets—" (p. 29), and we know that he has haslets like a hog rather than respectable internal organs.

To emphasize his animality, but also to connote a new creature through whose eyes the world will be refracted, Sut observes often that he has no soul: "I don't keer fur herearter, fur hits onpossible fur me tu hev ara soul" (p. 107).[9] He is, Sut repeats, a "nat'ral born durn'd fool"—"a poor ornary devil" (p. 58). He flaunts his soullessness, his wildness, and his animality. Others he sees as equally animal but less honest, taking refuge in convention's comfortable hypocrisy. Without really caring he meditates that if his legs hold out he might "turn human . . . that is sorter human, enuf to be a Squire ur school cummisiner" (p. 97). Soulless, Sut is free of responsibility, free from the necessity to be decent or good, but at the same time free to be honest about what he sees of himself and of his world.

Other clues to Sut's nature and consequently to his function as protagonist are offered by the images associated with his parentage. Early he observes that he is "one of dad's explites at makin cussed fool inventions, an' cum afore my time" (p. 107). Later he adds "I's nuffin but sum new-fangil'd sort ove beas', a sorter cross atween a crazy ole monkey an' a durn'd wore-out hominy-mill" (p. 107); perhaps, that is, child of a lascivious animal and a worn out kitchen machine. Thus, offspring of machine and animal, he is characterized as living or moving almost without mind or spirit—a suitable protagonist to celebrate the joys of action and the abandonment to the irrational, cruelty, hatred, and the euphoria of whiskey.

In his most fantastic explanation of his parentage, Sut explains to a stranger: "we kept a sand-hill crane, and Mam and him had a difficulty, and he chased her under the bed."[10] Sut is king of the fools, and the strange animal imagery of his birth connotes that he is fantastic and mythic, sired, like a Greek hero, by a wild bird on a wild hill country woman.

Even in accounts of his parentage less mythic and irrational, Sut is the figurative child of the sand hill crane. Once, speculating on his legitimacy, Sut muses:

My long laigs sumtimes sorter bothers me, but then mam tuck a pow'ful skeer et a san-hill crane a-sittin on a peel'd well-pole, an' she out-run her shadder thuty yards in cumin half a mile. I speck I owes my laigs an' speed tu that sarcumstance an' not tu eny fraud on mam's part. (p. 68)

At the level of plot, Sut's image of himself is of a "nat'ral born durn'd fool," delighting in liquor, women, food, practical jokes, and lazy story-telling. His pleasures are made possible to some extent by his conscious-ness of his own insignificance. Yet below his frequent confessions of worthlessness sounds a recurring theme of desperate misery. A few times Sut feels shame. Once, to satirize Abraham Lincoln, Harris pictures him as so disgustingly ugly and cowardly that Sut is ashamed for such a man to be President of the United States. Again, when community propriety in the person of Squire Hanley surprises Sut and his mother torturing the family father and husband, Sut suddenly sees the degradation of his life, and is ashamed:

A appertite tu run began tu gnaw my stumick, an' I felt my face a-swellin wif shame. I wer shamed ove dad, shamed ove mam's bar laigs an' open collar, shamed ove myself, an' dam, ef I minds right, ef I warn't a mossel shamed ove the pup. (p. 286)

Although at times Sut speculates that he might some day turn human, "That is, sorter human" (p. 97), he abandons himself to his animality in full consciousness of his misery and wretchedness. He expresses repeatedly in comic ambiguity his final despair: "I'll drownd mysef sum day" (p. 30); "I orter bust my head open again a bluff ove rocks, an' jis' wud du hit, ef I warnt a cussed coward" (p. 97); and "I'se a goner I 'speck, an' I jis don't keer a durn. I'm no count, no how, Jis' look at me! Did yu ever see sich a sampil of a human afore? I feels like I'd be glad *tu be* dead" (pp. 106-107). The conditions of his life make him liken himself to Old Stuffgut, his dog:

He wur skeered all the time, an' stud redy tu run ur tu steal, as the chances mout be; an' takin 'im altogether, he wur jis' the rite sort ove a dog tu belong tu me—not wurth a durn, an' orter been killed afore his eyes got open. (p. 151)

By denying Sut any transcendence, Harris consigns him to such complete insignificance that all violations are authorized.

Sut's father is protagonist in two sketches which, perhaps significantly, begin and end Harris's one published volume. In both tales the animal metaphor is extended to allegorical proportions. In the first, "Sut Lovingood's Daddy, Acting Horse," Sut's father plays the part of a domestic work animal. The family finds itself so poor that it has no horse to pull the plow. "Dad," "Mam," and the "childer" wait until almost strawberry time, hoping a stray will come by. None appears because, Sut observes, no such good luck "ever cums wifin reach ove whar dad is, he's so dod-dratted mean, an' lazy, an' ugly, an' savidge, and durn fool tu kill" (p. 22). But the old man is not without his sense of responsibility, and one night, as Sut recounts:

> he lay awake till cock-crowin, a-snorin, an' rollin, an' blowin, an' shufflin, an' scratchin hissef, an' a whisperin at mam a heap, an' at breckfus' I foun' out what hit ment. Says he, "Sut, I'll tell yu what we'll du: I'll be hoss *mysef*, an' pull the plow whilst yu drives me, an' then the 'Ole Quilt' (he ment that fur mam,) an' the brats kin plant, an' tend, ur jis let hit alone, es they darn pleze; I aint a carein." (p. 22)

However, merely to pull the plow is not enough; Sut's father decides he must be harnessed to play the character of a horse. While Sut buckles on the gear, the old man blows out his stomach to try the belly band, "chomps" the bit, tries to bite Sut's arm, whinnies like a mad horse, and drops on all fours to kick at his wife. Throughout, this fantastic paterfamilias works not as an obedient draft animal, but as a wild and fractious beast, driven to his task by cruelty and restraints. At the end, pursued by hornets, he overdoes the part of the horse and leaps over a cliff. In complaining that this was unhorselike, Sut introduces a new image:

> thars nara hoss ever foaldid durned fool enuf tu lope over eny sich place; a cussed muel mout a dun hit, but dad warn't actin muel, tho' he orter tuck that karacter; hits adzactly sooted to his dispersition, all but not breedin. (pp. 25-26)

Thus in this tale, Harris's customary animal metaphors are extended to become allegory, if one pleases: man, to feed his offspring, becomes a work animal. But he does not, like Chaucer's Bayard, resign himself with "Yet am I but an hors." He knows himself that he must be harnessed, curbed, and driven; still he remains wild and bestial.

At the end of the collection, in a story titled "Dad's Dog-School," Harris has Sut's father once more choose to play the part of an animal. For this adventure, the old man decides to teach the family bull pup, an animal "Ugly as a she ho'net an' brave es a trap't rat . . ." (p. 278), to bite and hang on. For the purpose Sut's father has himself sewed up in the hide of a newly slaughtered yearling bull, and has Sut sick the dog on him. Unexpectedly the dog goes in under the hide and fastens his teeth in the blood-besmeared nose and upper lip of Sut's father. As Sut gleefully describes it, "Dad's ole warty snout wer pull'd out tu a pint like ontu a mad bar's. . . ." The old man's obscenities and blasphemies are so distorted by the pup's hold that the family pretend not to know that he is crying for help. In the end Sister Sal separates the two with an ax, chopping away in her zeal the end of "Dad's" nose and a half-moon of his upper lip, along with the dog's snout and jaw. The dog, Sut observed, was "momoxed," and "Dad" remained long afterward "es tetchy about hit . . . es a sore-back hoss is 'bout green flies" (p. 277). Thus once again Sut's father chooses to become an animal, dressed, like an Indian shaman or a primitive Greek priest, in the skin of a bull to suffer an obscure and bloody penance, perhaps for the guilt of bringing children into the world.

Harris never explains logically why Sut should hate his father. In a tale written after the book was published, entitled "Well, Dad's Dead,"[11] the old man's death is treated with callous indifference by Sut and with relief by "Mam." George Washington himself, "Mam" observes, never had a better idea. But if "Dad" is a bull, or a fractious horse—more like a mule, except for the not breeding—perhaps the imagery connotes that condition the psychologists associate with sexual jealousy of the bull of the herd.

However that may be, the imagery associated with Sut's father—that of domestic animals, horse, mule, bull—connotes reluctant domesticity, cruel, fractious animality, laziness, and a desire for freedom, like Sut's, from inner and outer restraints.

One may add other objects of Sut's scorn to make a revealing list: he despises circuit riders, teachers, church-goers, sheriffs, judges, constables, Yankees ("they think that God eats half dimes for breakfus"),[12] Negroes, Republicans, Irishmen, Catholics, Jews, ugly women, old women, respectable women, and the woman as wife. Some of these groups are proper objects of prejudice for his place, time, and condition. The others generally represent respectability or authority. The imagery associated with them implies unattractiveness, an inclination and a power to suppress, and hypocrisy. One example, powerful and bitter, summarizes Sut's vision of man's condition and man's fate:

Whar thar ain't enuf feed, big childer roots littil childer outen the troff, an' gobbils up thar part. Jis' so the yeath over: bishops eats elders, elders eats common peopil; they eats sich cattil es me, I eats possums, possums eats chickins, chickins swallers wums, an' wums am content tu eat dus, an' the dus am the aind ove hit all. (p. 228)

Sut's hatreds, however, are not confined to symbols of oppressive authority and hypocritical respectability, or to outsiders. His dark philosophy is shown not only in his hatred of his ugly and guilty father but also in a series of hatreds culminating in a strange hatred of innocence worthy of the Marquis de Sade:

I hates ole Onsightly Peter, jis' caze he didn't seem tu like tu hear me narrate las' night; that's human nater the yeath over, an' yere's more univarsal onregenerit human nater: ef ever yu dus enything tu enybody wifout cause, yu hates em allers arterwards, an' sorter wants tu hurt em egin. An' yere's anuther human nater: ef enything happens [to] sum feller, I don't keer ef he's yure bes' frien, an' I don't keer how sorry yu is fur him, thar's a streak ove satisfackshun 'bout like a sowin thread arunnin all thru yer sorrer. Yu may be shamed ove hit, but durn me ef hit ain't thar. Hit will show like the white cottin chain in mean cassinett; brushin hit onder only hides hit. An' yere's a littil more; no odds how good yu is tu yung things, ur how kine yu is in treatin em, when yu sees a littil long laiged lamb a-shakin hits tail, an' a-dancin staggerinly onder hits mam a-huntin fur the tit, ontu hits knees, yer fingers *will* itch tu seize that ar tail, an' fling the littil ankshus son ove a mutton over the fence amung the blackberry briars, not tu hurt hit, but jis' tu disapint hit. Ur say, a littil calf, a-buttin fas' under the cow's fore-laigs, an' then the hine, wif the pint ove hits tung stuck out, makin suckin moshuns, not yet old enuf tu know the bag aind ove hits mam frum the hookin aind, don't yu want tu kick hit on the snout, hard enough tu send hit backwards, say fifteen foot, jis' tu show hit that buttin won't allers fetch milk? Ur a baby even, rubbin hits heels apas' each uther, a-rootin an' a-snifflin arter the breas', an' the mam duin her bes' tu git hit out, over the hem ove her clothes, don't yu feel hungry tu gin hit jis' one 'cussion cap slap, rite ontu the place what sum day'll fit a saddil, ur a sowin cheer, tu show hit what's atwixt hit an' the grave; that hit stans a pow'ful chance not tu be fed every time hits hungry, ur in a hurry? (pp. 245-246)

By imputing to Sut a hatred of ignorant innocence, Harris moves his
protagonist beyond the point of social criticism. Sut is honest in the way
Simone de Beauvoir contends the Marquis de Sade is honest: "He adhered
only to the truths which were derived from the evidence of his own actual
experience."[13] Further, also like the Marquis de Sade, Sut's choice seems
merely between conventional morality at its lowest, and violence. Sut
chooses pointless violence.

Franklin Meine,[14] F. O. Matthiessen, and other critics who have commented on Harris's work, praise Sut's love of joy, his Rabelaisian "jollity
of mind pickled in a scorn of fortune,"[15] and indeed Sut has joys and high
spirits. Matthiessen observes that the animal imagery connotes nature.[16]
If it does, it customarily connotes the nature of unrestrained and savage
beasts rather than the nature of beautiful animals and parklike country
side. It is the nature that seeks escape from all restraints. Harris's Sut and
his father are natural man unsoftened by humanity, unenlightened by intelligence, and unguided by religion: a terrible natural man who suffers
in his world, and who, like a stone age savage, renews his sense of power
and command by inflicting meaningless and endlessly repetitious pain
on whatever few he can find in his power.

For examples of the connotations and the artistry of Harris's more pleasant imagery, two women, minor characters in the *Yarns*, will serve. One
of the few times Harris allows Sut to be sentimental comes in his description of Sheriff Doltin's tubercular wife. The imagery associated with her
is the imagery of inanimate nature and of musical instruments. From nature
Sut draws comparisons to wells of water, the stars, the moon, and the like.
The finger cords in her hands, Sut observes, "wer mos' as high, an' look'd
es tight, and show'd es clar thru the skin es the strings ove a fiddil" (p. 257).
The second image, combining an insect and a musical instrument, describes
her coughing as "not much louder nor a crickit chirpin in a flute . . ."
(p. 257).

Another woman whom Harris describes to indicate Sut's approval of
her is the mountain girl Sicily Burns. In the images associated with her,
there are almost no animals, and of these none are ugly. Three references
to horses occur: Sicily's hair is "es long as a hoss's tail" (p. 76), she stands
"sixteen an' a 'alf hans hi" (p. 75), and could "du more devilmint nur a
loose stud hoss et a muster groun', ef she only know'd what tools she totes"
(p. 77), which women do know, Sut believes. Again describing the impact
of her appearance, Sut says that whenever he sees her his stomach feels
as it does when he has "seed the rattil-snake squar hissef tu cum at
me . . ." (p. 78). A dog collar could circle her waist (p. 76), her cheeks
and lips are as "rosey es a pearch's gills in dorgwood blossom time . . ."

(p. 76), and her hair is "black es a crow's wing et midnite" (p. 76). No other animal imagery is associated with Sicily.

The other images selected by Sut to describe her appearance and the nature of her effect on him are drawn from flowers, snow, ripe fruit, storms and lightning, fire in the mountains, plants, the clarity or foam of a rushing river, good whiskey, quicksilver, and music. When George observes that Sicily is handsome, Sut objects:

> Handsome! that ar word don't kiver the case; hit sounds sorter like callin good whiskey strong water, when yu ar ten mile frum a still-hous, hit a rainin, an' yer flask only haf full. She shows amung wimen like a sun-flower amung dorg fennil, ur a hollyhawk in a patch ove smartweed. Sich a buzzim! Jis' think ove two snow balls wif a straw-berry stuck but-ainded intu bof on em. (p. 75)

Sicily is described first in terms of her appearance, then in terms of a series of her actions, and finally in terms of her effect on Sut and on men in general. Of her smile, Sut says, "sich a smile! Why, when hit struck yu far an' squar hit felt jis' like a big ho'n ove onrectified ole Munongahaley" (p. 76). Again, Sut compares Sicily to a mountain storm:

> "I'se hearn in the mountins a fust rate fourth proof smash ove thunder cum onexpected, an' shake the yeath, bringin along a string ove litenin es long es a quarter track, an' es bright es a weldin heat, a-racin down a big pine tree, tarin hit intu broom splits, an' toof pickers, an' raisin a cloud ove dus', an' bark, an' a army ove lim's wif a smell sorter like the devil wer about, an' the long darnin needil leaves fallin roun wif a tif—tif—quiet sorter soun, an' then a quiverin on the yeath es littil snakes die; an' I felt quar in my in'ards, sorter ha'f cumfurt, wif a littil glad an' rite smart ove sorry mix'd wif hit." (pp. 77-78)

Sicily is also like the clear, cool water, white foam, and music of the Oconee River. When George objects to the final comparison, Sut insists:

> "Music; the rushin warter dus make music; so dus the wind, an' the fire in the mountin, an' hit gin me an oneasy queerness agin; but every time I look'd at that gal Sicily Burns, I hed all the feelins mix'd up, ove the litenin, the river, an' the snake, wif a totch ove the quicksilver sensashun a huntin thru all my veins fur my ticklish place." (p. 78)

The effects of Sicily on Sut lead him to another of his philosophical generalizations:

> "George, this worl am all 'rong enyhow, more temtashun than perventitive; ef hit wer ekal, I'd stand hit. What kin the ole prechurs an' the ugly wimen 'speck ove us, 'sposed es we ar tu sich invenshuns as she am?" (p. 77)

Thus in this sunken image Sicily Burns becomes the essence of female temptation which man cannot resist. She is as tempting as naked Eve, and like Eve, she is associated with serpents and the smell of the devil. The imagery communicates not merely the seductive beauty of the flesh, but the complexity of desire, fear, and the shaking power of sensual passion.

It may well appear that Harris's imagery will bear close scrutiny, that it is art of no mean order. Sut appears to seek sheer fun, but the imagery associated with him enlarges his stature to a figure ambiguously comic and mythic, hopelessly desiring an impossible freedom, pursuing intensity of experience in the flesh, and an abandonment to the obsessive and the irrational. Subtly communicated is the hint of large hopes of what man might be on the frontiers of the new world, and bitter disappointment in what he really was. Sut is hard and cruel because in the moral void of the American backcountry of his experience he can assert his individuality only through violence. The stories recount crude practical jokes; the imagery supplies the counterpoint, sounding a world only occasionally satisfying, but more often harsh, hypocritical, wicked, transitory, and meaningless.

NOTES

1. *Native American Humor* (New York, 1937), p. 96.
2. George W. Harris, *Sut Lovingood's Yarns* (New York, 1867), p. 158. Page references in the text are to this edition.
3. New York, 1924, p. 3.
4. *The American Adam: Innocence, Tragedy in the Nineteenth Century* (Chicago, 1955), p. 1.

5. "Sut Lovengood's Chest Story," Nashville *Union and American*, June 30, 1858, quoted from Donald Day, "The Life and Works of George Washington Harris" (unpublished doctoral dissertation, University of Chicago, 1942).

6. "Sut Lovengood Come to Life," Nashville *Union and American*, May 3, 1866, quoted from Day, p. 55.

7. The term is from Wells, pp. 76, 87, 172, and elsewhere.

8. Cf. Exodus 33: 15-19.

9. And again, "I hain't got nara a soul, nuffin but a whisky proof gizzard" (p. 172).

10. "Sut Lovengood Lands Old Abe Safe at Last," Nashville *Union and American*, March 5, 1861, quoted from Brom Weber's modernization of George W. Harris, *Sut Lovingood* (New York, 1954), p. 232.

11. Knoxville *Press and Herald*, November 15, 1868. See Day, pp. 61-62.

12. "Sut Lovengood Blown Up," Nashville *Gazette*, July 21, 1857, quoted from Day, p. 99.

13. Simone de Beauvoir, *The Marquis de Sade* (New York, 1953), p. 80.

14. *Tall Tales of the Southwest* (New York, 1930), p. xxiv.

15. *American Renaissance* (New York, 1941), p. 644, to describe Wirt Staples, one of Harris's more heroic creations.

16. *Ibid.* "Animal imagery of which Harris was so fond, since it brought man close to nature . . ." is Matthiessen's phrase.

Joseph Glover Baldwin:
Humorist or Moralist?

Eugene Current-Garcia

Joseph Glover Baldwin, author of *The Flush Times of Alabama and Mississippi*,[1] has long enjoyed a secure, if modest, reputation as an antebellum frontier humorist. So great was the success of this one book, in fact, that it served to overshadow his achievements in other fields—his authorship of various non-humorous publications,[2] for example, and his brilliant career as jurist and associate justice of the Supreme Court of California[3]—as well as to obscure altogether his major literary aims and aspirations. Thus, although scholars have carefully evaluated Baldwin's contribution to the field of Southern humor,[4] his career as a whole has been neglected.[5] No fully rounded critical study of his work exists in print,[6] and the only full-length biography of him remains unpublished.[7] Indeed, so little investigation of Baldwin has been published that one may still question whether he is to be regarded primarily as humorist, rather than as amateur social historian, jurist, or moralist.[8] A writer whose amusing portrayal of characters, scenes, and conditions of the old Southwest frontier attained the status of a minor classic, but whose ambition was to become the Macaulay of his age,[9] Baldwin seems to have suffered more than his share of obscurity.

This prolonged obscurity derives largely from a chain of untoward circumstances. Baldwin was cut off in the prime of life, just as he was on the point of turning the full power of his mind to writing.[10] In quick succession his three young sons, all of whom showed brilliant promise and who might have done much to enhance their father's reputation, likewise met untimely deaths.[11] His brother Cornelius, who had served as his editorial assistant in preparing his books for the press, never com-

From *The Alabama Review*, 5 (April 1952), 122-141. Reprinted by permission of the University of Alabama Press.

pleted the biography which he had undertaken to write after Joseph's death.[12] As a result, all the firsthand knowledge of Baldwin gathered together in the unpublished documents of the Baldwin family remained unexplored for many years, until a trained scholar, Mr. Robert M. Lester, obtained possession of these documents in the 1920's. Circumstances, however, also prevented Mr. Lester from fulfilling his desire to write the first biography of Baldwin, despite his immeasurably valuable efforts in assembling and cataloging the materials for it. Thus, it has only been within recent years that these essential materials, now known as the Lester-Gray Collection, have been made available to scholars.[13]

As the Lester-Gray Collection receives further attention, it is quite likely that a reappraisal of Baldwin's significance will result, since the various documents in the collection, especially the letters, throw much new light on both the man and his times. Here, in paragraphs which their author clearly never intended to show the world, one sees the unfolding record of Baldwin's struggles, anxieties, hopes, and fulfillments: his desire for wealth and professional prominence on the one hand and, these things achieved, his aspiration for literary prestige on the other. Equally significant, if slightly less revealing, are the various other documents in the collection, among which are several items offering eloquent proof of the high and serious respect which Baldwin had earned from his former colleagues in the California Supreme Court.[14]

In these tributes to his memory, formally bestowed by ranking members of the California Bench and Bar, the keynote to a proper evaluation of Baldwin's mind and character may be found.[15] For beneath their lofty phraseology runs the common sentiment, sincerely felt, that Baldwin had possessed a great legal mind and an almost inexhaustible capacity for sustained, serious effort. What counted primarily with these men was not the modest literary fame Baldwin had brought with him to California in 1854, though his authorship of *Flush Times* and *Party Leaders* was not to be overlooked, but rather the immense labors he had performed as a Supreme Court justice between 1858 and 1862. From their point of view his extra-legal writings were but the product of his leisure hours, just as his humor "was only the sportive play of a healthy, robust intellect —the recreation of a mind which, when girded for serious labor, was capable of keen analysis, comprehensive views and the clothing of correct opinion with the graces of elegant rhetoric;"[16] whereas "the business of his life was the law," which he "studied as a science [and] practiced as a high and honorable profession."[17] The chief monument to his ability, therefore, was to be found in the ten volumes of the *Reports* which coincided with his judicial career in California.[18] The majority of the opinions recorded therein were Baldwin's, but even more noteworthy than the amount of his labor was the manner in which he had performed it. "Probably no State in the Union," said the Chief Justice, "ever presented for legal investigation so many judicial problems, of so varied, novel and intricate a character as are found in the jurisprudence of California." Yet such was Baldwin's analytic grasp that, taking hold of this confused mass of litigation, within less than four years he had contributed more than any of his colleagues to clarifying the system of laws in the state.

In the face of this really sizeable accomplishment it is not surprising to find that Baldwin's judicial peers felt that his "literary reputation was singularly unjust to his actual merits." To be commonly classed because of the popularity of his *Flush Times* "with the rollicking humorists of the school to which Johnson J. Hooper . . . and Judge Longstreet belonged"[19] was from their standpoint less an asset than a liability. Hence it was that each of these jurists in turn took pains to single out for special commendation, not only the mirth-provoking but also the soberer qualities of *Flush Times,*[20] which helped to distinguish it sharply from "that careless and roystering and rollicking mass of ephemeral exudings with which the press has teemed." Hence too their mistaken belief that Baldwin's second book, *Party Leaders*, "the philosophic product of his maturer years," would in time provide the solider basis for his literary fame. To these men, who knew Baldwin intimately at the height of his intellectual power, it was plain that his bent lay not in the direction of humorous anecdote, but in that of political theory; and that had he lived the master effort of his career would have been a "philosophic history" of California.[21]

Viewed in the light of these testimonials, Baldwin's literary career takes on a new significance, which helps to explain some of the seeming incongruities noted in his supposedly humorous productions. For rightly or wrongly Baldwin's reputation has suffered the fate his fellow justices lamented. His *Party Leaders* has been forgotten, his ultimate aims have been unknown; while his value as writer, judged exclusively on the basis of *Flush Times*, has been determined by comparing his contributions to the literature of Southwest frontier humor with those of his fellow yarnspinners, Hooper, Longstreet, Harris, Thorpe, and Thompson.[22] Thus interpreted his offerings fall short of the feats of characterization and anecdotal tall tale narrative accomplished by those contemporaries. The generalized essay style in which they are written is sometimes too polished and leisurely, concludes Blair, "for an account of the brisk frontier and its rough inhabitants," while the omission of specific detail, and the paucity of direct discourse and of the actual rough and tumble episodes of frontier life often destroy their effectiveness. Though admittedly a diverting essayist who "laughingly perceives the comic topsy-turvy quality of law in a relatively lawless country [and] enjoys himself hugely as he writes the record of the strange assortment of men, ranging from rascals to statesmen,"[23] Baldwin has been labeled an "amateur story teller," whose wit and talent are "carelessly displayed."[24]

The charge is justified only so long as Baldwin is regarded as an amateur story teller whose sole motive in *Flush Times* was to record with gay abandon the age of litigation in a lawless country. That such was his primary motive is doubtless correct, but there is discoverable in Baldwin's writing, even in *Flush Times,* another motive which grows increasingly perceptible as one follows the known course of his life—that is, the motive of the moralist. Like Swift or Shakespeare, who often employ the comic for a deadly serious purpose, Baldwin too uses satire and irony, though far less trenchantly, to expose the shams and vices of society for correction. His earliest literary effort, says his brother, was a three-act comedy he wrote at the age of sixteen "to ridicule certain upstarts about Staunton (Virginia), who having got up in the world, put on all the vulgar and pretentious airs of the parvenue, and turned up their aristocratic noses at their old companions and occupations— a class of men he always held in supreme loathing and contempt."[25] Several years later, while assisting his eldest brother, then editor of the Lexington *Gazette,* Baldwin was again writing both satirical pieces and straight editorials for the newspapers;[26] and still later, shortly before his departure from Virginia in 1836, he was editing the Buchanan *Advocate* "with distinguished ability, often fearlessly and successfully encountering upon political and other issues, the veterans of the press . . . At least a page of every paper was filled with his pert, racy, and pointed editorials, highly flavored with wit and humor."[27]

Whether or not, as his brother believed, Baldwin would have become one of the country's leading editors if he had chosen journalism for his profession, is problematical. He chose instead the law and, having "left behind him the red hills of his native village in the valley of the Shenandoah,"[28] at the age of twenty-one headed for the fabulous Southwest frontier to seek his fortune in that field. The record of his quest is told in both ludicrous and poignant terms in such essays as "My First Ap-

pearance at the Bar," "The Bench and the Bar," "How the Times Served
the Virginians," and "The Bar of the South-West," which are among
the liveliest and most readable portions of *Flush Times*. Just as plainly
evident as the farce, buffoonery, and high spirits, however, there are in
these and other portions of the book the satire and moral earnestness
of one who cannot quite reconcile the excesses of humanity, however
diverting or profitable he finds them, with the promptings of his own
conscience.

Thus, although Baldwin lavishes upon his portrait of "Ovid Bolus,
Esq." the full force of his allusive humor,[29] his attitude toward that
Falstaffian liar and deadbeat remains consistently Shakesperian. Lest
it be misconstrued, he pauses in the midst of his panegyric to record it
overtly:

> "One thing in Ovid I can never forgive. This was his coming it
> over poor Ben. I don't object to it on the score of the swindle.
> That was to have been expected. But swindling Ben was degrading
> the dignity of the art. . . . It was little better than crude larceny."[30]

And in the end, for all his skill as liar and cheat, Bolus must pay the
penalty of all rogues who overwork their claims—exile from a community in which he need not ask to be remembered. "In every house he
had left an autograph, in every ledger a souvenir."[31] Again, in the
hilarious biography of an even more ingenious rascal, "Col. Simon Suggs,
Jr.,"[32] Baldwin's ironic characterization reveals a dual motive: the
moralist keeps step with the humorist. For in the record of this rogue's
progress almost every victory scored is made at the expense of individuals
only less skilled than Suggs himself in the arts of chicane: he outwits a
cruel schoolmaster, swindles his crooked father at cards,[33] illegally
establishes himself as a lawyer in a degenerate frontier community in
Arkansas, and rapidly rises to the top of his profession by defending
absconders, packing juries, subverting the criminal laws of the state, and
achieving the status of claims agent for the Choctaw Indians, whom he
defrauds on a grand scale. As he rounds off the portrait of Suggs making
his annual raids upon the Federal Treasury, the tone of Baldwin's
parting comment is unmistakable: "May his shadow never grow less; and
may the Indians live to get their dividends of the arrears paid to their
agent."[34] Suggs, in short, is the symbol of his time, the epitome of a
lawless, acquisitive society which had raised fraud and corruption to
the level of "super-Spartan roguery."[35]

Other instances of Baldwin's moral standards might be cited, as *Flush Times* is full of them.[36] In fact, it might be argued that the more ludicrous or hyperbolic the treatment of his scene or characterization, the more certain we are of the moral standards supporting his irony and jest. Behind the most hilarious of his situations[37] stands the attitude, not of the roystering clown or ring-tailed roarer, but of the sober, judicial citizen who perceived the comic aspects of human vice and pretentiousness without, however, condoning them. Though he can appreciate Falstaff, his hero is not Falstaff but Prince Hal; and like his hero Baldwin knew "how ill white hairs became a fool and jester." Having succeeded beyond expectation with *Flush Times*, which set the nation laughing,[38] he therefore had no wish to repeat himself and thus become identified, like his friend Hooper,[39] with the rascally creatures of his brain who had accounted for its success. Hereafter he would present only the serious side of his genius; he would demonstrate that the "scholarship" which had seasoned the biographical sketches of Bolus and Suggs, Jr. could be more worthily employed in writing the lives of really great men. The result of his decision was *Party Leaders,* a book which bears no trace of the high jinks of its predecessor, though the same fluent, allusive style is everywhere apparent in it.

In his preface to *Party Leaders* Baldwin states that his aim has been "to unite biography with political history; and by placing rival leaders in antagonism, to make events and principles stand out in bold relief, and to give a more striking expression to the characters he has ventured to sketch." Though frankly professing an ardent admiration for some of these "great personages," Baldwin insists that he "has sought to perform his task with candor, both in the narrative and criticism, and especially in entire freedom from all partisan bias." He makes no pretense of thorough or original research ("the events are matter of familiar history"), nor does he feel obliged to apologize for the lack of "sober gravity and subdued tone, by some supposed to be the only legitimate style of history," because he has tried also "to blend interest with instruction, and especially, to make his pages attractive to young men."[40] Surely, Baldwin the moralist is plain enough here, and in a day when partisan feeling still ran high there is much to be said for the even-tempered tone he maintained in fulfilling his purpose.[41]

Except for this individuality of style and tone, however, there is nothing remarkable about the contents of *Party Leaders*.[42] Beginning with a brief chapter on the Revolution, which develops the idea that two names emerged from it which were "destined to impress upon their country a more lasting influence than any other men" up to that time, Baldwin then reviews in alternating chapters the careers of Jefferson and Hamilton, each chapter offering him the opportunity of throwing one against the other. A similar scheme is followed throughout the book, although a weakness in its structure is apparent in the treatment of Randolph, who, as even friendly critics pointed out, was not the leader of a party.[43] But the essays do precisely what Baldwin intended, that is, blend instruction with entertainment: written on a high moral plane and in a smooth, sometimes colloquial style, they offer a popularization of American political history illustrating the interaction of men, events, and principles.

Fortunately, enough of the record of his authorship of both books survives to indicate that Baldwin felt that *Party Leaders*, rather than *Flush Times*, represented the kind of writing he was best fitted to do. Shortly after moving from Gainesville to Livingston, Alabama, in 1850, he had begun writing his humorous sketches of Southwestern society "chiefly as amusement at night and on rainy days when he was confined at home, scribbling often at the fire on a book, with his hat on and his children romping around him."[44] Most of them had been enthusiastically printed by Thompson in the *Southern Literary Messenger*, but when Baldwin went to New York in July, 1853, to arrange for their publication in book form, he was not very sanguine about the book's prospects,[45] however gratified he was to learn that his non-humorous biographical sketch of Prentiss had been highly praised and that Senator Mason was "a warm admirer of [his] writings."[46] And although the Appletons agreed to publish on a ten percent royalty basis, a high figure for an author's first book, Baldwin would in fact have been better satisfied at that time to settle for a specific sum on the first edition and "have something certain [rather] than be waiting for the sales of the work" to receive his share of the proceeds.[47] The main thing, however, he felt was to gain a reputation. Accordingly, by December 11 when the book was out, he began to look anxiously for reviews, and a week or so later he was elated to find it enjoying a brisk sale in Mobile. But his comment on its reception clearly shows what he valued more highly than a best-seller:

"I am beginning to think I stand a chance of being enrolled among the writers of the land; and that possibly my work will live to be thrown up to my children. I am glad to see that the notices of the book do not speak of it as a Suggs-like affair but as gentlemanly authorship."

By the following week *Flush Times* had become "the town talk" in Mobile, and Baldwin found himself "quite a lion—at least a cub . . . treated with a hospitality quite distressing." The attention lavished upon the author of a successful book delighted him; yet a more abiding pleasure was to have the book itself praised for its "elegance and beauty," to be told by people of "fine intellect—strong sense and cultivation" that its style resembled Charles Lamb's and that "Washington Irving might be gratified to write such a book." Moreover, the fact that much of this praise came entirely unsolicited from writers whom Baldwin did not even know,[48] convinced him as nothing else could that he possessed something of enduring worth. When Hooper wrote "a long review of the book" for his Chambers *Tribune* and spoke of it "as occupying a permanent place in literature,"[49] Baldwin felt certain that he now stood "a great deal better as a man of genius than . . . ever before." Thus, he confided to his wife:

> "On the whole so far, I am very much gratified with the take the book has had; more at the character of gentlemanly scholarship and elevated taste and vigorous thought."[50]

It was clearly this feeling that "gentlemanly scholarship and vigorous thought" were his forte which prompted Baldwin to push on with *Party Leaders* immediately after *Flush Times* had taken hold, although he had evidently made up his mind early in 1854 to leave Alabama for California and wanted to see his second book through the press before his departure.[51] He would thus be killing two birds with one stone, since the roundabout trip by way of New York offered the most feasible route to California. By pre-arrangement, he accordingly met his brother, Cornelius, in New York on July 18[52] and, having secured an excellent contract from the Appletons for fifty percent of the profits,[53] he left the manuscript with his brother for correction and proof-reading and embarked on July 20.[54] Unfortunately, the record of Baldwin's composition of *Party Leaders* is incomplete,[55] though it is apparent from references made to the book in his brother's *Memoir* that he was hard at work on revisions of his text during May and June because he was "more anxious about this book than [he] ever was about a speech when a life was up." Once the manuscript was out of his hands, however, his anxiety vanished; for he left New York in high spirits,[56] evidently convinced that *Party Leaders* could not but extend the fame he had already won with *Flush Times*. In his brother's mind, at any rate, there was no question of its success:

"Jo's book is going to rank among the ablest and most elegant productions of the kind in the English language. I think it superior to any of Macaulay's Essays—I will stake my head on its success. Appletons say it will sell."[57]

Baldwin left Alabama for California, as he had originally left Virginia, with the idea of making a fortune in the legal profession. Nor did it take him long to become a typical California booster, sending back full and glowing accounts to his family of the fabulous life that awaited them in El Dorado.[58] It was a "fine country as full of law as . . . of gold or fleas,"[59] where game, fish and fruit abounded and people talked and thought of money "by the twenty dollar gold pieces as they think of a five in Alabama." It was a place too where the legal fees ran as high as $5,000 a month for the energetic lawyer who could hustle for the business. Determined to reap his share of this rich harvest so that he might retire within three or four years (he was then only thirty-nine!) and yet leave his family secure,[60] Baldwin was willing to sacrifice everything, including personal comfort, to attain his goal. Obviously, there was little time for literary pursuits now. "I must work hard and make a fortune for my girls,"[61] he wrote.

> "I am in my office . . . not less than twelve hours a day; never go to the theatre or any amusements, and spend my time in active business. I am determined if hard work will do it, to make myself the first lawyer in S. F. and what I deem more important: to make money."[62]

The series of letters he wrote his family in 1854 and 1855 show that he was making it fast. For conditions in California in the mid-1850's were actually quite similar to those in Alabama in the mid-1830's: the full tide of the flush times was just beginning to ebb.[63] An enormous amount of litigation had piled up—claims and counter-claims over land titles and mining rights running into the millions—and speculation had rocketed to dizzying heights, a veritable bonanza for lawyers.[64] So Baldwin plunged into the thick of things, lived frugally till his family joined him, and made money. Within a few years, as his elder sons grew to manhood and his daughter married a smart lawyer, as enterprising as himself,[65] the entire Baldwin clan were growing rich in gold mining.[66]

Yet, throughout all this furor of money-making Baldwin kept a remarkably level head,[67] never losing sight of his second great goal—the achievement of permanent fame as a writer. The major object of his life was to establish the family's security. That done, he said:

> "I shall then be free to devote myself to literature, with a view of making a reputation which 'men will not willingly let die.' I think I can put myself on the roll of American authors somewhat above the names which are counted distinguished.[68]

Nor did he allow his talent to atrophy, but kept busy writing occasional pieces like the Aaron Burr essay[69] and, apparently even a humorous yarn now and then, which he served up for the delectation of his new friends among George Derby's circle of San Francisco wits.[70] Thus he kept up his dual career, and although the law as always remained his major interest, he managed to combine both his legal and literary talents. In 1855 he gave up, temporarily, writing for the press, partly because he was too busy but partly also because he was now unwilling to have his name associated with ephemeral literary productions.[71] The only literary fame he sought now was that born of serious writing, which he would not attempt unless the full power of his mind could be devoted to it. Hence his deep admiration for Dr. Samuel Johnson, whose vigor and force he found increasingly stimulating.[72] Hence too his sage advice to his son on the subject of style:

> "Avoid all exaggeration. Rise to the subject—but don't go beyond it. Overstatement is very generally worse than understatement. Don't strain after wit. Quiet wit is the best. Uproarious, bizarre humor is not the style of a gentleman or a scholar. The best speaking and writing is strong sense with the point of wit on it: like an axe made of iron with the edge steeled."[73]

Even though Baldwin could see by 1855 that *Party Leaders* would not equal *Flush Times* in popularity,[74] high praise of the book by men like Judge Mason[75] and President Fillmore[76] strengthened his determination to continue writing in that vein. He was repeatedly astonished to meet men of all classes, including even President Lincoln,[77] who praised the first book; for he felt that what he had written up to that time was far below the measure of his powers.[78] In the spring of 1856 came a challenge to demonstrate what he could do when aroused. A number of hot-headed San Francisco citizens, feeling that the authorities were incompetent to deal with certain criminal elements, had formed a vigilance committee which applied the Lynch law in the trial and execution of the outlaws; and Baldwin, "with his characteristic moral courage and love of order, justice, and law," vigorously condemned their actions.

> "Reckless of personal consequences he threw himself in front of a perfect hurricane of popular passion and fury, and calmly wrote for the editorial columns of the San Francisco Herald a number of masterly arguments upholding the supremacy of the law and denouncing law, (sic) vigilance committees and all self-constituted tribunals for the punishment of crime, as wholly unnecessary and inexcusable, as disgraceful to the civilization of the age, and fatal to the best interests of the country."[79]

But these editorials were but a foretaste of the brilliant series of opinions which, as we have seen, Baldwin was to leave behind him as a monument to both his legal and literary career on the Supreme Court of California.

Baldwin's progress in the law had thus been meteoric. Within four years of his coming to California he had attained his lifetime ambition of being recognized in two states as a brilliant, wealthy lawyer and had easily won a seat on the Supreme Court, not merely by knowing the right people but by giving proof of his capacities as a champion of justice and the law. Within eight years he had established himself as one of the foremost jurists in the land. Whether he would have achieved greater literary fame had he lived another decade, we can never know. For the fragmentary *Flush Times of California*, which his judicial colleagues referred to as his masterwork, is too brief and undeveloped to base any conjectures on, though it does show, not only the characteristic thoroughness with which Baldwin tackled all his serious literary labors, but also the deepening tone of a more mature and philosophic mind.[80] But his brother and his wife, of course, were sure he would have. "What would he have accomplished if ten years had been added to his days!" wrote Cornelius.

> "And had he lived, what better subject could he have desired for his philosophic mind and graphic pen than the tremendous war between the United States and the Confederate States, in its causes and its consequences, not yet half-developed, with its grand battles and romantic episodes, and with our illustrious chieftans, (sic) Davis, Lee, Jackson, Johnson, Stuart, as central figures?"[81]

If Joseph Glover Baldwin had lived his full span, and if he had carried out his plan to devote those years exclusively to literature, he may well have achieved a name in American literature which men would "not willingly let die." He may not have become the modern Thucydides of the War Between the States, as Mrs. Baldwin hoped and urged,[82] but neither would he have been relegated to the anthologies of frontier humor.[83]

NOTES

1. (New York, 1853, 1854, 1856; San Francisco, 1876, 1879, 1887, 1889; Americus, Ga., 1908).

2. *Party Leaders; Sketches of Thomas Jefferson, Alexander Hamilton, Andrew Jackson, Henry Clay, John Randolph* . . . (New York, 1854). W. B. Stewart, "Life of Joseph Glover Baldwin" (unpublished Ph.D. thesis, Vanderbilt University, 1941) lists several of these. See also Walter Blair, *Native American Humor (1800-1900)*, (New York, 1937), p. 85, n. 11.

3. Baldwin was elected, not appointed, to the Supreme Court of California in October, 1858. He served until January, 1862, at which time he resigned to devote his energies to private practice and to his writing. The period of his service was referred to by his fellow justices as a "judicial epoch," in which two systems of jurisprudence, the Spanish and the English Common Law, had to be blended together in the settlement of many complex cases. Baldwin's opinions in these cases were called "monumental." See "Proceedings in the U. S. Circuit Court, San Francisco, October 3, 1864, on the Occasion of the Death of the Late Hon. J. G. Baldwin," Sacramento *Daily Union*, October 5, 1864.

4. See Blair, *op cit.*, pp. 78-80; Arthur P. Hudson, *Humor of the Old Deep South* (New York, 1936), pp. 11-17; Franklin Meine (ed.), *Tall Tales of the Southwest* (New York, 1937), pp. i-xxxii; and Jennette Tandy, *Crackerbox Philosophers in American Humor and Satire* (New York, 1925), pp. 66 ff.

5. Trustworthy biographical sketches of Baldwin are few. Among the best are G. F. Mellen, "Joseph Glover Baldwin," in Edwin A. Alderman and Joel C. Harris (eds.), *Library of Southern Literature* (Atlanta, 1907), I, 175-181, and "Joseph G. Baldwin and Flush Times," *Sewanee Review*, IX, 171-181 (April, 1901); J. H. Nelson, "Joseph Glover Baldwin," *Dictionary of American Biography* (New York, 1928-1937), I, 538-539; and T. B. Wetmore, "Joseph G. Baldwin," *Transactions of the Alabama Historical Society, 1897-1898* (Tuscaloosa, 1898), II, 67-73.

6. Estimates of Baldwin's work as jurist may be found in H. H. Bancroft, *History of California* (San Francisco, 1888), VI-VIII, and *Works of Hubert Howe Bancroft* (San Francisco, 1882-1890), XXV.

7. See n. 2, above.

8. Only two references are listed in Lewis Leary, *Articles on American Literature Appearing in Current Periodicals* (Durham, 1947), p. 36.

9. See Letter, Cornelius Baldwin to Mrs. Joseph Baldwin, New York City, July 21, 1854. This letter, as well as all other MSS cited, are in the Lester-Gray Collection, New York Public Library. Microfilm copies are in the Alabama Collection, University of Alabama Library, Tuscaloosa.

10. Baldwin died September 30, 1844, aged forty-nine (see Cornelius Baldwin's unpublished "Memoir of Jo G. Baldwin," p. 29). Hereinafter referred to as Memoir.

11. The second son, Jo, Jr., aged twenty, died of tuberculosis shortly before his father; the third, Holly, died of the same disease, aged twenty-two, in 1868; and the oldest, Alexander, was killed in a train wreck in 1869 at twenty-eight. He had already attained a judgeship in Nevada and was headed for a brilliant career in law and politics.

12. See n. 10, above.

13. A native Alabamian, Mr. Lester has for many years been secretary of the Carnegie Corporation of New York. The Lester-Gray Collection (see n. 9, above) contains 220-odd family letters and many other legal documents, manuscripts, and miscellaneous items. Unfortunately, about forty letters written by or to Baldwin are known only through references made to them by his brother Cornelius (see n. 10, above).

14. These include a number of short fragmentary sketches and speeches and two important longer fragments, the "Memoir" by Cornelius and Baldwin's unpublished "Flush Times of California." Also included are handwritten fragments of legal opinions, the original of Baldwin's license to practice law in Alabama, personal notes, deeds, photographs, and newspaper clippings containing accounts of Baldwin's death and tributes paid to his memory by members of the California Bar.

15. Included among these were: Delos Lake, United States district attorney; W. W. Cope, former chief justice; Thompson Campbell, J. B. Crockett, S. J. Field, J. S. Hager, J. P. Hoge, and Gregory Yale.

16. Sacramento *Daily Union*, October 3, 1864.

17. *Ibid.,* October 5, 1864.

18. *Reports of Cases Agreed and Determined in the Supreme Court of the State of California* (1858-1862), X-XIX.

19. Nearly 600 cases were said to be pending on the court docket when Baldwin took his seat, four-fifths of which passed through his hands; and the docket was cleared when he left. "He combined unwonted industry with most consummate ability. His adjudications are models of clear and logical perception, and reveal the most extensive research, and stringent power of analysis, and copious and refined illustration, and are characterized by grace of style, and scholarly learning and sound deduction" (*Daily Union,* October 5, 1864).

20. Such as his biographical essays on Sargent S. Prentiss and Francis Strother Lyons.

21. This reference was doubtless to Baldwin's "Flush Times of California," the materials for which he was said already to have amassed. The existing fragment of this work, less than thirty typed pages, indicates that Baldwin had scarcely begun to organize his materials; however, the fragment may represent but a small portion of the work he had done on the project.

22. Tandy, *op. cit.*, pp. 65-96; Blair, *op. cit.*, pp. 62-101.

23. *Ibid.*, p. 79.

24. Tandy, *op. cit.*, p. 83.

25. Memoir, p. 6. The play was not published because the youthful author and his cronies could not raise the $40 needed to cover the printing costs. "Joe afterwards congratulated himself that the juvenile indiscretion never saw the light, and wisely threw the Ms. in the fire."

26. One of these pieces, written in collaboration with William Alexander Caruthers (author of *The Cavaliers of Virginia* and *The Kentuckian in New York*) was "a burlesque on the proceedings of the Democratic Convention . . . to nominate a candidate for Congress. They were ridiculed as kraut-eating Dutchmen, and a most amusing speech, high faluting, studded with dog-Latin and scripts of poetry [sic] was put into the mouth of the presiding Dutch officer" (*ibid.*, p. 8).

27. Memoir, p. 9.

28. *Flush Times*, p. 47.

29. *Ibid.*, pp. 1-19.

30. *Ibid.*, pp. 10-11.

31. *Ibid.*, p. 19. Though the original of Bolus has long been a matter of conjecture, Cornelius Baldwin avers that he was one of the three resident lawyers in DeKalb County (Miss.) at the time of Joe's arrival—"a very handsome and polite young man from South Carolina, who subsequently represented Kemper County in the Legislature" (Memoir, p. 11).

32. *Flush Times*, pp. 114-141.

33. His father was, of course, the famous Captain of the Tallapoosa Volunteers, created by Baldwin's good friend, J. J. Hooper, in *Some Adventures of Captain Simon Suggs* . . . (Philadelphia, 1845).

34. *Flush Times*, p. 141.

35. *Ibid.*, p. 238.

36. Compare, for example, Baldwin's climactic summaries of the saturnalia of speculation and corruption in the Southwest (*ibid.*, pp. 81-91; 236-239) with his straightforward, singleminded admiration for a man who in real life faced Sugg's temptation but honorably resisted it. Francis Strother (Lyons) "had passed through the strong temptations which beset a man in a new country, and *such* a country, unscathed, unsoiled even by suspicion, and ever maintained a reputation above question or challenge. It were easy to have accumulated an immense fortune by an agency for the Indians in securing their claims under the treaty of 1830; and he was offered the agency with a compensation which would have made him a millionaire; he took the agency but rejected the fortune" (*ibid.*, p. 253).

37. One of the most amusing sketches in the book, "Samuel Hele, Esq." (pp. 284-303) centers upon the episode in which a waspish old lawyer horrifies the Yankee schoolmarm of the village with his detailed account of the community's general debauchery so that she flees the town in fright and despair. The treatment given her, however, is no more than she deserves, and Baldwin's satire is nicely sustained.

38. *Southern Literary Messenger*, XX, 125 (February, 1854) noted that sales of *Flush Times* were passing 20,000 copies with demand still increasing.

39. See William Garrett, *Reminiscences of Public Men in Alabama, for Thirty*

Years (Atlanta, 1872), pp. 527-528, for an account of the embarrassment suffered by Hooper as a result of his being identified with Simon Suggs. Garrett's censorious tone, though perhaps extreme, was "more representative than one might suppose," states Blair (*op. cit.,* p. 109). "In the South and in the North, the 'better people' did not as a rule go for native humor."

40. *Party Leaders*, p. 8.

41. One has only to recall the tendency of American historiography in the 1840's to appreciate Baldwin's relatively unbiased analysis of his subjects. It was an age in which the prominent statesman was likely to be either deified or diabolized, depending on the writer's political affiliations. Bancroft's *History of the United States* is a case in point.

42. The book is divided into three sections, the first consisting of fourteen short chapters on Jefferson and Hamilton; the second, another fourteen chapters on John Randolph; and the third, five chapters on Jackson and Clay. Baldwin indicates that he had intended including an essay on Webster and Clay but omitted it because they were too recently dead. Only the essay on Jackson and Clay had been printed before.

43. *Sumter County Whig* (Livingston, Ala.), October 4, 1854. "Our Author labors hard to place the eccentric John Randolph, of Roanoke, in the galaxy of American statesmen. We demur. That he was a wit, a satirist, and an orator, we readily admit; but we cannot concede that these qualities united to bitter invective, sometimes of the purest and best men in the nation, made a statesman. His long political career is 'embellished by no monument of national utility.'"

44. Memoir, p. 15.

45. "From what I hear a first book never brings anything but dry fame to the author, so I don't expect much—indeed shall be satisfied if I get my expenses paid; but shall try to get as much as I can" (Baldwin to his wife, New York, July 22, 1853).

46. *Ibid.,* to *ibid.,* Richmond, July 5, 1853.

47. Baldwin to his son, Alexander (Sandy), New York, July 23, 1853.

48. Baldwin to his wife, Mobile, December 11, 22, 30, 1853. "I have been perfectly quiet, not doing anything to puff or be puffed—not even making the acquaintance of the writers of the press." He sent his wife a number of reviews, saying he did not know who had written them.

49. Though quite on the friendliest terms with Hooper, Baldwin neglected to thank him for this review until the following summer, when he sent Hooper a piece he had "just scribbled for the Mail," mentioning incidentally his plan to leave Alabama shortly (see Baldwin to Hooper, Livingston, June 10, 1854).

50. Baldwin to his wife, December 30, 1853.

51. In the Memoir (p. 17) Cornelius refers to a letter of Baldwin's dated Livingston, May 14, 1854, which revealed "that the California fever was raging in his veins."

52. *Ibid.,* p. 19.

53. Baldwin to his wife, New York, July 20, 1854.

54. Cornelius Baldwin to Mrs. Baldwin, New York, July 21, 1854: "We have made a very advantageous contract with the Appletons for the publication of *Party Leaders*. We get half the net profit. The Ms. is already in the hands of the compositors—at least a portion of it is—and the book will be out in about a month."

55. The Memoir, from which two sheets are missing (7-8), indicates that about twenty letters were written by Joseph to Cornelius during this period of parturition, most of them apparently having to do with problems of craftsmanship. None of these letters survive, however (see *ibid.*, pp. 16-19).

56. *Ibid.*, pp. 18-20. "About eleven o'clock on the morning of the 20th July 1854, . . . Joe took leave of his friends at the St. Nicholas, ordered a hack and in company with an intimate friend, Sen. Parsons of Alabama, . . . drove down to the steamer, Arago, then lying at her dock near the mouth of the North River. He was full of fun, joking and telling anecdotes all the way. "'Well, Joe,' said Sen. P. 'I am glad to see you go off in such high spirits'".

57. Baldwin to his wife, July 21, 1854.

58. Baldwin to his wife and others, October 11, November 15, 21, December 10, 15, 19, 1854; January 27, February 9, 22, 23, 1855.

59. Baldwin to "Dear Tom," San Francisco, October 11, 1854.

60. Baldwin to his wife, San Francisco, November 21, December 15, 19, 1854.

61. Baldwin to "My dear daughter Kate," December 19, 1854.

62. Baldwin to his wife, December 15, 1854.

63. "Flush Time of California," p. 1.

64. "A large land speculator proposed to me to undertake a very large number of suits involving two or three millions of money, giving me an interest in the result, besides a certain fee" (Baldwin to his wife, December 19, 1854).

65. *Ibid.*, to *ibid.*, Virginia City, September 25, 1862. Kate married John Brooks Felton, a Yankee from "Bosting," whose elder brother, C. C. Felton, was president of Harvard College. Baldwin and his son-in-law became partners.

66. *Ibid.*, to *ibid.*, Virginia City, August 20, September 25, 1862; Empire City, February 23, 1863.

67. " 'Keep money in your head, not in your heart,' said a wise man; and I do it" (*ibid.* to *ibid.*, August 20, 1862).

68. *Ibid.* to *ibid.*, San Francisco, December 19, 1854.

69. Memoir, pp. 22, 27.

70. Baldwin to his wife, San Francisco, November 21, 1854. Derby, whose pseudonym was John Phoenix, wrote *Phoenixiana* (New York, 1855) and *The Squibob Papers* (New York, 1859). He was at the time the best known humorist on the Pacific Coast. See Blair, *op. cit.*, pp. 102, 181, and G. R. Stewart, *John Phoenix* (New York, 1937). In this letter Baldwin called him "a fine fellow and a great admirer of mine; he looks up to me mightily, though I tell him he is a wittier man than I am: he hoots at the idea."

71. Memoir, pp. 22-23. See also Baldwin to his wife, San Francisco, February 22, 1855.

72. *Ibid.* to *ibid.*, October 16, 1854.

73. Baldwin to "My dear Sandie," San Francisco, February 23, 1855. At this time the boy was fourteen years old.

74. Baldwin to his wife, November 21, 1854.

75. J. M. Mason to C. C. Baldwin, November 2, 1854.

76. Millard Fillmore to C. C. Baldwin, November 2, 1854.

77. Baldwin to "My dear Felton," Baltimore, November 1, 1863. "Abe and I grew very pleasant and spent an hour together in the White House very cosily. He was very kind and affable and knew all about me and more about Flush Times (which seems to be one of his classics) than I knew myself. He says he is always

quoting me when he gets facetious (probably to restore gravity to his guests)." Baldwin had appealed to Lincoln, unsuccessfully, for permission to get through the lines to visit his family in Virginia.

78. Baldwin to his wife, San Francisco, February 22, 1855.

79. Memoir, pp. 24-25.

80. Unlike the *Flush Times of Alabama*, in which Baldwin was content largely to present the social scene as a variety of amusing but unconnected incongruities, his "Flush Times of California" indicates that he evidently intended this work to be the history of a vast movement of conflicting social forces. Flashes of the old humor and irony are present, but the underlying motive is more serious.

81. Memoir, p. 28.

82. Mrs. Baldwin to "My dear Husband," San Francisco, October 16, 1863.

83. Assistance in preparing this study was provided by a grant from the Research Grant-in-Aid program of the Alabama Polytechnic Institute.

Harden Taliaferro, Folk Humorist
of North Carolina

James H. Penrod

The humorous writings of Harden E. Taliaferro, who used the pen name "Skitt," have generally received only cursory notice by students of native American humor and folklore.[1] Born in 1818 in Surry County, North Carolina, adjoining three Virginia counties, Taliaferro moved in 1837 to Alabama, where he became a Baptist preacher and later edited *The Southwestern Baptist*. His chief contribution to American literature, *Fisher's River Scenes and Characters* (1859), was inspired by a return to his native county two years before its publication date. Taliaferro was also a contributor of humorous sketches to the *Southern Literary Messenger* in a period 1860-1863, but these quasi-literary efforts, which were collected and published by David K. Jackson in 1938 under the title *Carolina Humor*, added little or nothing to his reputation. Little is known of Taliaferro after the Civil War. He died in 1875 after returning to Surry County and was buried in that community.

Taliaferro's closest literary affiliations are with the humorists of the Old Southwest, although a strict geographical classification might disqualify him from membership in that distinguished group. Like the yarnspinners, Taliaferro wrote sketches which are of considerable interest today in several respects: (1) portrayal of folk character, (2) transcription of the folk tales of his region, (3) recording of social history of the Old South. Also as in the work of the yarnspinners, Taliaferro generally achieved a harmonious blend of these ingredients.

The characters portrayed in *Fisher's River Scenes and Characters* lived "near the foot of the Blue Ridge, on its spurs and ridges," and on the many rivers flowing from its base. Although most of the original inhabitants of the region had come from Virginia, the Fisher's River folk made no

From *Midwest Folklore*, 6 (Fall 1956), 147-153. Reprinted by permission of the author.

claims to membership in the First Families of Virginia.[2] Of all Taliaferro's characters, perhaps the most notable were a trio of artistic liars—Uncle Davy Lane, Oliver Stanley, and Larkin Snow—three raconteurs of marvelous hunting and fishing stories, whose literary counterparts are legion, but whom Taliaferro might well have created without ever hearing of Davy Crockett, Mike Fink, the "Big Bear of Arkansas," or many folk heroes of other continents.

Uncle Davy Lane was a lazy gunsmith, a glutton, and a hard drinker, but according to his own accounts, the mightiest hunter in the section. He always hunted with his trusty rifle, "Old Bucksmasher." Larkin Snow, the miller, was a more industrious, respectable sort, but he too was a "big story teller." Oliver Stanley was a good-natured, tobacco-chewing native who fished for small fry in actuality but cavorted with whales in his imagination. More will be said of the trio's tales anon.

Taliaferro resembles most of the best native American humorists (as well as such borderline realists as Balzac, Dickens, and Bret Harte) in combining a fondness for the grotesque with a more realistic bent in characterization. In Taliaferro's work both the grotesque and plain, simple folk are convincingly portrayed. The three artistic liars combine grotesquerie with realism both in their persons and their yarns. So does Johnson Snow, a glutton who loved turnip greens and "hog's gullicks" and who loved whiskey "as a thirsty ox does pond water." Johnson once disrupted a camp meeting with his loud snores but on another occasion won a night's lodging by quoting Scripture purposefully to Squire Taliaferro, presumably a relative of the author.[3] Of much the same type are Long Jimmy Thompson, a champion big-eater of the county, and the two backwoods bullies, Josh Jones and Hash Head Smith. Grotesque but credible is oafish Uncle Billy Lewis, the gullible dupe, who once shot the horses in a fire-hunt by mistake and who, during his brief career in the pulpit, was induced by pranksters to tell his congregation of a flying snake twelve feet long with a twelve inch stinger in his tail. His recall was inevitable even in such a primitive community.[4]

Taliaferro's only racial and national types are Reverend Charles Gentry, a Negro preacher whose interpretations of Scripture were slanted in favor of his own race, and Glassel, the superstitious Scotchman, who was convinced at one time that an owl was talking to him.

Taliaferro's treatment of regional character is generally distinguished from that of the foremost yarnspinners by one significant characteristic—sympathy. The obvious reason is that he was writing of his own people; whereas such classic Southern humorists as Longstreet, Baldwin, and

Hooper wrote in a consciously superior vein, reflecting alternately amused contempt and tolerance.[5] Another good reason for this difference is the fact that Taliaferro was writing of a stable, well-rooted society, whereas many Southwestern humorists wrote largely of the fluid frontier with its wide assortment of opportunists or "rapscallions." Conspicuously absent in his work are such venal swindlers as Hooper's Simon Suggs, and Baldwin's Ovid Bolus; neither are there hypocrites such as Sheriff Doltin and Parson Bullen of *Sut Lovingood's Yarns*. Perhaps the only unworthy characters in *Fisher's River Scenes* are the unqualified preachers, the insincere converts, and King, the independent idler, who decided to change his residence because the poll tax in Georgia was only fifty cents as against seventy-five cents in Alabama.[6] Even in such cases, the humor is rather kindly.

Taliaferro's most realistic, or normal, characters are his farmers, who are generally industrious, independent and honest; they generally have a dry sense of humor and the inevitable preference for "hoss sense" over book learning. For example, Uncle Frost Snow was a sturdy, poor farmer who eked out a living by hard work. He was proud of his humble status; he didn't care "a durn whether he b'longed to one of the fust famblys in Fudginny ur not."[7] Proud also of his simple language, Uncle Frost opined that "larnin' and big quality words is ruinin' on us fast. Even the niggers is a-ketchin big quality words."[8] His distaste for "quality talk," as well as his virtues, were shared by his son Dick, who got up to work before daylight after the birth of twins, saying, "When the family is 'creasin so fast, I must 'crease my wurk, by jingo." Considerable realistic detail is given about the farm life of the Fisher's River country in the sketch about John Senter and his son Sol, who lived in a crude log cabin and wore wooden-bottomed shoes.

Taliaferro also painted a memorable picture of an honest, untutored Alabama farmer in Ham Rachel, who lived near Eufaula. Ham lived mostly by raising cows, cotton, and corn; he went to market on an ox-cart. A garrulous, helpful, inquisitive sort, Ham was described as "letting fly a diarrhea of words and sentences."[9] The author's physical description of him emphasized his asymmetrical physique and his outlandish garb:

> There he stood, a lean, gaunt-looking specimen of freakish humanity, about five feet eight inches high, stoop-shouldered, long-armed, and knocked-kneed, with a peaked dish face, little, black, restless eyes, long keen nose, and big ears. His dress was cotton pants,

dyed black with copperas and maple bark, a coarse cotton shirt, collar large and open, no vest, coat, nor socks. His hat was old, broad-brimmed, and slouched down over his shoulders behind, and turned up before. His pants were 'gallused' to their utmost capacity, leaving considerable space between his knees and the tops of his old brogan shoes; not having on 'drawers' of course, the skin was exposed. His two jugs were part of his dress. They hung across his shoulders, before and behind, suspended to a wide black greasy leather strap, nearly down to his knees before and his calves behind.[10]

It is Taliaferro's transcription of the tall fishing and hunting yarns of his native county that has attracted most attention from literary historians and anthologists. Pattee referred to Taliaferro's stories as typical examples of humorous exaggeration.[11] B. A. Botkin included a yarn or two by Taliaferro in *A Treasury of American Folklore*. The tales spun by Taliaferro's mountain narrators were obviously patterned closely after popular folk tales of the region and period.[12] The close resemblance of several of these stories to those of the fabulous Baron Munchausen is striking.[13] Particularly does Uncle Davy Lane's story about the pigeon-roost smack of Munchausenism. In this yarn, Uncle Davy, having heard of a mighty pigeon-roost in the Little Mountains, hastened there and killed "about a thousand." He then discovered that he had hitched his horse to the limb "uv a tree bent to the yeth with pigeons . . . and when they riz the tree went up, and old Nip with it."[14] The resemblance to Munchausen's familiar story of the horse which was left dangling on the church steeple after the thaw following a big snow is obvious.

Most of Uncle Davy's yarns concerned meetings with fantastic animals. At one time he encountered a monstrous coach whip snake, whereupon he "jumped logs twenty foot high, clearin' thick bushes, and bush heaps, deep gullies, and branches." Another snake he encountered had a head "big as a sasser," a forked tongue, and a six-inch stinger in his tail. The creature rolled down the mountain like a hoop until his stinger got "stuv up" in a tree, whereupon the mighty hunter shot him. Following one of his hectic sessions with snakes, Uncle Davy tried milk as a remedy for snake-bite but became ill and had to settle his system with "at least two gallons of whiskey, the king cure-all."[15]

Even so prosaic an occupation as farming offered distinct possibilities to the artistic liar. Larkin Snow, the miller, told of his experience in farming a "track patch" near a river bank. Finding his crop of Crowder peas greatly depleted, Larkin sought in vain for an explanation until he discovered five hundred eels in the river nearby. He then devised a scheme to lure the eels into a barrel full of dry ashes, with the result that "the fryin' pan stunk fur months with fat eels, and we all got fat and sassy."[16]

In Taliaferro's only fanciful fishing yarn, Oliver Stanley played a variation on the Biblical story of Jonah and the whale. Oliver told of his being kidnaped while on a peaceful fishing expedition. Rather than shave with lather made of hog dung and turpentine, as his kidnapers did, Oliver chose to plunge into the ocean. Although pursued by sharks, the great swimmer eluded them for eight hours before being swallowed by a whale. Still undaunted, Oliver calmly lit his pipe and crossed his legs inside the cavernous belly, the smoke causing the whale to propel him a hundred feet into the air. Oliver then "swum fur a whole day with such verlocity that sea-sarpints, sharks, and uvry other vinimous monster uv the deep was no more to me than snails a-crawlin'."[17] That such a man should eventually arrive safely on shore was, of course, inevitable.

The mountaineer is traditionally a man who loves both solitude and social activity. In this respect Taliaferro's Blue Ridge characters are no exceptions. As a matter of fact, the subjects and incidents in *Fisher's River Scenes and Characters* closely parallel those in the best-known works of Old Southwestern humor, whether concerning the life of the highlanders (as in *Sut Lovingood's Yarns*) or that of the lowlanders. The value of these sketches as informal social history has been increasingly recognized in the last two decades. Probably none of the yarnspinners was more accurate in depicting social life than was Taliaferro.

One of the favorite pastimes of the Surry County folk, tale-swapping, has already been noted. Another was the militia muster. One recalls the sketches of rowdy, ludicrous militia drills by Oliver H. Prince and William T. Thompson in reading Taliaferro's "Famus or no Famus," which inevitably ends in social drinking and fighting. Night meetings and other varieties of religious experience not unnaturally predominate in Taliaferro's work. The author gently disapproves of the primitive though devout religion of the camp meeting. For example, Dick Snow, commenting ruefully on a meeting he had attended, declared: "They beat my back wusser nur a nigger beatin' hominy in a mortar, jist like religion could be beat inter a man, like maulin' rails out'n locked timber."[18] At another meeting the preacher made a boisterous but unsuccessful effort to convert Sol Hawkes, who almost came to love the Lord.[19] At still another gathering an emotional sinner stole the show from two Methodist ministers, one of whom was "traveling fast to Canaan. . . . five hundred miles ahead on anything on this grit."[20] Once Brother Walker's vivid description of the voice calling him convinced the brethren that he had "the right sort of call" and he was awarded a license to preach.[21]

The social aspects of rough-and-tumble fighting are emphasized by Taliaferro almost as much as by George W. Harris in *Sut Lovingood's Yarns*, indicating that fights really were notable social events in the Southern Highlands. Certainly Taliaferro provided one of the most vivid pictures of backwoods fighting in the following passage:

> Only such weapons as nature had given them would they use in attack and defense. They would knock with their fists like a Milo, kick with their feet like a horse, bite like loggerhead turtles, gouge like screw-augers, and butt like rams. Any method with the body was lawful. Bullies would keep their thumbnails oiled and trimmed as sharp as hawk's claws. Ask them why, they would reply, 'To feel fur a feller's eye-strings, and make him tell the news.'
>
> As you passed houses going home from musters and public gatherings, those who did not go would accost you thus: 'Who fout today?' If you replied 'No one,' there was evidently a disappointment.[22]

Rustic courtships, another staple of Old Southwestern humor (the most famous example is, of course, Thompson's *Major Jones's Courtship*), also were treated by Taliaferro. He described graphically the rivalry between Dick Snow and another suitor, particularly in the scene in which Dick out-maneuvers his rival on horseback, gets to escort the girl home, and decides to "make the big war talk to Sally."[23] As is usual in such cases, the battle is won when the hero summons the courage to propose.

A serious and tender love story is that of John Senter's crippled son Sol for Polly Spencer, who was also crippled. Old John has no time or money to waste on weddings, but at last grudgingly permits the marriage.[24] There is a sort of Old Testament dignity and simplicity in this account of the faithful, hard-working young lovers as well as the home-spun quality characteristic of Taliaferro's sketches.

A thorough search in Taliaferro's work for such conventional elements of folklore as songs, riddles, superstitions, potions, and magic cures might net a few interesting items, but Taliaferro's main concern was not with such matters. Less distinguished in style and technique than many American humorists of the nineteenth century, he yet preserved for posterity a rich storehouse of the folk tales of Surry County, North Carolina, portrayed vividly the folkways of his region, and presented a number of characters interesting for their oddities and normal traits, their wisdom and foolishness, their strengths and their weaknesses. Such a contribution should be enough to give him a secure niche in American literature and folklore.

NOTES

1. See, however, James E. Ginter, "Harden E. Taliaferro, A Sketch," *Mark Twain Quarterly (Winter, 1953)*, 13-15, 20.

2. Harden E. Taliaferro, *Fisher's River Scenes and Characters* (New York: Harper and Brothers, 1859), 14-16.

3. Johnson Snow," *ibid.*, 31-49.

4. "Uncle Billy Lewis," *ibid.*, 152-164.

5. For an excellent development of this point, see John Donald Wade, "Southern Humor," *A Vanderbilt Miscellany*, ed. Richmond C. Beatty (Nashville: Vanderbilt University Press, 1944), 193.

6. Taliaferro, "One of the People," *op. cit.*, 229-232.

7. "Uncle Frost Snow," *ibid.*, 94.

8. *Ibid.*, 96.

9. "Ham Rachel of Alabama," *ibid.*, 264.

10. *Ibid.*, 167.

11. Fred Lewis Pattee, *The First Century of American Literature, 1770-1870* (New York: D. Appleton-Century Company, 1935), 484-485.

12. See Ralph Steele Boggs, "North Carolina Folktales Current in the 1820's," *Journal of American Folklore*, XLVII (October-December, 1934), 269-288.

13. David K. Jackson (ed.), *Carolina Humor: Sketches by Harden E. Taliaferro* (Richmond: The Dietz Press, 1938), vi-vii.

14. Taliaferro, "The Pigeon Roost," *op. cit.*, 84.

15. "The Rattlesnake Bite," *ibid.*, 61.

16. "Story of the Eels," *ibid.*, 148.

17. "The Escape from the Whale," *ibid.*, 133.

18. "Dick Snow," *ibid.*, 122.

19. "The Convert," *ibid.*, 206-211.

20. "Outdone," *ibid.*, 239.

21. "A Call to the Ministry," *ibid.*, 233-236.

22. "Fighting," *ibid.*, 198.

23. "Dick Snow," *ibid.*, 120.

24. "A Declaration of Love," *ibid.*, 222-226.

III. Folk Figures

Mike Hooter—The Making of a Myth

John Q. Anderson

The Old Southwest produced several legendary heroes, who, through
the media of the oral tale and the printed story, passed from regional fame
to national popularity and thereby became part of the folklore of America.
Davy Crockett and Mike Fink are the most obvious examples of this
process.[1] Behind these great folk heroes stands a host of less widely
known though often equally fascinating figures whose exploits, if recorded at all, lie buried in weekly newspapers or long forgotten books.
Mike Hooter, Mississippi bear hunter and lay preacher, is one of these
almost forgotten figures. Though he was rather widely publicized in the
late 1850's, he has not flourished in the manner of Crockett and Fink,
though legends about him survive in Mississippi and tales about him
are still reprinted.[2] The evolution of the myth of Mike Hooter from a real
man to a legend is a good example of the myth-making process. To see
that process at work in this instance, it is necessary first to summarize
the legend of Mike Hooter as it appeared in print, next to present the
real Michael Hooter of family tradition and official records, then to
consider briefly the two writers responsible for the legend, and finally
to note how those writers transformed a living man into a legend.

Mike Hooter was the best bear hunter in Yazoo County. Everyone
was certain of that, for Mike had told them. In the pioneer days of northern
Mississippi the swamps along the Yazoo River were thick with bear,
and when Mike's wife wanted "a new bar-skin petticoat" or his daughter,
Sal, wanted "some bar's ile to slick her har with," Mike went on a bear
hunt. On one such hunt, as he described it, Mike, with his "old two-
shooter" and a pack of hounds, set off into the canebrake looking for
"bar sine." Soon his hounds, old Bumper and Echo, found the trail and

From *Southern Folklore Quarterly*, 19 (March 1955), 90-100. Reprinted by permission of
the publisher.

began "talking" to the bear, "most pertickler musical," as Mike put it, and, he added, "Tom Goin's fiddle and my Sal's singin, and all the camp meeting hallelujahs you ever hearn, warnt a patchin to it." But soon the dogs changed their tune and rushed out of the cane with the bear, "puffin and blowin like a young steamboat," right after them. Mike blazed away at the onrushing bear but only wounded him. The dogs soon had the bear at bay in a nearby creek. Thinking the animal could not escape, Mike, always eager to talk to whomever or whatever would listen, made a speech to the bear:

> Good mornin', Mister Bar. How did you leave Misses Bar and all the little Bars [Mike inquired]? Takin' a bath, I diskiver, with your breeches on! . . . You look hearty, Mister Bar. Good livin' up in Jim Stewart's punkin patch, I spose? . . . the ile what's in your hide would slick the har of all the galls in our neck of o' woods 'till the cows come home. You carrys a most too much dead capital in that ar skin of yourn, any how; and if it's the same to you, I'll jist peel the bark off'n you, and larn you the rudiments of perlitical economy . . . Mr. Bar, the tail of your jacket is a trifle too short for cold weather, and a feller might kalkilate the tailor that made your coat was an idee sparein of his cloth . . . [3]

The bear, apparently unappreciative of Mike's wit, attacked so furiously that Mike retreated and gave up the chase, and so there was no bear-skin petticoat for Mrs. Hooter and no bear oil for Sally's hair. The bear knew, of course, that his days were numbered and that he would not escape another day.

That the bear should get away from Mike that day was a result of the unique sagacity of Yazoo bears, for which Mike had the greatest respect. Unlike Tennessee bears which stupidly allowed Davy Crockett to kill one hundred and five of them in less than a year, Yazoo bears were the world's shrewdest. As Mike said:

> It's no use talkin' . . . bout your Polar Bar and Grisly Bar and all that sort of varmint what you read about. They ain't no whar, for the big black customer what circumlocated down in our neck o' woods beats 'em all hollow. I've hearn of some monsos [monstrous] explites kicked up by the brown Bars, sich as totein off a yoke o' oxen and eatin humans raw, and all that sort o' thing; and Capen Parry tells us a yarn 'bout a big white bar what 'muses hisself climbing up the

North Pole and slidin down again to keep his hide warm; but all that ain't a circumstance to what I've *saw*.[4]

Mike illustrated the peculiar cunning of Yazoo bears with a tale showing how one outwitted his neighbor, Ike Hamblin. Ike's dogs chased a bear in a thicket but would not go in after it. Ike leaned his gun against a sapling and went to gather rocks to chunk the dogs. The bear, unnoticed by Ike, took the gun, blew the powder out of the pan, took out the flint, and replaced the gun against the tree. When Ike recovered the gun and drew a bead on the bear, the animal stood "with the thumb of his right paw on the eend of his smeller, and wigling his tother fingers" while Ike snapped furiously.[5]

As the years went by, Mike's fame as a bear hunter spread, largely because of his boasting. He came to be known as the greatest bear hunter in the county, perhaps in the state. His name in the Indian language was said to signify "the grave of bears"; the ground around his homestead was white with the bones of bears he had killed; he could easily have dispatched the "Big Bear of Arkansas" without a flick of the eyelash; the whole bear population, in fact, was threatened with extinction. "When his horn sounded—so tradition ran—the bears began to draw lots to see who should die that day, for painful experience had told them the uselessness of all endeavoring to escape."[6] Mike Hooter, the Nimrod of the Yazoo bottoms, was indeed "a mighty hunter before the Lord."

And truly before the Lord did Mike hunt bear, for he was a pious man, an elder in the Methodist church, in fact, and something of a preacher. His chief chronicler said, ". . . at prayer and camp meetings, where bombast passed current for eloquence, and loud shouting for the fervor or sanctimonious zeal, he shone effulgent, chief of exhorters."[7] It was indeed debatable which Mike liked more, a good bear hunt or a camp meeting. Both provided the strenuous excitement he loved. In the summer, he packed his family off to the meeting grounds, where he could enjoy the loud and strong preaching. Describing such a meeting, Mike said:

> . . . Parson James, he was up on er log er preachin', an' er goin' it 'hard from the tomb!' I tell you what Brother James was loud that day! Thar he was, with the Bible on er board—stickin 'twene two saplins, an' he was er comin' down on it with his two fists worse nor maulin rails; an' er stompin his feet, an' er slobberin' at the mouth, an' er cuttin up shines worse nor er bob-tail bull in fly time![8]

Such preaching Mike enjoyed because it "convicted" the sinners with obvious results.

> Torrectly I spy the heatherns [Mike said] they commence takin' on, and the sperit it begin to move um for true—for Brother Sturte-vant's ole nigger Cain, an' all uv um, they 'gin to kinder groan an' whine, an' fell erbout like er corn stalk in er storm, an' Brother Bridle, he begin er rubbin his hands and slappin' um together, an' scramblin' about on his knees, an' er cuttin' up like mad![9]

Though he was not a full-time minister, Mike himself could deliver a "sarmint" when the occasion demanded. Evidently he could be "loud" too, as he said of Parson James, for the hill boys called him "Mike Shouter" and Arch Coony said, ". . . his preachin' ain't nuthin' but loud holerin' no how!" Mike almost "wolloped" Arch for that statement. When the two met on a bear hunt, Mike challenged Arch, in whom he saw "the devil big as a bull," "Then I pulled off my ole Sunday-go-to-meetin' coat," Mike said, "an' slammed it down on a stump, an' sez I, 'Lay thar, ole Methodist, till I learn this coon some sense!' " Arch backed down, for he was not about to fight Mike, whose fame as a rough-and-tumble fighter almost equalled that of his talent for bear hunting.

Mike's most annoying detractors were people in the towns in Yazoo County, some of whom whispered that "bear hunting was his devotion, and preaching his sport." Mike had an Old Testament prophet's antago-nism toward towns and frequently was caustic about "the mean folks" in Satartia, Mechanicsburg, and Yazoo City—Sodom, Gomorrah, and Ninevah, respectively. Satartia, he said, was the jumping off place and a mud hole of civilizations; Mechanicsburg was a nest of thieves, and Yazoo City was no better; in fact, it was worse. Even Texas, Mike said, was a better place. When the depression of the late 1830's caused the merchants to cut off Mike's credit, he was angry because he sometimes had to hunt bear on Sunday, which was against his religion. But when a store-keeper sold Mike a pint of whiskey that was half tobacco juice, Mike almost lost his religion, for liquor was as essential to him as food. Whether he was hunting bear, telling a tale, or preaching a sermon, Mike fre-quently interrupted himself with the friendly suggestion, "Les licker." Indeed of his trinity of hunting, preaching, and drinking, it was difficult to say to which he devoted the most time and affection. And whether he hunted bear on Sunday, hunted evil in the towns in Yazoo County, or hunted a "doggery" for liquor, Mike Hooter was surely "a mighty hunter before the Lord."

Behind this legendary Mike Hooter stands an actual man, Michael Hooter, stalwart pioneer of Yazoo County, a man whose industry and religious faith produced a fortune and family that even the destruction of the Civil War could not entirely sweep away. Michael Hooter was born on Red River in Louisiana in 1791.[10] His parents had been granted land on the Red River in 1772, to which they had moved from the vicinity of Natchez, then British West Florida. About 1800 the Hooters moved to Jefferson County, Mississippi, and by 1833 Michael Hooter was living in Yazoo County as his name appears on county tax rolls in that year. He was obviously a small planter at that time, for he owned six slaves. During the following years Hooter acquired land and additional slaves and became a planter. Yazoo County, rich in soil and easily accessible by steamboat on the Yazoo River, rapidly became one of the leading cotton growing sections of the ante-bellum South, as the 37,500 bales of cotton shipped from Yazoo City in 1839 indicate.[11] By 1857 Michael Hooter owned twenty-five slaves, and in 1860 his real estate was valued at $15,600 and personal property at $27,670—no small fortune.

A community-minded man, Michael Hooter was active in political and religious affairs in his part of the county. When the Whigs nominated the frontier hero, William Henry Harrison, to oppose Martin Van Buren, who was popularly blamed for bank failures and depression in the South and West, "Tippecanoe Clubs" sprang up all over the country in support of Harrison for president in the Presidential campaign of 1840. Several "Tippecanoe Clubs" were organized in normally Democratic Mississippi, and Michael Hooter was very active in the club organized in Satartia.[12] In addition, Michael Hooter was a loyal and faithful member of the historic Mount Olivet Methodist church, still in existence in the southwestern part of Yazoo County.[13] A devout man, he required his household servants and his slaves to attend evening prayer service held at the back door of his house. The brass bell which he used to call his people to worship is now in the possession of Harold C. Fisher of Yazoo City, a descendant.

The Civil War reduced Hooter to near poverty, as it did most Southern planters. At the beginning of the war, he lived in a large brick house called "Hooter's Inn" in Mechanicsburg, and he owned property in Satartia and a plantation nearby. When the Union army moved across the county south towards Vicksburg in June, 1863, Hooter's home was burned as were all other buildings in Mechanicsburg. At the time of his death, about 1865, Hooter was broken in health and almost penniless.[14] According to family tradition, he was buried in the Mechanicsburg cemetery, though no tombstone marks his grave, few people being able to afford markers at the time.[15]

The story of Michael Hooter in family tradition and official records is cryptic and sober. These preserve only the bones of the man, devoid of his personality, and they make no hero of him. It took two young men with imagination and a sense of humor to do that. Both William C. Hall[16] and Henry Clay Lewis[17] grew up in Yazoo County, where Mike Hooter, an older man, was a well known character by the time they began writing humorous sketches similar to those appearing weekly in the *Spirit of the Times*.[18] Since these sketches emphasized unique local scenes and characters, Hall and Lewis quite naturally turned to Mike Hooter whose eccentricities lent themselves to humorous treatment.

Mike Hooter of the legend is essentially the creation of Hall, for Mike is the central character of Hall's "Yazoo Sketches,"[19] the first of which was printed in the New Orleans *Delta* in October, 1849.[20] In this short, humorous sketch, "Mike Hooter's Fight with the 'Bar,' " Hall selected Hooter's outstanding character traits, which were developed more fully in four succeeding sketches. Hall emphasized Mike's passion for bear hunting and skillfully allowed that to conflict with his equally ardent religious convictions. Inside a brief introductory framework, Hall wisely lets Mike "tell his story his own way, and in his peculiar vernacular," thereby characterizing Mike more clearly than objective description might have done and at the same time producing a rapidly moving narrative suggestive of the oral tale. Mike dramatizes his encounter with the bear and leads up to the climax but cleverly withholds the resolution until a listener finally draws it out of him. The dialect, rhythm, and structure of the sketch suggests the oral tale as it might be told by a raconteur, the setting and characters are realistic,[21] and the framework and delayed climax enhance the dramatic effect.

"Mike Hooter's Bar Story," second of the Yazoo Sketches,"[22] is superior to the first structurally, for it is told entirely in Mike's amusing dialect. The tale describes Ike Hamblin's embarrassment when a bear stole his gun, removed the flint, and casually walked away while Ike snapped at him. In addition to further characterizing Mike, the tale introduces some of Mike's neighbors, and it exaggerates the native intelligence of Yazoo bears so that the story has a fantastic element characteristic of the tall tale. "Mike Hooter's Fight with the Panther,"[23] third of the series, is much longer than the first two tales, and though the digressions about steam doctors and country courting are typical of the oral tale, the story lacks the direct impact of the first "Yazoo" sketch. On the other hand, the tale further develops Mike's eccentricities, his boasting, drinking, and belligerance.

The fourth sketch in the series, "How Sally Hooter Got Snake-Bit,"[24] develops Mike's religious biases, introduces more fully members of his family, and graphically presents a backwoods camp meeting. Though the tale is told in Mike's words, his daughter, Sally,[25] who is as obstinate as her father, shares the action which centers around her attempt to be fashionably dressed at the camp meeting. In Mike's words:

> . . . you see the wimmin folks 'bout where I lives, is h-ll fur new fashions, an' one day one uv them ar all-fired yankee pedlars come er long with er outlandish kind uv er jigamaree to make the wimmin's coat sorter stick out in the 'tother eend, an' the she's, they all put on one, case they 'sposed the he's would love to see it. Well, my Sal, she got monsous stuck up 'bout it, an' axed me to give her one; but I told her she had no more use for one, nor er settin' hen had for a midwife, an' I wouldn't do no such er thing, case how she was big enough thar at first.[26]

Sally was not to be foiled by an obstinate father, however; she took the large sausage her mother had prepared for Parson James and laced it around her waist for a bustle. She was in the height of fashion until religious fervor led to dancing which caused the sausage to come loose and fall about her ankles. Sally mistook the sausage for a snake, but her indomitable father saved her from the "serpent."[27] Although this tale has been one of the most popular of the sketches, it is actually less well constructed than the first of the series.

The fifth and last of Hall's "Yazoo Sketches," "How Mike Hooter Came Very Near 'Wolloping' Arch Coony," develops further Mike's love of boasting, his religious zeal, and his willingness to fight those who criticized him. The tale is drawn out unnecessarily and lacks the dramatic climax of the first two sketches of the series.

Within five months all of the "Yazoo Sketches" appeared in New Orleans newspapers, and three of them[28] were immediately reprinted in the *Spirit of the Times*, the New York weekly which circulated so widely the humorous sketches of Thorpe, Thompson, Baldwin, and others of the Southwestern school of frontier humor. Hall for some reason wrote no more sketches about Mike Hooter. Tradition states that, when Hall returned to Yazoo County on a visit, Hooter threatened him with a beating. Hall retorted that he would retaliate with his pen and was not molested.

Although Henry Clay Lewis wrote only one sketch that is associated with the Mike Hooter legend, he contributed an element of fantasy to the cycle of tales. Lewis's "The Indefatigable Bear-Hunter" appeared in his book of humorous sketches in 1850[29] and was reprinted in the *Spirit of the Times* shortly thereafter.[30] "Mik-hoo-tah," allegedly an Indian name meaning "the grave of bears," is the central character of the sketch. Since Lewis, unlike Hall, used fictitious names in all his sketches, his "Mik-hoo-tah" is obviously Mike Hooter whom he had known when he lived in Yazoo County. Though the locale of Lewis's sketch is the swamps of northeast Louisiana where he was practicing medicine at the time it was written, the hunting tactics, dialect, and boasting show that he almost certainly had Michael Hooter in mind. Mik, child of the woods and of unknown parentage, had earned his Indian name because of his slaughter of bears. His ambition was to be called *the* "bear-hunter of Ameriky." So great was his prowess that the "Big Bear of Arkansas" would "not have given him an hour's extra work," and at the sound of his horn, the bears drew lots to see which one would die that day. Though the Swamp Doctor had to amputate with a bowie knife Mik's leg which a bear had mangled in a fight, Mik went on to even greater glory when he killed another bear in close combat with splinters of the wooden leg which the Doctor had made for him. Lewis lets Mik tell the tale in his own dialect, and Mik's use of exaggeration and fantasy give the story the tall tale flavor of heroic adventures of Mike Fink and Davy Crockett.

In selecting an actual man as the basis for their humorous sketches, Hall and Lewis were following a well established tradition in frontier humor.[31] Furthermore, oral tales about Mike Hooter's exploits were current, some of them still being told in Yazoo County. As Arthur P. Hudson has said of the frontier writers, ". . . they had the wit to realize that something old in talking might look new in writing."[32] Hall and Lewis, therefore, chose Mike's most obvious eccentricities, dramatized them, and surrounded him with characteristic actions and attitudes, though some were perhaps not originally his. Such a process almost inevitably leads to the elevation of a purely local character to national prominence.

Mike Hooter was well on his way to such distinction when Hall inexplicably stopped writing about him, and when Lewis died at the early age of twenty-five. As a result, Mike Hooter never attained the sustained popularity of the truly national folk hero. Nevertheless, the myth itself and the process by which it was created illustrate the manner by which such heroes as Davy Crockett, Mike Fink, and Paul Bunyan rose to national fame. Though Mike Hooter was not so destined, he nevertheless remains one of the most intriguing minor figures of the old Southwestern frontier.

NOTES

1. See Constance Rourke, *Davy Crockett* (New York, 1934), *passim.*, and *ibid.*, *American Humor* (New York, 1931), *passim.*; and Walter Blair and Franklin J. Meine, *Mike Fink, King of Mississippi Keelboatmen* (New York, 1933), *passim.*

2. The "Yazoo Sketches," of which Mike Hooter is the central character, appeared originally in 1849 and 1850 in the New Orleans *Daily* and *Weekly Delta* and were immediately reprinted in the *Spirit of the Times*, New York weekly sporting journal. One or more of the sketches were reprinted in such anthologies of humor as Thomas A. Burke's *Polly Peablossom's Wedding; and Other Tales* (Philadelphia, 1851); W. E. Burton's *Cyclopedia of Wit and Humor* (New York, 1858, 1866); and T. C. Halliburton's two extensive collections, *Traits of American Humor, by Native Authors* (London, 1852, 1866, 1873), and *The Americans at Home; or Byeways, Backwoods, and Prairie* (London, 1854, 1873; Philadelphia, 1854?). Four of the sketches were recently reprinted in V.L.O. Chittick's *Ring-Tailed Roarers; Tall Tales of the American Frontier, 1830-50* (Caldwell, Idaho, 1943).

3. "Mike Hooter's Fight with the 'Bar,' A Yazoo Sketch," *Spirit of the Times*, XIX (Nov. 10, 1849), 38.

4. *Ibid.*

5. Ike, by the way, was mortally wounded in a fight with a bear but lived three days afterwards, long enough to enjoy a nice, juicy bear steak before he died. Mrs. T. C. Guion of Phoenix, Yazoo County, Miss., had this version of Ike's death from a great niece of Ike's wife.

6. "The Indefatigable Bear-Hunter," by Henry Clay Lewis, in *Odd Leaves from the Life of a Louisiana Swamp Doctor* (Philadelphia, 1850), p. 165.

7. "Mike Hooter's Fight with the 'Bar.'"

8. "How Sally Hooter Got Snake-Bit," in *Polly Peablossom's Wedding*, pp. 71-72.

9. *Ibid.*, p. 72.

10. Biographical information on Michael Hooter was obtained from his descendants, Chancery Court records in Yazoo City, U.S. Census reports, and newspaper files. Harold C. Fisher of Yazoo City, a descendant of Michael Hooter, kindly furnished much information.

11. *Yazoo City Whig*, Dec. 17, 1841.

12. The *Yazoo Banner*, Whig weekly, published at Benton, county seat of Yazoo County, carried notices of political meetings throughout 1840 in which Hooter's name appears. On Jan. 5 he was appointed on the Committee of Vigilance of the "Tippecanoe Club" at Satartia. On May 15 he was appointed to a committee for nominating officers for the Club. On June 5 he was present for a Club meeting, and on Aug. 7 he was a member of the "Central Tippecanoe Club." At the public meeting of Whigs called at the death of President Harrison, Hooter was on the Committee of Correspondence.

13. J. B. Cain, *Methodism in the Mississippi Conference* (Jackson, 1939), p. 73, states that Michael Hooter was one of the trustees to whom a deed was made July 5, 1851, for property for a new church. Michael's brother, James, was also one of the trustees.

14. Family tradition records an instance of Hooter's deep sense of obligation. During the war he co-signed a note with a minister friend who soon thereafter fled the country. Hooter struggled to prevent foreclosure on the note but was unable to do so. At his death he instructed his children to sell enough of his property to pay the debt which was not his in the first place.

15. Sally Hooter, the daughter mentioned in the tales, built a house in Mechanicsburg about 1866 which is still occupied by her descendants.

16. Biographical information on Hall is meager. He was born in Yazoo County about 1819, son of John B. Hall, early settler, formerly of Nashville. He supposedly attended Transylvania University and then became a journalist in New Orleans. He died in Yazoo County about 1865. I am indebted to Mrs. T. C. Guion, Phoenix, Miss., for this information about her ancestor.

17. Born in 1825 in Charleston, S. C., Henry Lewis came to Yazoo City about 1836. He graduated from the Louisville Medical Institute, Louisville, Ky., in 1846 and practiced medicine in northeast Louisiana until his death in 1850. Under the pseudonym "Madison Tensas, M. D.," he published humorous sketches in the *Spirit of the Times* and in his one book, *Odd Leaves from the Life of a Louisiana Swamp Doctor* (1850). See my "Henry Clay Lewis, Alias 'The Louisiana Swamp Doctor,'" *Bulletin of the Medical Library Association*, XLIII (Jan., 1955), 58-73.

18. Many of these sketches were contributed from Mississippi. Among Mississippi contributors to the *Spirit* are "Obadiah Oilstone" (Phillip B. January), "The Turkey Runner" (Gov. A. G. McNutt), "Falconbridge" (Jonathan Falconbridge Kelley), in addition to the unidentified "Azul," "The Man in the Swamp," "Yazoo," "Kurnell Shingle Splitter," and "Curnill Jenks."

19. Identification of Hall as the author of these sketches is based on Judge Robert Bowman's "Yazoo County's Contribution to Mississippi Literature," *Publications of the Mississippi Historical Society*, X (1909), 301-303, and on a letter written by Mary Bonney Fields, niece of Hall, published in the *Yazoo Sentinel*, Yazoo City, Jan. 20, 1926, and reprinted in the *Yazoo City Herald*, Aug. 7, 1952. Chittick in *Ring-Tailed Roarers*, p. 307, states that W. E. Burton named Hall as the author in the *Cyclopedia of Wit and Humor*, and speculates that Hall "is quite possibly" the author of all the "Yazoo" sketches.

20. The *Delta*, a Democratic organ, was started by Denis Corcoran in 1845 as a rival of George W. Kendall's famous *Picayune*. The *Delta* staff split in 1849

and the *Daily True Delta* was established. Hall's sketches appeared in the *True Delta* and the *Weekly Delta* over the signature "H." or "Printer's Devil." Some were unsigned.

21. U.S. Census reports for 1840 and 1850 list most of Mike Hooter's neighbors who appear under their own names in the "Yazoo Sketches," including John Potter, Samuel Dilley, Archibald Coody (Coony in the tales), Moses Hambelin, and Dr. C. D. Bonney.

22. *Delta*, Jan. 6, 1850.

23. *Ibid.*, Feb. 17, 1850. The editor wrote the day before, "Our paper of Sunday will contain a great amount of valuable, interesting and varied matter. Among other original articles, there will be an excellent Panther Story, by our popular sketch writer."

24. *Ibid.*, March 25, 1850.

25. Chittick, *Ring-Tailed Roarers*, p. 307, erroneously calls Sally Mike's sister.

26. *Polly Peablossom's Wedding*, p. 71.

27. Mrs. Guion states that an old-timer in Yazoo County swears that Sally actually wore the sausage bustle.

28. "Mike Hooter's Bar Story," Jan. 26, 1850; "Mike Hooter's Fight with the Panther," March 9, 1850; and "How Sally Hooter Got Snake-Bit," April 13, 1850.

29. *Odd Leaves from the Life of a Louisiana Swamp Doctor*, pp. 164-175.

30. XX (April 20, 1850), 9. Lewis had previously published four sketches in the *Spirit*: "Cupping on the Sternum; Or, A Leaf from the Life of a Medical Student," XV (Aug. 16, 1845), 25; "A Tight Race Considerin'," XVI (Nov. 28, 1846), 40; "A Leaf from the Life of a 'Swamp Doctor,'" XVII (May 29, 1847), 14 [reprinted in his book as "Valerian and the Panther"]; and "Winding up a Mississippi Bank," XVII (Oct. 2, 1847), 2.

31. Most of the major Southwestern humorists maintained that they were writing about real people and actual conditions. See, for example, A. B. Longstreet's preface to *Georgia Scenes* (New York, 1840), p. iv, and W. T. Thompson's "To the Reader," *Major Jones' Courtship* (Philadelphia, 1879), pp. 5-7. William T. Porter expresses the same conviction in his preface to *The Big Bear of Arkansas, and Other Sketches* (Philadelphia, 1858), pp. viii-xii.

32. *Humor of the Old Deep South* (New York, 1936), pp. 16-17.

David Crockett, The Legend and the Symbol

James Atkins Shackford

The explanation for Crockett's becoming and remaining a national legendary figure has six primary facets: the imaginative temper of the unsettled West; the imaginative temper of the settled East; the qualities of the man himself with reference to the tempers of the time; the political culture of the period; the use of David as a symbol by both political parties, and their employment of a *national press* to establish that symbol clearly in the minds and thoughts of a whole nation; Crockett's dramatic death at the Alamo, which raised him to the level of national martyr; and the pursuit by latter-day writers of "Davy of the typescript."

What we may call the *imaginative* temper of the backwoods, as distinct from its economic, political, pragmatic aspects, may perhaps best be viewed by looking at the "tall tale" of Western literature. Those who go with life and limb into the unknown wildernesses of a strange and forbidding land, necessarily develop both elastic horizons and elastic imaginations. Strange sights, strange animals, unaccustomed noises, unforeseen experiences, and completely novel combinations of life continually confront this social creature in his solitary backwoods fastness. His imagination must be prepared to face anything, he must be able to believe in the possibility of all things.

Counterbalancing that credulous imagination is a trait characteristic of the thinking animal, a sense of play, of funning—an anchor and a balance which pulls him back toward center when he moves too far forward on the peripheral extreme. The physical basis for this lies perhaps in the tension and reflex of the neuron itself.

The unsocial situation of separation and isolation in which the backwoods family spent its nights and days stimulated this sense of play by making special demands upon it. Entertainment was scarce, opportunities

From *David Crockett: The Man and the Legend* by James Atkins Shackford. Chapel Hill: University of North Carolina Press, 1956. Reprinted by permission of the publisher.

for convivial get-togethers infrequent. Necessarily, therefore, every harvest or house-raising became a social and playful occasion, and ordinary prosaic affairs were cast in the entertaining form of the "tall tale." Political speeches in the backwoods were no more to be divorced from entertainment, from tall tales, from picnic, frolic, barbecue, stomp-down, than freckles from a boy who lives in the sun. Woe be to the political candidate who did not know this need for entertainment or who, knowing it, could not cater to it naturally. This urgent need for social entertainment is also a partial explanation of the fact that the tall tale was *so* tall. Yet, though the imagination had to be elastic so as to be prepared for any danger, it was necessary also to guard against magnifying minor danger to the proportions of major peril—against making a bear of a rat, a lion of a bob cat, and thus creating fear and paralysis in place of courage and action.

It was necessary to preserve balance and sanity by joking about danger, to prick the taut nerve and thus return bursting tensions to normal. And so the wonders were made *ridiculously* wonderful. Each hunter must outlie every other about the nature of the marvels which had personally befallen him, until one bestrides a tornado and is immediately outclassed by another who makes a perambulator of the sun, in a sharpening of those faculties in play which, in the backwoods, must ever be sharp in dead earnest. Hence that strange array of "varments" in backwoods folklore: the creature so curiously adapted to the steepest mountains, with legs shorter on one side than on the other, to be caught only on one of its infrequent visits into the lowlands, where it could only run in circles; or that other, even more difficult to catch, that could dig a hole in a flash, plop into it, and pull it in after him.

I feel sure that this temper characterized our backwoods at a very early time in our history. It lived for a long time only in the unwritten cultural heritage of the isolated Southern and Western wonderlands of the forests, and up and down the rivers, the highways of that day. About 1830 it began to become literate and vocal, and to get into the quick-freeze mediums of print. Two of the very earliest products of this new literacy were David Crockett's *Autobiography*, by a real backwoodsman himself; and Augustus Longstreet's *Georgia Scenes*, by a literary man making use of those materials for his own literary purposes. It developed through a long line of humorists, and finally culminated in Mark Twain. The original strain at last petered out as the primitive conditions of life out of which it had grown disappeared.

What was there about David Crockett that tended to typify those qualities characteristic of the imaginative, tall-tale temper of the backwoods?

First of all, he was one of them. To use one of their own expressions, appropriately modified for print, he was "common as coon spore in a barley patch." He was a "gentleman from the cane." He had a keen sense of humor in the Western tradition—the broad and exaggerated, the hyperbolic and vast, or the same in reverse, the sly and dry understatement, as revealed in numerous incidents ("he beat me exactly *two* votes . . .though I have always believed that many other things had been as fairly done as that same count"). Further, he had certain characteristics which were strange, different—which made people talk. I think of his unusual determination to cross that swollen river in midwinter to get his keg of powder, his going after the bear at night alone and not turning back until he had got it, his setting out as a child through knee-deep snow in the dark to walk miles in order to escape from his employer. Society today may look upon such adventures as more foolhardy than wise. In the backwoods the qualities of unusual strength, unusual perseverance, extraordinary courage, unbelievable determination, even in connection with what may *now* appear to be relatively trivial matters, were the measures of a man because they were in a very real sense the measures of life. Crockett so excelled in these qualities that when an incredible story was to be told, the fixing on Crockett about whom to tell it lent it that air of reality and credibility which made the story delicious to its hearers.

Also, there were other qualities about the man which simply made him a "character"—the relation of his life as early as 1833 had been titled "The Eccentricities of," and incidentally had been quite popular; and the defense of him by a paper in his own district had granted his "eccentricities."

There were the lovable qualities of good sportsmanship and good showmanship (the occasion when S. H. Stout as a small boy stared at him in church) which made it *fun* to tell a story "on him" because of his reaction to the stories ("I'd wring *his* tail off!"), or because of the titillation of the listener in his imagining of David's reactions, either to the story or to the situation in which the imaginary story placed him. Yet these were not qualities which tended to make him a butt of a joke, for not of such is a lovable legend made.

In brief, Crockett possessed in the extreme many of those abilities which the backwoods required and admired, and in terms of which it judged a man. He possessed also the personable qualities which led tall tellers to make him the center of their tales. There was that in the man which tended to make him a *local* tradition and character long before literature or the press began to catch him up. Being, in his person, the essence of the backwoods of his locale, since his locale was the nucleus of the whole tradition he was the apt representative and symbol of the whole Western culture.

The imaginative temper of the East, however different from that of the West, was in a sense complementary and easily capable of accepting David Crockett, *properly spruced up*, as the symbol of its concept of the Westerner. The age was romantic. Eastern society, as compared with the West, was relatively settled and uneventful. The backwoods was almost as far, in spirit, from the drawing rooms of New York society as from the ball rooms of London. Yet it was close enough geographically and in the pages of the newspaper, to be especially piquant to jaded but uncritical imaginations. James Fenimore Cooper picked up the tales of a romantic age, transferred them to a local setting, and supplied pabulum for the hungry maw of a romantic East. His *Spy* (1821), *Pioneers* (1823), *Last of the Mohicans* (1826), and *Prairie* (1827) not only fed the romantic appetite, but helped to set the pattern for and to stimulate avid interest in a highly romanticized picture of the backwoods where David was actually living. We have never been able to erase from our literature, and I suppose now we never shall, this romantic young girl's dream of all the beauties and glories of the backwoods and of backwoodsmen who talk like little Lord Fauntleroys in buckskin, though any three words from the real vocabulary of an actual backwoodsman would send the blood to her cheeks and cruelly shock her artificial modesty.

The *literary* versions of the backwoods, then, had come into being as a delightful new and stimulating toy with which to escape the "vapours" of a settled society. As the backwoods flowed into print, the gentleman and the lady became adventurers-on-their-own-terms in a backwoods the more real because physically closer than Irving's halls of the Alhambra in lands beyond the sea. There resulted an orgiastic revelling in the romantic backwoods. Into the literature of the East went this local legend, this David Crockett of the West, out of ephemeral tradition into solid print. This was the situation, the imaginative temper in which the legend grew. Other factors, of course, helped it to grow—helped an historical figure, David Crockett, to replace, so to speak, the literary creation, Natty Bumppo, as the national symbol of the backwoodsman.

The next most important factor, I believe, aside from the historical juncture which made the backwoods play such a dominant theme and occupy such an essential role in the affairs of the moment, was David's rise to prominence in politics and the consequent manipulations by the press of his "public person." This aspect of the fable has been developed by Professor Walter Blair in his article "Six Davy Crocketts."[1] Four of the six Crockett's that he discusses—the two Crocketts produced by the

Jackson papers, one while David was pro-Jackson, the other when he became anti-Jackson; and the two produced similarly by the Whig papers before and after his "switch"—are the political Crockett of fiction produced by the press. In the light of the story that lies behind us, elaboration on that point is unnecessary here. Simply stated, while Crockett was a Jacksonian, the Democratic press polished him up with little reference to the true man, and the Whig papers, with just as little regard for fact, tried to laugh him out of Congress as a blundering bull in the sanctified halls of gentlemen. When David changed his allegiances, the Democratic papers were prone to take up the old line initiated by the Whigs and enlarge upon that, while the Whigs refined upon the earlier tradition which the Democrats had so carefully built up.

The point of our explanation here is that through all of this, coming as it did at a time when the American press had just vanquished all barriers, extending itself even into the far reaches of the backwoods, the name of David Crockett, scattered to the four corners of the America of that day, slipped willy nilly into that image which Western and Eastern minds alike, Whig as well as Democrat, carried about in their realistic or romantic imaginations—the idea or *ideaform* of the American backwoodsman. David became the body. He fitted into the realistic Western concept as he was. He was dressed up, first by the Democrats and then by the Whigs, to fit into the romantic concepts of the East. The whole tradition was furiously stirred by Charles Brockden Brown, by Fenimore Cooper, by many others, in fact, by history itself. The speeches which Easterners carefully wrote for him on his Eastern tour, speeches peppered with the condiments of backwoods vernacular, humor, and homeliness, yet smooth enough not to offend any romantic sensibility; were but one of the more obvious and conscious exploitations of a popular public taste. The theoretical backwoodsman was present in the minds of all, East and West. David won his right to represent his class in his own neighborhoods in a succession of localities as he moved across the state. The exploitation on a national scale of the public taste, and of Crockett to satisfy that taste, had a tremendous effect in establishing him in the minds, thoughts, and conversations of people all over America. It played, that is, a tremendous part in fixing him as the symbol in the cultural tradition that lives in a people's talk and memories. In that early exploitation of a national taste, the early Crockett books and such a play as *The Lion of the West* contributed their significant parts.

To attempt to say which factor was of greatest importance is meaningless. Without the newspapers David would have been a local legend, and would doubtless have survived as such for a time. Whether that tradition would have grown or dwindled one cannot positively state. Watching what has happened to it, even with the help of the press, I suspect that it would not have survived to our day, except in the most isolated and occasional instances. The historical man would have survived for his *Autobiography*—if for no other reasons because he symbolizes aspects of our history. On the other hand, the newspapers could not pick up just any man as a symbol of the West. Without David's personification of the backwoods, without the man himself, his experience, his slow rise to the point where he had become, with all his native endowments, *capable* politically and personally of *being exploitable* as the national symbol of the type, the mere universality of the press unaided would not alone have sufficed to initiate a legend. He had to be authentic to be acceptable to the West. Given David and what he was, the press did create a temporary, more or less homogeneous national tradition of the backwoods, with David as its central figure. Yet its success was predicated upon the imaginative tempers of both East and West, nor could it have occurred at any very far-removed juncture of our history.

Finally, David's death at the Alamo at approximately the height of his greatest renown in a fight that itself seemed to symbolize the growing, expanding, liberating destiny of America, a death that seemed to be the final bravest act of which a brave man was capable, the giving of all material things even unto his own body and blood in defense of a spiritual idea—so fired the imagination of America as to bring to volcanic heat the miscellaneous sediments of the times and to fuse the softer and rather evanescent materials of a local age into the granite or obsidian which appears for awhile to outwear time itself. The peculiar circumstances of that battle likewise allowed the imagination free play, for no reliable witness of much of what happened there survived, and history was incapable of cluttering up the event with fact. History, indeed, came to the aid of the imagination in its record of the pass of Thermopylae, and helped to glorify the Alamo in similes as grand as the records of man could supply.

These seem to be the most important factors which have created and kept alive the mythological "Davy," so far as he is alive. There is another type of mythological "Davy" who seems to live principally in the carols of folklore romanticizers. He lives in literature mainly at the expense of the historical Crockett, and in recent years he has crowded the *Autobiography* out of anthologies and the historical person out of literary histories. This contemporary literary romanticism is, I think, a variety of sentimental romanticism indulged in by sedentary folk to escape dull reality. The exciting and untempered zeal of rediscovering our origins all clothed in the quaintness and charm of time and distance stimulates imaginations dulled by the prose of fact. Such "rediscovery" also appeals to the self-interest of the conventional patriot of my town, my state, my section, my nation, and all of the other multitudinous ramifications of *me.* In an age which combines the loss of a physical backwoods (or even of a simple rural life that would accord with the nature and instincts of man) with a nationalism in which self-interest is stretched tight by powerful national rivalries, I suppose it was, and is, in a sense, inevitable. I will not, therefore, say more about it here. It is only necessary to trace briefly the path of the literary myth for those who may wish to pursue their folklore in literary adaptations.

We have noted in the appendix the initial play which helped to fuse a backwoods tradition, both real and literary, with the person of David, *The Lion of the West.* We have noted the excessive tall-tale elements of an exaggerated literary sort which were incorporated into the first *Life* of Crockett, in its original issue and in its reissue as the *Eccentricities,* and which partially created and partially helped to perpetuate the literary legend. We have further cited the various newspaper creations, and such novels as those of William Alexander Caruthers and James Strange French which also helped to give sustenance to the literary figure. We have pointed out in appendix three the creation of spurious lore in the *Texas Exploits* of Richard Penn Smith, guessing that this was perhaps the first purely literary exploitation, completely unconcerned with politics. One very important early medium, probably only slightly related to political motives, we have not heretofore discussed—the "Davy" Crockett Almanacs.

Miss Rourke's bibliographical chapter devotes a great deal of space to giving an almost complete list of these "Davy" almanacs, and I will not repeat the list here. The first Almanac issued, Volume I, Number I, published in Nashville, Tennessee, was *not* copyrighted in the name of the man whose life we have undertaken to tell, the *David* Crockett in whose name the *Autobiography* was copyrighted: rather, it was copyrighted in the name of that hallmark of the myth, "Davy" Crockett. The masthead motto read, "Go ahead, or Davy Crockett's Almanac of Wild Sports of the West and Life in the Backwoods." It was published by Snag and Sawyer! This Almanac is a veritable mare's nest of fictional tall tales coupling the names of Davy, Ben Hardin, Black Hawk (Adam Huntsman), and others. It is as disrespectful of or indifferent to fact as the fabricators of children's bedtime stories. Indeed, it is their very power to create gargantuan hoax that has so endeared the Almanacs to lovers of the tall-tale and patriot ferreters after the Great American Epic.

Huntsman's wooden leg has taken on flesh and blood in the Almanac woodcuts. The "autobiographical" details of Davy snub David's own account which had come off the press six or seven months earlier—but that is fitting, seeing that David had just as completely ignored, in his correspondence or in anything else he wrote or said, the "Davy" almanacs. The first issue had been copyrighted late in 1834 for 1835; the second, copyrighted in late 1835 for 1836, was printed this time not *by* "Davy," but *for* him, inasmuch as all the world knew that David had been gone from Tennessee since the preceding November. The third issue I have not seen, but the fourth, published in late 1837 for 1838, was printed, according to the title page which for some reason the lovers of the almanac tall tales suddenly decided to take quite literally, by "his heirs." The fifth (Number I of Volume 2), was published by "Ben Harding," as was the next issue. By 1842 (Volume 2, Number 4), the publication had moved to "New York and Philadelphia," though fortunately Ben Harding had now learned the correct spelling of his own name and writes it *Hardin*. For some reason this native Kentuckian copyrighted it in the eastern district of twpennsylvania! The Davy myth was now widespread, especially had the seed been sown in Pennsylvania, and it afforded a plentiful harvest in many places.

From this point on, it had not even the identity of geographical locale to connect it with David, and I refer the interested reader to Miss Rourke for further bibliography on the subject. Yet I must point out one fact: even so recently as the middle of the Twentieth Century, Mr. Joseph Leach, in a published adaptation from a book he is writing, could say: "These [almanac] sketches may indeed represent a kind of collaboration because, before leaving for Texas, Crockett himself *reportedly* had prepared enough material to fill six full issues." And: "The [almanac] sketches faithfully transcribe the backwoodsman's realistic vernacular."[2] I have pointed out to Mr. Leach the total error of both statements, as well as the "slanting" in his use of the word "reportedly." For I have not found even the slightest suspicion of a trace of a connection between David Crockett and the Davy almanacs, except of course in the claims of the almanacs themselves. As for the vernacular, its realism is as spurious and artificial as the faked Crockett vernacular in the 1833 *Life*.

In my opinion, David neither sponsored nor in any way contributed to these almanacs, nor were they issued for David or by or for his heirs. They were part of the exploitation of his renown which yet goes on; and they represented that point, I think, at which a low type of literary exploitation joined hands with the economic need of inferior literary ability. It was a sort of shot-gun marriage of the economic and literary motives, and could hardly be expected to be of a very high quality, though some folklorists profess to see in it pristine specimens of the native American Legend out of which the Great National Epic *almost* arose.[3] Perhaps my own taste is at fault. Fine or poor, as history they were completely false and spurious, and as such here deserve, at the very most, a questionably honorable mention. However, in the creation and perpetuation of the literary "Davy," they were one among a number of important mediums.

This is the field which the Twentieth Century Scholar has chosen to pitch upon and to cultivate to the exclusion of the real Crockett. If one cares to pursue the literary mythological figure in the present century, he may add such names to those I have given him as Vance Randolph, John A. and Alan Lomax, B. A. Botkin, Julia Beazley, Carl Sandburg, Irwin Shapiro, V. L. O. Chittick, Edwin Justice Mayer, Franklin J. Meine, and Walter Blair. Peace be to them. But let them be reminded that the historical David and his classic *Autobiography* need, and strongly deserve, their interest in history. Let them recall V. L. Parrington's observation that the best joke David and his exploiters ever played, they "played upon posterity that has swallowed the myth whole and persists in setting a romantic halo on his coonskin cap."[4]

Our narrative began with the ending of the old, old story of man's long migration westward from his cradle somewhere in central Asia a million years ago. Slowly and feebly he moved outward. Millennia by millennia he crept onward. Finally, only in the last century and on our own North American continent, he at length completed, in a dramatic burst of speed, his thousands-of-years-old transmigration of a planet, and conquered the final geographical boundaries of this globe. One frame for David Crockett's biography is the vanishing frontier—the frontier vanishing not simply from America, but from the world; not merely from the scene of a nation or of a time, but from the scene of all mundane nations and of all earthly time.

David Crockett is a significant figure in terms of that old story. To follow his career from North Carolina across that great Appalachian barrier to east Tennessee, then to middle Tennessee, thence to the mighty Mississippi, and finally to Texas is to follow the last far-flinging lines of the frontier in its concluding marches back to the Pacific. To follow his life is to see repeated therein much of the history of the old kind of man and his old frontiers—the barbarous rudiments of his beginnings, where brute force hewed roughly at the inimical environments; his quench-less wanderlust for new, and ever new physical horizons; his slow and tedious advance in knowledge, in understanding, and in the creation of a primitive culture; his gradual rise out of a blind wilderness into elemen-tary forms of social living and law; and finally his subduing all physical boundaries until the continents had been reduced into national constitu-tions and governments. David Crockett is the archetype of the age-old pioneer, slowly mastering the world's physical frontiers.

In another real sense this narrative concludes with the beginning of a new story and so is pitched within a new frame. By the very act of con-quering geographical barriers, man created a different sort of world and set himself upon a new and entirely different sort of quest. Having learned to live with, then to master, all physical frontiers until he reduced the world and the nations to one small demesne, man must now learn to live with and to master the frontiers of the human mind, heart, and spirit until he reduces that demesne to one home. Man's new frontier is the spiritual frontier of universal brotherhood where all men are their brothers' keep-ers. Not until he masters this frontier will man make a home of his narrowed world.

David Crockett's greatest value is as a symbol of the new man striking into this new and spiritual frontier. His life and career depict the great formative struggles in the birth of this new philosophy on this new conti-nent. Crockett did not espouse the philosophy of the old physical man who judged people in terms of externals—ancestry, caste, riches, or fame —holding some men of value and some worthless and setting one group to war against another. Instead, he grasped the philosophy of the new spiri-tual man who judges a people intrinsically in terms of their inherent worth and their divine potential in a universe where all are the sons of God and where all before God are of inalienable value and entitled to equal dignity and justice. This passionate spiritual faith in the worth of all personality, extending beyond religious shibboleths to legal, social, political, and economic areas, is the faith of the new and spiritual frontier —and the only faith which can make man's shrunken world his home. This faith is so new that to date it has prevailed only among small groups and for limited periods. The furthest advance along this new frontier on any grand scale in all history is the story of the rise of the American civili-zation. Even that civilization has fallen far below its aim, and sometimes seems to prefer its own destruction to a radical reaffirmation of that new faith. David Crockett symbolizes the essential man, that vital "common stock," that has played a most important part in this new land in the shaping of that philosophy of the new spiritual frontier.

Here, then, is Crockett: symbol both of the pioneer of that old world of physical frontiers, just ended; and of the pioneer of the new spiritual frontier just beginning, attacking those barriers that separate man from his fellows and that threaten to make of his world a Buchenwald. To our own generation has been bequeathed the decision as to whether we shall follow David Crockett into this new and unconquered spiritual wilderness, master it, and make of our world a home; or shall violently explode back into barbarism and begin anew that weary, age-old pioneering of the old physical man along the blind, physical boundaries of a creature existence.

NOTES

1. W. Blair, "Six Davy Crocketts," *Southwest Review*, XXV (July, 1940), 443-462.

2. J. Leach, "Crockett's Almanacs and the Typical Texan," *Southwest Review*, Summer, 1950. Italics added by author.

3. R. M. Dorson, in *Davy Crockett: American Comic Legend*, has published a volume of these almanac stories to which the reader may refer. Professor Howard Mumford Jones in a preface to Dorson's book assures us that they have truly epic proportions, comparing them to the Maginogion. Dorson Followed Jones' suggestion and made the comparison elaborate: "Davy Crockett and the Heroic Age," in the *Southern Folklore Quarterly*, VI (June, 1942), 95-102.

4. V. L. Parrington, *Main Currents in American Thought*, II, 179.

Who Wrote "The Harp of a Thousand Strings"?

George Kummer

Of the eccentrics who flourished in the backwoods areas of America in the first half of the nineteenth century, the Hardshell Baptist preachers were among the most amusing to outsiders. Travelers through the South and West found diversion in contemplating the oddities of these sermon-izers, who, unlike the clergy of most other denominations, made no bones about chewing tobacco or drinking whiskey in public.[1] Dead set against reformers who wished to deprive man of his innocent worldly comforts like mint juleps, they were sometimes called "Ten-Gallon Baptists" or "Whiskey Baptists." According to Edward Eggleston, who was both literary local colorist and social historian, the travesty of Calvinism by which they justified their liberal principles was expressed somewhat as follows: "Ef you're elected you'll be saved; ef you a'n't you'll be damned. God'll take keer of his elect. It's a sin to run Sunday-schools or Temp'rence s'cities, or to send missionaries. You let God's business alone. What is to be will be, and you can't hender it."[2]

Depending for a livelihood on such secular activities as trading on the Mississippi and its confluents, most Hardshell preachers were only part-time clergymen. As a rule they were poorly trained and their sermons were frequently so fantastic that the temptation to mimic them was irresistible. Of the many burlesques which resulted, perhaps the best known is "The Harp of a Thousand Strings." The scene of this harangue was the reputedly rowdy village of Waterproof, Louisiana (then in Missis-sippi), and the preacher was an old flatboat captain, who had brought his broadhorn there to trade with the gamblers, river pirates, and other reck-less characters said to infest the place. As a preacher he may have been somewhat deficient in homiletics, but as a businessman he had a deep

From *Ohio Historical Quarterly*, 67 (July 1958), 221-231. Reprinted by permission of the publisher.

understanding of the great science of advertising. The subtlety with which he departed from his text to remark that speaking of liquor, he had on board "as good an artikel uv them kind uv sperits . . . as ever was fotched down the Mississippi" is proof that he knew almost as much about the technique of the commercial as present-day radio and television sponsors know.

His sermon enjoyed widespread and long-drawn-out popularity. During the late 1850's it appeared in newspapers in every section of the Union. Versions of it crossed two oceans and circulated in both England and Australia.[3] In 1882 Henry Watterson declared that it was "one of the notable stories which have gone the rounds of the American press in the last forty years, which yet linger on the stage, appearing and reappearing at intervals, as if to take a fresh lease on life, and which are thoroughly characteristic in tone, color, and action of the era to which we owe Simon Suggs and Sut Lovingood."[4] Even in our own day, oral versions of "The Harp" are still extant in rural areas; as recently as the summer of 1946 one folklorist heard it preached in Moberly, Missouri.[5]

Authorities disagree as to the authorship of the sermon. The influential *Literary History of the United States* gives the piece to the Rev. Henry Taliaferro Lewis, a Methodist minister from Mississippi,[6] but Jay B. Hubbell, in his careful and accurate *The South in American Literature, 1607-1900*, says it is by William Penn Brannan.[7] Though the piece has been claimed for still other writers, among them Andrew Harper and Joshua S. Morris, most of the evidence points to either Lewis or Brannan. The present paper attempts to show that Brannan, an itinerant portrait painter and journalist from Cincinnati, has the better title.[8]

Probably the earliest appearance of "The Harp" in book form occurred in Thomas Powell's *Chit-chat of Humor, Wit, and Anecdote* in 1857.[9] Powell indicated no source, but William Evans Burton, who printed the sermon the following year in his *Cyclopaedia of Wit and Humor*, said that it "first appeared in a New Orleans paper."[10] Both Powell and Burton seem to have reproduced the version found in the *Spirit of the Times* for September 29, 1855, which attributes the waif to "a New Orleans paper." This was likely the *Daily Crescent*; at least "The Harp" appeared there with no indication of its source on September 10, 1855. But it had appeared elsewhere before that. As early as July 10, 1855, it had found its way into the *Ohio State Journal*, where it was credited to the Brandon, Mississippi *Register*, certainly an error, as the only paper published in Brandon at that time was called the *Republican*. No file of the *Republican* for 1854 or 1855 has survived, but in 1879 Colonel A. J. Frantz, then editor of that paper, reprinted "The Harp" there with the following introduction:

> This celebrated Hard-Shell sermon was first published in the *Brandon Republican* in the year 1854—twenty-five years ago. Its authorship has been claimed by various persons in all sections of the country, but it was first written out in full for the press by Rev. Henry T. Lewis in our office, and first made its appearance in the *Republican*. Mr. Harper [the editor in 1854] only assisted in "fixing up the description of the preacher," which accompanied the publication.[11]

That Colonel Frantz's phrase, "first written out in full for the press," implies that oral versions of "The Harp" were in circulation before its appearance in the *Republican* will, I believe, become clear in the course of the discussion.

The chief source of information about the Rev. Henry Taliaferro Lewis is a small book entitled *Harp of a Thousand Strings, with Waifs of Wit and Pathos*, compiled by Lewis' daughter, Mrs. Anne Roberts, copyrighted in 1907, but printed without indication of place. From this we learn that Lewis (1823-1870) was not only a Methodist minister of parts but also a successful temperance lecturer, and that though he "never provoked a smile" in the pulpit, he was an irresistible comedian on the lecture platform (pp. 7-10). In support of her father's claim to "The Harp," a version of which she printed in her volume, Mrs. Roberts cited the following clipping, which she says appeared in the *Louisville Courier-Journal* in the summer of 1881:

> A resident of Frankfort, writes to This and That: "I am satisfied that the author of 'The Harp of a Thousand Strings' sermon, was the Rev. Henry T. Lewis, formerly living in Memphis, Tenn., but afterwards a citizen of Homer, La.
>
> Mr. Lewis was a gentleman of rare ability; a poet, and a wit and humorist of the first order. He was also a Methodist clergyman of the highest standing; of unimpeachable integrity. He has hosts of friends, all over the Southern States and South West; from Tennessee to the Gulf, and from Florida to Texas, in many parts of which region he labored, as lecturer and preacher. When he resided in Memphis, a few years before the war, I heard him repeatedly say (or rather, admit, in answer to the direct question), that he was the author of that sermon.

In answer to an inquiry of my own, he made substantially, the following statement: As a matter of fact, he supposed that an old Hardshell Baptist preacher, navigating a trading broadhorn, or flat boat, down the Mississippi to New Orleans, away back in the second or third decade of the Nineteenth Century, did tie up one Sunday, at Waterproof, La., and delivered [sic] a sermon, something like, or rather having a distant resemblance to the one written out by Mr. Lewis, and published in a Mississippi paper. At all events, such was the purport of an anecdote that circulated from mouth to mouth, for a long time in that region, previous to any publication. At last, after having heard the story, told in a hundred different ways, by a hundred different people, Mr. Lewis concluded to write it out and make it as absurdly humorous as he could. After having done so, he read it to the editor of a country paper (Andrew Harper), of the 'Brandon Republican,' Brandon Miss., 1854, who was living on the circuit, that he was then traveling. Finding it such a grand hit, others claimed its authorship, but Mr. Lewis cared nothing for this; his ambition was to do good to his fellow men and not to win renown as a humorist." (pp. 19-20)

On the basis of "a resident of Frankfort's" testimony Professor Arthur Palmer Hudson in his *Humor of the Old Deep South* gave the sermon to Lewis.[12] But the text of "The Harp" which Professor Hudson reproduced in this anthology is from the *Spirit of the Times* rather than from Mrs. Roberts' book, a puzzling inconsistency in view of the fact that Mrs. Roberts' text contains several passages not found in the *Spirit of the Times*. Thus at the end of the seventh paragraph of the sermon as printed by Professor Hudson,[13] Mrs. Roberts presented the following text:

And then thar's the Presbyterians; they ar' a high-minded kind uv folks. They bleeve in edicating their preachers, and so they remind me uv a paper kite, fur the stronger the wind blows the higher the kite flies, until the string breaks or it loses its tail, and then it dashes headlong, down, down, slap dash right into a brier patch; and that is just the way uv the Presbyterians, my brethring, fur the more edication they have the higher they fly, an' you know a kite has to have ballast to make it fly level; and, my dear brethring, that's just the way uv the Presbyterians, for their salary is their ballast, and the more you give 'em the levelar are their heads an' the higher they fly, an' ef you lighten their ballast they kick up a dust and skedaddle away like a wild hoss running away in harness until they find some place whar thar's plenty uv ballast, fur the text says: "He played on a harp of a thousand strings—sperits uv just men made perfeck." (p. 18)

Hitherto, the word "skedaddle" as used in this passage has not been found in print before 1861, though it may have existed in the vocabulary for some time.[14] The passage, therefore, looks like an accretion. In any event, Professor Hudson is to be congratulated on his fine literary taste in choosing to reproduce the shorter text from the *Spirit of the Times* rather than the longer and less effective one given by Mrs. Roberts. Indeed, there is reason to think that Professor Hudson may have had some doubt about Lewis' claim. At least in commenting on still another burlesque sermon, "Brother Crafford's Farewell Sermon," which he printed under the name of "Bill Easel," he stated that in diction, style, and organization, "Brother Crafford's Farewell" is so like "The Harp" as "to suggest the same author for both."[15]

Like Professor Hudson, Professor Walter Blair in anthologizing "The Harp" reproduced under Lewis' name the version of the sermon which had been printed anonymously in the *Spirit of the Times*.[16] In a cautionary note, however, he said he doubted Lewis' authorship, pointing out that Lewis "showed little of the [same] skill in his other writings."[17] But some influential later books overlook this warning; B. A. Botkin's *A Treasury of Southern Folklore*, for example, attributes the sermon to Lewis without caveat.[18]

Let us now examine the case for William Penn Brannan. An obituary in the *Cincinnati Commercial* for August 10, 1866, says that he was born in 1825 in Cincinnati, the son of a farmer, and that he became a self-taught portrait painter, who devoted his leisure to literature.[19] As an itinerant artist, according to the same source, he traveled up and down the Mississippi Valley from Maysville to New Orleans, and it was on one of these journeys through the deep South that he wrote the famous sermon "The Harp of a Thousand Strings," a masterpiece of humor, which "will carry his name to posterity." Another Cincinnati newspaper, the *Daily Union*, on which Brannan had been an associate editor in 1865, said that he was the author not only of "The Harp" but also of many other "waifs still floating on the sea of literature," that he had published pieces under various pen names, and that some of his best work had been signed either Van Dyke Brown or Bill Easel.[20]

Now Professor Hudson thinks, as we have seen, that Bill Easel's "Brother Crafford's Farewell Sermon" and "The Harp" are so alike in diction, style, and organization as "to suggest the same author for both."

If, then, the Bill Easel who wrote "Brother Crafford's Farewell Sermon" and William Penn Brannan were one and the same man, Brannan's title to "The Harp" would seem to be very strong indeed. Such is the case; in 1856 Brannan, who was then living in Louisville, where he had a studio at the corner of Fifth and Jefferson streets,[21] contributed frequently to the *Courier*, sometimes using his own name, sometimes his pseudonym, "Bill Easel." On January 10, 1856, under the name of Easel, he published "Brother Crafford's Farewell Sermon" there; and on January 30, 1856, that paper, apropos of a parody on "Hiawatha" by "Easel," noted that "Easel" was the author of "The Harp":

> "Fire Water":—Our correspondent, "Bill Easel," enables us to present to the readers of the *Courier* this morning by all odds the best thing in the season. It is entitled "Fire-Water," is done up in genuine Longfellow "Hiawatha" fashion, and is full of capital hits. By the way, our readers are not probably aware that "Bill Easel" is the author of the sermon of the Hard Shell Baptist who "played upon a harp of a thousand strings, sperits of just men made perfect." . . . His "Brother Crafford's Farewell Sermon," which appeared in the *Courier* a few weeks ago, is going the rounds of the press, and promises to have a run equal to the "Harp of a Thousand Strings."

This claim was challenged by Joshua S. Morris, editor of the *Port Gibson* (Mississippi) *Reveille*, who claimed the paternity of "The Harp" for himself. In answer to Morris the Louisville *Daily Democrat* printed the following letter, July 28, 1856:

> "The Harp of A Thousand Strings"
>
> Messrs Editors: As I have seen one or two paragraphs going the rounds of the papers lately questioning the authorship of the "Sermon" bearing the above title, I desire, with your permission, to lay a few facts before your readers, which are well known, not only to myself, but to every gentleman of Mr. Brannan's acquaintance, who resided in the South during 1851, '52, '53. The authorship of the sermon is, perhaps of no consequence to Mr. Brannan, as he has written too many beautiful things to care for so small a matter; but when this man, Morris, charges him, through prominent papers, with being a "literary" thief and "plagiarist" it is due to himself and his friends that some correction be made. On my own part, I have found Mr.

B's writings remarkable for originality—and I am intimately acquainted with almost everything he has written. The "Harp of a Thousand Strings" was written in August 1853. I saw the manuscript. It was first entitled the "Arkansas Preacher." It was produced for the benefit of a few friends and preached on festive occasions.

When Mr. B. left Mississippi, his numerous friends wished copies of the "Sermon," and he gave the manuscript to Morris for publication, and he has ever since claimed it as his own. There is a bit of revenge at the bottom of the affair, on the part of Morris. He took offense at some harmless satires, which occurred in a series of articles called the "Sharpsburgh Letters," written by Mr. Brannan for the Port Gibson Herald in 1851. In conclusion, we would advise Mr. Morris to be more sparing of his delicate epithets in future; and, if he wishes to lay claim to literary distinction, to send some of his own productions forth to the world.

Maulstick.

As I have been unable to find a complete file of the *Port Gibson Herald* for 1851, I cannot substantiate Maulstick's statement about the "Sharpsburgh Letters." Several items in the available numbers of the newspaper do, however, bear out Maulstick to the extent of placing Brannan in the vicinity of Port Gibson in the summer of 1851.[22]

Maulstick was not alone in his defense of Brannan. The *Courier* vigorously protested against the "vain, braggart, and indecent card" in which Morris had urged his claim and asserted:

We have the most irrefragable testimony that Mr. W. P. Brannan, now of this city, is the author, having conceived and executed that masterpiece of humor alone. This is the assurance we have from a gentleman of the South and from documentary evidence.

Mr. Brannan appears in our paper this morning in a card relative to the matter. He considers it a small affair, and is disposed to treat it as such. It is well, however, to crush out Morris's pretentions [*sic*] at once. Indeed it is wrong that he should aspire to the production of anything, having never published a line worthy of reprint, whereas Mr. Brannan's effusions form a delightful portion of our current literature.[23]

In his own defense, Brannan asked Morris to produce a list "of the thousand and one wonderful productions of his able and witty pen" and sarcastically thanked him "for not claiming all the other writings that have appeared over his [Brannan's] signature and *nom de plume* ('Bill Easel')." Then to show that he could produce writings in the same vein as "The Harp," whereas Morris couldn't, Brannan added the following letter from Jabez Flint, the Hardshell preacher himself:

Peggys holler Injeanar, July 21, 1856

Mr. Brannan—Sir: My nabor squire jinkins, who is a scholar—i never had no edication—tells me that you and a man named Mor-ass ar claimin to be orthors of my great sarmont which I preached from the tex And he played on the harp of a thousand strings—sperits uv just men made perfek.

Squire jinkins is a man of larnin and a good hard shell baptist. He says i o it to myself to speak out in meatin and let the people no that i am the only orthor of that selybrated sarmont. When I preached it to the benighted heathen of Waterproof i didn't know that you writin chaps was thar—and it's well for you I didn't; I wouldn't have left a hold bone in ure bodies—for i play on the harp of a thousand strings, sperits uv just men made perfek.

Sence i quit flatboatin, i have kep a respectable grocery in peggy's holler, where hard shell baptists and them as isn't will find me constantly on hand. In the first place, i hev a leetle of the best corn meal, a lztle of the best bacon, a leetle of the best whisky, and a leetle of the best saft soap—made by my wife, betsey—that perhaps you ever seed—and i play on the harp of a thousand strings, sperits uv just men made perfek.

Now don't understand by my keepin' sperits that i hold any communion with the whisky baptists. No, sir! The whisky baptists are a low-flung drunken set that like unto the hogs that wallow in the mire return again to their vomick. I am no sech a person as to drink sperits and throw 'em up to the man who sold 'em—for i play on the harp of a thousand strings, sperits of just men made perfek.

Now i want you and that Mor-ass man to own up that you stole my grate sarmont, for the commandment expressly says, render unto ceaser the things that is ceasers, and they went and done so likewise—for the time will cum when u will both go to that lake where the fire never dies and the worm is not squenched. Then will i be rejoicing in the land of Canaan, playn' on the harp of a thousand strings world without end.

JABEZ FLINT
hard-shell baptist.

Since Morris was unable to answer Brannan's challenge by pointing to other writings of his comparable to "The Harp," his claim may—until further evidence is forthcoming—be disregarded. As for Lewis' claim, the fact that he wrote out the sermon in the office of the Brandon *Republican* is no proof of his authorship. "A resident of Frankfort," the staunchest witness on Lewis' side, admits that the story "had circulated from mouth to mouth for a long time in that region, previous to any publication" and that Lewis had heard it "told in a hundred different ways by a hundred different people" before writing it out for Harper.

If Maulstick is correct about the sermon's having been circulated in manuscript after August 1853, Lewis might well have picked it up for use in his temperance lectures. This theory is strengthened by the fact that "Brother Crafford's Farewell Sermon" was used in just that way by another temperance lecturer, John B. Gough, who, after altering the title to "Brother Watkins" and making several other changes, convulsed large audiences with Brannan's mutilated sketch.[24]

Whether or not this conjecture as to how Lewis came to know "The Harp" is correct, Brannan's claim to the sermon seems much stronger than Lewis'. Certainly the testimony of old and generally trustworthy reference books like Howe's *Historical Collections of Ohio* and Sabin's *A Dictionary of Books Relating to America*, [25] both of which attribute the piece to Brannan, ought to carry as much weight as the clipping cited in Mrs. Roberts' volume. Furthermore, the text of the sermon in Mrs. Roberts' book is garbled. Moreover, in "Brother Crafford's Farewell Sermon" Brannan produced a burlesque whose diction, style, and organization are, as Professor Hudson has said, so like those of "The Harp" as "to suggest the same author for both." Finally, in his known writings Lewis shows no skill comparable to that seen in "The Harp." Professor Blair's doubt as to Lewis' title, therefore, seems well-founded. Indeed, the weight of the evidence thus far accumulated points to Brannan's authorship.

NOTES

1. J. S. Buckingham, *The Slave States of America* (London, 1842), I, 197.

2. Edward Eggleston, *The Hoosier School-Master* (New York, 1883), 102.

3. Edward William Cole, comp., *Cole's Fun Doctor: The Funniest Book in the World* (Melbourne and London, 1886), 193-198.

4. Henry Watterson, *Oddities in Southern Life and Character* (Boston, 1882), 474.

5. Jack Conroy, *Midland Humor: A Harvest of Fun and Folklore* (New York, 1947), 2.

6. Robert E. Spiller and others, eds., *Literary History of the United States* (New York, 1948), II, 741.

7. Jay Broadus Hubbell, *The South in American Literature, 1607-1900* (Durham, N. C., 1954), 661.

8. I wish to thank the following persons for supplying helpful information for this paper: Professor Walter Blair, Mrs. H. F. Broyles, Miss Norma Cass, Mr. H. H. Crisler, Mr. John F. Fierson, Miss Edna Grauman, Mrs. Alice P. Hook, Mr. William D. McCain, Mr. Franklin J. Meine, Mrs. Adlia Morgan, and Mr. W. C. Morris. Officials at the University of Kentucky Library, the Louisville Free Public Library, the Mississippi Department of Archives and History, and the Western Reserve Historical Society Library were especially helpful.

9. Thomas Powell, *Chit-chat of Humor, Wit, and Anecdote* (New York, 1857), 190-191.

10. William E. Burton, ed., *The Cyclopaedia of Wit and Humòr* (New York, 1858), 476.

11. Charles B. Galloway, "Henry T. Lewis—Humorist, Poet, Preacher, Reformer," *Quarterly Review of the Methodist Episcopal Church, South*, new series, XV (1894), 375.

12. Arthur Palmer Hudson, *Humor of the Old Deep South* (New York, 1936), 234.

13. *Ibid.*, 236-237.

14. See H. L. Mencken, *The American Language, Supplement I* (New York, 1945), 239; see also "skedaddle" in William A. Craigie, ed., *A Dictionary of American English on Historical Principles* (Chicago, 1938-44).

15. *Humor of the Old Deep South*, 234.

16. Walter Blair, *Native American Humor* (New York, 1937), 388-389.

17. *Ibid.*, 557.

18. B. A. Botkin, *A Treasury of Southern Folklore* (New York, 1949), 100.

19. See also William T. Coggeshall, *Poets and Poetry of the West* (Columbus, 1860), 186.

20. *Daily Union*, August 9, 1866.

21. *Louisville Courier*, May 27, 1856.

22. On August 1, 1851, the *Herald* noted that "Mr. William P. Brannan is in the vicinity for the summer painting landscapes and fancy pieces. He expects to return to New Orleans after the sickly season passes." The *Herald* also published "Song of the Inebriate," a poem by Brannan (June 27, 1851), and "Frank Sommers," a burlesque novel by Bill Easel (August 15, 1851).

23. *Louisville Courier*, July 29, 1856.

24. "Brother Watkins" is printed in Phineas Garrett, ed., *One Hundred Choice Selections, No.* 7 (Philadelphia, 1903), 50. The most convenient text of "Brother Crafford's Farewell Sermon" is that found in Hudson, *Humor of the Old Deep South,* 236.

25. Henry Howe, *Historical Collections of Ohio* (Cincinnati, 1900), I, 858 Joseph Sabin and others, eds., *Bibliotheca Americana: A Dictionary of Books Relating to America* (New York, 1868-1936), II, 417.

IV. Impact on American Literature

Mark Twain and the Humor of
the Old Southwest

Pascal Covici, Jr.

Mark Twain's relationship to the humor of his region is probably less direct than it is usually thought to be. That the humor of the old Southwest is indeed part of his heritage can be, and has been, demonstrated; the proposition is by now axiomatic. Mark Twain transcends this tradition. Faced with the literary problem of presenting many of the themes and moods that in various ways attracted such diverse minds as Poe, Hawthorne, Melville, Henry James, and Henry Adams, Twain, to be sure, found solutions different from theirs. But this difference is not to be measured solely by the scale of Twain's adherence to the models of his southwestern predecessors.

Nevertheless, to understand Mark Twain's use of humor is, at least partly, to put oneself in tune with the early frontier and western humor of America. Many scholars, among them Franklin Meine, Mody C. Boatright, Bernard De Voto, and, most recently, Kenneth S. Lynn, have shown in a multitude of ways how oral humor became more than mere pastime for hunters and keelboatmen confronting violence and loneliness, and for any raw westerner confronting the snickering East. Such personal uses of humor only gradually became literary, however, for the literate tellers of tales in the pre-Civil War Southwest almost without exception were newcomers to the regions in which their stories were set. As a result, they were moved by compulsions different from those of the "natives." Lawyers, judges, and doctors, educated on the Atlantic seaboard and suddenly thrust into the continent, they looked with wonder at the "manners, customs, amusements, wit, dialect" so different from what they had left behind.

From *Mark Twain's Humor: The Image of a World* by Pascal Covici, Jr. Dallas, Texas: Southern Methodist University Press, 1962. Reprinted by permission of the publisher.

The stories that flowed from this wonderment were largely organized around two impulses: a need to belittle and a desire to report. The gentlemen from the East looked upon their presence in the West—Alabama, Georgia, Mississippi—as a blessing to the barbarous natives from whom the Gentleman must always be careful to distinguish himself, at least in print. The lawyer might slap backs all he chose, but his duty was to make sure that the barbarian knew his place, that the political and economic fortunes of the new country were safeguarded by his own kind from public ravishment. An illuminating and just emphasis is Kenneth Lynn's on the political bias revealed through the framework of countless yarns in which a "Self-controlled Gentleman"[1] presents the actions of an uncouth lout. Lout and gentleman are separated by dialect as well as by action; there is no chance that a reader might confuse the two.

This need of gentlemanly authors to establish a moral and cultural distance between themselves and the places where they earned their living was at one with, and perhaps even helped to develop, the second impulse behind the humorous tales of the Southwest, that of realistic description. A writer who views his environment from a distance is less likely to take that environment for granted than is one wrapped up in the mores of the people he is observing. The living habits of the folk—how they talk, the pranks they play, what interests them—will seem worth reporting in proportion to their variation from the "normal" life left behind. One can see now that the striving for objectivity implicit in the aim of setting down the oddities of a new sort of civilization—or lack of one—clashed with the feeling of superiority so meticulously cultivated by the writers. Brutality and coarseness were blown up out of all proportion in order to solidify the position of the detached witness; most of the events narrated could never have been enacted by mere human beings: the half-horse, half-alligator men of the Mississippi, in fact, a whole menagerie of frontier titans, were used to accommodate the Gentleman's need for low behavior from which to disassociate himself.

But beneath the violence and exaggeration of mid-nineteenth-century southwestern humor there lies an impulse toward realism, toward a faithful presentation of the life of the region. Repeatedly, the stories about Simon Suggs, Sut Lovingood, Major Jones, and their picaresque brethren are introduced as offering intimate knowledge of a particular locality and its particular citizens. William Tappan Thompson, as he says in his preface to *Major Jones's Chronicles of Pineville* (1843), "endeavored, in a small way, to catch [the Georgia "cracker's"] 'manners living as they rise' . . . I claim no higher character for my stories" than that they present "a glance at characters not often found in books, or

anywhere else, indeed, except in just such places as *'Pineville,'* Georgia."
The vividness with which the frontier and the backwoods live for Americans today is at least partial testimony to the realistic bent of Thompson and his fellows. Although they dealt in exaggeration, tall tales, impossible violence, satire, and other distortions of reality, their intention to be faithful to the felt quality of life in their region cannot be mistaken.

The realism in the stories of George Washington Harris, W. T. Thompson, Augustus Longstreet, Johnson J. Hooper, *et al.* implies more than close observation and a nice ear for the spoken word. The expressed intention "to supply . . . the manners, customs, amusements, wit, dialect, as they appear in all grades of society to an ear and eye witness of them"[2] yielded time and again to the more subtle, less often articulated, pressure to crack the local yokels, or the damn-yankees, on their presumptuous and ill-bred snouts. The content of these satiric thrusts was apt to be anything but realism, narrowly considered, yet the distance, or disengagement, from local life that provided the perspective for satire also fostered the careful reporting of minute detail. But no sense of a transcendental oversoul, infusing both squatter and sophisticate, pervades the realism of the Southwest. Although the writers described the commonplace, they did not, with Emerson, embrace it. The effect of their stories upon a reader is to insulate him from any emotional involvement or identification with events, characters, or region.

These pre-Howells realists present the externals of action and dialogue. Had they explored through their fiction interior states of being, or even acknowledged through analysis the existence of human feelings in their characters, we could not laugh at the predicaments set before us. A concern limited to the realistic surface of behavior is made almost obligatory in the case of the southwestern humorists by the nature of the humor which the "school" employed. If a reader is asked to respond to victimized protagonists, or to protagonists' victims, as though they were of the same flesh and spirit as himself, he is not going to laugh as he watches their cruel and exaggerated suffering. When Sut Lovingood leaves half of his skin stuck to his shirt by some newfangled, gluelike starch, one can laugh only if Sut is nothing more than the "nat'ral born durn'd fool" he represents himself to be. The quality of Sut's humanity is so removed from ours that the distance between the two is never bridged, nor was it meant to be. On the other hand, were Huck Finn to be comparably flayed, the reader would wince, not smile; no one laughs when Nigger Jim is bitten by a snake, or when Huck hides out from the Sherpherdsons by climbing a tree.

The realism of the southwestern humorists consists, then, of content—

a report on what life looks like in the sticks—and of an aesthetic distance, or psychological detachment, from the object of scrutiny. The juxtaposition of educated gentry and boorish locale goes far toward accounting for the content and the attitude that shaped so much of the writing which poured out of the region. But the seeds of this village realism in a still more important way came from outside, just as did the writers themselves. Behind the attitude of objective disdain lies an assumption right out of the rationalistic eighteenth century: that a man of common sense can distinguish truth from falsehood, reality from appearance, can know what is right, can see with clarity and dispassion the world around him. The unambiguous treatment of material reinforces the epistemology of realism: direct sense-impressions are to be trusted; what seems to be, is.

For the reader who aligns himself with the rational author, the world is no mystery. Sut Lovingood shatters the slumber of an unwelcome intruder by tying a nine-foot length of intestines to the man's shirttail: the terrified "snake-bit Irishman" lights out for home, convinced that " 'a big copper-headed black rattil-snake is crawlin up [his] britches,' "[3] but the reader never for a moment needs to doubt the reliability of his own senses. The boorish victims, on the other hand, repeatedly suffer from an inability to distinguish between the real and the pretended, for the discrepancy between what seems to be and what actually exists forms the crux of numerous pranks perpetrated by southwestern scalawags. It is not only Simon Suggs among them whose "whole ethical system lies snugly in his favorite aphorism—'IT IS GOOD TO BE SHIFTY IN A NEW COUNTRY.' "[4] Repeatedly, characters are victimized because they fail to recognize that "reality" has been altered for their special benefit. William Tappan Thompson's "How to Kill Two Birds with One Stone"[5] ironically applauds young lawyer Jenkins' wisdom in persuading two men that each has stolen from the other when the lawyer himself has hidden Si Perkins' wagon in Absalom Harley's cellar, in turn loading Si's wagon with Harley's bacon and other articles, in order to foment a double lawsuit and pocket double fees. The ruse works perfectly, and the reader appreciates with a Whig's awareness the "democratic" acuteness of Thomas Jefferson Jenkins while condemning with a laugh the litigious pretensions of his victims. The characters are fooled; the reader is not.

The refined reader is encouraged to trust his sense of ethics as well as his sense of what is real. The behavior of the fictional characters is held up against an implicit standard accessible to all men of reason. Again, simply the surface of what happens, the mere action, speech, and setting as they impinge upon the senses of the realist, is adequate to the purpose of the writers. What really counts is "manners"; the way in which the characters act is of more import than what they do or why they do it. When Sut Lovingood works himself into that fancily-starched shirt which subsequently rips the hide off him, he isn't being unethical, but, rather, pretentious. His pretensions to city grandeur do not mesh with his backwoods ignorance, and one laughs because Sut is ridiculous.

If there is any one pattern basic to the humor of the Southwest it is precisely this: a character is pushed by the author into a situation in which he either exposes the pretensions of others or himself emerges as ridiculous because of his pretentious behavior. The eighteenth-century concept of decorum comes to mind in this connection; what is being criticized more often than not is a failure to adhere to the standards of a cultivated civilization, a failure—so annoyingly common in raw, frontier democracy—to recognize and to accept one's inferior position in society. By considering himself to be as good as the next man, the country democrat becomes pretentious, at least in the eyes of the transplanted easterners whose aloof standards shaped the Southwest humor of the nineteenth century.

The satire embedded in this humor is a satire of the ridiculous, which means that when we talk about the humor of the American Southwest we are really talking about the kind of humor described by Henry Fielding in his preface to *Joseph Andrews*, the humor of eighteenth-century England. The tales so often and so delightfully anthologized that Americans think of as so particularly their own are American in content but English in theory and in organization. Through affectation, "the only source of the true ridiculous," according to Fielding, characters are made into figures of fun. Sometimes the affectation is motivated by vanity, "which puts us on affecting false characters, in order to purchase applause," sometimes by hypocrisy, which "sets us on an endeavor to avoid censure by concealing our vices under an appearance of their opposite virtues." Hypocrisy and vanity—under which headings outsiders could lump almost all attempts to transcend the unmannerly boorishness of a frontier community—lead to affected behavior, and "from the discovery of this affectation arises the Ridiculous—which always strikes the reader with surprise and pleasure." Fielding had no need to add that the reader's pleasure depends on his identifying with the objective viewer rather than with the vain or hypocritical character, for the very attribution of vanity or hypocrisy automatically establishes the proper aesthetic distance between author and reader on the one hand, ridiculous character on the other.

A careful reading of southwestern "American" humor will give substance to the suggestion that this particularly American tradition is in fact derived explicitly from English theory and practice of the eighteenth century. Hooper, Harris, Thompson, and others show a keen sense of the ridiculous as Fielding defines it. Repeatedly, their humor embodies Fielding's contention that "from affectation only, the misfortunes and calamities of life, or the imperfections of nature, may become the objects of ridicule." The victims of Simon Suggs's camp meeting, for example, endure considerable misfortune and calamity when the worthy Captain rides off with the dollars they have donated toward his pretended efforts to establish a church. One might expect to find a reader's sympathies aroused for the swindled congregation, but, instead, one finds oneself chuckling along with wicked old Simon as he canters off at the end of the story. Simon's victims are ridiculous, not because of what they are, necessarily, but rather because the reader has been made to observe them from the point of view of a refined and rational being.

As Hooper leads his reader into the camp meeting, he first describes realistically and objectively the various kinds of religious hysteria manifested by the throng. Then he kills off any incipient identification with the masses that may have sprung up in the reader's open mind: "The great object of all seemed to be, to see who could make the greatest noise—

> 'And each—for madness ruled the hour—
> Would try his own expressive power.' "[6]

One of the ministers, under the guise of religious zeal, is "lavishing caresses" upon the prettier among the young women. The Negro woman who is most profoundly moved by religious emotion is "huge" and "greasy," adjectives which cast doubt on the delicacy of her spiritual awakening. The minister to whom Simon attributes his spectacular—though bogus—conversion is a presumptuous ass; the whole crew get what's coming to them.

> 'I—I—I can bring 'em!' cried the preacher . . . in a tone of exultation—'Lord thou knows ef thy servant can't stir 'em, nobody else needn't try—but the glory aint mine! I'm a poor worrum of the dust,' he added, with ill-managed affectation.[7]

Affectation renders the people ridiculous and permits one to laugh at them. At the very moment when Simon is cajoling them into contributing money so that he can found a church "in his own neighborhood" and "make himself useful as soon as he could prepare himself for the ministry," his smooth talk is aimed not at their religious enthusiasm but at their desire to appear wealthy and generous before their neighbors: "Simon had excited the pride of purse of the congregation, and a very handsome sum was collected in a very short time."[8]

Nineteenth-century Americans not only ridiculed the affectations of louts, but also went still farther into eighteenth-century English practice when aiming at more specific targets. By pretending that the object of attack was simply affecting the qualities that made him dangerous— courage, intelligence, power, or whatever—Jonathan Swift, and many others, could cut their enemies down to size, denying in the process that the enemy was worth taking seriously in the first place. George Washington Harris, for one, borrows a page from Swift when he recounts Sut Lovingood's travels with "Old Abe Linkhorn"[9] in a way that "diminishes" Lincoln to the disappearing point. The leader of the antislavery faction so inimical to Harris is too stupid to be dangerous, too cowardly to be feared. Moreover, his ugliness is inhuman enough to suggest that he can be disposed of as easily as any other harmless amphibious reptile:

> I ketched a ole bullfrog once [says Sut] and drove a nail through his lips into a post, tied two rocks to his hind toes and stuck a darnin needle into his tail to let out the moisture, and left him there to dry. I seed him two weeks after'ards: and, when I seed old Abe, I thought it were an awful retribution come onto me, and that it were the same frog—. . . same shape same color same feel (cold as ice), and I'm damned if it ain't the same smell.[10]

This technique of belittling the object of attack is by no means limited to eighteenth-century England, but belongs to a tradition of literary satire familiar to any classically educated American of the nineteenth century. Since *meiosis*,[11] whether applied to northern Presidents or backwoods boobs, was so frequently and deliberately and even characteristically employed, it is fair to say that no matter how firmly anchored to American experience their lives and writings might be, the pre-Civil War humorists of the Southwest had at least one eye on foreign literary sources.

II

The characteristics of southwestern humor, then, are those of realism in content and in epistemology. Even the satirical intentions behind the humor call upon the reader to agree to the existence of clearly defined standards, identically visible to all thinking men. Instead of the moral hesitancies to be found on a frontier where old codes are daily called in question by the exigencies of a new life, this humor reflects the bland assurance of eighteenth-century men of reason that the cultivated mind can measure all things.

But to Mark Twain there was little, if any, validity in the realistic assumptions behind the humor of the frontier. When, in *Mark Twain at Work*,[12] Bernard De Voto asserts that Twain's aim in writing *Huckleberry Finn* was to record life by the banks of the Mississippi, his comment is less applicable to the complex and ambiguous novel Twain wrote than to the literary tradition from which most of Twain's work emerges. Twain uses the materials of realism—the events and objects of the daily life of the region—but in a way that Americanizes American humor and puts it more closely in touch with the metaphysical facts of life in a new land and in our modern world: his effects do not, ultimately, depend on a detached objectivity that permits the reader to look upon scoundrels and boors as nonhuman beasts of no importance, or on a sense of the ridiculous as it arises from affectation, but, instead, on a knowledge— paid for by experience—that human reason is cruelly limited, too often unable to discriminate between what is and what seems; that the shibboleths of one generation are the jests of another; and that the powers of irrationality, rather than the deliberate exercise of will, make people appear to be other than what they are.

This is, to be sure, taking humor seriously. Yet even in the simplest episodes of Twain's narrative humor lies the basis for such a contrast between what Twain does and what his predecessors did with similar raw material. In Chapter XX of *Huckleberry Finn* (1885), the king attends a camp meeting at Pokeville much like the one to which Johnson J. Hooper had sent Simon Suggs forty years earlier. Both meetings are minutely described, and both congregations are subtly robbed. The essential difference is between the frailties that in each case lead the people to allow themselves to be cheated. Simon Suggs defrauds those who are guilty of affectation: the laity are purse-proud, and the clergy are concerned either with taking up the collection or with hugging the prettiest girls. Simon's benefactors give money to create the impression of wealth; their show of pious charity is transparently hypocritical and vain, and they are made to seem ridiculous because of affection. Mark Twain's king exploits a very different sort of meeting: his victims, not "ridiculous through affectation," neither hypocritical nor vain, are victimized because they share humanity's penchant for romantic excitement. The king, improbably representing himself as a pirate, succeeds completely in taking in the communicants because they want to believe that an Indian Ocean pirate could brush against their own dull lives. In exchange for this fatuous belief they are willing to pay their money: "The king said . . . it warn't no use talking, heathens don't amount to shucks alonside of pirates to work a camp meeting with" (XIII, 184-85).[13] This has nothing to do with vanity or hypocrisy—and, therefore, has no connection with affectation, either. The gulled ones are just as charitable and religious as their actions suggest, but they are motivated less by charity and zeal than by their desire to share in a sensation. This, however, they do not know about themselves. In contrast to the earlier tradition, the people of Pokeville are not trying to appear to be what they are not. Rather, they are by their very nature other than they seem.

Mark Twain's fictional world is different from that of his immediate regional predecessors because it is organized around a real, and not a contrived, discrepancy between reality and appearance. The orderly and comprehensible universe presided over by the Self-controlled Gentleman is one in which author and readers can all relax together, assured that only those who stand outside their circle can be deceived by the contrived accidents that befall frontier clowns. Sut Lovingood gladly swallows Sicily Burns's "love-potion," with terrific results, but the civilized reader knew all along that it was soda. Such assurance is foreign to the nineteenth-century American fiction most cherished today. Nathaniel Hawthorne's explorations of the effects of sin on the human heart force one to reorganize one's sense of what sin itself is, and Melville's presentation of the Mount of Titans in *Pierre*, and of Moby Dick himself, compels one to question the seeming beneficence of smiling nature. More to our immediate purpose, Mark Twain, using the materials and surroundings of his southwestern literary progenitors, throws into doubt—as they never do—a reader's complacent evaluation of common sense as applied first to daily human behavior, and finally to man's role in the universe.

Twain's preoccupation with revealing a discrepancy between seeming and reality is central, not peripheral, to his work. A striking example, built from bits of Twain's frontier heritage, is Huck's trip to the circus to counterpoint through humor one of the most somber episodes in *The*

Adventures of Huckleberry Finn. In Chapter XXI, Old Boggs, a harmless drunk, is shot down in cold blood by the ruthless but gentlemanly Colonel Sherburn. Huck Finn is the one sympathetic witness of the slaying. An orphan himself, Huck is especially touched by the pathos of Bogg's daughter as she weeps over the dying man. "She was about sixteen, and very sweet and gentle looking, but awful pale and scared." The other witnesses are totally detached. In fact, "the whole town" watches callously as Boggs breathes his last in a drugstore window, a weighty Bible laid upon his chest to ease his departing soul and increase his agony. They might be watching a show, to hear the people farther back from the window talk to those hogging the front row: " 'Say, now, you've looked enough, you fellows; 'tain't right and 'tain't fair for you to stay thar all the time, and never give nobody a chance; other folks has their rights as well as you' " (199).

Huck subsequently (Chapter XXII) watches another drunk at a local circus whose life is endangered not by pistol-fire but by his insistence that he be permitted to attempt equestrian acrobatics. Finally the patient ringmaster acquiesces; amid howls of laughter and derision, the drunk mounts a horse, "his heels flying in the air every jump, and the whole crowd of people standing up shouting and laughing till tears rolled down." The horse breaks loose from the roustabouts, and the drunk seems headed for certain death, to the vast delight of the audience. "It warn't funny to me, though," says Huck; "I was all of a tremble to see his danger" (206). The seeming "drunk" turns out to be a seasoned performer, a member of the circus-troupe who rides like an angel, and the laugh is on naïve Huck Finn, so easily taken in by a circus act. Huck has been sentimental, the reader may feel, in separating himself from the crowd that first jeers, then laughs at the performer. His delicacy of feeling is worthless, for the crowd's callous merriment has injured no feelings. The laughers, indeed, have added to the effect of the circus routine. As for the heartlessness of their instinctive response, well, their sympathies were as unsought as they were unstirred.

But when the reader remembers the similar excitement of this same toughened crowd when it witnessed the murder of Boggs and the drama of his death, he sees that though Huck is naïve, his simple compassion is preferable to the "smart" sensation-seeking of the empty-headed mob. Not only had the people clustered around the store window in which Boggs lay dying, but they also had had the cold-blooded detachment to enjoy a re-enactment of the slaying after the event, even offering their flasks to the "long, lanky man" who "done it perfect . . . just exactly the way it all happened" (200). In each case, Huck's reaction differs from the crowd's. Moreover, Huck's sympathy for Boggs arises from the same qualities of spirit that make Huck a gull at the circus, just as the same shallow craving for excitement motivates the crowd in both instances. Thus, although Huck's attitude at the circus appears to stem from a foolish and valueless naïveté, its true source is his fineness of soul. The reader, therefore, is compelled to reinterpret the "reality" that has been set before him. What has seemed to be and what is are inexorably opposed.

We know that Twain's murder of Boggs is in itself "realistic," for it is "almost without a hairsbreadth of variation" a duplication of Judge John Clemens' account of the shooting of "Uncle Sam" Smarr by William Owsley in Hannibal, when Sam Clemens was just over nine years old.[14] Moreover, the circus incident itself was borrowed from an earlier southwestern writer. What is at issue here, though, is something more than a question of how photographic the writer's memory happens to be. The murder and the circus not only are events in themselves; they also reveal hidden duplicities in the world. The analogue of Twain's circus scene, however, concerns itself with no such opposition between what seems and what is; it never challenges the reader to revise his first impressions. William Tappan Thompson's circus in "The Great Attraction! or The Doctor Most Oudaciously Tuck In"[15] anticipates by some forty years the one Huck attends: in each case, a conventional equestrian act precedes the pseudo-drunken "head-liner"; a witty clown cracks jokes of surpassing cleverness; and then comes the rider who turns out to be sober after all and astonishes his beholders by rising to his feet on the horse's back, then stripping off assorted suits of clothes, "twenty or more" for Thompson's hero, a mere seventeen for Twain's.

The effect of Thompson's circus is considerably simpler than that of Twain's. It appears to be, and it is, a short satire on pretension. Doctor Jones, the unhappy protagonist of the piece, is insufferably impressed with his own sophistication. Denizen of Pineville though he be, he has once visited Augusta, "that Philadelphia of the South," and feels that he is "—to use one of his own polished expressions—'bully of the tanyard.' "[16] Everything about Augusta is immeasurably superior to whatever Pineville has to offer, and Jones, because of his exposure to the metropolis, includes himself among its wonders. He has seen everything, done everything; and he knows everything, too. When he guides the untutored young ladies of Pineville to their first circus, he assures them that what they are seeing is "nothing to what he had seen in Augusta."

Thompson's attitude toward Jones is one of ironic scorn, as any reader quickly perceives. The Doctor is pretentious. Vanity leads him to affect a sophistication, a *savoir-faire*, that he doesn't really possess, and the circus proves to be his undoing. When the "drunk" tries to ride, thus interrupting the performance, Doctor Jones rushes to the ring, intent on being the hero of the hour. Despite explicit warning by two of the towns-folk that "that chap belongs to the show," he tries valiantly to prevent the ride, only to be rudely rebuked by the clown and finally jostled into the colored section. The Doctor has failed to understand the niceties of circus shenanigans, and so is made a laughingstock, "oudaciously tuck in." Needless to say, the citizens of Pineville rejoice in his downfall. " 'Is that the way they does in Augusta?' . . . and a hundred other such jeers" bring both the story and the Doctor's local glory to a close.

Thompson's story is excellently organized and accomplishes the effect that one can assume Thompson meant it to have. Because his aim was not Twain's is no reason to criticize Thompson, whose consciousness of theme is embodied even in his language. Doctor Jones's refinement is called into question by a report of his own coarse epithet for himself—"bully of the tan-yard"—a bit of backwoods lingo echoed in the description of big Bill Sweeney as the rough and tough "bully of the county." Mr. Sweeney, whose place in the story is quite subordinate, shares with Jones the fault of pretentiousness. His pretensions are not to sophistica-tion, however, but to gentility. When he refuses to remove his hat so that others can see the show, the ensuing fracas reveals that he has no right to sit among gentlefolk, just as the main action of the story annuls the Doc-tor's claims to intellectual supremacy. Both men, each in his different way, have striven to "purchase applause,". in Fielding's words, by "affect-ing false characters." There are no hidden subtleties in the story, no extraneous reverberations. Its satiric impact is obvious and direct. The motives of the characters appear clearly at the start, and one never needs to revise his estimate. This is not true of the king's camp meeting victims or of Huck Finn at his circus.

The two examples of the circus and the camp meeting suggest that although Mark Twain's writing draws upon the traditions and materials utilized by earlier southwestern humorists, its humor goes beyond an exposure of deliberate affectation. In psychological awareness, Twain is closely akin to Melville and Henry James, for he presents human beings as more disposed to misunderstand themselves, as do Pierre and the first-person protagonists of *The Turn of the Screw* and *The Sacred Fount*, than to mislead others deliberately. Consequently, his technique, his literary organization of material, is more concerned with laying bare the human heart than with presenting the rogue's world as it was at a given time and place. Anyone who reads carefully the introduction to the king's camp meeting cannot help but be impressed by the meticulous acuteness of the description, even down to the benches "made out of outside slabs of logs, with holes bored in the round side to drive sticks into for legs" (XIII, 181). To say that Twain is not concerned at all with the surface appearance of the life surrounding his characters is clearly to overstate the point. It is his particular use of appearances that sets him off from his humorous predecessors.

III

The most direct way to suggest the unique quality in Twain's use of surface, or reportorial, realism is to turn from specific analogues to a technique as general as the use of spoken language. That Twain·cared about reproducing the exact inflections of dialect, and that he was proud of his abilities in this direction, the author's "Explanatory" to *Huckleberry Finn* makes clear. Seven distinct varieties of speech are mentioned, and, we are reminded, "The shadings have not been done in a haphazard fashion . . . but painstakingly, and with the trustworthy guidance and support of personal familiarity with these several forms of speech" (XIII, xxi). Repeatedly he tries to make his people talk as their environment and training might make them talk in real life, adopting the vocabulary and imagery that will most precisely evoke the varieties of backwoods experience.

His westerners, for example, repeatedly speak the language of the poker table, and in this respect they are not alone in nineteenth-century fiction. Poker talk was a common device of local-color characterization in the writings of the transplanted lawyers and judges who found rural Tennessee, Georgia, Alabama, and Mississippi strikingly different from the metropolitan East they had left behind. There were many stories about gamblers in the new country, and the vocabulary of gambling provided a quick metaphorical index to the habits and origins of the speaker. " 'No matter what sort of a hand you've got . . . take stock!' " exhorts Simon Suggs. " 'Here am *I*, the wickedest and blindest of sinners—has spent my whole life in the sarvice of the devil—has now come in on *narry pair* and won a *pile!*' "[17] That Simon presents his recent "conversion" in poker language serves to place him as a backwoods con man; also, one notes the dramatic irony of his words, for Simon's auditors interpret "narry pair" as a reference to Simon's sinful life prior to the camp meeting, his newly-won "pile" as a joyful allusion to God's free grace which Simon appears to be experiencing, whereas the reader is aware that Simon is planning to win a "pile" of money on the strength of his pretended conversion, his bluff "hand" with "narry pair" in it. When he urges unrepentant sinners to join him on the mourners' bench, he reassures them that " 'The bluff game aint played here! No runnin' of a body off! Every body holds four aces, and when you bet, you win!' "[18] Summing up his achievement at the end of the story, Simon concludes that " 'Ef them fellers aint done to a cracklin, . . . I'll never bet on two pair agin!' "[19] The principal effect of this terminology is to present Simon as a cardsharper, willing to gamble on the gullibility of the average man. But this the reader knew from the opening pages of the story. The poker talk has revealed nothing new about the Captain; it is simply part of the author's impulse toward realism, toward presenting the audible surface of the time and place.

In a bit of Mark Twain's earlier writing the same limited effect appears: poker vocabulary denotes the westerner but tells nothing specific about him as a man. Describing a rising river in 1859, Sergeant Fathom "would suggest to the planters, as we say in an innocent little parlor game, commonly called 'draw,' that if they can only 'stand the raise' this time, they may enjoy the comfortable assurance that the old river's banks will never hold a 'full' again during their natural lives."[20] This is an amateur's imitation of a technique: the effort to westernize the speaker is unsupported by dialect, and the humor is heavy-handed. Fathom is a stick figure who never comes to life. But Twain was to discover the possibilities latent in simple speech: the preparations for Buck Fanshaw's funeral in *Roughing It* not only amuse one but present a fully-drawn character as well. Scotty Briggs and the minister converse for seven pages of western slang and eastern elegance where a single page of less characteristic talk might have sufficed, but one finds that Scotty emerges in the round because of the way he talks.

The first stage of the interview presents Scotty's effort to tell the minister that Buck is dead and that the "boys" would appreciate a few comforting words at the funeral:

" 'Are you the duck that runs the gospel-mill next door?' " (IV, 45) asks Scotty. After the minister counters that he is, rather, " 'the spiritual adviser of the little company of believers whose sanctuary adjoins these premises,' " Scotty "scratched his head, reflected a moment, and then said: 'You ruther hold over me, pard. I reckon I can't call that hand. Ante and pass the buck.' "

Scotty's perplexities increase. The minister asks for simpler language, but the request is too complexly worded. " 'I'll have to pass, I judge.' " " 'How?' " " 'You've raised me out, pard' " (46).

Eventually the two understand each other. But the minister wonders about Buck Fanshaw's religious affiliations in language that leads Scotty to complain, " 'Why, you're most too many for me, you know. . . . Every time you draw, you fill; but I don't seem to have any luck. Let's have a new deal.' " " 'How? Begin again?' " " 'That's it.' " " 'Very well. Was he a good man, and—' " " 'There—I see that; don't put up another chip till I look at my hand' " (50).

Apart from giving the western flavor that Twain explicitly means to impart (42-43), poker terminology here accomplishes two ends. First, the metaphoric equation of chips and cards with words ties the episode together by providing a secondary story line. The inability of Scotty and the minister to communicate becomes as much the subject of the brief scene as is the arranging of Buck Fanshaw's funeral. The two confuse each other with their language, and a reader wonders how long their differences of terminology will keep each from "seeing" the other's point. The minister, slick though sickly easterner that he is, keeps on talking, and Scotty is "raised" out of several conversational "pots" by his flow of words. Finally, however, Scotty can "call"—" 'I see that' "—and the episode comes to a close with mutual comprehension.

Secondly, Scotty's poker vocabulary displays his character. Never does he try to bluff. He admits the minister's ability to "draw and fill"; he quickly acknowledges the inadequacy of his own "hand"—his comprehension of language—and forthrightly "passes," having "raised out." When he understands the minister's words—the "bet"—he will "see that," but he wants to "look at [his] hand" before any more chips—words—fall. Scotty's discourse is scrupulously honest and manly; his terms never suggest that he thinks the minister's ignorance is pretended—a suspicion that the reader cannot help entertaining—and he never tries to run a bluff of his own. Scotty's self-revelation prepares the reader for Twain's concluding presentation of him as a sympathetic Sunday-school teacher whose rendition in slang of Bible stories "was listened to by his little learners with a consuming interest" (53). The contrast between East and West is clearly presented, but the story differs from most western stories of the time in that the contest and victory are moral and are presented through language, not through violent action: the rough westerner, in the terms of his own rough game, shows himself to be a more honest man than the educated easterner. The language of poker ties Scotty's character and story together into a simple, kindly unit.

Scotty's simplicity of 1871 contrasts with the simple-minded duplicity of Saladin Foster in "The $30,000 Bequest" (1904). The anecdote of Scotty and the minister is more or less a "set piece," an exhibition of language for its own sake. The story of the Fosters, on the other hand, has a definite plot organized around a specific theme; its concern is not to demonstrate speech but to use it to reveal character. Saladin's use of poker metaphor establishes him as an unpretentious, rather common-place man—which is important for the total effect of the story, since the reader is supposed to feel that what happens to Saladin might happen to anyone—and simultaneously reveals his understanding of himself. The effect of the device is double: it both vivifies him and foreshadows his actions.

Saladin exhibits more self-awareness than Scotty. When his wife expresses joy at the news that his rich uncle—from whom they expect to inherit $30,000—is still living, Saladin derides her for being " 'immorally pious' " (XXIV, 12). Electra is tartly certain that " 'there is no such thing as immoral piety,' " and Saladin is soon overwhelmed because he doesn't know when to stop talking. He multiplies his excuses, only to entangle himself still further. "Then, musingly, he apologized to himself. 'I certainly held threes—I *know* it—but I drew and didn't fill. That's where I'm so often weak in the game. If I had stood pat—but I didn't. I never do. I don't know enough' " (13).

Saladin, one sees, laments two things. Superficially, he bemoans his unavoidable failure to "fill"—and superficially the story is built upon the Fosters' expectations (doomed to disappointment) that the uncle will make the bequest that he promised. No one can control the run of the cards at poker; likewise, Saladin is not responsible for his uncle's malicious deceit. But Saladin does have a weakness and sees it clearly: he knows that he cannot bluff successfully, whether before or after the draw. Later, as the Fosters come to live more and more in their imaginations, daydreaming about their lives as millionaires once the bequest shall have been invested a few dozen times, Saladin sinks to degrading debaucheries. He gambles; he drinks; he fornicates. His transgressions are purely mental, but Electra detects the glazed eyes and the slack face as he sits lost in fantasy. He is unable to "bluff" her; he cannot deny what in imagination he has been up to, and the happiness of their marriage is blighted. The misery that results from his failure to "stand pat" is a direct outgrowth of the character revealed through the poker-talk monologue.

Finally, to choose an example near the chronological middle of Twain's career, when Hank Morgan presents himself in Arthur's dining hall near the beginning of *A Connecticut Yankee in King Arthur's Court* (1889), one finds an intensive use of American frontier, or "Yankee," poker talk not only to characterize the protagonist but also to anticipate theme and prepare for the satiric irony behind the story. Faced with the dismal fact that he is either in the sixth century or in a lunatic asylum, with no way to determine which until an eclipse occurs or fails to occur, Hank decides to dismiss the problem from his mind: "One thing at a time, is my motto— and just play that thing for all it is worth, even if it's only two pair and a jack" (XIV, 16). Ironically, Hank Morgan's career as "The Boss" will be an attempt to inculcate the masses of Great Britain with the habits of rationality and the attributes of reflective intelligence; his whole program will be one of education in the "Man-factory." But here, he shows that he is a man who will play a bluff with the best, and foreshadows his successful eclipse-bluff, his repeated "miracles," and his final saturnalia of destruction when his "bluff" is called. The conflict between reason and irrationality, between, one may say, the doctrines of the perfecti- bility of man and of innate human depravity, is played off against the background of Hank's poker-faced opportunism. In the great tourna- ment between the "magic of fol-de-rol" and the "magic of science" (396), the magic of science triumphs, but "it was a 'bluff' you know. At such a time it is sound judgment to put on a bold face and play your hand for a hundred times what it is worth; forty-nine times out of fifty nobody dares to 'call,' and you rake in the chips" (395).

Such a passage is of the frontier tradition; it is the realistic speech of an uneducated man who, by speaking the way he does, convinces a reader of the existence of his environment. Yet it accomplishes a good deal more. Hank Morgan's use of poker terminology is more significant than that of Captain Simon Suggs at his camp meeting. Suggs's poker metaphors come at the end of his story, when the reader already knows all about the Captain, but Hank's "two pair and a jack" serves to intro- duce both his character and the essential conflicts to be presented in his story. Hooper's satire, moreover, has nothing to do with the charac- terization of Simon Suggs through poker talk. Simon is no outsider whose entrance into a previously stable society disrupts the status quo. He is immediately recognized as "the very 'chief of sinners' in all that region,"[21] his physiognomy as familiar as his reputation. His vocabulary adds little to the meaning of the story, because Simon's function—to victimize the affected—does not depend on his origin as signaled by his talk. Hank Morgan, however, is an unknown quantity. His very clothing seems miraculous, and his vocabulary repeatedly sets him off from his captors. His mere presence in Arthur's court will serve to contrast Yankee ingenuity and energy with Arthurian romance and sloth; the contrast between his American language and sixth-century, knightly habits of thought will be essential to the development of the book's theme.

IV

Even when Hank Morgan is roaming the streets of Old England, his Americanism is guaranteed by his poker talk. Of even broader usefulness in suggesting nationality is the poker face, more a way of saying something, or nothing, than a vocabulary. Because it embodies an attitude rather than a regional heritage, the frontiersman's poker face was more widely appropriated than his slang by writers presenting an American to the outside world; and from the very beginning, the outside world was inescapably present in the American consciousness. Distant though he was, the frontier settler was fair game for the polished easterner, the easterner himself open to wisecracks from abroad. The conflict embodied in such antitheses as country and city, West and East, became a theme common to writers as far removed from the conventional eighteenth- and nineteenth-century nature-civilization dichotomy as Twain, Henry James, and Sinclair Lewis. In many cases, what began as western humor was quickly pressed into service on behalf of the national honor.

One may think of the tall tale as a traditionally western way of cutting the pompous outsider down to size. The heaping up of exaggerations by a narrator who never cracks a smile, or in any other way indicates that he is joking, stretches to the breaking point the stranger's predisposition to assume the worst about the new region. The Texan who disdainfully put a braggart in his place by saying, " 'Only after my fourth killing, gentlemen, did I consider myself worthy of becoming a citizen of Texas,' "[22] is satirizing an unthinking acceptance of malicious anti-Texas gossip; the previous speaker, with but one corpse to his credit, plays the role of straight man.

This is folk humor hot off the range, but the technique antedates the frontier. As a defense against slander, the tall tale and the poker face enabled no less a man than Benjamin Franklin to counteract falsehoods about America that were circulating in London in 1765. Rather than attack detractors in passionate rage, Franklin quietly admitted in a letter to a London newspaper that no story, however extravagant it seemed, could give a false picture of America, which was itself so grandiose. He went on to speak of the cod and whale fishing on the Great Lakes, concluding that

> Ignorant People may object that the upper Lakes are fresh, and that Cod and Whale are Salt Water Fish: But let them know, Sir, that Cod, like other Fish when attack'd by their Enemies, fly into any Water where they can be safest; that Whales, when they have a mind to eat Cod, pursue them wherever they fly; and that the grand Leap of the Whale in the Chase up the Fall of Niagara is esteemed, by all who have seen it, as one of the finest Spectacles in Nature.[23]

In fiction, however, the development of a poker-faced manner was a sophisticated refinement that occurred only after more violent techniques of presenting western antipathy toward eastern elegance had been fully explored. The rough squatter of Hannibal, in Sam Clemens' "The Dandy Frightening the Squatter" (1852), wastes no words, forthrightly punching the overarmed but unmanned Dandy into "the turbid waters of the Mississippi."[24] Sut Lovingood frightens his intrusive Irishman right back across the ocean, to the land where there are no snakes. Thompson's Doctor Jones is led to the circus for the single purpose of being "oudaciously tuck in," for Augusta, "the Philadelphia of the South," has rendered him objectionable to his fellows at Pineville. Even in real life, the young men of Hannibal, incensed at the citified airs of one of their number who had returned from Yale in all the appurtenances of eastern fashion, turned to action, not talk: they "dressed up the warped negro bell ringer in a travesty of him—which made him descend to village fashions."[25]

The country resents the city, the West resents the East, and the theme of this hostility toward what is different—and therefore threatening—is expressed in countless stories, first by those who were intent on capturing the feelings of the folk around them, regardless of where their own sympathies lay, and, later, by men who identified themselves at least partially with their adopted, or even natal, home on the frontier. This same opposition found its way into serious fiction as a contrast between America and Europe, although as early as Revolutionary times Royall Tyler's comedy—titled, of course, *The Contrast*—was elevating the manly

American above the effete Englishman. By the last third of the nineteenth century, though, the contrast had become considerably more complex. For many writers, to place an American in a European context was to provide the *donnée* for infinitely suggestive adventures. This confrontation carries with it a minor, but interesting, literary problem: how shall the author establish implicitly the particular qualities of his characters' nationality without writing an essay? Mark Twain, in *The Innocents Abroad* (1869), points the way to one sort of solution through characters whose use of a poker face stamps them as Americans from a frontier rawer than a genteel reader will approve yet worthy of respect for its clear-sighted resistance to humbug.

The immediate impulse of Twain's traveling Yankee is to disguise emotion, whether fear of Europe as it threatens an American's self-image or awe of Europe as it suggests unexplored possibilities of experience. Accomplished poker-players that they are, they deceive for gain on the byways of the Continent as expertly as they might at the card table. When Twain-the-character and his friends in *The Innocents* plague a series of guides, all rechristened "Ferguson," the iron-visaged idiocy displayed leads to one very specific gain: "The guide was bewildered—nonplussed. He walked his legs off, nearly, hunting up extraordinary things, and exhausted all his ingenuity on us, but it was a failure; we never showed any interest in anything" (I, 306). By criticizing "Christopher Columbo's" poor penmanship, by asking if an Egyptian mummy is dead, the Doctor—who "asks the questions, generally, because he can keep his countenance, and look more like an inspired idiot, and throw more imbecility into the tone of his voice than any man that lives" (303)—forces the guide of the moment on to ever greater exertions.

Like any clever poker-player, the Doctor is versatile. When a guide persists in taking Twain, Dan, and the Doctor to silk stores rather than to the Louvre, the masquerade of boredom changes to one of simulated enthusiasm. As "Ferguson" foolishly persists in his commercial scheming, the Doctor's mounting anger expresses itself as aesthetic pleasure: " 'Ah, the palace of the Louvre; beautiful, beautiful edifice! Does the Emperor Napoleon live here now, Ferguson?' " (115) And at the third silk store: " 'At last! How imposing the Louvre is, and yet how small! how exquisitely fashioned! how charmingly situated! Venerable, venerable pile—' " (116). This reaction is, strictly speaking, irony, but as an attitude adopted by the Doctor for slicing through a foreigner's deceit, it also belongs to the species "poker face."

When the Doctor stonily asks, " 'Is, ah—is he dead?' " before every statue, he is clearly deceiving for gain. The guide, intent on drawing a conventional show of enthusiasm from the passive Doctor, works much harder than he is paid to do in the hopes of shattering his employer's calm. But there is another side to the coin. The Innocents are impressed by what they see, for if they were not, they would find no practical advantage in pretending to be bored. "We came very near expressing interest, sometimes—even admiration—it was very hard to keep from it" (306). But the pretense means more than just a desire to gain additional sights, as one sees when the group visits the vault beneath the Capuchin Convent. The walls are decorated by the dismembered skeletons of dead monks. The guide—in this case one of the monks who will some day add his mite to the communal fresco—has shown them everything, and now they stop to examine in particular one skeleton, robed and intact, whose skull has preserved "a weird laugh a full century old!" "It was the jolliest laugh, but yet the most dreadful, that one can imagine" (II, 5). Terror and humor coalesce: "At this moment I saw that the old instinct was strong upon the boys, and I said we had better hurry to St. Peter's. They were trying to keep from asking, 'Is—is he dead?' " (5)

In this instance, the poker face gains a very real but immaterial advantage for its user: it allows him to inject humor into a situation that frightens him. Certainly this is a common technique all through *The Innocents Abroad*. When Twain, the American narrator, is overwhelmed by Europe, he can find relief by laughing at it, or simply by laughing, a response similar to that of Melville's Ishmael who emerges from his first violent brush with a whale to conclude that life's vicissitudes, from "small difficulties" to "extreme tribulation" and "peril of life and limb," must be taken "for a vast practical joke" if sanity is to be retained.[26] That Twain's American laughs does not mean, always, that he is happily at ease in his world.

Twain's awareness of the impact of Europe on Americans abroad is hardly the central theme of his fiction. Still, he helped to develop the terms through which American writers were to confront the Old World with representatives of the New. The fears and insecurities that Twain revealed through humor became the clichés of the future tourist class, whether from Lewis' Zenith or from James's New York City. The materials of the humorist became touchstones of allegiance for the novelists.

Like other Americans in Europe, the Innocent Abroad is troubled; the "dreadful" laugh that is "a full century old"—older than the town of Samuel Clemens' birth, or of most nineteenth-century Americans' birth —is different from anything Mark Twain has ever known. The very existence of the skeleton suggests a way of looking at life that is foreign, for the fashions of American interior decoration have never emulated the Capuchin vaults. Twain's fascination with that ancient, that noticeably "un-American," laugh suggests Lewis' Sam Dodsworth, who is at first intrigued by and attracted to the laughter of the Count von Obensdorf, his wife's future lover: " 'Kind of like an American, this fellow—this count,' said Sam. 'Got a sense of humor. . . .' " But Sam is wrong.

> "Oh no, it's a very different thing," Fran [Sam's wife] insisted. "He's completely European. Americans are humorous to cover up their worry about things. They think that what they do is imme- diately important and the world is waiting for it. The real European has a sense of a thousand years . . . behind him."[27]

Dodsworth does "worry about things." He cannot keep from himself "a deep and sturdy recognition of his own ignorance,"[28] and on many occasions we are told, more or less directly, that "he suddenly felt insecure."[29] When he successfully orders French station-attendants around, "he admitted that he was possibly being the brash Yankee of Mark Twain."[30] But Sam Dodsworth eventually chooses a European way of life, and Lewis pointedly foreshadows Sam's un-Americanism by contrasting his unexpected appreciation of art with "the Mark Twain tradition," in which "the American wife still marches her husband to galleries from which he tries to sneak away."[31] His appreciation is unexpected because Sam Dodsworth is first presented as being very much in the tradition: "He liked whiskey and poker,"[32] and his fondness for poker is referred to often enough and in the proper contexts to make it a metaphor of his desire to be with and like Americans.[33]

Now the American poker-player's approach to European art is established for all time by Mark Twain, and the establishment sanc- tioned by no less a pontiff than Henry James. Twain's Innocent tells us that he "could not help noticing how superior the copies were to the original. . . . Wherever you find a Raphael, a Rubens, a Michael Angelo, a Caracci, or a Da Vinci (and we see them every day) you find artists copying them, and the copies are always the handsomest" (I, 190). Henry James gives us, in his *The American* (1877), the transitional step between the completely westernized narrator of *The Innocents Abroad* and the potential renegade of *Dodsworth*. Christopher Newman is a synthesis of American types. He looks back upon the isolated spirit of Natty Bumppo as "he laughed the laugh in which he indulged when he was most amused—a noiseless laugh, with his lips closed."[34] He shows a more sociable sort of frontier experience, too, for—like Twain—"Newman had sat with Western humorists in knots, round cast-iron stoves, and seen 'tall' stories grow taller without toppling over, and his own imagination had learned the trick of piling up consistent wonders."[35] Finally, he is mythologized as an American titan in the "*légende*" of western wealth and power that the stout Duchess, Madame d'Outreville, invents for him,[36] a myth that will be echoed by Lewis in Dodsworth's determination, at the start of his travels,[37] to return to America and create such a city as is attributed to Newman.

In our first view of him, Newman is presented most simply as the "specimen of an American," as "the American type," and although his visit to the Louvre fills him, "for the first time in his life, with a vague self-mistrust,"[38] his habitual front possesses "that typical vagueness which is not vacuity, that blankness which is not simplicity."[39] He is aware of his fears, but, good American that he is, he is poker-faced. Like Sam Dodsworth, he has gambled quite literally, in business and in sport, "glad enough to play poker in St. Louis."[40] Unlike Twain's *persona*, he has come to Europe—as so many of James's people do—to learn; but his European education does not begin until after his first stroll through the Louvre, when he is most pointedly still the American: Newman looks "not only at all the pictures, but at all the copies that were going forward around them, . . . and if the truth must be told, he had often admired the copy much more than the original."

Newman's poker-faced admiration of Mlle Nioche's copies soon gives way to an acknowledged emotional involvement with Claire de Cintré, and to Newman's efforts to register directly on his feelings a sense of Europe. Mark Twain, playing the game of the American in Europe, retains the poker face that Newman struggles to put off, that is torn from Dodsworth by fate. (Dodsworth is not trying to educate himself into an involvement with Europe; events conspire to educate and to involve him despite himself.) For Lewis and James as well as for Twain, the American approaching Europe is poker-faced, and his reactions to European culture and customs are similar, initially, for all three writers. As James's and Lewis' protagonists succumb in their respective ways to the lure of the Continent, they lose their poker-faced detachment that has served as a defense against involvement, but their point of departure is defined by Twain's Innocent.

The three authors are concerned with tracing three variations of their common theme. For James, the impact of Europe as a civilizing force on the visiting American—Christopher Newman, Isabelle Archer, Lambert Strether, et al.—is the central concern, whether the force initiates a progression that culminates in grandeur or in futility. Lewis' *Dodsworth*, as one of the many novels in which Lewis presents America as seen through the eyes of H. L. Mencken, stresses the tawdry quality of American society, touching on the world of George F. Babbitt and focusing on the insubstantial character of Fran Dodsworth's worship of all things European. The actual impact of Europe on Sam Dodsworth is great—he chooses to leave America and live in Italy—but the weight of Europe itself is felt less throughout the book than is the density of the America from which Sam turns. The behavior of Mark Twain's Innocent merely suggests the rejection of America, and even the suggestion is only occasional. Most of the time, he appears brashly complacent in his Americanism. Indeed, his fear of Europe drives him happily back to his native shores, although he captures undertones that will become more significant in Twain's later work.

Twain's protagonist is really the most subversive of the three. Happy though the traveler returned may be, his first official act is to summarize the pilgrimage for the New York *Herald*, as Twain in fact did do, and his summary is not flattering to his fellow-Americans. His sarcastic irony—"We always took care to make it understood that we were Americans—Americans!" (II, 401)—evokes such samples of nationalism as the expedition's criminal archeological activities among the pyramids and their bad manners among the French. Boorishness and ignorance are the two most conspicuous qualities of these wandering representatives of God's latter-day Chosen People, as their spokesman's newsletter paints them. There clearly is more to Twain's treatment of America than simpleminded adulation. His ambivalence is as real as James's and Lewis', although one must see it in a more finished work to appreciate it.

Twain's use of the theme—Europe and America, East and West—and the central image for embodying this theme (the poker face) both arise from his immediate background in the humor of the Southwest, of the frontier. The same theme and the same image became equally part of the equipment of writers totally removed from both the frontier and the Southwest. Twain's use of this material differs from that of James and Lewis; the gap between Twain and his own tradition is equally significant. To be clear on this point one has only to remember Hank Morgan in Arthur's Court and Simon Suggs at his camp meeting: they are both slang-slinging adventurers, out for what they can get, but Hank's use of poker talk achieves effects that Simon's does not even suggest. Mark

Twain's adaptation of the standard elements of frontier humor enlarged their usefulness for literary art. How radical some of his departures were we have yet to see.

NOTES

1. See *Mark Twain and Southwestern Humor* (Boston: Atlantic-Little, Brown, 1959), pp. 61 ff.

2. Quoted from Augustus B. Longstreet by Donald Day, "The Humorous Works of George W. Harris," *American Literature*, XIV (January, 1943), 393.

3. George Washington Harris, *Sut Lovingood: Yarns Spun by a 'Nat'ral Born Durn'd Fool'* (New York, 1867), p. 111.

4. Johnson J. Hooper, *Simon Suggs' Adventures* (1845, reprinted Philadelphia, 1881), p. 26.

5. *Major Jones's Chronicles of Pineville* (Philadelphia, 1843), pp. 99-135.

6. Hooper, *op. cit.*, p. 132.

7. *Ibid.*, p. 138.

8. *Ibid.*, pp. 142, 143-44.

9. Reprinted from the Nashville *Union and American*, February 28, March 2, and March 5, 1861, in *Sut Lovingood*, ed. Brom Weber (New York: Grove Press, 1954), pp. 219-37.

10. *Ibid.*, pp. 221-22.

11. The "technique of rendering devils flabby is a common literary device which was discussed in rhetorical handbooks under the Greek title, *meiosis*, meaning, literally, 'belittling' or 'diminuation.' Diminuation may be described briefly as the use of any 'ugly or homely images' which are intended to diminish the dignity of an object. . . . diminuation is any kind of speech which tends, either by the force of low or vulgar imagery, or by other suggestion, to depress an object below its usually accepted status." (John M. Bullitt, *Jonathan Swift and the Anatomy of Satire: A Study of Satiric Technique* [Cambridge: Harvard University Press, 1953], p. 45.)

12. *Mark Twain at Work* (Cambridge: Harvard University Press, 1942), p. 69.

13. All volume and page references, unless otherwise indicated, are to *The Writings of Mark Twain*, "Definitive Edition" (37 vols.; New York: Harper & Bros., 1922-25).

14. Dixon Wecter, *Sam Clemens of Hannibal* (Boston: Houghton Mifflin, 1952), pp. 107-8.

15. In *Major Jones's Chronicles of Pineville*. Twain, says De Voto, "was thoroughly familiar with Thompson's work" (*Mark Twain at Work*, p. 68n).

16. *Major Jones's Chronicles of Pineville*, p. 18.

17. Hooper, *op. cit.*, p. 141.

18. *Ibid.*, pp. 141-42.

19. *Ibid.*, pp. 144-45.

20. In Edgar M. Branch, *The Literary Apprenticeship of Mark Twain* (Urbana: University of Illinois Press, 1950), p. 227.

21. Hooper, *op. cit.*, p. 136.

22. In Mody C. Boatright, *Folk Laughter on the American Frontier* (New York: Macmillan, 1949), p. 22.

23. Quoted in F. O. Matthiessen, *American Renaissance* (New York: Oxford University Press, 1941), p. 639.

24. Reprinted in Branch, *op. cit.*, p. 218.

25. Quoted from the Mark Twain Papers by Henry Nash Smith in "Mark Twain's Images of Hannibal," *Texas Studies in English*, XXXVII (1958), 3.

26. *Moby Dick*, chap. xlix, "The Hyena."

27. *Dodsworth* (New York: Modern Library ed., 1929), p. 231.

28. *Ibid.*, p. 121.

29. *Ibid.*, p. 76.

30. *Ibid.*, p. 112.

31. *Ibid.*, p. 119.

32. *Ibid.*, p. 11.

33. *Ibid.*, pp. 139, 140, 188, 190.

34. *The American* (Rinehart ed.; New York: Rinehart, 1949), p. 332. See Cooper's *The Prairie* for Natty's silent laugh (Rinehart ed.; New York: Rinehart, 1950), pp. 437 and *passim*.

35. *The American*, p. 98.

36. *Ibid.*, p. 212.

37. *Dodsworth*, p. 23.

38. *The American*, p. 2.

39. *Ibid.*, p. 3.

40. *Ibid.*, p. 21.

Faulkner and Certain Earlier
Southern Fiction

Carvel Collins

Some critics have said that Faulkner's fiction often falls into the patterns of two earlier kinds of writing produced in the South: the fiction
which presented a glamorous view of ante-bellum and Civil War life, and
the fiction written by the humorists of the Old Southwest, Faulkner's immediate region.

Several critics present the view that Faulkner's works which deal with
the Southern past usually make it glamorous and are basically in the
literary tradition of Cooke's *Surry of Eagle's Nest* and Page's *In Ole
Virginia* if not actually on a level with the novels of Beverly Tucker, Mrs.
Southworth, or Mary Holmes. These critics say that Faulkner, in
essence, subscribes to the commemorative view of the ante-bellum
plantation as the domicile of invariably cultured men of honor, inevitably
fair ladies, and the happy slave. These commentors also see Faulkner as
lost in a rosy fog about the Civil War, chiefly an affair of cavalry.

It is quite true that Faulkner is strongly drawn to these romantic
conceptions of the Southern past. He has been exposed to them not only
by the literary tradition but even more strongly by the rest of his environment. As he has one character say in *Intruder in the Dust*: "For
every Southern boy fourteen years old, not once but whenever he wants
it, there is the instant when it's still not yet two o'clock on that July
afternoon in 1863, the brigades are in position . . . the furled flags are
. . . loosened to break out and Pickett himself with his long oiled
ringlets . . . looking up the hill waiting for . . . the word . . . and
it's all in the balance, it hasn't happened yet . . . we have come too far

From *College English*, 16 (November 1954), 92-97. Copyright 1954 by the National Coun-
cil of Teachers of English. Reprinted with permission. The version published here has been
revised by the author.

with too much at stake and that moment doesn't need even a fourteen-year-old boy to think *This time*. *Maybe this time* with all this much to lose and all this much to gain: Pennsylvania, Maryland, the world, the golden dome of Washington itself to crown . . . the desperate gamble."

So Faulkner does present romantic conceptions of the Civil War and the Southern past. But it is interesting to note that in these works and in his fiction in general these conceptions are usually expressed by the most nearly expository passages, while the imaginative parts of those same works—the fables, if you will—usually portray different and often opposite ideas.

For Faulkner is by no means starry eyed about the South, past or present. Though like any of us he resents criticism from outside his own region, he is himself extremely critical, not only in his fiction but occasionally in public letters. Not long ago, at the time of a widely publicized trial of three Mississippi white men for the murder of a negro family, Faulkner wrote one of these rare letters to the *Memphis Commercial Appeal*, saying in part: "And those of us who were born in Mississippi and have lived all our lives in it, who have continued to live in it forty and fifty and sixty years at some cost and sacrifice simply because we love Mississippi and its ways and customs and soil and people; who because of that love have been ready and willing at all times to defend our ways . . . from attack by the outlanders whom we believed did not understand them, we had better be afraid too—afraid that we have been wrong; that what we had loved and defended not only didn't want the defense and wasn't worthy of the love, but worse: [was] incapable of the one and indefensible of the other."

More important to us here, however, is what Faulkner's fiction shows about his conception of the Southern past. In the novel *Sartoris* the Civil War gallantry of one member of the Sartoris family, though in some ways presented as romantically inspiring, is shown to be at best humorous and at worst selfish and fool-hardy when he is killed in the gesture of a single-handed raid for anchovies from the Federal stores. In *Light in August*, a book which some critics falsely consider to consist of two parts without unity, a unifying character, Hightower, is shown to reach psychological maturity at the end of the book only because he puts aside his life-long romantic vision of his grandfather's gallantry as a Confederate cavalryman and accepts both the reality of his grandfather's death while raiding a hen-coop and the reality of his own selfish immaturity in having deserted the present for a fixation on the supposedly glamorous past. In *Absalom, Absalom*, Faulkner, writing under intense personal grief and omitting much of his usual leavening humor, reports his conception of the ruthless means by which one ante-bellum plantation was created. *Go Down Moses* gives the ante-bellum South biting treatment in Ike McCaslin's examination of his family's past, which had included so much misuse of human beings and of the earth that Ike repudiates his heritage and will not accept the plantation left to him by his ancestors.

It is true that Faulkner usually shows a preference for the rural, less heavily populated, less hurried, less commercial life of an earlier time; but he is by no means committed to the ideas of the earlier authors who wrote shimmering novels about the Southern past.

Many critics say that Faulkner is closely in another literary tradition, that of the humorists of the Old Southwest. It is impossible to say just how much he has been influenced by his reading of these humorists, such as Augustus Longstreet, George W. Harris, Johnson Hooper, and Thomas Thorpe, and how much he has been influenced by his intense personal exposure to a later phase of the life and oral tradition on which those authors drew. Augustus Longstreet lived out his years in Faulkner's town of Oxford and is buried in the Oxford cemetery. His book *Georgia Scenes* (1835), a pioneering and influential work of its type, is known there. Parallels between episodes in Faulkner's novels and in *Georgia Scenes* have been pointed out by scholars. But if Longstreet and his contemporaries picked up a great deal of their material by watching the daily life and listening to the tales of the region, Faulkner has done as much of this as they. When a university student once asked Faulkner for advice about how to write, Faulkner replied, "Listen when other people talk." He has been following his own advice since the mid-nineteen-twenties when he decided that his *metier* was not poetry derived from Keats, Swinburne, Housman, and Aiken but was fiction. I was surprised not long ago when by chance I came upon more evidence of just how sharp that change was. In sorting through the debris at the site of a house which had burned ten years previously with some of Faulkner's apprentice manuscripts in it, I found a hundred few pages written when he was in his early twenties. Along with a number of his early unrecorded published works which I have been able to find, these charred papers show little sign of the interest in the local and observable Mississippi which has since been the starting point of much of his best fiction. But with his decision to try a different kind of writing, he presumably began much more consciously to listen and observe—on the court house square, in the houses of the country people whom he has come to know well, and in the hunting camps of which he has long been an active member.

So whether or not he has borrowed from the books of Longstreet and the other Old Southwestern humorists, he has been exposed to the remains of the experiences to which they were exposed; and his fiction contains much which has the flavor of the older works. I do not want here to discuss Faulkner's humor in general; that has been done in several articles and in a chapter of a recently published book on Faulkner. Instead I want to speak only about the use he makes of three elements characteristically found in the writings of the humorists of the Old Southwest. These three elements are 1) especially flamboyant humor, 2) violence, and 3) folklore.

The flamboyant humor of Davy Crockett, Simon Suggs, and Sut Lovingood appears in many of Faulkner's works. And, I might add parenthetically, it is interspersed with the ironical humor of his conversation. In the satirical and self-defensive way of the older Southwesterners he once reported, "I was born in 1826 of a negro slave and an alligator. . . ." But in Faulkner's works this exaggerated humor, with almost no exception, is never presented for itself alone. It is often excellent humor, valuable enough for itself, but Faulkner uses it for important additional purposes. The well-known piece called "Spotted Horses" has seemed to many readers uproariously funny, but when fitted into the novel *The Hamlet* it is not the diversion many readers have considered it to be, but is an important contribution to the movement of the novel as a whole. This episode, in which flamboyant humor and great pathos astonishingly mix and effectively interact with each other, increases our disgust with Flem Snopes; for in his rapacious commercialism he here corrupts nature yet again and ironically does it by using the wild and natural broncos as his tools. Exaggerated episodes of this sort appear throughout Faulkner. For example, we are entertained at one level by the fantastic humor of the convict's experiences with the flood in *The Wild Palms*, but unlike most of this sort of thing when written by the humorists of the Old Southwest, these experiences do not appeal to us at that level only but go on to contribute to a significant and complex comment on the human condition.

Critics have suggested that in Faulkner's portrayal of violence he may not only be following a general trend in modern literature—with its multifarious causes—but may have found some precedent in the violence of this older literature of his region: for example the gougings of Longstreet's "The Fight" or the violent practical jokes and calamities of George Harris' Sut Lovingood. Whether or not it is true that Faulkner's violence owes anything to this earlier Southern fiction, it is certainly true that, as with flamboyant humor, he does not use it for itself alone. In Longstreet the gouging during a fight is local color presented for itself, the author essentially saying merely, "Isn't this remarkable!" In *Sut Lovingood's Yarns*, which I consider a fine book on many other grounds, the violence begins to pall after a time and becomes in itself little more appealing than a series of elaborate hot-foots. But in Faulkner's fiction the violence is woven into the story in order to contribute to the total effect which is almost invariably well beyond the hot-foot or local color.

To take a particular, extreme example because it has aroused so much hostile comment: In *Light in August* Joe Christmas cuts Miss Burden's throat with a razor. When her body is wrapped up and carried out of the house and unwrapped in the yard, the spectators see that her head is turned backward on her body. Most readers have considered this to be an unnecessary twist, entirely gratuitous and differing from the cruelties of Longstreet's "Fight" only as it causes more revulsion. But the episode is an integral part of the elaborate and successful symbolism of the novel. In *The Divine Comedy*, Canto XX of "The Inferno," Dante and Virgil come upon a group of sinners whose punishment is to have their heads turned backward on their bodies. They are the prophets, Tiresias and others—they who have sinned by looking into the future. *Light in August* is a novel dealing in great part with time. The major characters are carefully given a relationship with time. Miss Burden is the character concentrated on the future, and it is her elaborate plans for the future of the reluctant Joe Christmas that prepare the situation in which he cuts her throat. I cannot prove that Faulkner draws on Dante for this episode and thus give some weight to this interpretation. But Faulkner is extremely well-read and frequently does this sort of thing—to an extent which would surprise the critics who continue to regard him as an unlettered barefoot country boy, a concept he has fostered after the fashion of these Southern humorists, who also sometimes feigned illiteracy. Whether or not Faulkner drew on Dante or, like Dante himself, had no known source for this motif, the fact remains that even this episode of extreme violence, selected for illustration here because it often has been singled out for its supposedly gratuitous horror, is almost certainly not for itself alone but for a larger purpose.

Another of the contributions of the humorists of the Old Southwest was the reshaping and transmission in print of a considerable amount of folklore. Faulkner also does this, but here again I believe that he never presents folklore just for itself. The critics' failure to see this has often lead them to erroneous judgments about an entire Faulkner novel. *The*

Hamlet, which is full of elements common to the humor of the Old Southwest, offers a useful example. In one of its sections, Houston, a resident of the small hamlet of Frenchman's Bend lies with his wife naked in the moonlight in the folk belief that this will insure pregnancy. Critics who keep repeating that *The Hamlet* is not a unified novel but a collection of sketches have cited this episode as one of the proofs of their contention. But it is by no means presented as a bit of folklore interesting to the reader solely for its quaintness or its local-color charm. Its function in the book is to add its small share to the opposition between the natural, emotional people of Frenchman's Bend and the Snopes tribe which is destroying them under the leadership of the unemotional, commercialized, and sterile Flem. Immediately after the novel shows the widowed Houston in the act of recalling how he and his bride had lain in the moonlight in the interest of fertility, it goes on to tell us that Houston is shot and killed by one of the Snopes.

A larger and more important sample of the difference between the use of folklore in Faulkner's work and that in the work of the early humorists is the long section entitled "The Bear" in *Go Down Moses*. This story has a great deal in common with the best piece of its kind produced by the humorists of the Old Southwest: Thomas Thorpe's excellent story, "The Big Bear of Arkansas," which was published in *The Spirit of the Times* during 1841 and which Faulkner in conversation once made clear to me that he knew well.

Both of these stories are related to a long line of folklore on which many pieces of literature are considered to have drawn, among them *The Odyssey, Beowulf*, and *Moby Dick*. In Thorpe as in Faulkner the hunted animal is extraordinarily large, competent, and mysterious. Its hunters, with varying intensity, see it as supernatural and an embodiment of large principles. Even in minor matters the two works are parallel with each other and with the basic folktale: these details include a plunge through water at a climax of the hunt, the temporary substitution of an inferior for the real quarry, and the inability of the hunters to confront the bear when they are conventionally prepared for the hunt (in Faulkner the hunter, Ike McCaslin, confronts the bear only after he has put aside his rifle, compass, and other tools of civilization much in the fashion of Melville's Captain Ahab on his hunt for the great whale; in Thorpe the hunter, though he has his rifle nearby, finally and most closely confronts the bear only when he is in the woods not to hunt but for another natural purpose which the story presents with ribaldry).

Both works are excellent, but Thorpe's does not attempt to do much more than tell an entertaining tall-tale. It has great attraction for us in its conventionally analyzable surface story, and presumably has as much or more in what psychologists would consider to be its less well-understood latent content, which apparently is considerable. But Faulkner's story has most of these qualities and more besides. Here Faulkner is using folklore as he uses violence and exaggerated humor: for larger purposes than did the humorists of the Old Southwest. Ike McCaslin's experience in the mysterious bear hunt, though extremely well told, does not end there. One possible subtitle for Faulkner's bear story is "The Education of Ike Mc-Caslin." During the hunt and its aftermath Ike becomes initiated into the way of maturity. As a result of what he learns in the hunt and what he knows of the corrupt history of his family, he repudiates his family's ante-bellum past and refuses to inherit the plantation. Thorpe's story of "The Big Bear of Arkansas" is excellent; but Faulkner, using the same basic folklore, adds other themes and goes far beyond his predecessor.

To both of these literary traditions of the South—the humor of the Old Southwest, and the romantic fiction about the Southern past—Faulkner's work stands in a similar relationship. He is drawn to their essentials and uses many of their devices and motifs, but fundamentally his work is quite removed from them in both purpose and method.

William Faulkner and George Washington Harris: In the Tradition of Southwestern Humor

M. Thomas Inge

The importance of the work of the group of writers known as the South-western Humorists to the mainstream of American Literature received only slight critical recognition until it was observed that it furnished a literary background for and influenced much of the writings of Mark Twain. Among the names of the better known writers in this group, one was of paticular importance to Twain—the Tennessee humorist, George Washington Harris. Harris had created a fun-loving, hell-raising, whiskey-guzzling East Tennessee comic character, the inimitable Sut Lovingood, who apparently meant much to Twain's creation of Huckleberry Finn. The innovation which Harris negotiated, that set him apart from the other humorists and made him the forerunner of Mark Twain, was his accurate transcription of a Southern vernacular or dialect in the mouth of a native. He allowed a representative of the East Tennessee moun-taineers and backwoods folk to recount his pranks and tall tales in his own person, in his own language, and from his own viewpoint.

Another factor which has brought Harris, and other Southwestern humorists as well, into the critical spotlight is the number of studies now being made on the techniques of humor in the work of another notable American writer—William Faulkner.[1] That Faulkner has used much of the material and techniques of frontier humor was first pointed out by Malcolm Cowley, who wrote in his introduction to *The Portable Faulkner:*

> In his later books, . . . there is a quality not exactly new to Faulkner . . . but now much stronger and no longer overshadowed

From *Tennessee Studies in Literature*, Volume VII, edited by Alwin Thaler, Richard Beale Davis, and John Livesay, by permission of The University of Tennessee Press. Copyright 1962 by The University of Tennessee Press.

by violence and horror. It is a sort of homely and sobersided frontier humor that is seldom achieved in contemporary writing (except by Erskine Caldwell, another Southerner).[2]

Faulkner has used the forms and material of the tradition in a new and original way, so that they become a part of the complex structure of the whole of his work. Although surely he did, Faulkner need not even have read the humorists. Robert Penn Warren says of this strain of humor in Faulkner's work, "it is probable that he got it from the porches of country stores and the courthouse yards of county-seat towns and not from any book. . . ."[3] The tall tales and ribald anecdotes told by men standing around on street corners while passing around a jug of corn liquor were the very sources in another day of the Southwestern humor tradition. Faulkner grew up amidst the remains of these elements surviving from a past era, and any attempt to utilize this environment in a fictional manner could hardly avoid containing something of the flavor of the older tradition. Thus, Carvel Collins comments:

> If Longstreet and his contemporaries picked up a great deal of their material by watching the daily life and listening to the tales of the region, Faulkner has done as much of this as they. When a university student once asked Faulkner for advice about how to write, Faulkner replied, "Listen when other people talk."[4]

What distinguishes Faulkner from the traditional humorists is the fact that he uses the material as an effective device for achieving a more serious artistic end. It has a schematic purpose in his work, and it is not written merely for its comic value. Faulkner himself wrote in 1926: "We have one priceless universal trait, we Americans. That trait is our humor. What a pity it is that it is not more prevalent in our art."[5] By presenting the humorous as well as the tragic aspects of life, and thus displaying the whole fabric of existence, he is perhaps in accord with his stated aim of the writer, "to help man endure by lifting his heart."[6] Interestingly enough, George Washington Harris claimed a similar purpose in his writing, in the preface to his only collection of tales, *Sut Lovingood's Yarns*. He has Sut say:

> "Ef eny poor misfortinit devil hu's heart is onder a mill-stone, hu's raggid children am hungry, an' no bread in the dresser, hu is down in the mud, an' the lucky ones a-trippin him every time he

struggils tu his all fours, hu hes fed the famishin an' is now hungry hissef, hu misfortins foller fas' an' foller faster, hu is so foot-sore an' weak that he wishes he wer at the ferry—ef sich a one kin fine a laugh, jis' one, sich a laugh as is remembered wif his keerless boyhood, atwixt these yere kivers—then, I'll thank God that I *hes* made a book an' feel that I hev got my pay in full."[7]

But a relationship of even greater depths exists between the work of George Washington Harris and William Faulkner. In a comparative study of Nathaniel Hawthorne and Faulkner, Randall Stewart has written:

Each . . . has certain important lineal relations, as a writer, to the regional literature which preceded him. If Hawthorne's relation to his New England predecessors (to Cotton Mather, for example) is clearer than Faulkner's relation to his Southern predecessors (to G. W. Harris, for example), it is because the former subject has been a good deal more studied than the latter. The latter subject—a whole new field—has scarcely been studied at all.[8]

We do not know for a certainty whether Faulkner ever read any of the sketches of Augustus Baldwin Longstreet, Johnson Jones Hooper, Joseph Baldwin, Thomas Bangs Thorpe, William Tappan Thompson, or any of the other Southwestern humorists, but by his own admission, we know that he read the yarns of Harris. In fact, he has singled out Sut Lovingood as one of his favorite fictional characters. When he was asked in 1956 to cite some of his favorite fictional characters in literature, he concluded with:

And then I like Sut Lovingood from a book written by George Harris about 1840 or '50 in the Tennessee mountains. He had no illusions about himself, did the best he could; at certain times he was a coward and knew it and wasn't ashamed; he never blamed his misfortunes on anyone and never cursed God for them.[9]

In view of Faulkner's temperament, it is easy to see why a character of Sut's nature would appeal to him, but there is also reflected in one aspect of Faulkner's comic technique what would seem to be a sure influence of Harris's style, which would denote a more than cursory reading of Harris.
One of Harris's greatest achievements lies in his vivid imagery based

upon a frequent, wild, and complex use of epithets, similes and metaphors. One critic has written of Harris's style:

> The first effect of this frequency of imagery is speed and intensity. The reader is whirled into the illusion of sheer delight in motion and wild action. Racy colloquialism, nonce words, corruption of names and of bookish terms, compression of details, astonishing expansion of connotation, and controlled changes in the tensions of the action and of the language, shifting from litotes to the wildest hyperbole, give a constant illusion of speed and movement. Images are expanded by piling detail upon detail until the reader is bewildered in a complexity of emotions and ideas.[10]

This, in part, is what accounts for the impression of fast-moving action one perceives in the reading of a Sut Lovingood yarn. It is what F. O. Matthiessen was referring to when he wrote, "Harris possesses on the comic level something of what Melville does on the tragic, the rare kind of dramatic imagination that can get movement directly into words. This brings a wonderfully kinetic quality to whole situations. . . ."[11] The artistry of this "kinetic" quality is easily seen in an example of this style at its best. It can be seen in this picture of the awkward, lanky Sut seeking a kiss:

> "Purty soon Sal Yardley started fur the smoke-'ous, so I jis' gin my head a few short shakes, let down one ove my wings a-trailin, an' sirkiled roun her wif a side twis' in my naik, stepping sidewise, an' a-fetchin up my hinmos' foot wif a sorter jerkin slide at every step." (146)

It is clear how the bird imagery, suggested by "wings" and "sirkiled," adds to the imparted action.

The imagery of Faulkner, in several passages in *The Town*, is highly reminiscent of that employed by Harris; this is particularly true of that highly comic and technically admirable section which describes the escaped mules of I. O. Snopes which Old Het and Mrs. Hait chase around the yard of the latter. Many passages here come near the same "kinetic" quality that Harris achieved. For instance:

> Mrs. Hait set the scuttle down on the edge of the brick coping of the cellar entrance and she and old Het turned the corner of the

house in time to see the mule coincide with a rooster and eight white-leghorn hens coming out from under the house. Old Het said it looked just like something out of the Bible, or maybe out of some kind of hoodoo witches' Bible: the mule that came out of the fog to begin with like a hant or a goblin, now kind of soaring back into the fog again borne on a cloud of little winged ones.[12]

It is possible that Faulkner might have been influenced by a scene in one of the Sut yarns when he wrote of the wild horse who entered Mrs. Littlejohn's house in the "Spotted Horses" episode in *The Hamlet*, a book particularly full of the elements of Southwestern humor. In Harris's version, Sock, a bull, blinded by a basket and plagued by bees, backs into the Burns' house where a wedding dinner is being held for the former Sicily Burns and her new husband, Clapshaw; Sut gleefully relates:

"He cum tail fust agin the ole two story Dutch clock, an' fotch hit, bustin hits runnin geer outen hit, the littil wheels a-trundlin over the floor, an' the bees even chasin them. Nex pass, he fotch up agin the foot ove a big dubbil injine bedstead, rarin hit on aind, an' punchin one ove the posts thru a glass winder. . . . Clapshaw's ole mam wer es deaf es a dogiron, an sot at the aind ove the tabil, nex tu whar ole Sock busted thru the wall; tail fus' he cum again her cheer, a-histin her an' hit ontu the tabil . . . an' thar sot ole Missis Clapshaw, a-straddil ove the top ove the pile, a-fitin bees like a mad wind-mill, wif her calliker cap in one han, fur a wepun, an' a cract frame in tuther, an' a-kickin, an' a-spurrin like she wer ridin a lazy hoss arter the doctor, an' a-screamin rape, fire, an' murder, es fas' es she cud name 'em over." (92-3)

Faulkner writes:

They saw the horse . . . whirl and dash back and run through the gate into Mrs. Littlejohn's yard and run up the front steps and crash once on the wooded veranda and vanish through the front door. . . . A lamp sat on a table just inside the door. In its mellow light they saw the horse fill the long hallway like a pinwheel, gaudy, furious and thunderous. A little further down the hall there was a varnished yellow melodeon. The horse crashed into it; it produced a single note, almost a chord, in bass, resonant and grave, of deep and sober astonishment; the horse with its monstrous and antic shadow whirled again and vanished through another door. It was a bedroom; Ratliff, in his underclothes and one sock and with the other sock in his hand and his back to the door, was leaning out the open window facing the lane, the lot. He looked back over his shoulder. For an instant he and the horse glared at one another. Then he sprang through the window as the horse backed out of the room and into the hall again. . . . It whirled again and rushed down the hall and onto the back porch just as Mrs. Littlejohn, carrying an armful of clothes from the line and the washboard, mounted the steps.[13]

Unlike Mrs. Clapshaw, who simply screamed "rape, fire, an' murder, es fas' as she cud name 'em over," Mrs. Littlejohn strikes back with a washboard and a very unladylike exclamation. When Ratliff is discussing the episode later, he says, " 'Maybe there wasn't but one of them things in Mrs. Littlejohn's house that night. . . . But it was the biggest drove of just one horse I ever seen. It was in my room and it was on the front porch and I could hear Mrs. Littlejohn hitting it over the head with that washboard all the same time.' "[14] Sut, speaking of the basket which Old Burns is swinging and hitting the bull over the head with on his bull ride, says, " 'I'll jis' be durn'd ef I didn't think he hed four ur five baskits, hit wer in so meny places at onst' " (94).

There is also an event in another Sut yarn similar to the scene in *The Hamlet* where one of the spotted horses meets the Tull family wagon on a bridge, overturns his wife and daughters, and leaves Mr. Tull's unconscious body on the bridge:

Then the front end of the wagon rose, flinging Tull, the reins now wrapped several times about his wrist, backward into the wagon bed among the overturned chairs and the exposed stockings and under-garments of his women. The pony scrambled free and chased again on the wooden planking, galloping again. The wagon lurched again; the mules had finally turned it on the bridge where there was not room for it to turn and were now kicking themselves free of the traces. When they came free, they snatched Tull bodily out of the wagon. He struck the bridge on his face and was dragged for several feet before the wrist-wrapped reins broke. Far up the road now, distancing the frantic mules, the pony faded on. While the five women still shrieked above Tull's unconscious body, Eck and the little boy came up, trotting, Eck still carrying his rope. He was panting. "Which way'd he go?" he said.[15]

In the Harris yarn, Sut has caused a horse to go berserk with a Yankee lawyer named Stilyards upon it. On its wild dash, it encounters an "ole baldheaded, thick-sot feller a-cummin in frum [the] mill," riding a "blaze-face hoss," with "a 'oman behine him." Sut describes the ensuing catas-trophe:

> "Well, yu kin sorter take in the tremenjus idear ove that spot ove sandy road, whar Stilyards met the bald-headed man. That onlucky ole cuss lit twenty foot out in the woods, never look'd back, but sot his trampers tu work, an' distributed hissef sumwhat towards the Black Oak Ridge. The 'oman hung by wun foot in the fork ove a black-jack, an' a-holdin tu a dogwood lim' wif her hans, an' she hollerin, surter spiteful like—'Split the black-jack, ur fetch a quilt!' . . . Stilyards wer ni tuther side ove the road, flat ontu his back, fainted cumfortabil, and quiet as a sick sow in a snowstorm, his arms an' laigs stretched till he look'd like a big letter X." (42-4)

There is also an interesting parallel between the treatment, in terms of imagery, by Faulkner of Eula Varner and Harris of Sicily Burns, Sut's sweetheart who jilted him to marry Clapshaw, the circuit-rider. The hyperbole and epithets Faulkner applies to Eula, to suggest the Hellenic appeal of her physical attractions, are more sophisticated than Harris's, but no less vivid. Faulkner combines this style of writing with the device of showing the effect she has on the men who come in contact with her— thus evading a direct description which could not do justice to the beauty he wishes to portray. This combination is seen in the first impression of Eula on the young schoolteacher, Labove, who later abandons all his hopes for a law career, for which he has labored so hard, merely to prostrate himself before this supernal earth-goddess:

> Then one morning he turned from the crude blackboard and saw a face eight years old and a body of fourteen with a female shape of twenty, which on the instant of crossing the threshold brought into the bleak, ill-lighted, poorly-heated room dedicated to the harsh functioning of Protestant primary education a moist blast of spring's liquorish corruption, a pagan triumphal prostration before the supreme primal uterus.[16]

Faulkner writes, ". . . her entire appearance suggested some symbology out of the old Dionysic times—honey in sunlight and bursting grapes, the writhen bleeding of the crushed fecundated vine beneath the hard rapacious trampling goathoof."[17] In other places she is called the "drowsing maidenhead symbol's self," "at once supremely unchaste and inviolable: the queen, the matrix," and "Venus."[18] Eula is compared to a fertile field:

> The fine land rich and fecund and foul and eternal and impervious to him who claimed title to it, oblivious, drawing to itself tenfold the quality of living seed its owner's whole life could have secreted and compounded, producing a thousandfold the harvest he could ever hope to gather and save.[19]

Harris, like Faulkner, has Sut describe Sicily Burns mainly in terms of the effect she has on Sut and men in general, though he does employ some colorful and vivid imagery to indicate her appearance. When someone suggests Sicily is handsome, Sut exclaims:

> "Handsome! that ar word don't kiver the case; hit sounds sorter like calling good whiskey strong water, when yu ar ten mile frum a still-hous, hit a rainin', an' yer flask only haf full. She shows amung wimen like a sunflower amung dorg fennil, ur a hollyhawk in a patch ove smartweed. Sich a buzzim! Jis' think ove two snow balls wif a strawberry stuck but-ainded intu bof on em." (75)

"Her har's es black es a crow's wing at midnite," Sut says, ". . . an' her cheeks an' lips es rosy es a pearch's gills in dorgwood blossom time— an' sich a smile! why, when hit struck you far an' squar hit felt jis like a big ho'n ove onrectified ole Munongahaley . . . " (76). Of her effect on men, Sut says, "Sich an 'oman cud du more devilmint nur a loose stud hoss et a muster groun', ef she only know'd what tools she totes, an' I'se sorter beginin tu think she no's the use ove the las' durnd wun, tu a dot" (77). Sut philosophizes on Sicily's seductive charms: ". . . this worl am all 'rong enyhow, more temtashun than perventitive; ef hit were ekal, I'd stand hit. What kin the ole prechurs an' the ugly wimen 'spect ove us, 'sposed es we ar tu sich invenshuns es she am?" (77).

Harris also resorts to the world of nature to allow Sut to describe the effect of Sicily on him. She is compared to a storm in the Tennessee mountains:

> "I'se hearn in the mountins a fus rate fourth proof smash ove thunder cum onexpected, an' shake the yeath, bringin along a string

ove litenin es long as a quarter track, an' es bright es a weldin heat, a-racin down a big pine tree, tarin hit intu broom-splits, an' toof pickers, an' raisin a cloud ove dus', an' bark, an' a army ove lim's wif a smell sorter like the devil wer about, an' the long darnin needil leaves fallin roun wif a tif—tif—quiet sorter soun, an' then a quiverin on the yeath es littil snakes die; an' I felt quar in my in'ards, sorter ha'f cumfurt, wif a littil glad an' rite smart ove sorry mix'd wif hit."

"I'se sed the rattil-snake squar hissef tu cum at me, a saying ze-e-e-e, wif that nisey tail ove his'n, an' I felt quar agin—mons'rous quar. I've seed the Oconee River jumpin mad frum rock tu rock wif hits clear, cool warter, white foam an' music . . . , an' hit gin me an oneasy queerness agin; but every time I look'd at that gal Sicily Burns, I hed all the feelins mix'd up, ove the litenin, the river, an' the snake, wif a totch ove the quicksilver sensashun a huntin thru all my veins fur my ticklish place." (77-8)

Thus Sut communicates the queer, unnerving power of sensual passion and the fear of fleshly delights, by likening them to the inspirational and fearful beauty of nature. By association with the procreative force of Mother Nature, Sicily, like Eula, becomes the seductive earth-goddess, the eternally creative female.

Faulkner not only utilizes a style similar to Harris's upon occasion, but they have both written upon similar themes. The Fonzo and Virgil Snopes episode in *Sanctuary* is another variation on the country yokels come to town theme, which had been treated by Harris, in an unribald manner, in a pre-Sut Lovingood sketch called "There's Danger in Old Chairs."[20] And, as in the imaginative Faustian allegory in *The Hamlet*, when Flem goes to hell to retrieve his soul, Sut also once went to hell, or dreamed he did, for voting the "Radikil ticket," in a yarn called "Sut Lovingood's Dream."[21] It is true that these two sketches by Harris appeared in contemporary newspapers only, and were not included in the collected *Yarns*. The chances are Faulkner could never have seen them, despite wide reprinting.

This is likewise true of one of Harris's last and best yarns, which appeared in only one newspaper as far as is known, which nevertheless is strikingly similar in material to one of Faulkner's best novels, *As I Lay Dying*. The yarn referred to is called "Well! Dad's Dead."[22] It was written three years after the close of the Civil War and approximately one year before Harris's sudden and mysterious death. The sketch is a perfect example of how embittered and morbid minded Harris had become after the conclusion of the sectional conflict. Harris had allied his sympathies with the Southern Democrats early in his career, and he never budged an instant from his stand. He had always vilified Northern politicians and he later began to ridicule, through his satires, his Knoxville neighbors for their treasonous anti-secessionist attitude. When the Union Forces moved into Knoxville in February of 1862, Harris joined the general exodus of Southern sympathizers with his wife and children.

Most of the writing Harris did after the war held political implications. In very few of his non-political pieces did he achieve any semblance of his old vivid and lively style, and only then when he wrote of his nostalgic memories of pre-war days. The yarn, "Well! Dad's Dead," which tells of the death and interment of Sut's "King Fool" Dad, and describes the Lovingoods' burlesque funeral procession, uses the same characters from some of Sut's most hilarious adventures, but the material is handled so morbidly and grotesquely, that it is humor only of a macabre sort. It uses the same material of Southwestern humor, but has none of the wild abandon and comical elements of Harris's old work.

In this respect, *As I Lay Dying* is like the yarn, as it too treats of the material and characters of Southwestern humor converted to a somberness and grotesqueness. In his brief book on Faulkner, Ward L. Miner relates the novel to folk humor in this way:

> The novel is a folk comedy embodying tragedy, despair and futility. These overtones are those particularly appropriate to southwest folk humor, which has been noted for its violence and cruelty. Faulkner has applied modern subjective techniques to the violent material of the regional folklore.[23]

On the social level, the Bundrens and the Lovingoods are equal. The main concern of both pieces is a funeral procession which becomes a ridiculous or macabre spectacle. The journeys in both become bizarre caricatures of what such sacred missions should be like. It is only the preponderant cosmic pessimism of the novel which keeps it from becoming as farcical as Harris's sketch.

Sut's lack of concern over his father's death is shown in the opening lines of the yarn:

> Thar never wer a man yet, so mean, but what some time or other, done at least one good thing. Now, my Dad, put off doing his good thing, for an awful long time, but at last he did hit, like a white man.

He died by golly! prefeckly squar—strait out, an' for keep. Aint you glad?

Sut's mother is likewise unconcerned, who only complains that her husband didn't "ketch the idear twenty years sooner, for then she mout 'a done sumthin.' But no, he hilt on, jist to spite her, ontil she broke off her last tooth, crackin' a corn bread crust, an' then he immegintly went." While the old man is dying, she is outside fighting with a neighbor:

> Old Muddleg's wife come to the fence an' call'd mam out, to know if she cudent spar the frock she had on, in pay for sixty cents, that dad owed her husbun'. . . . she thought mam mout afford to run in her petticoattail a while, as the weather wer good, an' hit bein' black, would pass for fust rate mournin . . . she jist bleated like an' ole ewe, an' jump'd the fence to her. An' don't you believe! mam kicked her bustle clean off ove her, the passun, an' his wife a ridin' apast at that. Her nose bled, an' mam cried, an sich a snortin' as they had. The las' words dad ever spoke, were "Which whip'd?"

There is also a lack of appropriate concern for the death of Addie Bundren in *As I Lay Dying*. Cora Tull says she will not die like Addie does:

> Not like Addie Bundren dying alone, hiding her pride and her broken heart. Glad to go. Lying there with her head propped up so she could watch Cash building her coffin, having to watch him so he would not skimp on it, like as not, with those men not worrying about anything except if there was time to earn another three dollars before the rain come and the river got too high to get across it.[24]

Addie is no sooner gone than Anse's first reaction is to think of the opportunity afforded by the coming funeral journey to town: "God's will be done. . . . Now I can get them teeth."[25] Like Sut's mother, he too has apparently lost his last tooth.

When Sut's father is "cool, an' stiff enuf to handle," he is wrapped in an old, black bed spread and placed in an old accoutrement box. The makeshift coffin is loaded onto a big, shingle sled, which is hitched to a couple of steers. As the funeral procession begins, Sut says:

> I sot in front an' was driver, an' a feelin' come over me, like I think a durn'd, starvin', one-hoss lawyer mus' a had, when he fust foun'

hisself Captain ove Company A, at the beginnin' ove the war. I'd a cuss'd a man in a minit, but fortinatly for any man, he warnt about jist then. So, when I promised mam that I would "go slow," I did hit, with dignerty and 'sponsibility. I'd a liked durn'd well to a hearn anybody venture to order me to go fast, or to go at all, for that matter. I meant to make the most out ove that persession, an' my persition in hit, you understan'.

There is a similar sense of pride in Anse, in Faulkner's novel, who enjoys the position of importance the funeral gives him; Tull first notices this pride when he and the neighbors arrive to pay their respects: "He looks folks in the eye now, dignified, his face tragic and composed, shaking us by the hand as we walk up on to the porch and scrape our shoes. . . ."[26] And he admonishes several of his children for their conduct, as the journey begins, with "It ain't respectful," and "It ain't right," or "It's a flouting of the dead."[27] Olga W. Vickery notes:

> . . . the Bundrens are expected to assume the traditional role of mourners, a role which carries with it unspoken rules of propriety and decorum. Only Anse, for whom Addie never existed as an individual, finds such a role congenial. His face tragic and composed, he easily makes the proper responses to condolences and recites his litany of grief, though somewhat marred by irrepressible egotism. There is even a sense in which Anse thoroughly enjoys the situation since as chief mourner he is, for the first time in his life, a person of importance.[28]

Thus both Anse and Sut feel pride for the first time in their lives.

The troubles encountered by the Lovingoods on the journey are not as diverse and numerous as those the Bundrens meet with, but they arise in part from the same source: the stench of the rotting corpse. Sut relates:

> Now, durn'd fool like, in my big strut, I never tho't wonst about the smell ove the corpse a skeerin' the steers—hit always does, you know. So, jist as soon as they cotch the first whif ove hit, they snorted —bawl'd—histed their tails up strait, an', with one mind, run away, hoss fashion.

A wild cross-country ride follows which throws the family from the wagon and leaves Sut's mother hanging in a tree. As the sled speeds past the graveyard, Sut kicks the coffin into the grave, without any formal rites or words:

> One thing I sorter hated, he fell with his head to the east, an' I'm feared, that will make him a little late in a risein'. But, by golly! I cudent help hit, for we come in from the west. . . . Thars one little comfort in hit tho'—he'l rise with his back to the danger, an' I'll bet he hooves it frum thar.

As I Lay Dying closes on a wry, ironic, humorous note when Anse gets himself another wife, with Addie having been in the ground for only a matter of minutes. Harris's yarn likewise ends on a wry, macabre note:

> That night, when we wer all hunker'd round the hearth, sayin' nothin', an' waitin for the taters to roast, mam, she spoke up—"oughtent we to a scratch'd in a little dirt on him, say?" "No need, mam" sed Sall [Sut's sister], "hits loose yeath, an' will soon cave in enuff." "But, I want to plant a 'simmon sprout at his head," sed mam, "on account ove the puckery taste he had left in my mouth. Law sakes alive! haint hit so pervokin, that we never kin do enythin like eny body else?"

To Anse, Addie had just as well never been born, once she is dead: he can forget that easy. Were she presented with the opportunity, Sut's mother would probably get her a new husband just as quickly as Anse did a new wife; then perhaps the "puckery taste" in her mouth would pass. But at least Sut's Dad left some sort of memory with his wife, no matter how distasteful it is. As much cannot be said for Addie.

Thus, many marked similarities are apparent between *As I Lay Dying* and "Well! Dad's Dead." This does not necessarily imply that Harris's tale was used or even seen by Faulkner. But Ward L. Miner makes some interesting comments on the possibility of there having been some original source material used by Faulkner:

> This burial journey story is one found in many legends and tales since medieval times. Though I have been unable to locate the particular one, I feel fairly sure that what the author has done has been to start with the basic story in one of these legends, transplant it to Frenchman's Bend, and then present it by modern subjective methods. How closely the author stuck to an original story we can never tell

until the hypothetical original has been found. Indeed it may very well be true that he was only following a general folklore pattern although his having written *As I Lay Dying* in six weeks leads one to suspect the existence of a more particular source.[29]

Perhaps not Harris's yarn but one similar to it in material, or a source common to both of them, may have been followed by Faulkner.

There are no definite conclusions to be drawn from the number and variety of similarities between the material, and method or style of treatment, in the writings of George W. Harris and William Faulkner. The fact that Faulkner has read and admires Harris denotes the possibility of influence, but it is hard to determine exactly how much any one favorite author could shape the work of a writer. If an influence exists, it is not as clear and certain, for instance, as is the effect of Harris on Mark Twain. Whatever material Faulkner has used, from Harris or any other Southwestern humorist, it has been transmuted in his hands to convey more significance and meaning than its originator could have achieved. By becoming a part of the total scheme of Faulkner's work, it is given a more lasting and enduring quality.

NOTES

1. See, for example: Carvel Collins, "Faulkner and Certain Earlier Southern Fiction," *College English*, XVI (1954), 92-7; Frank M. Hoadley, "Folk Humor in the Novels of William Faulkner," *Tennessee Folklore Society Bulletin*, XXIII (1957), 75-82; Cecil D. Eby," Faulkner and the Southwestern Humorists." *Shenandoah*, XI (1959), 13-21. Among unpublished studies are: Bettye Field, "William Faulkner and the Humor of the Old Southwest," Master's thesis, Vanderbilt University, 1952; Herman O. Wilson, "A Study of Humor in the Fiction of William Faulkner," Doctoral dissertation, University of Southern California, 1956.

2. In *William Faulkner, Two Decades of Criticism*, ed. Frederick J. Hoffman and Olga W. Vickery (Michigan State College, 1954), pp. 80-1. See also by Cowley, "William Faulkner's Human Comedy," *New York Times Book Review*, October 22, 1944.

3. In *Two Decades of Criticism*, 93.

4. "Faulkner and Certain Earlier Southern Fiction," *College English*, XVI (1954), 94.

5. Cited by John Arthos, "Ritual and Humor in . . . Faulkner," in *Two Decades of Criticism*, 106.

6. "The Nobel Prize Address," in *The Faulkner Reader* (New York, 1954), p. 4.

7. *Sut Lovingood's Yarns* (New York, 1867), p. xi. Page references to this book will hereafter be included within parentheses in the text, following quoted matter. Cecil D. Eby recently stated that, "No such ideological purposes [as those of Faulkner] characterized the work of any Southwestern humorist. . . . they were more interested in transcribing the flavor of the frontier than in questioning its values." "Faulkner and the Southwestern Humorists," *Shenandoah*, XI (1959), 20. Harris was intensely concerned at times, however, with the very values of existence itself, particularly during the bitter post-war years.

8. "Hawthorne and Faulkner," *College English*, XVII (1956), 259.

9. Cited by Kenneth S. Lynn, *Mark Twain and Southwestern Humor* (Boston, 1959), p. 137.

10. Milton Rickels, "The Imagery of George Washington Harris," *American Literature*, XXI (1959), 175.

11. *American Renaissance* (New York, 1941), p. 643.

12. *The Town* (New York, 1957), 238. Notice also that "kinetically" effective paragraph running from page 237 to 238.

13. *The Hamlet* (New York, 1957), 307-8. Since this study was originally written, it has come to my attention that William Van O'Conner has already taken notice of these analogous passages in his book *The Tangled Fire of William Faulkner* (Minneapolis, 1954), pp. 122-3.

14. *Ibid.*, p. 314.

15. *The Hamlet*, p. 309.

16. *Ibid.*, p. 114.

17. *Ibid.*, p. 95.

18. *Ibid.*, pp. 115, 116, 119.

19. *Ibid.*, p. 119.

20. *Weekly Nashville Union,* October 6, 1847; reprinted in *Knoxville Standard*, October 10, 1847, and *Spirit of the Times* (New York), December 4, 1847.

21. *Lynchburg Daily Virginian*, January 23, 1867.

22. *Knoxville Press and Herald*, November 15, 1868.

23. *The World of William Faulkner* (Durham, 1952), p. 116.

24. *As I Lay Dying* (New York, 1946), pp. 353-4.

25. *Ibid.*, p. 375.

26. *Ibid.*, p. 399.

27. *Ibid.*, pp. 409-10.

28. *The Novels of William Faulkner* (Baton Rouge, 1959), p. 52.

29. *The World of William Faulkner*, p. 117.

Tidewater and Frontier

Randall Stewart

Southern literature from the beginning has been more diverse, more varied, than the literature of New England, or of the Middle West. There have been greater extremes in Southern literature, and the basic difference is that which separates two traditions, which one may call the Tidewater tradition and the Frontier tradition. There is no such division in New England literature, for the frontier in New England was never very pronounced or articulate; nor in the literature of the Middle West, because that region has been more homogeneously democratic. But in the South, the contrast has been marked, indeed. It would be difficult to find writers more different than William Byrd of Westover and George Washington Harris, the author of the *Sut Lovingood Yarns*; or, to take more recent examples, Ellen Glasgow of Richmond and Jesse Stuart of W-Hollow, in the Kentucky mountains. It is a remarkable fact about Southern literature that both traditions have had a great deal of vitality, and have flourished side by side.

In modern times, the Tidewater tradition is represented by (among others) the Virginians, Ellen Glasgow and James Branch Cabell; by John Crowe Ransom and Allen Tate of the Nashville School; by Mississippians Stark Young and Eudora Welty. These writers stem spiritually and culturally from William Byrd's Tidewater: they are courtly, sophisticated, intellectual; they cultivate "wit" in the older sense, and a fine irony; they address an inner circle; they possess restraint, dignity, a sense of form; they are classicists.

The Frontier first found expression in the early Nineteenth Century. This was a full one hundred years after Byrd's *History of the Dividing Line*, but it is remarkable that the Frontier should have been represented

From *Georgia Review*, 13 (Fall 1959), 296-307. Reprinted by permission of the publisher.

in literature at all, let alone so early. The Frontiersman—whether in the mountains of East Tennessee or the canebrakes of Arkansas—was a pretty lively fellow, and he has his niche—and a secure one it is turning out to be—in such writings as Longstreet's *Georgia Scenes*, *The Autobiography of David Crockett*, Harris's *Sut Lovingood Yarns*, Hooper's *Adventures of Captain Simon Suggs*, Baldwin's *Flush Times in Alabama and Mississippi*, Thorpe's *Big Bear of Arkansas*. In modern times, the tradition is represented by such literary descendants as Erskine Caldwell and Jesse Stuart. Thomas Wolfe, who came from the same mountain region as George Washington Harris, belongs with the members of this Frontier school in some respects, though he lacked their sense of humor and their mastery of the vernacular.

The two traditions—Tidewater and Frontier—have maintained a good deal of separateness from each other down to our time, though Faulkner and Warren, as I shall suggest presently, have combined elements from both. You will find, as a general thing, little truck between writers of the two schools. I shouldn't expect Ransom to have a high opinion of Wolfe, and I shouldn't expect Jesse Stuart to think very well of James Branch Cabell. (I mean, of course, of their writings.) I doubt if Tate admires Caldwell, and I should be surprised if Caldwell reads Tate. Tidewater and Frontier are still Tidewater and Frontier.

William Byrd, of course, is the grand prototype in literature of the Tidewater, and he is best seen in his delightful *Progress to the Mines* (1732). The journey was undertaken to investigate the state of the mining industry in Virginia, and the account shows that Byrd was a most painstaking investigator, but the more lively parts of the narrative concern the social entertainment along the way. The *Progress to the Mines* was indeed a royal progress, for Byrd was most hospitably received by the neighboring gentry. The account of his visit with the Spotswoods is revealing:

> Here I arrived about three o'clock, and found only Mrs. Spotswood at home, who received her old acquaintance with many a gracious smile. I was carried into a room elegantly set off with pier glasses, the largest of which came soon after to an odd misfortune. . . . A brace of tame deer ran familiarly about the house, and one of them came to stare at me as a stranger. But unluckily spying his own figure in the glass, he made a spring over the tea table that stood under it, and shattered the glass to pieces, and falling back upon the tea table, made a terrible fracas among the china. This ex-

ploit was so sudden, and accompanied with such a noise, that it surprised me. and perfectly frightened Mrs. Spotswood. But it was worth all the damage, to show the moderation and good humor with which she bore this disaster.

The moderation and good humor with which Mrs. Spotswood bore the disaster is clearly the point to underscore. She was, as Alexander Pope put it in that most elegant of all compliments to a gentlewoman, "mistress of herself though china fall."

Col. Spotswood, whom Byrd called the "Tubal Cain of Virginia," and who modestly substituted for "Virginia" in the appellation, "North America," was generous with his knowledge of the mining and smelting of iron ore; like many a Southerner after him, he was a great talker. After business, which was not scanted, came the social hour with the ladies, Mrs. Spotswood and her spinster sister, Miss Theky. The conversation with the ladies (Byrd recorded in this private narrative; the *Progress* was not published until after his death) was "like whip sillabub—very pretty, but nothing in it." Southern gallantry, it would seem, was not incompatible with a certain amount of masculine condescension toward the ladies.

At the home of the Chiswells, Bryd was shocked to discover that the twenty-four years which had passed since he last saw Mrs. Chiswell

had made great havoc with her pretty face, and plowed very deep furrows in her fair skin. It was impossible to know her again, so much the flower was faded. However, though she was grown an old woman, yet she was one of those absolute rarities, a very good old woman.

Of Col. Jones's plantations, situated nearby, Byrd recorded:

The poor negroes are a kind of Adamites, very scantily supplied with clothes and other necessaries; nevertheless (which is a little incomprehensible), they continue in perfect health, and none of them die, except it be of old age. However, they are even with their master, and make him but indifferent crops, so that he gets nothing by his injustice, but the scandal of it.

During his visit at the Flemings, the company were confined indoors all day by rainy weather, and Byrd, always the agreeable guest, "began to talk of plays," and, he goes on to say,

> finding Mrs. Fleming's taste lay most towards comedy, I offered my service to read one to her, which she kindly accepted. She produced the second part of the Beggar's Opera [*Polly*, 1729], which had diverted the town [London Town] for forty nights successively, and gained four thousand pounds to the author. . . . After having acquainted my company with the history of the play, I read three acts of it, and left Mrs. Fleming and Mr. Randolph to finish it, who read as well as most actors do at a rehearsal. Thus we killed the time, and triumphed over the bad weather.

I resist with difficulty the temptation to quote further from this classic of the colonial South. The *Progress to the Mines* contains most of the essential elements which will recur, with modifications of course, as we attempt to trace the history of the Tidewater tradition: the good manners, the decorum, the sense of community, the sense of justice, the interest in polite literature, the gallantry, the wit. Byrd has never had justice done him as a writer. His taste and style were formed under Restoration and early Augustan auspices, and his writing as writing compares favorably with some of the best in contemporary London. Particularly noteworthy is the wit, which illustrates well enough Addison's definition in *Spectator* No. 62. Wit, Addison says, involves a turn of surprise, as in the statement, "My mistress' bosom is as white as snow, *and as cold.*" Byrd has similar turns of surprise: "Though she was grown an old woman, yet she was one of those absolute rarities, *a very good old woman*"; "So that he gets nothing by his injustice *but the scandal of it.*"

If we divide the Nineteenth Century South into two periods—the ante-bellum and the post-bellum—we find that the best book in each period to illustrate the Tidewater tradition is still, appropriately enough, a product of Virginia: I refer to John Pendleton Kennedy's *Swallow Barn* (1832), and Thomas Nelson Page's *In Ole Virginia* (1884).

Kennedy was a Baltimorean, but his mother's family were Virginians, and Kennedy, like his narrator Mark Littleton, was a welcome guest in the Old Dominion. In writing *Swallow Barn*, the author, therefore, enjoyed the double advantage of detachment and sympathy. His picture is faithfully drawn. Kennedy is less witty than Byrd; his closest literary affinity seems to have been with Irving. But (like Irving) he is a good observer, he has a sense of humor, and he can be, and often is, amusing.

"Swallow Barn," he says, "is an aristocratic old edifice which sits, like a brooding hen, on the Southern bank of the James River." "It gives," he says, "the idea of comfort." Frank Meriwether, "the master of this lordly domain," is "a very model of landed gentlemen." He is most hospitable: "a guest is one of his daily wants." He is a good citizen and attends to business, but, contrary to the expectation and desire of his friends, "he has never set up for Congress." "He is not much of a traveller. He has never been in New England, and very seldom beyond the confines of Virginia. He makes now and then a winter excursion to Richmond, which he considers the center of civilization" (matching Dr. Holmes' view of Boston as the hub of the solar system). He is a Jeffersonian Agrarian, thinking "lightly of the mercantile interest," and believing that those who live in large cities are "hollow-hearted and insincere." He opposed the re-election of John Quincy Adams to the Presidency in 1829, and voted for Andrew Jackson, without, I imagine, being an ardent Jacksonian. "He piques himself upon being a high churchman, but is not the most diligent frequenter of places of worship, and very seldom permits himself to get into a dispute upon points of faith." "He is somewhat distinguished as a breeder of blooded horses." These are some of the main points in Kennedy's "character" of the Virginia planter of the 1830s.

There is less elegance at Swallow Barn than at Westover, a hundred years earlier. The life seems homespun in comparison. A self-contained provincialism has taken the place of the cosmopolitanism of Byrd, who was as much at home in London Town as in Williamsburg. There is an even greater emphasis on neighborliness and family life: Swallow Barn fairly swarms with relatives and neighbors. There are dinner parties, and the drinking of toasts. There is still the practice of polite learning: interlocutors quote Virgil and Horace. Negro slavery has become a controversial question by 1832 (though not so much so as it was soon to become, after the Abolitionists took over), and Kennedy's book contains a statement on the subject which seems more judicious than propagandistic. "No tribe of people," says Mark Littleton, "have ever passed from barbarism to civilization whose middle stage of progress has been more secure from harm, more genial to their character, or better supplied with mild and beneficent guardianship, adapted to the actual state of their intellectual feebleness, than the Negroes of Swallow Barn." We recall that Byrd spoke of the "scandal" attached to mistreatment of Negroes in the Tidewater of his time, and it is interesting to see the same view expressed a hundred years later in Kennedy's book: "Public opinion is stronger than law," Meriwether declares, "and no man can hold up his head in this community who is chargeable with mal-treatment of his slaves." As if to prove the point, one of the more prominent characters in *Swallow Barn* is Old Carey, the much-indulged, crochety, loyal family retainer, whose progeny in Southern fiction was to be legion.

If *Swallow Barn* was realistic and objective, though sympathetic with the life described, *In Old Virginia* was romantic and propagandistic. The War had come between, and Thomas Nelson Page wrote out of a profound nostalgia for the ante-bellum days. "Dem wuz good ole times, de bes Sam uver see! Dey wuz, in fac!" Page's hero, Marse Chan, is a paragon of all the virtues: "de peartes scholar ole Mr. Hall hed," and at the same time, "de head in all debilment dat went on." He is the soul of chivalry, fighting for his lady fair and for his father's good name. There is just one false touch in the portrait of this manly young knight, namely, his statement to the heroine that he has kept himself "pure" for her sake. There is nothing objectionable in the "purity," but it is the kind of statement which a young man doesn't ordinarily make to a young woman, for fear (if for no other reason) that she may think the less of his manhood. Page knew this, of course, as does every man, but he was willing to sacrifice verisimilitude to propaganda; willing to go to this extreme length in an attempt (useless though it was) to refute the stock accusation of miscegenation.

The narrator is the faithful darkey, Sam, Marse Chan's "body-servant." I am not at all disposed to deprecate Carey, Sam, and the others. The relationship which they represent would be anachronistic today, but it was a lovely one in its time and place. It was based upon personal loyalty, and the loyalty was reciprocal. Mutuality and irrevocableness (that is, permanence) are the important characteristics. Nothing of the sort exists in the modern world, such relationships having long ago been superseded by what Carlyle, long ago, called the "cash-nexus."

I am not at all disposed, either, to deprecate chivalry. I am not willing to dismiss the literature of chivalry as nonsense, merely because the age of chivalry is gone, and that of sophisters, economists, and calculators has succeeded. And still less am I disposed to deprecate a sense of honor. Allen Tate raised the question some years ago as to whether there is any such thing in the modern world as a sense of honor. It is a serious question.

The literary work of the modern period which best embodies the Tidewater tradition is Stark Young's *So Red the Rose* (1934). It would be interesting to examine the relation of this work to the earlier works which

I have been discussing. A few observations must suffice here. We note the presence of wit, Augustan wit, a quality conspicuous in Byrd, but not much emphasized in Kennedy, and absent from Page, where the Tidewater tradition is thoroughly sentimentalized. The remark, for example, in *So Red the Rose*, by Cynthia Eppes, a cousin from New Orleans, "I get my hats and my absolutions in Paris," recalls the wit of *The Rape of the Lock*: "Dost sometimes counsel take, and sometimes tea"; "Or stain her honour, or her new brocade." The recovery of wit was a valuable recovery. Page's sentimentality was a debasing of the tradition. The true aristocrats were not sentimentalists.

The prominence given to family ties, neighborliness, community life, recalls *Swallow Barn*. The Bedfords and the McGehees resemble in their neighborly rivalry (though "rivalry" may be too strong a word—there is no envy between them) the Meriwethers and the Traceys of Swallow Barn. Nearly everybody is somebody's cousin. Young Duncan Bedford has some of Marse Chan's chivalry, and William Veal, the family butler at Montrose, resembles Marse Chan's Sam. Agnes McGehee, who journeyed in a wagon to the battle-field of Shiloh, accompanied only by William Veal, to recover and bring home the body of her dead son, recalls in her heroic, quiet firmness the poised Mrs. Fleming of Byrd's narrative; the unobtrusive, efficient mistress of Swallow Barn, Lucy Meriwether; and the heroine, though sentimentalized, of Page's story. The Southern gentlewoman was not a clinging vine, a weak sister. On the contrary.

Hugh McGehee, who regards the changing world with a philosophic mind (he had been opposed to secession), is an ampler and wiser Frank Meriwether. "The way I've been obliged to see it is this," he says to his son: "Our ideas and instincts work upon our memory of these people who have lived before us, and so they take on some clarity of outline. It's not to our credit to think we began today, and it's not to our glory to think we end today. All through time, we keep coming in to the shore like waves—like waves. You stick to your blood, son; there's a certain fierceness in blood that can bind you up with a long community of life." "And think with passion," he added: "it's the only kind of thought that's worth anything." "In Hugh McGehee," says the book's best interpreter, Donald Davidson, "Southern society has produced a fine example of the unified personality, in tune with its environment, while also commanding it." Davidson comments also on the oral quality in *So Red the Rose*. "The tones of the speaking voice," he says, "ring throughout the book as in few other novels." Young has caught, he thinks, "the characteristic tone of Southern speech, its variation in pitch, its rhythms, as well as the idioms, vocabulary, archaisms, and oddities of pronunciation." The naturalness, the leisureliness and desultoriness of good talk are found not only in Young's novel, but in the works (though perhaps to a less degree) which I have taken to be the principal antecedents of *So Red the Rose*. There is also, in these works, an anecdotal quality, which reflects the Southern habit of telling stories—stories which, for the most part, have come out of the community life.

We must look now at the other tradition—the tradition of the Frontier.

The Frontier referred to is, first of all, that of the Old Southwest, which comprised the states now known as the South, if we exclude Virginia and the Carolinas. The literature which flourished in this region between 1830 and the Civil War is the opposite, in most respects, of the literature which we have been considering. Instead of courtliness, sophistication, restraint, there is uninhibited nature. Instead of chivalry, gallantry, polite learning, there is rough-and-tumble. Instead of wit, there is slapstick. The region in this period specialized in the tall tale. The liveliest and most amusing of the frontier humorists is George Washington Harris, author of *Sut Lovingood Yarns*, published in 1867.

The 1867 edition is long since out of print, and now difficult to come by. A new edition has been recently published, but the editor committed the unpardonable error of revising the language and orthography. The intention was to make the tales more intelligible to the general reader. The original work *is* difficult for many educated Northerners, but the difficulty is not insuperable (not greater, for example, than in Chaucer), and to revise a Sut Lovingood tale is to destroy it.

On the occasion of the appearance of the "revised" edition, Mr. Edmund Wilson wrote a long article in the *New Yorker* on the Sut Lovingood yarns in which he deals so harshly with his subject that one suspects he does not rightly understand what is going on. The work is, he says, "by far the most repellant book of any real merit in American literature." He objects to the "crude and brutal humor." Sut, he says, "avenges his inferiority by tormenting other people; his impulse is avowedly sadistic." He quotes as an example of the sadism the following statement by Sut about "universal onregenerit human nater":

> Ef enything happens to some feller, I don't keer ef he's yure bes frien, an I don't keer how sorry you is for him, thar's a streak ove satisfachun 'bout like a sowin thread a-runnin all thru yer sorrer. Yu may be shamed ov hit, but durn me ef hit aint thar.

Can it be that Mr. Wilson is so unaware of "universal onregenerit human nater"—possesses indeed so little of it himself—that this is a shockingly new thought to him? If so, he needs a course in Original Sin, and I suggest that he read, as a starter, Robert Penn Warren's poem entitled *Original Sin*, where he will find the accusing line: "You hear of the deaths of friends with sly pleasure."

The truth is that the Lovingood yarns are rowdy slapstick fun, the most hilarious, uninhibited compositions in American literature, and the broadest humor written in Nineteenth Century America; and if time permitted I would prove it to you by reading one—I should like nothing better. They were not printed in the *Atlantic Monthly*, but in a subliterary journal, the *Spirit of the Times* (published in New York), whose importance has only recently been discovered by the historians. The fun is often rough, but we read these yarns, if we read them correctly, with the willing suspension of the sentimental-humanitarian attitude, which is as inappropriate here as a Puritan-moralistic attitude toward a comedy by Congreve or Noel Coward. As for sadism, and taking pleasure in spoiling other people's fun, Sut is himself as often as not the butt. Many of the funniest things, moreover, do not involve physical pain at all. "Rare Ripe Garden Seed" might easily be mistaken for a Chaucerian fabliau, and the discourse on the "points" of young widows is hardly surpassed anywhere for its appreciation of sexual pleasures.

Mr. Wilson's crowning error is the statement that Sut is a direct ancestor of Flem Snopes. Faulkner, as I shall suggest presently, does owe a good deal to Harris, but Sut and Flem are as unlike as two human temperaments can very well be. Did Flem Snopes ever go to a party, get drunk, spark the girls? Flem never had any good healthy fun in his life—he was mercenary, calculating, and impotent. Sut, on the other hand—indiscreet, fun-loving, practical joker extraordinary—wasn't exactly the kind to get himself elected president of a bank.

Bernard DeVoto pointed out twenty-five years ago, in his *Mark Twain's America*, Mark Twain's debt to the Old Southwest humorists. Sut belonged in the East Tennessee mountains, in the neighborhood where Mark Twain's parents lived before they moved to Missouri. Mark Twain was almost certainly *conceived* in Sut's neighborhood, and if he had been born there, and had not gone East and come under the dispiriting influence of Livy, Howells, and the Reverend Mr. Twitchell, he might have become the great Rabelaisian author whom Van Wyck Brooks, with a good deal of insight, thought him capable of being.

One must recognize the bearing of Southern topography on these mat-

between the Shenandoah and the Tidewater, the up-country and the low-country in South Carolina, the Kentucky mountains and the Blue Grass, East Tennessee and Middle Tennessee. The Southern Appalachians—comprising Eastern Kentucky, East Tennessee, and Western North Carolina—are a homogeneous region, and a kind of modern Frontier. This region was Union in sympathies during the Civil War, and is still Republican. There were no plantations in these mountains and few slaves. The Clemenses had one Negro slave, a girl, who accompanied the family to Missouri, and today there are in this region comparatively few Negroes. The mountain people are, or have been, less restrained than their neighbors in the lowlands. They are, or have been, characterized by a special kind of wildness, and it is worth noting in this connection that Tom Wolfe's Altamont is just over the range from the Sut Lovingood country. Wolfe, of course, attended Chapel Hill, studied drama in Professor George Pierce Baker's 47 Workshop at Harvard, taught English in N.Y.U., Washington Square, lived in Brooklyn, read Shelley and Walt Whitman, and came under other "corrupting" influences, but he was a Southern mountaineer, and the mountain wildness is the most autochthonous fact about him. There is a particularly interesting passage in *Of Time and the River*, where Eugene and his cronies go for an automobile ride, drinking as they ride, careering from the hills to the plains, and landing in jail after a wildly drunken time of it. The passage, except for the somewhat Shelleyan treatment of landscape, recalls Lovingood.

ters, and the age-old distinction between the highlands and the lowlands:

It must have been, in part at least, Faulkner's admiration for the mountain wildness which led him to rank Wolfe first among the American novelists of the Twentieth Century (placing himself second). For this wildness—whether of the mountains or the plains—is an important part of Faulkner's inheritance, and it comes out in some of his best writing. Perhaps the best example is the story *Spotted Horses* (later incorporated in *The Hamlet*). Complete pandemonium can be carried no further than in Faulkner's account of what happens after the Texas ponies (the liveliest ever created by God or man) break out of the corral, and run pellmell down the country roads, upsetting many a cart, wagon, and surrey, and trampling their occupants under foot. For a sheer all-hell-broke-loose narrative, it has no equal unless in one of Sut Lovingood's farm-yard escapades. Faulkner's yarn, like many of Sut's, is hilariously funny, despite the fact that several people get hurt, and I don't quite see how Mr. Wilson can escape his old difficulty here. But the difficulty, in fact, is quite common. Non-Southerners often react to the Southern wildness in the wrong way.

If I may be permitted the pedantry of a footnote (without actually relegating the matter to the bottom of the page) on Southern folklore in general, and in particular the special kinship of Faulkner and Wolfe, I should like to quote from each author (from *Of Time and the River*, and from *Sartoris*) a description of the proper way to drink moonshine out of a jug. It is an important subject, and the correct technique is a matter of importance. Each author is obviously proud of this bit of connoisseurship. Wolfe says: "They hooked their thumbs into the handle of the jug, and brought the stuff across their shoulders with a free-hand motion, and let the wide neck pour into their tilted throats with a fat thick gurgle. . . ." Faulkner says: "Bayard was already drinking, with the jug tilted across his horizontal forearm, and the mouth held to his lips by the same hand, as it should be done." The methods are not quite identical, but basically similar. An allowance can be made for a small variation between North Carolina and Mississippi. (Young Sartoris, at the time, is hob-nobbing with the neighboring farm boys, and one of them is saying to another, "I knowed he was all right.") In each case, it is a ritual, not to be familiar with which marks one as lacking the proper initiation into good Frontier society.

We have been considering two traditions in the literature of the South—the Tidewater and the Frontier—and we have seen that they have flourished side by side, and somewhat separate from each other. There is just one more point which I wish to suggest: it is that the two traditions are united in the works of the writer who, all agree, is the greatest in the South today, and possibly this is one important reason why he *is* the greatest. For like Shakespeare, Faulkner embraces the high and the low, the aristocratic and the plebeian, the courtly and the uncouth, the educated and the illiterate, the literary and the vernacular, the traditional and the modern. I have already glanced at his affinity with the Frontier tradition. His sympathetic interest, on the other hand, in the Sartorises, the Compsons, and other aristocrats (Faulkner's treatment of these people can rise to the high-tragic mode) allies him with the Tidewater. It is this comprehensiveness, among other things, which sets Faulkner apart from his contemporaries in the South, though I should add that Robert Penn Warren has some of this same comprehensiveness.

I hope these remarks have at least suggested a genetic relationship (I believe not much appreciated) between the new literature of the South, and the old. However important various influences from outside the South may have been in the present century (and it has not been my intention to deal with these), modern Southern literature—both Tidewater and Frontier—has had a long background in Southern writing.

Suggs and Sut in Modern Dress:
The Latest Chapter in Southern Humor

Willard Thorp

Three summers ago I was working on a chapter about the renascence of writing in the South during the past thirty years. Having got the Southern Agrarians out of the way—not an easy thing to do because they are always up there in the front row, sitting for their photographs —I went on to try to account for the various subjects and themes the writers of fiction in the South today have employed and how they differ from what one finds in, say, Fitzgerald, Dos Passos, Steinbeck, Farrell, Cozzens, and others. The Southern novelists have not been much concerned with social problems, with the exception of the racial issue. Nor is there more than a handful of city novels to compare with *Manhattan Transfer* or *Studs Lonigan*. The tradition of historical fiction is still strong in the South and it is notable that several Southern novelists —Tate, Lytle, and Hamilton Basso, for example—have written historical works or biographies of historical figures. What once would have been called "local color" fiction also persists, though there is a world of difference between the mountain people of Miss Murfree and Miss Roberts. I had to say a good deal, of course, about the increasing interest in Negro life and the relations between the two societies, an interest which becomes marked in the 1920's in the fiction of DuBose Heyward, Julia Peterkin, and E. C. E. Adams and still continues with unbated strength. Having disposed of these matters and some others, including separate consideration of Thomas Wolfe and Faulkner, I had a residue of fiction on my hands which was difficult to classify in the neat, schematic fashion preferred by literary historians. A good deal of contemporary

From *Mississippi Quarterly*, 13 (1960), 169-175. Reprinted by permission of the publisher.

Southern fiction, evidently, is intended to be humorous though its humor varies all the way from Faulkner's rogue stories about the Snopes clan and Erskine Caldwell's raffish treatment of the Lester family and the exploiters of God's little acre to the fantastic humor of Truman Capote and the grim and grotesque humor of Flannery O'Connor. The strain is there, unmistakably, and so this question presented itself: is this strain something new in Southern writing or is there a tradition behind it? In the days when the literary comedians flourished, the South had a tradition of humorous writing which was the most vigorous in the country. Are there any connections to be traced between these two traditions or if no direct connections can be found, are there parallels striking enough to be worth talking about?

Until Carson McCullers confesses that she has been an assiduous reader of Henry Junius Nott's *Odds and Ends from the Knapsack of Thomas Singularity, Journeyman Printer* or Johnson J. Hoopers' *Adventures of Simon Suggs*, or Flannery O'Connor admits that she treasures copies of *Odd Leaves from the Life of a Louisiana Swamp Doctor* and George Washington Harris' *Sut Lovingood Yarns* it may be impossible to document the flow of the one tradition into the other.[1] I do want to take a moment, however, to point out that public demand for the writings of the older humorists lasted much longer than has generally been supposed. It is true that most of the work of Joseph G. Baldwin, Davy Crockett, Harris, Hooper, Longstreet, Nott, William Tappan Thompson (the creator of Major Jones of Georgia), and T. B. Thorpe was in print before the Civil War. George William Bagby and "Bill Arp, So Called" came along soon after. But the popularity of these humorists down through the remaining decades of the century and, in some instances, even into this century has not been sufficiently explored. This older Southern humor did not merely cradle Mark Twain and when this important function was performed, vanish up attic. Editions of Joseph G. Baldwin's *Flush Times in Alabama and Mississippi* continued to appear in the '80's and '90's and there was an edition published in Americus, Georgia (the Americus Book Co.) in 1908. For some reason the book was especially popular on the West Coast when it was first issued in 1876 (San Francisco) and went through at least four more printings, the last being in 1899.[2] Reprintings of the T. B. Peterson edition of Johnson J. Hooper's *Some Adventures of Captain Simon Suggs* continued to appear until 1881 and Americus honored Captain Suggs with an edition as late as 1928. The Harper and Brothers issues of A. B. Longstreet's *Georgia Scenes* continued until 1897, and there was an edition by J. O. Culpepper at Quitman, Georgia in 1894. William Tappan Thompson's *Major Jones* books were popular into the '80's. I have seen one curious edition (not listed by Blair) published by the W. L. Allison Company in 1893, with a made-up title, *Major Jones's Georgia Scenes*. The paper and binding are so cheap that the edition must have been got up to sell for a few cents. Blair lists only three editions of *Odd Leaves from the Life of a Louisiana Swamp Doctor, by Madison Tensas, M. D.* (1846, 1856, 1858), but I have seen a notice of it among the twenty-seven humorous works advertised at a dollar each in the 1881 Peterson reprint of Hooper's *Simon Suggs* and another in the 1879 Peterson reprint of *Major Jones's Courtship*. Possibly the longest survivor of these Southern humorous works is George Washington Harris's *Sut Lovingood's Yarns*. The old Dick and Fitzgerald edition is listed in the 1928 edition of the *United States Catalog*. My friend James B. Meriwether bought a copy recently. The imprint reads: Fitzgerald Publishing Corporation, Successor to Dick and Fitzgerald. The old plates were holding up well.

But this catalogue is not the complete story of the survival of interest in these writers. Henry Watterson's anthology, *Oddities in Southern Life and Character*, appeared first in 1882 but was in print as late as 1928. And if you will look in the *Library of Southern Literature*, that ambitious work in seventeen volumes which was issued between 1907 and 1923, you will find that the humorists are given a generous amount of space (only the Swamp Doctor is missing) and the biographies which introduce the selections are full and appreciative.

Meanwhile, we need to ask, did the tradition persist in fiction written after the Civil War? This is a crucial question and I wish I had a more satisfactory answer to it than I do. Here is a place where some extensive research needs to be done. Shields McIlwaine in his *The Southern Poor-White from Lubberland to Tobacco Road* (1939) treats the matter only incidentally. He was concerned first with trying to define as exactly as he could that slippery term "poor white," and then with following the fortunes of the poor whites through all Southern literature. But the older humor literature says next to nothing about class. The "take-home pay" and "income bracket" of Sut Lovingood and Simon Suggs are impossible to determine and you will recall that the narrator (it is Hooper of course) of "Taking the Census" was baffled at every turn in his attempt to make a statistical survey of the poultry population in Tallapoosa County. As a result, McIlwaine's necessary insistence on the criterion of class requires him to omit some writers who might be useful to us in this discussion. A good case in point is Miss Murfree, who is not mentioned in his book because, I gather, her mountaineers are a bracket above the poor whites. But Professor Parks, in his excellent biography of Miss Murfree, has pointed out that she probably knew and was influenced by the humorists, particularly Longstreet and Harris. It is worth noting that many of her stories begin with setting, dialogue, and theme which suggest that the tale will be developed in the humorous vein. This is true, for example, of "Old Sledge at the Settlemint" and "Dancin' Party at Harrison's Cove." But invariably the practical joke or incipient knock-down fight is stopped off in time for a sentimental ending, just as, in her novel *The Prophet of the Great Smoky Mountains*, the gander-pulling (a stock episode with the humorists) is not permitted to take place.

But it is high time that I came to grips with the question whether the parallels between the older Southern humor and the new are numerous and striking enough to warrant the use of the word revival, if not tradition. First to be noted is the fact that most of the characters in these tales—both the old and the new—move outside the society of people who are conventional, well-behaved, hard-working, God-fearing. In the older humor they are rogues, brawlers, con-men, gamblers, natural-born durned fools, hunters escaping from civilization into the wilderness. In the newest humor they are the Snopeses and the Ty Ty Waldens, the credulous, the un-educated, the religious fanatics; sometimes they are children or child-like adults and their Negro companions. In both literatures there is a war going on—a war between the untamable ones and the upholders of law and order. Simon Suggs' father, you will remember, was a "hard-shell" Baptist preacher who endeavored to rear his boys according to "the strictest requisitions of the moral law." But Simon, while he was still a "shirt-tail" boy, had begun to prepare himself for warfare against society. He had stolen his mother's roosters to fight them at Bob Smith's grocery and his father's plough-horses to enter them in "quarter" matches at the same place. He was already adept at "old sledge" and "seven up," weapons he used in his later skirmishes. When you come down to it, the central situation in Truman Capote's *The Grass Harp* is still another of these little wars against society. The escaped ones, who live in their tree house and do battle with rocks and mason jars against the ranks drawn up below them, are a dotty old woman, Dolly Talbo, her staunch Negro friend Catherine Creek, a young boy who never brought anyone home with him and never wanted to, and a senile judge who has nothing to do but stop in at the bank where his prissy-mouthed sons work, men who might have been twins "for they were both marshmallow-white, slump-shouldered, watery-eyed." Even in so mild a collection of humorous tales as the Major Jones series we find that the Major never can get on to the highfalutin' ways of his mother-in-law or his wife and doesn't really wish to.

Since there is a battle going on here most of the time between the ins and the outs (who have nothing but contempt for the way the ins lead their lives), in the humor of both periods there is a good bit of incidental satire of the occupations, manners, and recreations of respectable folk. I say incidental because social satire is by no means the main intention of these humorists, old or new. But we do get pleasantly distorted versions of genteel behavior as seen through the slant eyes of these outsiders. Major Jones is suspicious of the book learning his Mary Stallings is acquiring at the Female College in Macon and his awe-struck but somewhat contemptuous account of the graduation exercises there is good fun. One can find many matching passages in the contemporary humorists. Let me cite one example. In the course of his zany wanderings Haze Motes, head of the Church without Christ, in Flannery O'Connor's *Wise Blood*, has to contend with the amorous advances of Sabbath Lily Hawks. *Her* chief worry is that she is a bastard and therefore "shall not enter the kingdom of heaven." She has sought counsel from a columnist who gives advice to the love-lorn: "Do you think I should neck or not? I shall not enter the kingdom of heaven anyway so I don't see what difference it makes." This answer comes back to her:

> Dear Sabbath, Light necking is acceptable, but I think your real problem is one of adjustment to the modern world. Perhaps you ought to re-examine your religious values to see if they meet your needs in Life. A religious experience can be a beautiful addition to living if you put it in the proper prespective and do not let it warf you. Read some books on Ethical Culture.

Sabbath needs more advice and tries again. "I says, 'Dear Mary, What I really want to know is should I go the whole hog or not? That's my real problem. I'm adjusted okay to the modern world.'"

In assessing the humor of both periods it is important, I believe, to remember that much of the reader's pleasure comes from this battle between the ins and the outs, between respectability and instinctual, irrational behavior. To make the battle more furious the humorists often resort to a grim and outlandish fantasy which carries their writing way beyond realism. In discussions of the older Southern humor the realistic aspects have, I believe, been over-stressed. You know how the argument goes. (I have used it often enough, myself.) These writers were close to the life of the common people, enjoyed the raciness of their talk, their sports and pastimes, and their rude horseplay. This argument will hold well enough for Baldwin's *Flush Times* and Longstreet's *Georgia Scenes* but it cannot be stretched to cover some of the more nightmarish adventures of Sut Lovingood—his maltreatment of the Negro's corpse in "Frustrating a Funeral" for instance—or some of the episodes from the Louisiana Swamp Doctor's *Odd Leaves*. In the Doctor's story called "The Day of Judgment," he and some of his prankish friends provided the apocalyptic climax to a Negro camp meeting by saturating a mule's hide with turpentine and tar and sending him in flames through the singing and screaming congregation. The most blood-chilling of the Doctor's stories describes his fight with a crazed and horrible-vizaged Negro dwarf who is conducting him through a swamp to visit a patient. His life is saved only because the Negro jumps into their camp fire and burns to death. And then there is the Doctor's gently humorous story of how the too curious boarding-house keeper is presented with a well-wrapped infant's corpse from which the face has been sliced away. George Harris, the creator of Sut, knew well enough that the violence and the grim humor of some of his stories were bound to offend. He makes Sut say, in the preface to *Sut Lovingood's Yarns:*

> I dusn't 'speck this yere perduckshun wil sit purfeckly quiet ontu the stumicks ove sum pussons—them hu hes a holesum fear ove the devil, an' orter hev hit, by geminey. Now, fur thar speshul well-bein hereafter, I hes jis' this tu say: Ef yu ain't fond ove the smell ove cracklins, stay outen the kitchin; ef yu is fear'd ove smut, yu needn't climb the chimbley: an' ef the moon hurts yer eyes, don't yu ever look at a Dutch cheese. That's jis' all ove hit.

In the writing of contemporary Southern humorists there are a good many episodes which one "dusn't 'speck . . . sit purfeckly quiet ontu the stumicks ove sum pussons." To be quick about it I can instance the love affair between Ike Snopes and the cow and the hanging of the mule in Truman Capote's *Other Voices Other Rooms*. And then there is that pretty little love idyll, Flannery O'Connor's "Good Country People," about the sexually precocious young Bible salesman who obligingly seduces the female Ph. D. in the hay loft so she will let him unfasten her wooden leg and add it to various other sexual trophies packed in his blue-lined suit-case. Even less well calculated to "sit purfeckly quiet ontu the stumicks ove sum pussons" are the goings-on in Carson McCullers' *The Ballad of the Sad Cafe:* the strange marital life of the Amazonian Miss Amelia and the husband she discards; the arrival of the hunchback cousin whom she loves in her fashion; the league between Cousin Lymon and the husband, just returned from the penitentiary; and the final destructive fight between the husband and wife, another of those house-destroying, community-shattering battles which Southern humorists, old and new, write about.

There is no doubt that this aspect of life in the South (be it true or false) to which no satisfactory name has yet been given, has fascinated readers for a long time. The most persistent and possibly least qualified recorder of this variety of Southern life is Erskine Caldwell whose books sell in the millions and who is regarded by some French critics as a major American writer. He began well—I still think parts of *Tobacco Road, God's Little Acre,* and *Trouble in July* are genuinely funny—but he has poured words into the mould of Sister Bessie too many scores of times and the later product is brittle and cheap. But one will have to admit that Jean-Paul Sartre when he became aware of the fact that there was French gold in these Southern hills and wrote *The Respectful Prostitute* to prove it, took Caldwell for his model rather than Faulkner. It is all very unfortunate, but what can the South do about it? Carson McCullers and Flannery O'Connor are as culpable or as valuable as Sut Lovingood and the Swamp Doctor and they are likely to have progeny.

NOTES

1. Two critics have tackled the question of William Faulkner's possible indebtedness to the Southern humorists. In the tenth chapter ("Frenchman's Bend and the Folk Tradition") of *The Tangled Fire of William Faulkner* (1954), William Van O'Connor traces one episode in *The Hamlet* to A. B. Longstreet's "The Horse Swap" and another to "Sicily Burns's Wedding," one of the stories in

George W. Harris's *Sut Lovingood's Yarns*. Carvel Collins, in "Faulkner and Certain Earlier Southern Fiction" *(College English*, XVI [Nov., 1954], 92-97) is more sceptical of any direct influence. The general purport of his article is that though parallels can be found, Faulkner used humor and violence for larger purposes than did the humorists of the Old Southwest. "He is drawn to their essentials and motifs, but fundamentally his work is quite removed from them in both purpose and method."

2. For information about the printing history of these Southern humorists I am indebted to the Bibliography in Walter Blair's *Native American Humor*, New York, 1937, and to his "The Popularity of Nineteenth-Century American Humorists" *(American Literature*, III [May, 1931], 175-194).

V. Bibliography

Humor of the Old Southwest:
A Checklist of Criticism

Charles E. Davis and Martha B. Hudson

The following checklist of criticism on Old Southwestern humor is divided into three parts. Parts I and II consist of general studies which appear in books and journals, respectively, and part III lists books and articles on individual authors. Except for the omission of brief introductory biographical sketches and routine discussions in anthologies, encyclopedias, and histories of literature, we have attempted to compile as thorough and comprehensive a listing of secondary sources as possible.

I

GENERAL STUDIES: BOOKS

Anderson, John Q. *With the Bark On*. Nashville: Vanderbilt Univ. Press, 1967. Pp. 3-11 and *passim*.

Babcock, C. Merton, ed. *The American Frontier*. New York: Holt, Rinehart and Winston, 1965. Pp. 391-392 and *passim*.

Baldwin, Oliver P., ed. *Southern and South-Western Sketches*. Richmond: J. W. Randolph, 1855. Pp. 3-4.

Bier, Jesse. *The Rise and Fall of American Humor*. New York: Holt, Rinehart and Winston, 1968. Pp. 52-76.

Blaine, Harold A. "The Frontiersman in American Prose Fiction, 1800-1860." Diss. Western Reserve 1936.

Blair, Walter. *Horse Sense in American Humor*. Chicago: The Univ. of Chicago Press, 1942. Pp. v-ix and *passim*.

_____. " 'A Man's Voice Speaking': A Continuum in American Humor." *Veins of Humor*. Ed. Harry Levin. Cambridge: Harvard Univ. Press, 1972. Pp. 185-204.

From *Mississippi Quarterly*, 27 (1974), 179-199. Reprinted by permission of the publisher. The checklist has been updated by the compilers.

——————. *Native American Humor*. New York: American Book Company, 1937. Pp. 62-101, 163-196.

——————. *Tall Tale America*. New York: Coward McCann Inc., 1944.

—————— and Franklin J. Meine, eds. *Half Horse Half Alligator: The Growth of the Mike Fink Legend*. Chicago: The Univ. of Chicago Press, 1956. Pp. 33-34 and *passim*.

—————— and Franklin J. Meine. *Mike Fink: King of the Mississippi Keelboatmen*. New York: H. Holt and Company, 1933. Pp. 261-263, 273-283.

Boatright, Mody C. *Folk Laughter on the American Frontier*. New York: The Macmillan Company, 1949.

——————. *Tall Tales from Texas*. Dallas: The Southwest Press, 1934. Pp. vii-xx.

Botkin, B. A., ed. *A Treasury of American Folklore*. New York: Crown Publishers, 1944. Pp. 2-9, 272-273.

——————, ed. *A Treasury of Southern Folklore*. New York: Crown Publishers, 1949. Pp. 418-420.

Brevard, Carolina M. *Literature of the South*. New York: Broadway Publishing Company, 1908. Pp. 35, 40-41.

Bridgman, Richard. *The Colloquial Style in America*. New York: Oxford Univ. Press, 1966. Pp. 23-30 and *passim*.

Brinley, Francis. *Life of William T. Porter*. New York: D. Appleton and Company, 1860.

Chittick, V. L. O., ed. *Ring-Tailed Roarers: Tall Tales of the American Frontier, 1830-1860*. Caldwell, Idaho: Caxton Printers, 1946. Pp. 13-25, 305-311 and *passim*.

Clark, Thomas D. *The Rampaging Frontier: Manners and Humors of Pioneer Days in the South and the Middle West*. Indianapolis: The Bobbs-Merrill Company, 1939.

Cohen, Hennig, and William B. Dillingham, eds. *Humor of the Old Southwest*. Boston: Houghton-Mifflin Company, 1964. Pp. ix-xxiv and *passim*. Athens: Univ. of Georgia Press, 1975.

Collins, Carvel E. "The Literary Tradition of the Southern Mountaineer, 1824-1900." Diss. Univ. of Chicago 1944.

Covici, Pascal, Jr. *Mark Twain's Humor: The Image of a World*. Dallas: Southern Methodist Univ. Press, 1962. Pp. 3-109.

Cox, James M. "Humor of the Old Southwest." *The Comic Imagination in American Literature*. Ed. Louis D. Rubin, Jr. New Brunswick, New Jersey: Rutgers Univ. Press, 1973. Pp. 101-112.

DeVoto, Bernard. *Mark Twain's America*. Boston: Little, Brown and Company, 1932. Pp. 92-99, 240-245, 252-260, 335-339.

Dodd, William E. *The Cotton Kingdom: A Chronicle of the Old South*. New Haven: Yale Univ. Press, 1921. Pp. 71-96.

Dorson, Richard M. *American Folklore*. Chicago: Univ. of Chicago Press, 1959. Pp. 49-73.

Durham, Phillip C. "The Objective Treatment of the 'Hard-Boiled Hero' in American Fiction: A Study of the Frontier Background of Modern American Literature." Diss. Northwestern Univ. 1949.

Eaton, Clement. *The Freedom-of-Thought Struggle in the Old South.* New York: Harper and Row, 1964. Pp. 51-52 and *passim.*

——————. *The Mind of the Old South.* 2nd ed. Baton Rouge: Louisiana State Univ. Press, 1967. Pp. 130-151.

Flanagan, John T., and Arthur P. Hudson, eds. *Folklore in American Literature.* Evanston, Illinois: Row, Peterson, and Company, 1958. Pp. 236-237 and *passim.*

Fowler, Bill F. "Hell-Fire and Folk Humor on the Frontier." *Tire Shrinker to Dragster.* Ed. W. M. Hudson. Austin: Encino Press, 1968. Pp. 51-62.

Fussell, Edwin. *Frontier: American Literature and the American West.* Princeton: Princeton Univ. Press, 1965. Pp. 133-134.

Gohdes, Clarence, ed. *Hunting in the Old South: Original Narratives of the Hunters.* Baton Rouge: Louisiana State Univ. Press, 1967. Pp. 113-114 and *passim.*

Gooch, Margaret M. "Point of View and the Frontier Spirit in the Old South-western Tales of Baldwin, Longstreet, Hooper, and G. W. Harris." Diss. Univ. of North Carolina at Chapel Hill 1968.

Haliburton, Thomas C. *The Americans at Home.* London: Hurst and Blackett, 1854. I, v-ix.

Hall, Wade. *The Smiling Phoenix.* Gainesville: The Univ. of Florida Press, 1965. Pp. 1-18, 357-368.

Harris, Isabella Deas. *The Southern Mountaineer in American Fiction, 1824-1910.* Lexington: The Univ. of Kentucky Press, 1956. Pp. 59-92, 239-273.

Harris, Joel Chandler. *Stories of Georgia.* New York: American Book Company, 1896. Pp. 240-251.

Hauck, Richard Boyd. *A Cheerful Nihilism: Confidence and 'the Absurd' in American Humorous Fiction.* Bloomington: Indiana Univ. Press, 1971. Pp. 40-76.

——————. "The Literary Content of the New York *Spirit of the Times,* 1831-1856." Diss. Univ. of Illinois 1965.

Havens, Charles B. "Mark Twain's Use of Native American Humor in His Principal Literary Works." Diss. Vanderbilt Univ. 1954.

Hoffman, Daniel G. *Form and Fable in American Literature.* New York: Oxford Univ. Press, 1961. Pp. 53, 57, 62-78.

——————. *Paul Bunyan.* Philadelphia: Temple Univ. Publications, 1952. Pp. 66-73.

Holliday, Carl. *A History of Southern Literature.* New York: Neale Publishing Company, 1906. Pp. 117-355.

Howe, William D. "Early Humorists." *The Cambridge History of American Literature.* Ed. William P. Trent, *et al.* New York: Macmillan, 1933. II, 148-159.

Hubbell, Jay B. *The South in American Literature, 1607-1900.* Durham: Duke Univ. Press, 1954. Pp. 658-662.

——————. *Southern Life in Fiction.* Athens: The Univ. of Georgia Press, 1960. Pp. 71-78.

Hudson, Arthur Palmer. *Humor of the Old Deep South.* New York: Macmillan, 1936.

Hunter, Edwin Ray. *"The American Colloquial Idiom."* Diss. Univ. of Chicago 1925.

Kerlin, Charles Martin, Jr. "Life in Motion: Genteel and Vernacular Attitudes in the Works of the Southwestern American Humorists, Mark Twain and William Faulkner." Diss. Univ. of Colorado 1968.

Kitch, John Charles. "Dark Laughter: A Study of the Pessimistic Tradition in American Humor." Diss. Northwestern Univ. 1964.

Krapp, George P. *The English Language in America.* New York: The Century Company, 1925. I, 261, 300-314.

Link, Samuel Albert. *Pioneers of Southern Literature.* Nashville: M. E. Church, 1899. II, 465-470.

Lynn, Kenneth S., ed. *The Comic Tradition in America.* Garden City: Doubleday and Company, 1958. Pp. 104-107 and *passim.*

——————————. *Mark Twain and Southwestern Humor.* Boston: Little, Brown and Company, 1959.

McIlwaine, Shields. *The Southern Poor-White from Lubberland to Tobacco Road.* Norman: The Univ. of Oklahoma Press, 1939. Pp. 40-74.

Major, Mabel, and T. M. Pearce. *Southwest Heritage: A Literary History with Bibliographies*, 3rd ed. Albuquerque: The Univ. of New Mexico Press, 1972. Pp. 58-63.

Masterson, James R. *Tall Tales of Arkansas.* Boston: Chapman and Grimes, 1943. Pp. 299-305 and *passim.*

Meine, Franklin J. *Tall Tales of the Southwest: An Anthology of Southern and Southwestern Humor, 1830-1860.* New York: Alfred A. Knopf, Inc., 1930. Pp. xv-xxxii.

Meriwether, Frank. "The Rogue in the Life and Humor of the Old Southwest." Diss. Louisiana State Univ. 1952.

Miles, Elton. *Southwest Humorists.* Austin: Steck-Vaughn, 1969.

Milner, Joseph. "The Social, Religious, Economic and Political Implications of the Southwest Humor of Baldwin, Longstreet, Hooper, and G. W. Harris." Diss. Univ. of North Carolina at Chapel Hill 1971.

Mims, Edwin, ed. *History of Southern Fiction.* In *The South in the Building of the Nation.* Ed. J. A. C. Chandler, *et al.* Richmond: The Southern Historical Publication Society, 1909. VIII, xl-xlvii.

Moore, William E. "Mark Twain's Techniques of Humor." Diss. Peabody 1947.

Moses, Montrose J. *The Literature of the South.* New York: Thomas Y. Crowell and Company, 1910. Pp. 229-238.

Page, Thomas Nelson. *The Old South.* New York: Charles Scribner's Sons, 1908. Pp. 67-109.

Paine, Gregory, ed. *Southern Prose Writers: Representative Selections.* New York: American Book Company, 1947. Pp. lxxiv-lxxix and *passim.*

Parks, Edd Winfield. *Ante-Bellum Southern Literary Critics.* Athens: The Univ. of Georgia Press, 1962. Pp. 60-65.

Pattee, Fred L. *The First Century of American Literature, 1770-1870.* New York: D. Appleton-Century Company, 1935. Pp. 477-485.

Penrod, James H. "Character Types and Humorous Devices in the Old Southwest Yarns." Diss. Peabody 1952.

Phillips, Robert L., Jr. "The Novel and the Romance in Middle Georgia Humor and Local Color: A Study of Narrative Method in the Works of Augustus Baldwin Longstreet, William Tappan Thompson, Richard Malcolm Johnston and Joel Chandler Harris." Diss. The Univ. of North Carolina at Chapel Hill 1971.

Porter, William T., ed. *The Big Bear of Arkansas and Other Sketches.* Philadelphia: Carey and Hart, 1845. Pp. vii-xii.

Quinn, Arthur H. *American Fiction: An Historical and Critical Survey.* New York: D. Appleton-Century Company, 1936. Pp. 100-101 and *passim*.

───────────, *et al. The Literature of the American People: An Historical and Critical Survey.* New York: Appleton-Century-Crofts, 1951. Pp. 235-236 and *passim*.

Robertson, Thomas L., Jr. "The Unfolding Magnolia: A Literary History of Mississippi until 1876." Diss. Vanderbilt Univ. 1960.

Rogers, Edward R. "Four Southern Magazines." Diss. Univ. of Virginia 1902.

Rourke, Constance. *American Humor: A Study of the National Character.* New York: Harcourt, Brace, 1931. Pp. 37-69 and *passim*.

Rubin, Louis D., Jr., ed. *A Bibliographical Guide to the Study of Southern Literature.* Baton Rouge: The Louisiana State Univ. Press, 1969. Pp. 67-71 and *passim*.

───────────. *The Writer in the South: Studies in a Literary Community.* Athens: The Univ. of Georgia Press, 1972. P. 62 and *passim*.

Rutherford, Mildred L. *The South in History and Literature.* Atlanta: The Franklin Turner Company, 1906. Pp. 6-7 and *passim*.

Scott, Harold P. "Mark Twain's Theory of Humor: An Analysis of the Laughable in Literature." Diss. Univ. of Michigan 1917.

Skaggs, Merrill M. *The Folk of Southern Fiction.* Athens: The Univ. of Georgia Press, 1972. Pp. 25-35.

Smith, Henry Nash. "Origins of a Native American Literary Tradition." *The American Writer and the European Tradition.* Ed Margaret Denny. Minneapolis: The Univ. of Minnesota Press, 1950. Pp. 63-77.

Spiller, Robert E., *et al.*, eds. *Literary History of the United States.* 3rd ed. New York: Macmillan, 1963. I, 609; II, 703-741.

Tandy, Jennette. *Crackerbox Philosophers in American Humor and Satire.* New York: Columbia Univ. Press, 1925. Pp. 65-102.

Thorp, Willard. *American Humorists.* Minneapolis: The Univ. of Minnesota Press, 1964. Pp. 11-17.

Trent, William P., ed. *Southern Writers: Selections in Prose and Verse.* New York: Macmillan, 1905. Pp. 75-76 and *passim*.

Turner, Arlin, ed. *Southern Stories.* New York: Holt, Rinehart and Winston, 1960. Pp. xi-xl and *passim*.

Wade, John Donald. "Southern Humor." In *Culture in the South.* Ed. W. T. Couch. Chapel Hill: The Univ. of North Carolina Press, 1934. Pp. 159-182.

Walser, Richard, ed. *Tar Heel Laughter.* Chapel Hill: Univ. of North Carolina Press, 1974. *Passim*.

Watterson, Henry, ed. *The Compromises of Life.* New York: Fox, Duffield and Company, 1903. Pp. 59-101.

——————, ed. *Oddities in Southern Life and Character*. Boston: Houghton Mifflin Company, 1882. Pp. v-ix, 1-2 and *passim*.

Weber, Brom, ed. *The Art of American Humor: An Anthology*. Foreword Lewis Leary. New York: Thomas Y. Crowell, 1962. New York: Apollo, 1970. *Passim*.

Williams, Benjamin. "A Literary History of Alabama to 1900." Diss. Vanderbilt Univ. 1971.

Wilson, Edmund. *Patriotic Gore*. New York: Oxford Univ. Press, 1962. Pp. 507-528.

Wilt, Napier. *Some American Humorists*. New York: Thomas Nelson, 1929. Intro. Martin Roth. New York: Johnson Reprint Corporation, 1970. Pp. v-xxxv and *passim*.

Yates, Norris. "William T. Porter and the Development of Frontier Writing, 1831-1861." Diss. New York Univ. 1953.

——————. *William T. Porter and the Spirit of the Times: A Study of the Big Bear School of Humor*. Baton Rouge: The Louisiana State Univ. Press, 1957.

Zanger, Jules. "The Frontiersman in Popular Fiction, 1820-1860." In *Frontier Reexamined*. Ed. John Francis McDermott. Urbana: The Univ. of Illinois Press, 1967. Pp. 141-153.

II

GENERAL STUDIES: ARTICLES

Allen, G. Wilson. "Humor in America." *Sewanee Review*, 40 (Jan.-March 1932), 111-113.

Anderson, John Q. "Folkways in Writing about Northeast Louisiana before 1865." *Louisiana Folklore Miscellany*, 1 (Jan. 1960), 18-32.

——————. "Scholarship in Southwestern Humor—Past and Present." *Mississippi Quarterly*, 17 (Spring 1964), 67-86.

Austin, James C. "The Cycle of American Humor." *Papers on English Language and Literature*, 1 (Winter 1965), 83-91.

Baskervill, W. M. "Southern Literature." *Publications of the Modern Language Association*, 7 (1892), 89-100.

Bettersworth, John K. "The Humor of the Old Southwest: Yesterday and Today." *Mississippi Quarterly*, 17 (Spring 1964), 87-94.

Betts, John R. "Sporting Journalism in Nineteenth Century America." *American Quarterly*, 5 (Spring 1953), 39-56.

Blair, Walter. "Burlesques in 19th Century American Humor." *American Literature*, 2 (Nov. 1930), 236-247.

——————. "Inquisitive Yankee Descendents in Arkansas." *American Speech*, 14 (Feb. 1939), 11-22.

——————. "The Popularity of Nineteenth-Century American Humorists." *American Literature*, 3 (May 1931), 175-194.

——————. "Traditions in Southern Humor." *American Quarterly*, 5 (Summer 1953), 132-142.

Boatright, Mody C. "The Art of Tall Lying." *Southwest Review*, 34 (Autumn

1949), 357-363.

Bradley, Sculley. "Our Native Humor." *North American Review*, 242 (Winter 1937), 351-362.

Brashear, Minnie M. "The Missouri Short Story as It Has Grown out of the Tall Tale of the Frontier." *Missouri Historical Review*, 43 (April 1949), 199-219.

Budd, Louis J. "Gentlemanly Humorists of the Old South." *Southern Folklore Quarterly*, 17 (Dec. 1953), 232-240.

Cardwell, Guy A. "The Duel in the Old South: Crux of a Concept." *South Atlantic Quarterly*, 66 (Winter 1967), 50-69.

Carlisle, Henry. "The Comic Tradition." *American Scholar*, 28 (Winter 1958-1959), 96-108.

Chittick, V. L. O. "Ring-Tailed Roarers." *Frontier*, 13 (May 1933), 257-263.

Clark, Thomas D. "The American Backwoodsman in Popular Portraiture." *Indiana Magazine of History*, 42 (March 1946), 1-28.

——————. "The Common Man Tradition in the Literature of the Frontier." *Michigan Alumnus Quarterly Review*, 63 (1957), 208-217.

——————. Humor in the Stream of Southern History." *Mississippi Quarterly*, 13 (Fall 1960), 176-188.

——————. "Manners and Humors of the American Frontier." *Missouri Historical Review*, 35 (Oct. 1940), 3-24.

Collins, Carvel. "Faulkner and Certain Earlier Southern Fiction." *College English*, 16 (1954), 92-97.

——————. "Nineteenth Century Fiction of the Southern Appalachians." *Bulletin of Bibliography*, 17 (1942-1943), 186-187, 217-218.

Colville, Derek. "History and Humor: The Tall Tale in New Orleans." *Louisiana Historical Quarterly*, 39 (1956), 153-167.

——————. "A Rich Store of Southern Tall Tales." *Bibliographical Society of the Univ. of Virginia Soc. News Sheet*, No. 33 (June 1955).

Current-Garcia, Eugene. "Alabama Writers in the *Spirit*." *Alabama Review*, 10 (Oct. 1957), 243-269.

——————. " 'Mr. Spirit' and *The Big Bear of Arkansas:* A Note on the Genesis of Southwestern Sporting and Humor Literature." *American Literature*, 27 (Nov. 1955), 332-346.

——————. "Newspaper Humor in the Old South, 1835-1855." *Alabama Review*, 2 (April 1949), 102-121.

——————. " 'York's Tall Son' and His Southern Correspondents." *American Quarterly*, 7 (Winter 1955), 371-384.

Dillingham, William B. "Days of the Tall Tale." *Southern Review*, 4 (Spring 1968), 569-577.

Dondore, Dorothy A. "Big Talk! The Flyting, the Gabe, and the Frontier Beast." *American Speech*, 6 (Oct. 1930), 45-55.

Dorson, Richard M. "The Identification of Folklore in American Literature." *Journal of American Folklore*, 70 (1957), 1-8, 21-23.

Durham, Frank. "The Southern Literary Tradition: Shadow or Substance?" *South Atlantic Quarterly*, 67 (Summer 1968), 455-468.

Eastman, Max. "Humor and America." *Scribner's*, 100 (July 1936), 9-13.

Eaton, Clement. "The Humor of the Southern Yeoman." *Sewanee Review*, 49 (April-June 1941), 173-183.

Eberstadt, Lindley. "The Passing of a Noble Spirit." *Papers of the Bibliographical Society of America*, 44 (1950), 372-373.

Eby, Cecil. "Faulkner and the Southwestern Humorists." *Shenandoah*, 11 (1959), 13-21.

Ferguson, J. D. "On Humor as One of the Fine Arts." *South Atlantic Quarterly*, 38 (April 1939), 177-186.

————. "The Roots of American Humor." *American Scholar*, 4 (Winter 1935), 41-49.

Flanders, B. H. "Humor in Ante-Bellum Georgia: The Waynesboro *Gopher*." *Emory Univ. Quarterly*, 1 (Oct. 1945), 149-156.

Foster, Ruel E. "Kentucky Humor: Salt River Roarer to Ol' Dog Tray." *Mississippi Quarterly*, 20 (Fall 1967), 224-230.

Freeman, D. S. "The Tonic of Southern Folklore." *American Scholar*, 19 (Spring 1950), 187-193.

Gilmer, Gertrude. "A Critique of Certain Georgia Ante-Bellum Literary Magazines Arranged Chronologically and a Checklist." *Georgia Historical Quarterly*, 18 (Dec. 1934), 293-334.

Hauck, Richard B. "Predicting a Native Literature: William T. Porter's First Issue of the *Spirit of the Times*." *Mississippi Quarterly*, 22 (Winter 1968-69), 77-84.

Havard, William C. "Mark Twain and the Political Ambivalence of Southwestern Humor." *Mississippi Quarterly*, 17 (Spring 1964), 95-106.

Hill, Hamlin. "Modern American Humor, the Janus Laugh." *College English*, 25 (Dec. 1963), 170-176.

Hubbell, Jay B. "The Old South in Literary Histories." *South Atlantic Quarterly*, 48 (July 1949), 452-467.

Hyde, Stuart W. "The Ring-Tailed Roarer in American Drama." *Southern Folklore Quarterly*, 19 (1955), 171-178.

Inge, M. Thomas. "Literary Humor of the Old Southwest: A Brief Overview." *Louisiana Studies*, 7 (Summer 1968), 132-143.

Ives, Sumner. "A Theory of Literary Dialect." *Tulane Studies in Literature*, 2 (1950), 137-182.

Johnston, Charles. "Old Funny Stories of the South and West." *Harpers Weekly*, 57 (4 Jan. 1913), 21.

Jones, Howard M. "The Generation of 1830." *Harvard Library Bulletin*, 13 (1959), 401-414.

Jordan, P. D. "Humor of the Backwoods, 1820-1840." *Mississippi Valley Historical Review*, 25 (June 1938), 25-38.

Kummer, George. "Who Wrote 'The Harp of a Thousand Strings'?" *Ohio Historical Quarterly*, 67 (July 1958), 221-231.

Leisy, E. E. "Folklore in American Literature." *College English*, 8 (Dec. 1946), 122-129.

————. "Folklore in American Prose." *Saturday Review of Literature*, 34 (21 July 1951), 6-7, 32.

Loomis, C. Grant. "The American Tall Tale and the Miraculous." *California Folklore Quarterly*, 4 (1945), 109-128.

————. "A Tall Tale Miscellany, 1830-1866." *Western Folklore*, 6 (1947), 28-41.

Lukens, Henry C. "American Literary Comedians." *Harper's Magazine*, 80 (1890), 783-797.

Maclachlan, John M. "Southern Humor as a Vehicle of Social Evaluation." *Mississippi Quarterly*, 13 (Fall 1960), 157-162.

Mendoza, Aaron. "Some 'Firsts' of American Humor, 1830-1875." *Publisher's Weekly*, 119 (21 March 1931), 1603-1605.

Moore, Arthur K. "Specimens of the Folktales from Some Ante-Bellum Newspapers of Louisiana." *Louisiana Historical Quarterly*, 32 (Oct. 1949), 723-758.

Moses, M. J. "The South in Fiction: The Trail of the Lower South." *Bookman*, 33 (April 1911), 161-172.

Paine, Gregory. "The Frontier in American Literature." *Sewanee Review*, 36 (April 1928), 225-236.

Parks, Edd Winfield. "The Intent of the Ante-Bellum Southern Humorists." *Mississippi Quarterly*, 13 (Fall 1960), 163-168.

_____. "The Three Streams of Southern Humor." *Georgia Review*, 9 (Summer 1955), 147-159.

Pearce, James T. "Folk Tales of Southern Poor Whites, 1820-1860." *Journal of American Folklore*, 63 (1950), 398-412.

Penrod, James H. "Characteristic Endings of Southwestern Yarns." *Mississippi Quarterly*, 15 (Winter 1962), 27-35.

_____. "The Folk Hero as Prankster in the Old Southwestern Yarns." *Kentucky Folklore Review*, 2 (1956), 5-12.

_____. "The Folk Mind in Early Southwestern Humor." *Tennessee Folklore Society Bulletin*, 18 (1952), 49-54.

_____. "Folk Motifs in Old Southwestern Humor." *Southern Folklore Quarterly*, 19 (June 1955), 117-124.

_____. "Military and Civil Titles in the Old Southwestern Yarns." *Tennessee Folklore Society Bulletin*, 19 (1953), 13-19.

_____. "Minority Groups in Old Southern Humor." *Southern Folklore Quarterly*, 22 (Sept. 1958), 121-128.

_____. "Teachers and Preachers in the Old Southwestern Yarns." *Tennessee Folklore Society Bulletin*, 18 (1952), 91-96.

_____. "Two Aspects of Folk Speech in Southwestern Humor." *Kentucky Folklore Record*, 3 (Oct.-Dec. 1957), 145-152.

_____. "Two Types of Incongruity in Old Southwestern Humor." *Kentucky Folklore Record*, 4 (1958), 163-173.

_____. "Women in the Old Southwestern Yarns." *Kentucky Folklore Record*, 1 (April-June 1955), 41-47.

Rickels, Milton. "The Humorists of the Old Southwest in the London *Bentley's Miscellany*." *American Literature*, 27 (Jan. 1956), 557-560.

Rourke, Constance. "Examining the Roots of American Humor." *American Scholar*, 4 (Spring 1935), 249-252.

_____. "Miss Rourke Replies to Mr. Blair." *American Literature*, 4 (May 1932), 207-210.

_____. "Our Comic Heritage." *Saturday Review of Literature*, 7 (21 March 1931), 678-679.

Sederberg, Nancy B. "Antebellum Southern Humor in the *Camden Journal*:

1826-1840." *Mississippi Quarterly*, 27 (Winter 1973-74), 41-74.

Shepherd, Esther. "The Tall Tale in American Literature." *Pacific Review*, 2 (Dec. 1921), 402-414.

Simms, William G. "Southern Literature: Its Conditions, Prospects and History." *Magnolia*, 3 (Jan.-Feb. 1841), 1-6, 69-74.

Simpson, Lewis P. "The Humor of the Old Southwest." *Mississippi Quarterly*, 17 (Spring 1964), 63-66.

Smith, Charles F. "Southern Dialect in Life and Literature." *Southern Bivouac*, n. s. 1 (Nov. 1885), 343-351.

Snyder, H. N. "The Matter of Southern Literature." *Sewanee Review*, 15 (April 1907), 218-226.

Spotts, C. B. "The Development of Fiction of the Missouri Frontier (1830-1860)." *Missouri Historical Review*, 28 (April-July 1934), 195-205, 275-286; 29 (Oct. 1934-Jan. 1935), 17-26, 100-108, 186-194, 279-294.

————————. "Mike Fink in Missouri." *Missouri Historical Review*, 28 (Oct. 1933), 3-8.

Stein, Allen F. "Return to Phelps Farm: *Huckleberry Finn* and the Old Southwestern Framing Device." *Mississippi Quarterly*, 24 (Spring 1971), 111-116.

Stewart, Randall. "Tidewater and Frontier." *Georgia Review*, 13 (Fall 1959), 296-307.

Thompson, W. F. "Frontier Tall Talk." *American Speech*, 9 (Oct. 1934), 187-199.

Trent, W. P. "A Retrospect on American Humor." *Century*, 63 (Nov. 1901). 45-64.

Turner, Arlin. "Realism and Fantasy in Southern Humor." *Georgia Review*, 12 (Winter 1958), 451-457.

————————. "Seeds of Literary Revolt in the Humor of the Old Southwest." *Louisiana Historical Quarterly*, 39 (1956), 143-151.

Tyner, Troi. "The Function of the Bear Ritual in Faulkner's *Go Down, Moses*." *Journal of the Ohio Folklore Society*, 3 (1968), 19-40.

Weaver, R. M. "Scholars or Gentlemen?" *College English*, 7 (Nov. 1945), 72-77.

Weber, Brom. "American Humor and American Culture." *American Quarterly*, 14 (Fall 1962), 503-507.

West, James L. W. III. "Early Backwoods Humor in the Greenville *Mountaineer*, 1826-1840." *Mississippi Quarterly*, 25 (Winter 1971), 69-82.

Wheeler, Otis B. "Some Uses of Folk Humor by Faulkner." *Mississippi Quarterly*, 17 (Spring 1964), 107-122.

Wilkinson, C. W. "Backwoods Humor." *Southwest Review*, 24 (Jan. 1929), 164-181.

Wright, Lyle H. "A Statistical Survey of American Fiction, 1774-1850." *Huntington Library Quarterly*, 2 (April 1939), 309-318.

Yates, Norris W. "Antebellum Southern Humor as a Vehicle of Class Expression." *Bulletin of the Central Mississippi Valley American Studies Association*, 1 (Spring 1958), 1-6.

————————. " 'The Spirit of the Times': Its Early History and Some of Its Contributors." *Papers of the Bibliographical Society of America*, 48 (1954), 117-148.

III

INDIVIDUAL AUTHORS
JOSEPH GLOVER BALDWIN

Alderman, Edwin A., *et al.*, eds. *Library of Southern Literature.* Atlanta: The Martin and Hoyt Company, 1907-08. I, 175-181.

Baldwin, Joseph G. *The Flush Times of Alabama and Mississippi.* Ed. William A. Owens. New York: Sagamore Press, 1957. Pp. v-ix.

————————. *The Flush Times of California.* Ed. Richard E. Amacher and George W. Polhemus. Athens: The Univ. of Georgia Press, 1966. Pp. 1-10, 65-78.

Blanck, Jacob. "Joseph Glover Baldwin." *Bibliography of American Literature.* New Haven: Yale Univ. Press, 1955. I, 116-117.

Current-Garcia, Eugene. "Joseph Glover Bladwin: Humorist or Moralist?" *Alabama Review,* 5 (April 1952), 122-141.

Farish, H. D. "An Overlooked Personality in Southern Life." *North Carolina Historical Review,* 12 (Oct. 1935), 341-353.

Hubbell, *The South* . . . , pp. 675-678.

Link, *Pioneers* . . . , II, 486-504.

McDermott, John F. "Baldwin's 'Flush Times of Alabama and Mississippi'— A Bibliographical Note." *Papers of the Bibliographical Society of America,* 45 (1951), 251-256.

Mellen, G. F. "Joseph G. Baldwin and the 'Flush Times.' " *Sewanee Review,* 9 (April 1901), 171-184.

Stewart, Samuel B. "Joseph Glover Baldwin." Diss. Vanderbilt Univ. 1941.

Wetmore, T. B. "Joseph G. Baldwin." *Alabama Historical Society Transactions,* 2 (1916), 67-73.

JOHN GORMON BARR

Hoole, W. Stanley. "John Gormon Barr: Forgotten Alabama Humorist." *Alabama Review,* 4 (April 1951), 83-116.

JOSEPH B. COBB

Buckley, George T. "Joseph B. Cobb: Mississippi Essayist and Critic." *American Literature,* 10 (May 1938), 166-178.

Hubbell, *The South* . . . , pp. 637-639.

Mohr, Clarence L. "Candid Comments from a Mississippi Author." *Mississippi Quarterly,* 25 (Winter 1972), 83-93.

Rogers, Tommy W. "The Folk Humor of Joseph B. Cobb." *Notes on Mississippi Writers,* 3 (1970), 13-35.

————————. "Joseph B. Cobb: Antebellum Humorist and Critic." *Mississippi Quarterly,* 22 (Spring 1969), 131-146.

——————. "Joseph B. Cobb: Continuation of a Distinguished Lineage." *Georgia Historical Quarterly*, 56 (Fall 1972), 404-414.

——————. "Joseph B. Cobb: The Successful Pursuit of Belles Lettres." *McNeese Review*, 20 (1971-72), 70-83.

DAVID CROCKETT

Alderman, *Library* . . . , III, 1083-1088.

Arpad, Joseph J. "David Crockett, an Original Legendary Eccentricity and Early American Character." Diss. Duke Univ. 1969.

——————, ed. *Narrative of the Life of David Crockett*. New Haven: College and Univ. Press, 1972.

Bezanson, W. E. "Go Ahead Davy Crockett." *Journal of Rutgers Univ. Library*, 12 (June 1949), 32-37.

Bishop, H. O. "Davy Crockett—Bear Hunter." *National Republic*, 17 (Aug. 1929), 31-37.

Blair, *Horse Sense* . . . , pp. 24-50.

——————. "Six Davy Crocketts." *Southwest Review*, 25 (July 1940), 443-462.

Bright, Verne. "Davy Crockett Legend and Tales in the Oregon Country." *Oregon Historical Quarterly*, 51 (1950), 207-215.

Crockett, David. *The Autobiography of David Crockett*. Ed. Hamlin Garland. New York: Charles Scribner's Sons, 1923. Pp. 3-10.

Crockett, David. *A Narrative of the Life of David Crockett of the State of Tennessee*. Intro. James A. Shackford and Stanley J. Folmsbee. Knoxville: The Univ. of Tennessee Press, 1973. Pp. v-xx and *passim*.

Crowell, C. T. "Davy Crockett." *American Mercury*, 4 (Jan. 1925), 109-115.

Davis, Curtis C. "A Legend at Full Length." *Proceedings of the American Antiquarian Society*, 69 (1959), 155-174.

Dorson, Richard M. *Davy Crockett: American Comic Legend*. New York: Spiral Press, 1939. Pp. xi-xxvi.

——————. "Davy Crockett and the Heroic Age." *Southern Folklore Quarterly*, 6 (June 1942), 95-102.

——————. "The Sources of Davy Crockett, American Comic Legend." *Midwest Folklore*, 8 (1958), 143-149.

Foster, A. D. "David Crockett." *Tennessee Historical Magazine*, 9 (1925), 166-177.

Hoffman, Daniel G. "The Deaths and Three Resurrections of Davy Crockett." *Antioch Review*, 21 (Spring 1961), 5-13.

Hubbell, *The South* . . . , pp. 662-666.

Link, *Pioneers* . . . , II, 534-540.

Masterson, *Tall Tales* . . . , pp. 21-28.

Miles, Guy S. "David Crockett Evolves, 1821-1824." *American Quarterly*, 8 (Spring 1956), 53-60.

Null, Marion M. *The Forgotten Pioneer: The Life of Davy Crockett*. New York: Vantage, 1954.

Parrington, Vernon L. *Main Currents in American Thought: The Romantic Revolution in America, 1800-1860.* New York: Harcourt, Brace and Company, 1927. II, 172-179.

Rourke, Constance. *Davy Crockett.* New York: Harcourt, Brace and Company, 1934.

——————. "Davy Crockett: Forgotten Facts and Legends." *Southwest Review,* 19 (Jan. 1934), 149-161.

Shackford, James A. "The Author of Davy Crockett's Autobiography." *Boston Public Library Quarterly,* 3 (1951), 294-303.

——————. *David Crockett: The Man and the Legend.* Ed John B. Shackford. Chapel Hill: The Univ. of North Carolina Press, 1956.

Shapiro, Irwin. *Yankee Thunder: The Legendary Life of Davy Crockett.* New York: Julian Messner, Inc., 1944.

Stiffler, Stuart A. "Davy Crockett: The Genesis of Heroic Myth." *Tennessee Historical Quarterly,* 16 (1957), 134-140.

WILLIAM ELLIOTT

Alderman, *Library* . . . , IV, 1569-1571.

Hubbell, *The South* . . . , pp. 564-568.

Jones, Lewis Pinckney. "Carolinians and Cubans: The Elliotts and Gonzales, Their Work and Their Writings." Diss. Univ. of North Carolina at Chapel Hill 1952.

——————. "William Elliott: South Carolina Non-Conformist." *Journal of Southern History,* 17 (Aug. 1951), 361-381.

C. N. B. EVANS

Hubbell, Jay B. "Charles Napoleon Bonaparte Evans: Creator of Jesse Holmes the Fool-Killer." *South Atlantic Quarterly,* 36 (Oct. 1937), 431-446.

WILLIAM C. HALL

Anderson, John Q. "Mike Hooter: The Making of a Myth." *Southern Folklore Quarterly,* 19 (June 1955), 90-100.

GEORGE WASHINGTON HARRIS

Alderman, *Library* . . . , V, 2099-2102.

Bass, William W. "Sut Lovingood's Reflections on His Contemporaries." *Carson-Newman College Faculty Studies,* 1 (1964), 33-48.

Blair, *Horse Sense* . . . , pp. 149-157.

——————. "Sut Lovingood." *Saturday Review of Literature,* 15 (7 Nov. 1936), 3-4, 16.

Blanck, *Bibliography* . . . , III, 384-386.

Current-Garcia, Eugene. "Sut Lovingood's Rare Ripe Southern Garden." *Studies in Short Fiction*, 9 (Spring 1972), 117-129.

Day, Donald. "The Humorous Works of George W. Harris." *American Literature*, 14 (Jan. 1943), 391-406.

——————. "The Life and Works of G. W. Harris." Diss. Univ. of Chicago 1942.

——————. "The Life of George Washington Harris." *Tennessee Historical Quarterly*, 6 (March 1947), 3-38.

——————. "The Political Satires of George W. Harris." *Tennessee Historical Quarterly*, 4 (Dec. 1945), 320-338.

Harris, George W. *High Times and Hard Times: Sketches and Tales*. Ed. M. Thomas Inge. Nashville: Vanderbilt Univ. Press, 1967. Pp. 3-8, 34-43, 105-118, 222-231, 319, 321.

——————. *Sut Lovingood*. Ed Brom Weber. New York: Grove Press, 1954. Pp. ix-xxix.

——————. *Sut Lovingood Travels with Old Abe Lincoln*. Intro. Edd Winfield Parks. Chicago: The Black Cat Press, 1938. Pp. 7-18.

——————. *Sut Lovingood's Yarns*. Ed. M. Thomas Inge. New Haven: College and Univ. Press, 1966. Pp. 9-24.

Howell, Elmo. "Timon in Tennessee: The Moral Fervor of George Washington Harris." *Georgia Review*, 24 (Fall 1970), 311-319.

Hubbell, *The South* . . . , pp. 678-679.

Inge, M. Thomas, ed. "Early Appreciations of George W. Harris by George Frederick Mellen." *Tennessee Historical Quarterly*, 30 (June 1971), 190-204.

——————. "George Washington Harris and Southern Poetry and Music." *Mississippi Quarterly*, 17 (Winter 1964), 36-44.

——————. "G. W. Harris's 'The Doctor's Bill': A Tale about Dr. J. G. M. Ramsey." *Tennessee Historical Quarterly*, 14 (1965), 185-194.

——————. "The Satiric Artistry of George W. Harris." *Satire Newsletter*, 4 (1968), 63-72.

——————. "Sut Lovingood: An Examination of the Nature of a 'Nat'ral Born Durn'd Fool.' " *Tennessee Historical Quarterly*, 19 (1960), 231-251.

——————. "The Uncollected Writings of George Washington Harris: An Annotated Edition." Diss. Vanderbilt Univ. 1964.

——————. "William Faulkner and George Washington Harris: In the Tradition of Southwestern Humor." *Tennessee Studies in Literature*, 7 (1962), 47-59.

Leary, Lewis. *Southern Excursions: Essays on Mark Twain and Others*. Baton Rouge: Louisiana State Univ. Press. 1971. Pp. 111-130.

Long, E. Hudson. "Sut Lovingood and Mark Twain's *Joan of Arc*." *Modern Language Notes*, 64 (Jan. 1949), 37-39.

McClary, Ben Harris, ed. *The Lovingood Papers*. 4 vols. Knoxville: The Univ. of Tennessee Press, 1962-1965.

——————. "The Real Sut." *American Literature*, 27 (March 1955), 105-106.

——————. "Sanky and Sut." *Southern Observer*, 9 (Jan. 1962), 13.

_____. "Sut Lovingood Views 'Abe Linkhorn.' " *Lincoln Herald*, 56 (Fall 1954), 44-45.

_____. "Sut Lovingood's Country." *Southern Observer*, 3 (Jan. 1955), 5-7.

McKeithan, D. M. "Bull Rides Described by 'Scroggins,' Harris, and Mark Twain." *Southern Folklore Quarterly*, 17 (Dec. 1953), 241-243.

_____. "Mark Twain's Story of the Bull and the Bees." *Tennessee Historical Quarterly*, 11 (Sept. 1952), 246-253.

Matthiessen, Francis Otto. *American Renaissance: Art and Expression in the Age of Emerson and Whitman*. London: Oxford Univ. Press, 1941. Pp. 603, 637, 641-645.

Parks, Edd Winfield. *Segments of Southern Thought*. Athens: Univ. of Georgia Press, 1938. Pp. 215-222.

Penrod, James. "Folk Humor in Sut Lovingood's Yarns." *Tennessee Folklore Society Bulletin*, 16 (1950), 76-84.

Plater, Ormonde. "Before Sut: Folklore in the Early Works of George Washington Harris." *Southern Folklore Quarterly*, 34 (June 1970), 104-115.

_____. "The Lovingood Patriarchy." *Appalachian Journal*, 1 (Spring 1973), 82-93.

_____. "Narrative Folklore in the Works of George Washington Harris." Diss. Tulane Univ. 1969.

Rickels, Milton. *George Washington Harris*. New York: Twayne, 1966.

_____. "The Imagery of George Washington Harris." *American Literature*, 31 (May 1959), 173-187.

Thorp, Willard. "Suggs and Sut in Modern Dress: The Latest Chapter in Southern Humor." *Mississippi Quarterly*, 13 (Fall 1960), 169-175.

_____, ed. *A Southern Reader*. New York: Alfred A. Knopf, 1955. Pp. 661-662.

Williams, Cratis. "Sut Lovingood as a Southern Mountaineer." *Appalachian State Teacher's College Faculty Publications*, 44 (Apr. 1966), 1-4.

Wilson, Edmund. "Poisoned!" *New Yorker*, 31 (7 May 1955), 138-142, 145-147.

JOHNSON JONES HOOPER

Alderman, *Library* . . . , VI, 2489-2491.

Brannon, Peter A. "Hooper's Influence in Early State Literature." Montgomery *Advertiser*, Centennial Edition, 15 March 1928.

Current-Garcia, "Alabama Writers . . . ," pp. 243-269.

Hollingsworth, Annie Mae. "Johnson Jones Hooper, Alabama's Mark Twain, Champion of the Creeks." Montgomery *Advertiser*, 23 March 1931.

Hoole, W. Stanley. *Alias Simon Suggs: The Life and Times of Johnson Jones Hooper*. University, Alabama: The Univ. of Alabama Press, 1952.

Hooper, Johnson Jones. *Adventures of Captain Simon Suggs, Late of the Tallapoosa Volunteers*. Intro. Manley W. Wellman. Chapel Hill: The Univ. of North Carolina Press, 1969. Pp. ix-xxiv, 181.

Hopkins, Robert. "Simon Suggs: A Burlesque Campaign Biography." *American Quarterly*, 15 (Fall 1963), 459-463.

Hubbell, *The South* . . . , pp. 672-675.

Inge, M. Thomas. "Simon Suggs Courts a Widow: A New Sketch." *Alabama Review*, 17 (April 1964), 148-151.

Link, *Pioneers* . . . , II, 505-524.

Smith, Howard Winston. "An Annotated Edition of Hooper's *Some Adventures of Captain Simon Suggs.*" Diss. Vanderbilt Univ. 1965.

——————. *Johnson Jones Hooper: A Critical Study*. Lexington: The Univ. of Kentucky Press, 1963.

——————. "Simon Suggs and the Satiric Tradition." *Essays in Honor of Richebourg Gaillard McWilliams*. Ed. Howard Creed. Birmingham: Birmingham Southern College Press, 1970. Pp. 49-56.

Thorp, "Suggs and Sut . . . ," pp. 169-175.

West, Harry C. "Simon Suggs and His Similes." *North Carolina Folklore*, 16 (May 1968), 53-57.

HAMILTON CHAMBERLAIN JONES

Walter, Richard. "Ham Jones: Southern Folk Humorist." *Journal of American Folklore*, 78 (Oct.-Dec. 1965), 295-316.

GEORGE WILKINS KENDALL

Copeland, Fayette. *Kendall of the Picayune*. Norman: The Univ. of Oklahoma Press, 1943.

Coulter, E. Merton, ed. *The Other Half of Old New Orleans: Sketches of Characters and Incidents from the Recorder's Court of New Orleans in the Eighteen Forties as Reported in the Picayune*. Baton Rouge: Louisiana State Univ. Press, 1939. Pp. 1-8.

Kendall, John. "George Wilkins Kendall and the Founding of the New Orleans *Picayune*." *Louisiana Historical Quarterly*, 11 (April 1928), 261-285.

HENRY CLAY LEWIS

Anderson, John Q. "Folklore in the Writings of 'the Louisiana Swamp Doctor.' " *Southern Folklore Quarterly*, 19 (Dec. 1955), 243-251.

——————. "Henry Clay Lewis, Alias 'Madison Tensas, M.D., the Louisiana Swamp Doctor.' " *Bulletin of the Medical Library Association*, 43 (Jan. 1955), 58-73.

——————. "Henry Clay Lewis, Louisville Medical Institute Student, 1844-1846." *Filson Club Historical Quarterly*, 32 (1958), 30-37.

——————. "Louisiana 'Swamp Doctor.' " *McNeese Review*, 5 (1953), 45-53.

——————. *Louisiana Swamp Doctor: The Life and Writings of Henry Clay Lewis, Alias "Madison Tensas, M.D."* Baton Rouge: The Louisiana State Univ. Press, 1962. Pp. v-viii, 3-70, 259-279.

Rose, Alan H. "The Image of the Negro in the Writings of Henry Clay Lewis." *American Literature*, 41 (May 1969), 255-263.

BARTOW LLOYD

Figh, Margaret G. "Bartow Lloyd, Humorist and Philosopher of the Alabama Back Country." *Alabama Review*, 5 (April 1952), 83-99.

AUGUSTUS BALDWIN LONGSTREET

Alderman, *Library* . . . , VII, 3241-3244.

Bridgers, Emily. *The South in Fiction*. Chapel Hill: The Univ. of North Carolina Press, 1948. Pp. 8-10.

Davidson, James Wood. *The Living Writers of the South*. New York: Carleton Publishers, 1869. Pp. 337-342.

Fitzgerald, Bishop Oscar Penn. *Judge Longstreet: A Life Sketch*. Nashville: Methodist Episcopal Church, South, 1891. Pp. 9-192.

Ford, Thomas W. "Ned Brace of *Georgia Scenes*." *Southern Folklore Quarterly*, 29 (Sept. 1965), 220-227.

Gilbert, Creighton. "Emory Portrait II: Four Figures of the College Campus." *Emory University Quarterly*, 4 (March 1948), 40-54.

Harkey, Joseph H. "A Note on Longstreet's Ransy Sniffle and Brackenridge's Modern Chivalry." *West Pennsylvania Historical Magazine*, 52 (1969), 43-45.

Hubbell, *The South* . . . , pp. 666-669.

Johnson, John W. "Augustus Baldwin Longstreet." *Mississippi Historical Society Publications*, 12 (1912), 122-135.

King, Kimball. "Regionalism in the Three Souths." *Transactions of the Wisconsin Academy of Sciences, Arts and Letters*, 54 (1965), 37-50.

Knight, Lucian Lamar. *Reminiscences of Famous Georgians*. Atlanta: Franklin-Turner Company, 1908. II, 174-184.

Link, *Pioneers* . . . , II, 471-485.

Longstreet, Augustus B. *Georgia Scenes*. Ed. B. R. McElderry, Jr. New York: Sagamore Press, 1957. Pp. v-x.

Parrington, *Main Currents* . . . , II, 166-172.

Poe, Edgar Allan. "Georgia Scenes." *Southern Literary Messenger*, 2 (1836), 287-292.

Rutherford, *The South* . . . , pp. 153-159.

Silverman, Kenneth. "Longstreet's 'The Gander Pulling.' " *American Quarterly*, 18 (Fall 1966), 548-549.

Smith, Gerald. "Augustus Baldwin Longstreet and John Wade's 'Cousin Lucius.' " *Georgia Historical Quarterly*, 56 (Summer 1972), 276-281.

Swanson, William J. "Fowl Play on the Frontier." *West Georgia College Review*, 1 (1968), 12-15.

Wade, John D. "Augustus Baldwin Longstreet." Diss. Columbia Univ. 1923.

──────────────. "Augustus Baldwin Longstreet." *Southern Pioneers in Social Interpretation*. Ed. H. W. Odum. Chapel Hill: The Univ. of North Carolina Press, 1925. Pp. 117-140.

──────────────. *Augustus Baldwin Longstreet: A Study of the Development of Culture in the South*. New York: Macmillan, 1924. Ed. M. Thomas Inge. Athens: The Univ. of Georgia Press, 1969.

——————. "Old Books: *Georgia Scenes*." *Georgia Review*, 14 (Winter 1960), 444-447.

Weber, C. J. "A Connecticut Yankee in King Alfred's Country." *Colophon*, 1 (Spring 1936), 525-535.

ALEXANDER G. McNUTT

Foote, Henry S. *Casket of Reminiscences*. Washington: Chronicle Publishing Company, 1874. Pp. 198-215.

Howell, Elmo. "Governor Alexander G. McNutt of Mississippi: Humanist of the Old Southwest." *Journal of Mississippi History*, 25 (May 1973), 153-165.

CHARLES F. M. NOLAND

Masterson, *Tall Tales* . . . , pp. 29-54.

Noland, Charles F. M. *Pete Whetstone of Devil's Fork*. Ed. Ted R. Worley and Eugene A. Nolte. Van Buren, Arkansas: The Press-Argus, 1957. Pp. i-xxxvi.

Shinn, Josiah H. "The Life and Public Service of Charles Fenton Mercer Noland." *Publications of the Arkansas Historical Association*, 1 (1906), 330-343.

JAMES KIRKE PAULDING

Alderman, Ralph M. "James Kirke Paulding, Forgotten Letter Writer." *Manuscripts*, 9 (1957), 77-85.

——————. "James Kirke Paulding's Contributions to American Magazines." *Studies in Bibliography: Papers of the Bibliographical Society of the Univ. of Virginia*, 17 (1964), 141-151.

——————, ed. *The Letters of James Kirke Paulding*. Madison: The Univ. of Wisconsin Press, 1962.

Adkins, N. F. "James K. Paulding's *Lion of the West*." *American Literature*, 3 (Nov. 1931), 249-258.

Arpad, Joseph J. "John Wesley Jarvis, James Kirke Paulding, and Colonel Nimrod Wildfire." *New York Folklore Quarterly*, 21 (1965), 92-106.

Conklin, W. T. "Paulding's Prose Treatment of Types and Frontier Life before Cooper." *University of Texas Studies in English*, 19 (1939), 163-171.

Henry, Joyce. "Five More Essays by James Kirke Paulding." *Papers of the Bibliographical Society of America*, 66 (1972), 310-321.

Herold, Amos L. *James Kirke Paulding: Versatile American*. New York: Columbia Univ. Press, 1926. Pp. 98-99, 105, 148-160.

Hodge, Francis. "Biography of a Lost Play: *Lion of the West*." *Theatre Annual*, 12 (1954), 48-61.

Mason, Melvin R. "*The Lion of the West*: Satire on Davy Crockett and Frances Trollope." *South Central Bulletin*, 29 (1969), 143-145.

Parrington, *Main Currents* . . . , II, 212-221.

Pattee, *The First Century* . . . , pp. 289-293.

Paulding, James K. *The Lion of the West.* Ed. James N. Tidwell. Stanford: Stanford Univ. Press, 1954. Pp. 7-14.

Paulding, William Irving. *The Literary Life of James K. Paulding.* New York: Charles Scribner and Company, 1867. Pp. 216-233.

Taylor, William R. *Cavalier and Yankee: The Old South and American National Character.* New York: G. Braziller, 1961. Pp. 225-259.

Watkins, Floyd C. *James Kirke Paulding, Humorist and Critic of American Life.* Nashville: The Joint Univ. Libraries, 1952. Pp. 10-12.

——————————. "James Kirke Paulding and the South." *American Quarterly,* 5 (1953), 219-230.

——————————. "James Kirke Paulding's Creole Tale." *Louisiana Historical Quarterly,* 33 (1950), 364-379.

——————————. "James Kirke Paulding's Early Ring-Tailed Roarer." *Southern Folklore Quarterly,* 15 (Sept. 1951), 183-187.

Wegelin, Oscar. "A Bibliography of the Separate Publications of James Kirke Paulding, Poet, Novelist, Humorist, Statesman, 1779-1860." *Bibliographical Society of America, Papers,* 12 (1918), 34-40.

JOHN S. ROBB

McDermott, John Francis, ed. "Gold Fever:- The Letters of 'Solitaire,' Goldrush Correspondent of '49." *Missouri Historical Society Bulletin,* 5 (1949), 115-126, 211-223, 316-331; 6 (1949), 34-43.

Robb, John S. *Streaks of Squatter Life, and Far-West Scenes.* Ed. John F. McDermott. Gainesville: Scholars' Facsimiles and Reprints, 1962. Pp. v-xxii.

HARDEN E. TALIAFERRO

Boggs, Ralph S. "North Carolina Folktales Current in the 1820's." *Journal of American Folklore,* 47 (Jan.-March 1934), 269-288.

Coffin, Tristam P. "Harden E. Taliaferro and the Use of Folklore by American Literary Figures." *South Atlantic Quarterly,* 64 (Spring 1965), 241-246.

Ginther, James E. "Harden E. Taliaferro, A Sketch." *Mark Twain Quarterly,* 9 (Winter 1953), 13-15, 20.

Penrod, James H. "Harden Taliaferro, Folk Humorist of North Carolina." *Midwest Folklore,* 6 (1956), 147-153.

Taliaferro, Harden E. *Carolina Humor.* Ed. David K. Jackson. Richmond: The Dietz Press, 1938. Pp. iii-viii.

Whiting, B. J. "Proverbial Sayings from Fisher's River, North Carolina." *Southern Folklore Quarterly,* 11 (Sept. 1947), 173-185.

Williams, Cratis D. "Mountain Customs, Social Life, and Folk Yarns in Taliaferro's *Fisher's River Scenes and Characters.*" *North Carolina Folklore,* 16 (Nov. 1968), 143-152.

WILLIAM TAPPAN THOMPSON

Alderman, *Library* . . . . XII, 5283-5286.

Ellison, George R. "William Tappan Thompson and the *Southern Miscellany*, 1842-1844." *Mississippi Quarterly*, 23 (Spring 1970), 155-168.

Flanders, Bertram H. *Early Georgia Magazines: Literary Periodicals to 1865.* Athens: The Univ. of Georgia Press, 1944. Pp. 30-35 and *passim*.

Hubbell, *The South* . . . , pp. 669-672.

Link, *Pioneers* . . . , II, 525-533.

McKeithan, Daniel M. "Mark Twain's Letters of Thomas Jefferson Snodgrass." *Philological Quarterly*, 32 (Oct. 1953), 353-365.

Miller, Henry P. "The Authorship of *The Slave-Holder Abroad*." *Journal of Southern History*, 10 (Feb. 1944), 92-94.

——————————. "The Background and Significance of *Major Jones's Courtship*." *Georgia Historical Quarterly*, 30 (Dec. 1946), 267-296.

——————————. "The Life and Works of William Tappan Thompson." Diss. Univ. of Georgia 1942.

Rutherford, *The South* . . . , pp. 372-375.

Thompson, Maurice. "An Old Southern Humorist." *Independent*, 50 (20 Oct. 1898), 1103-1105.

Thompson, William T. *Major Jones's Chronicles of Pineville*. Philadelphia: Getz and Buck, 1852. Pp. 5-7.

THOMAS BANGS THORPE

Blair, Walter. "The Techniques of the Big Bear of Arkansas." *Southwest Review*, 28 (Summer 1943), 426-435.

Callow, James. *Kindred Spirits: Knickerbocker Writers and American Artists, 1807-1855*. Chapel Hill: The Univ. of North Carolina Press, 1967. Pp. 9-10, 171, 235.

Current-Garcia, Eugene. "Thomas Bangs Thorpe and the Literature of the Ante-Bellum Southwestern Frontier." *Louisiana Historical Quarterly*, 39 (1956), 199-222.

Hayne, Barrie. "Yankee in the Patriarchy: T. B. Thorpe's Reply to *Uncle Tom's Cabin*." *American Quarterly*, 20 (Summer 1968), 180-195.

McDermott, John F. "T. B. Thorpe's Burlesque of Far West Sporting Travel." *American Quarterly*, 10 (Summer 1958), 175-180.

Masterson, *Tall Tales* . . . , pp. 56-61.

Rickels, Milton. "A Bibliography of the Writings of Thomas Bangs Thorpe." *American Literature*, 29 (May 1957), 171-179.

——————————. *Thomas Bangs Thorpe, Humorist of the Old Southwest*. Baton Rouge: Louisiana State Univ. Press, 1962.

——————————. "Thomas Bangs Thorpe in the Felicianas, 1836-1842." *Louisiana Historical Quarterly*, 39 (1956), 169-197.

Simoneaux, Katherine G. "Symbolism in Thorpe's 'The Big Bear of Arkansas.' " *Arkansas Historical Quarterly*, 25 (Fall 1966), 240-247.

Weber, Brom. "American Humor and American Culture." *American Quarterly*, 14 (Fall 1962), 503-507.

MASON LOCKE WEEMS

Adams, R. G. "It Was Old Parson Weems Who Began It." *New York Times Magazine*, 80 (5 July 1931), 10.

Alderman, *Library* . . . , XIII, 5731-5737.

Hart, A. B. "American Historical Liars." *Harper's*, 131 (Oct. 1915), 732-734.

Ingrahim, C. A. "Mason Locke Weems: A Great American Author and Distributor of Books." *Americana*, 25 (Oct. 1931), 469-485.

Kellock, Harold. *Parson Weems of the Cherry Tree*. New York: The Century Company, 1928.

Purcell, James. "A Book Pedlar's Progress in North Carolina." *North Carolina Historical Review*, 29 (Jan. 1952), 8-23.

Skeel, Emily E. F. "Mason Locke Weems: A Postscript." *New Colophon*, 3 (1950), 243-249.

————————. *Mason Locke Weems: His Works and Ways*. New York, 1929.

Van Tassel, David D. "The Legend Maker." *American Heritage*, 13 (Feb. 1962), 58-59, 89-94.

Weems, Mason Locke. *Three Discourses*. Intro. Emily E. F. Skeel. New York: Random House, 1929. Pp. 3-8.

Wroth, Lawrence C. *Parson Weems*. Baltimore: The Eichelberger Book Company, 1911.

Index

(Excludes entries in the Checklist of Criticism)